DHOL

DHOL

DRUMMERS, IDENTITIES, AND MODERN PUNJAB

GIBB SCHREFFLER

UNIVERSITY OF ILLINOIS PRESS
Urbana, Chicago, and Springfield

Publication supported by a grant from Pomona College.

1 2 3 4 5 C P 5 4 3 2 1

∞ This book is printed on acid-free paper.

Library of Congress Cataloging-in-Publication Data
Names: Schreffler, Gibb, author.
Title: Dhol: drummers, identities, and modern Punjab / Gibb Schreffler.
Description: Urbana: University of Illinois Press, 2021. | Includes bibliographical references and index.
Identifiers: LCCN 2021037413 (print) | LCCN 2021037414 (ebook) | ISBN 9780252044076 (hardback) | ISBN 9780252086120 (paperback) | ISBN 9780252053016 (ebook)
Subjects: LCSH: Dholi—Social aspects—India—Punjab. | Music—Social aspects—India—Punjab. | Drummers—India—Punjab. | Panjabis (South Asian people)—Music—History and criticism. | Panjabis (South Asian people)—Social life and customs.
Classification: LCC ML3917.I4 S35 2021 (print) | LCC ML3917.I4 (ebook) | DDC 780.954/552—dc23
LC record available at https://lccn.loc.gov/2021037413
LC ebook record available at https://lccn.loc.gov/2021037414

For the dholis of Punjab—May the work go on.

CONTENTS

List of Figures ix

List of Audiovisual Examples xi

Note on Translation and Transliteration xiii

Preface xv

Introduction: Drumming to the Beat of a Different March 1

1 The Short End of the Stick: Strategies of Identification 35

2 Dhol Manifested: Body, Sound, and Structure 59

3 Asking Rude Questions: Dholi Ethnicity 92

4 A Portrait of a Dholi and His Community 128

5 Becoming and Being a Dholi 148

6 Dhol Players in a New World 172

7 Return to Punjab, Turning Punjab 193

Notes 217

Bibliography 229

Index 241

FIGURES

0.1 The dholi neighborhood in Amritsar 3
0.2 Administrative divisions of the Punjab region and surrounding areas 15
2.1 *Dhamāl* rhythm 72
2.2 *Ḍabal* of *dhamāl* 72
2.3 Wedding procession rhythm 75
2.4 Wrestling matches in the village of Dadu Majra 77
2.5 Wrestling rhythm 78
2.6 Wrestling rhythm 78
2.7 Wrestling rhythm 78
2.8 *Kabaḍḍī* rhythm 78
2.9 Original-style *bhangṛā* rhythm 81
2.10 Stage-style *bhangṛā* rhythm 82
2.11 *Toṛā* for *bhangṛā* 82
2.12 *Luḍḍī* rhythm 83
2.13 *Tuṇkā* rhythm 83
2.14 *Multānī luḍḍī* rhythm 84
2.15 *Siālkoṭī* rhythm 84

2.16 *Mirzā* rhythm 85
2.17 *Bhalvānī* or "*ṭikā-ṭik*" rhythm 85
2.18 *Jhummar* rhythm 87
2.19 *Lahirīā* rhythm 88
2.20 Men's *giddhā* rhythm 88
3.1 Bal Kishan 98
3.2 Tilak Raj and family 103
3.3 Faqir Ali at the shrine of Haider Shaikh 108
3.4 Akhtar Dhillon and nephew 112
3.5 Valmiki dholis of Dadu Majra Colony 118
3.6 Lacchman Singh 126
4.1 Bazigar-style *jhummar* dancing 135
4.2 Portrait of Bhana Ram 137
4.3 Bahadur Singh 138
4.4 Biru Ram and son 139
4.5 Bazigar dholis waiting for roadside clients 140
4.6 Garib Dass exhibiting the "Kerala" technique 144
6.1 Lal Singh Bhatti 181
7.1 Dev Raj Vartia and son 199
7.2 Harbans Lal Jogi 201
7.3 A bhangra dance team at the 1970 Republic Day celebration 208
7.4 Cassette cover with artist's revisions 209

AUDIOVISUAL EXAMPLES

Items may be found on the YouTube channel, *Dhol: Drummers, Identities, and Modern Punjab,* https://www.youtube.com/c/DholBook.

1 Excerpts from the 2004 Zonal Youth Festival, Chandigarh, https://www.youtube.com/watch?v=5yD9T9nQeMc

2 Annual fair in honor of Sitla Devi, village of Jarg, 2005, https://www.youtube.com/watch?v=KCfAIb2J7gQ

3 "Calls" (*sadd*), https://www.youtube.com/watch?v=ZujwxoFvGcQ

4 Wedding procession rhythm, https://www.youtube.com/watch?v=mNGMO7-CXR0

5 Wedding processions, https://www.youtube.com/watch?v=3rtqr88sECg

6 Wheat-cutting rhythm, https://www.youtube.com/watch?v=m2S4r2Y7n10

7 Hola Mahalla in Anandpur Sahib, 2005, https://www.youtube.com/watch?v=MuTxB7cfBco

8 Wrestling rhythms, https://www.youtube.com/watch?v=rpvldf7OZRc

9 Kabaddi rhythm, https://www.youtube.com/watch?v=M39ZW4KKXi8

10 The shrine of Haider Shaikh in Malerkotla, https://www.youtube.com/watch?v=NaFZnyeCamg

11 Mother Goddess rhythm, https://www.youtube.com/watch?v=3pI-Bss7zWA

12 Lakhdata Pir rhythms, https://www.youtube.com/watch?v=7JxMHjfQVjo

13 Bhangra rhythms, https://www.youtube.com/watch?v=AlMVJG_6tbs

14 Tunka rhythm, https://www.youtube.com/watch?v=IO671ifyI-s

15 Sialkoti rhythm, https://www.youtube.com/watch?v=Nx88Q_nqsDI

16 Mirza rhythm, https://www.youtube.com/watch?v=Zd3hCE9nnl8

17 Jhummar rhythms, https://www.youtube.com/watch?v=NzGWrTNIN3A

18 Men's giddha, https://www.youtube.com/watch?v=uVk3HV8EwoU

20 Dadra tal, https://www.youtube.com/watch?v=fIlyXymklLM

21 Bharai dholi Muhammad Sabi, https://www.youtube.com/watch?v=HlodHb8adoc

22 Pilgrimage to Goga Meri, https://www.youtube.com/watch?v=sFoOLPw6kQA

23 Ravidasia nagar kirtan, https://www.youtube.com/watch?v=3PrFPwB1PrY

24 Garib Dass in his own words, https://www.youtube.com/watch?v=YozMp7tLo3A

25 Bazi performance in Jalandhar, https://www.youtube.com/watch?v=cH2hw9IwIao

26 Jagat Ram dancing jhummar, https://www.youtube.com/watch?v=vlSjPpSbpFk

27 Children learning dhol, https://www.youtube.com/watch?v=Y-oDghPoy4U

28 Comparison of swing in dholi style, https://www.youtube.com/watch?v=dgZvW2uhuGI

29 Jago procession, https://www.youtube.com/watch?v=2p3tHNbhAjk

NOTE ON TRANSLATION AND TRANSLITERATION

All quotations from speech and print in languages other than English have been translated into English by the author. Non-English terms appear in native singular forms and are made plural according to English rules. Except for frequently or commonly used terms (e.g. dhol, bhangra, gurdwara, tabla), Indic words represented in Roman script are transliterated according to the International Alphabet of Sanskrit Transliteration, with a few modifications. Nasalization of long final vowels is indicated by /ṅ/ after the vowel. Directly before consonants, all nasal stops in the dental, palatal, and velar placement are represented by /n/. The voiceless palatal sibilant is represented by the digraph /sh/. Personal names, the names of organizations, and place names appear in the idiosyncratic Romanized spellings used by the respective parties and in local maps.

PREFACE

Ḍhol. A beloved word—a musical word, even, when spoken with the intonation of the Punjabi language. It is a beloved instrument, as well. The sight of this colorful, fat-bellied drum, provokes smiles. Its sound, deep, strong, and insistent, invites people—irresistibly, some say—to gather and to move.

Dhol: Drummers, Identities, and Modern Punjab interrogates the gap between the unbridled love for dhol and the equivocal love for its players. It asks: *who* are the dhol's players? *Where* are they positioned in relation to the cultural formations in which the instrument has an emblematic place? In combination: what are the *identities* of Punjab's dhol players, situated with respect to both their positions in local communities and a broadly conceived Punjabi nation?

Inquiry into the identities of dhol players is driven by documentary, intellectual, and ethical interests. This book documents rich ethnographic data about diverse ethnic communities of Punjabi origin whose continued social and discursive marginalization has rendered them less visible. Because they are most visible in musical contexts, musicological study brings these communities and their cultural formations to the fore. Intellectually speaking, analysis of the identities of dhol players yields insight into Punjab-based concepts of musical performance and how these concepts work to create or articulate social structure. Modern Punjab, as a case study, contributes to thought about identity construction at the intersections of ethnicity, class, and nationality, both locally realized and extrapolated internationally. Addressing current ethical concerns, this work engages debates on cultural appropriation by illustrating how questions about ownership of cultural practices are complicated by competing existential and ideological struggles over identity.

It asserts that to reveal the identities of dhol players—as they have been, typically and historically—is an ethical necessity that acknowledges their place in Punjabi cultural history and helps to repair their representation.

This work is the fruit of two decades of research and critical observation. The bulk of data derives from fieldwork on the participant-observation model. I made extended trips to India in 2000, 2001, 2004–2005, 2006, and 2019, and short trips to Pakistan in 2001 and 2006. The extremities of my research area in South Asia were the edge of Balochistan in the West, central Uttar Pradesh in the East, Jammu in the North, and Delhi in the South. In 2009, 2018, 2019, and 2020, I worked with dhol players of diaspora communities in London (U.K.), California, New York, Ontario, and British Columbia. In the gap years of 2003 and 2007, I brought my primary mentor, Ustad Garib Dass, to my home for several weeks. Over the years, I also engaged sporadically with artists in North America in-person and via distance communication.

I cannot tell all sides of the story. For both reasons of argument focus and research limitations, though this work discusses Punjabi dhol broadly, the phenomena it addresses belong most to the modern Indian constituent state of Punjab. Dhol players and the culture of that place constitute the center of focus, out from which the work deals with uneven emphasis on other locations. Additionally, in emphasizing data obtained from hereditary-professional musicians, the study is weighted towards male perspectives and historical phenomena.

I have tried to balance my scholarly interest in presenting a full picture with an ethical charge to advocate for my teachers' positions. As the book articulates, the identities of traditional drummers have much to do with participating in adhering to and transmitting a set of values and sharing a perspective born of life experiences that are particular to them. This book, therefore, privileges views from the traditional drummers' "marginal" perspective and the emphases associated with their values. While also validating the voices of "mainstream" Punjabis, I operate from the position that their voices may often be heard elsewhere while it is the voices of the marginalized that demand amplification at this time.

Because of the expansive scope of my inquiry and the long period entailed to formulate the ideas herein, I owe debts to many people. First and foremost, I give thanks to (late) Ustad Garib Dass ji, my guru in the study of dhol and Punjabi culture. I thank him for his willingness to open his home and his heart, and for his generosity to share so much of his time and wisdom. I am grateful, too, for the hospitality of the master's family. Thank you, Auntie Labh Kaur, Des Raj, Raj, Bhappi, Sunny, Honey, Sandeep, Jass, Chichu, Neha, Geeta, Darshan, Rano, and the rest of the Vartia family.

In my formative years as a doctoral student at UC Santa Barbara, I was inspired to high standards of ethnomusicological scholarship by Music Department mentors Scott Marcus, Timothy Cooley, Dolores Hsu, and Cornelia Fales. The mentor to whom I owe the most in graduate studies on Punjab was Gurinder Singh Mann, Chair of the Center for Sikh and Punjab Studies. I thank my Punjabi language teacher, Gurdit Singh, from whom I received first instruction in 1999. My classmates at UCSB created an invigorating community of Punjab scholars with complementary interests. They included: Rana Ajrawat, Anna Bigelow, Randi Clary, David Fowler, Mary Garcia, Rahuldeep Singh Gill, Pawan Rehill, Ami Shah, John Warneke, and Justin Weaver. I was fortunate, too, to interact with an international complement of scholars of South Asia from other universities, including Satwinder Bains, Amarjeet Chandan, Patrick Frölicher, Will Glover, Joyce Hughes, Jim Kippen, Laura Leante, Chloe Martinez, Farina Mir, Nicola Mooney, Kristina Myrvold, Michael Nijhawan, Caroline Sawyer, Ashveer Pal Singh, Harpreet Singh, Shinder Thandi, and Richard K. Wolf. There are many others. I acknowledge, too, the support of my classmates in graduate studies at Santa Barbara: Kara Attrep, Jason Busniewski, Revell Carr, Sonja Downing, Emilee Getter, Denise Gill, Lillie Gordon, Tom Greenland, Jim Grippo, Ken Habib, Robert Hodges, Max Katz, Alan Kirk, Karen Liu, Ralph Lowi, Katherine Meizel, Phil Murphy, Baharam Osqueezadeh, Malia Roberson, Nasir Sayid, Justin Scarimbolo, Barbara Taylor, and Rob Wallace. Special thanks go to Daniel Michon, who assisted my transition into fieldwork in Punjab and provided feedback on the manuscript.

Pomona College has been my home as this work developed. I am grateful for the mentorship and administrative support of Music Department colleagues Graydon Beeks, Elizabeth Champion, Alfred Cramer, Cathy Endress, Tom Flaherty, Melissa Givens, Donna Di Grazia, Katherine Hagedorn, Genevieve Lee, Eric Lindholm, Gwendolyn Lytle, Bill Peterson, and Joti Rockwell. Much of this work was completed in Claremont among the camaraderie of Pong's CK Café, with the moral support of Kevin Bryan, John Eichinger, Paul Roberts, Greg Smith, and other friends.

A period of one year's research in India was funded by a Fulbright-Hays Doctoral Dissertation grant and with the help of the United States Educational Foundation in India. Follow-up fieldwork in India was supported by a Pomona College Faculty Research Grant, as was preparation of the final version. The Sikh Foundation and the UCSB Center for Sikh and Punjab Studies provided significant additional funding during early research trips.

I received academic support at educational institutions and archives in India. During my one-year residence in India, I had the pleasure of calling

Dr. Nahar Singh (Panjab University) my advisor. Other academic advisors and interlocutors were Surjeet Singh Lee, Harvinder S. Bhatti, Rajinder S. Gill, Gurnam Singh, Gurcharan Singh, Iqbal Singh Dhillon, Indu Banga, and J. S. Grewal. Many individuals at government organizations aided my research, including: Adam Nayyar and Iqbal Saeed Ansari, Pakistan National Council of the Arts (Islamabad); Naseemullah Rashid, Lok Virsa (Islamabad); Prit Pal Singh, R. S. Malhotra, and J. P. Bengeri, Sangeet Natak Akademi (New Delhi); Alka Pande, India Habitat Centre; Shubha Chaudhury, AIIS Archive and Research Center for Ethnomusicology; Kuldeep Singh, Dept. of Cultural Affairs (Chandigarh); Indu Kaur and Parminder Kaur, Punjab State Archives; and Jagjit Singh and Mohd. Rafi, North Zone Cultural Centre. I especially want to thank the staff at the Kala Bhavan (Chandigarh) and in particular Prof. Rajpal Singh and Anil Sharma.

None of this work would have been possible without the musicians, dancers, and community members. This book is dedicated to them. For as many of those I can name in the following list of primary interlocutors, however, there are more who must go unnamed who provided hospitality and safety. Notably, among the predominately male cast, there were many women whose names I did not have the privilege of knowing.

Ambala: Dalip Vartia; *Amritsar*: Harbans Lal Jogi, Manohar Lal, Gulab Chuch Mahi, Tilak Raj, Gosha Shiva, Dev Raj; *Amroha*: Haji Qamar ud-Din, Anis Ahmad; *Bathinda*: Vishnu; *British Columbia*: Rayman Bhullar, Gurp Sian and South Asian Arts, Rupee Kainth, Vijay Yamla, Gora Longowalia, Tejinder Singh, Daljinder Johal, Hardeep Sahota, Harjinder Sandhu, Jasbir Poonia; *California*: Lal Singh Bhatti, Jim and Surinder Singh Dhanoa, Raju Bhangar; *Chandigarh*: Tara Chand, Kala, Puran, Sonu, Gulab Singh, Shamsher Singh, Sethi, Golu, Vicky, Pathani Ram, Dilbag Singh, Mahinder, Jagat Ram, Sardari Lal, Prem Chand, Ramesh Kumar, Sewa Singh, Kartar Singh Ghanot, Raju, Balbir Singh Sekhon, Narinder Nindi, Avtar Singh Chana, Parmjit Padda, Mohinder Singh, Neelam Mansingh Chowdhry, Saroop Singh; *Firozpur*: Joginder Chota, Lacchman Singh, Mahinder, Nidhan Singh; *Gurdaspur*: Ramesh Chand, Harbhajan Singh; *Hoshiarpur*: Balvindar Ram, Jagesh Gill; *Jalandhar*: Charan Das, Harbans Lal Kaku and sons, Kala Takhi, Anil Takhi, Inderjit Singh; *Jammu*: Madan Lal Balgotra, Bal Kishan; *Jarg*: Sher Khan, Muhammad Shukardin, Gaga, Rafi; *Jhelum*: Saghir Ali Khan; *Khanna*: Mahindar Pal Lalka, Jaimal Ram; *Ludhiana*: Janak Raj, Ravi Malhotra, Des Raj, Ramesh Kumar Meshi, Ravi Kumar Dana, Surinder Kumar Chindu, Naresh Kukki, Jagdish Yamla, Sant Ram Khiva, Faqir Chand Patanga, Tehal Singh Khiva, Raju Khiva, Makkhan Ram, Ashok Khiva, Gobind Khiva, Gopal Khiva, Kamla, Mesho, Dev Raj, Kala, Pappu; *Malerkotla*: Akhtar, Anwar, Majid Ali, Sultan, and Ehsan Dhillon, Faqir Ali, Liaqat Ali, Dilshad, Salamat Ali, Muhammad Sabi, Balbir Singh; *Meerut:* Zamir Amar; *Mohali*:

Mangat Ram, Dev Raj, Charni, Vijay Kumar, Shivcharan, Mahinder; *New York*: Mali Ram, Jarnail Singh, Muhammad Boota, Sher Boota, Amit Aulakh; *Ontario*: Manvir Hothi, Aaron Sahota, Gaurav Sharma, Gurjot Dhanjal, Rajvir Reehal, Gaurav Sidhu; *Patiala*: Biru Ram, Manak Raj, Paramjit Singh Sidhu; *Sunam*: Bahadur Singh; *United Kingdom*: Gurvinder Kambo, Ravinder Ghattora, Hardeep Singh Sahota, Jas Bhambra; *Washington DC*: Dave Gupta, Amrinder Pannu.

Thank you to Laurie Matheson and the Press for their patient guidance. Two anonymous readers went above and beyond during the height of a pandemic to offer careful feedback. Any mistakes and remaining shortcomings in this publication are entirely my own.

My family are now no strangers to Punjabi culture and the seven-syllabled field of ethnomusicology. I thank my parents, stepparents, J., J., B., and N. for their unconditional love and patience during a difficult time for all. Lastly, I could not have made it across the finish line without the unrelenting cheers of Xiao Fei.

DHOL

INTRODUCTION

Drumming to the Beat of a Different March

"The dholis are facing the toughest time ever," claimed a 2005 article in the Amritsar *Tribune* about the city's residents who practiced the profession of drummer: *ḍholī* (Bagga 2005). One might wonder why drummers warranted such attention. The answer has to do with the fact that in the late twentieth century, the drummers' instrument, a barrel drum called *ḍhol*, had emerged as an emblem of modern Punjab. So, whereas elsewhere a report on the condition of drummers might be of interest only to music fans, any person broadly connected to Punjab might relate to a story invoking this veritable *national* drum. Better considered as a cultural phenomenon—"instrument," alone, cannot do it justice—"dhol"[1] has long been part of everyday and seasonal public functions across the region's rural landscape. Beaten by men of a distinct occupational class, the rhythms of dhol accompanied wedding processions, community dances, harvest activities, and worship. Dhol acquired prominence in a broader political sphere after India won independence in 1947. From that point, the drum began to appear in various forms of heritage performance through which Punjabis in restructured sociopolitical landscapes remembered their past to buffer the changes of modernity.

Chief among these heritage performance forms was bhangra, a staged presentation of village-style harvest dance. Since its advent in India's Punjab state in the 1950s, bhangra has been treated as a crucible in which to meld combinations of remembered movements and sounds with newly composed elements. Bhangra has developed almost continually for seven decades, across which it has been used to mark political events, deployed in ambassadorial contexts, and embedded in educational curricula as a means of inculcating young people with a consciousness of their heritage. It has been incorporated into films representing Punjabi life to India and the world and formed the conceptual backdrop (although only the partial musical basis) of a commercial music genre. Bhangra forms have evolved to cater to evolving Punjabi values at home and abroad, always retaining the evocation of a rural, agricultural ethos that is presumed to be at the heart of Punjabi experience. At the center of bhangra's sound is dhol, whose rhythm ties together its disparate compositional elements and loudly proclaims a Punjabi presence.

With the development of bhangra and similar representative heritage forms, dhol has ever expanded its network, being incorporated into globally consumed commercial media that carry a sound recognized as *Punjab*'s sound. Ubiquitously heard in both the traditional ritual sphere and the modern political sphere, whether live or mediated, dhol synchronizes the heartbeats of Punjabis around the world. For these reasons, one might feel concern for the people who gave birth to and sustain dhol traditions and, by extension, might consider what their condition might portend for the condition of Punjab. Yet, although the sound of dhol continues to invigorate and fascinate, little actual attention has been paid to those individuals who articulate it, the dholis. This book aims to change that.

OF LAMENTS

I read the report on Amritsar's dholis at the midpoint of a decade during which I was engaged in documenting dhol traditions, at which time I filed it along with many news articles that painted a dismal picture of the state of Punjabi performing arts. I was wary (and weary) of the discourse's grand narrative of dying traditions. I was, more optimistically, invested in documenting the rich (and growing) cultural significance of dhol. Looking back, I wonder: at that historical moment, what had I been seeing about the dhol's *players*? Yes, the instrument itself was gaining a higher profile and richer significance but, with respect to practitioners, was this, indeed, the beginning of some sort of decline? Was I observing the start, whether consequent or concurrent, of a new tradition? Were the changes I was seeing responsible for a net negative outcome for the dholis? And when I am the one to say, now, that dholis today are facing the toughest time, will anyone heed me?

My earlier work on dhol uncovered recently created concepts, rhythms, dance movements, and so on, many of which had passed into the domain of perceived authenticity that earned them the label "traditional." It was not their recent creation that did so but rather their ability to comport with notions of what was essential to what they were imagined to represent. Nevertheless, the usual implication of the perception of authenticity in South Asia,

FIGURE 0.1 The dholi neighborhood in Amritsar, 2019. Photo by the author.

that a phenomenon is ultimately rooted in the distant past and that its value scales to its conformity to past forms, makes many inclined to see a tradition either as continuing the status quo or as a decline. I therefore viewed with skepticism this habit of painting change as decline—often configured as a fall from a state of a preindustrial ideal to modern disarray. There must also be room for narratives of increase and creation. Was the dholis' tradition really in such dire circumstances as the default discourse of dying traditions would suggest?

At that point in my journey, I would have answered in the negative. I had been seeking older individuals in hopes of seeing both how traditions were practiced contemporaneously and how they had changed. Changes in the traditions of dhol were not, however, something to which I aimed to ascribe positive or negative value. The notion of academic objectivity prescribed that

I take a neutral position, accepting the inevitability of change. Moreover, laments such as I assumed to be instantiated by the *Tribune* article not only invoke a trope of "loss of heritage" but also do it from the subject position of a Punjabi person. The mourners are Punjabis speaking on behalf of a narrative concept in which a person in my subject position cannot make an investment: Punjabi heritage. To mourn the loss of heritage, for me, risked striking a tone that was extraneous to serious scholarship. Perhaps more significantly, my work of that time centered on an inanimate object and abstract concept: dhol in Punjab. Observing inevitable changes to a thing and ideas freed me from excessive expression of value, for less was at stake.

With more time, however, my personal working relationship with dholis bound me increasingly to individuals affected by change. This position engendered not greater sympathy for constructs of Punjabi heritage as such but rather greater empathy for the people for whom issues of heritage cultivation are important. As a singular scholar engaged in presenting their stories, I felt a responsibility to be their advocate. Thus, I began to ask, is there anyone speaking up for the dholis? The drummers' voices are caught in an iteration of Spivak's double-bind of the subaltern, unheard behind local walls of caste segregation and buried beneath a liberal nationalist discourse that celebrates music in the abstract (divorced from the musician), as a source of social capital. Cosmopolitan Punjabis may, in Spivak's terms, masquerade as "native informants" (1999, 6) while their voices collude with outsider voices to mask our view of Punjab's most marginalized. It remains not my position to speak as a Punjabi for Punjabi heritage, and thus my work continues to refrain from typical strains of "loss of heritage." Nevertheless, I find myself positioned to amplify what Punjab's dholis have to say about their place within narratives of heritage and nationhood. They are the people whom, in this work, I move to the center of the story. Consequently, my narrative, while not embracing the trope of culture loss per se, is underscored by lamenting tones.

It was following my shift in position that I reread the *Tribune*'s gloomy report on Amritsar's dholis. I now see it not as a conventional lament for a grandly conceived Punjabi heritage but rather a lament for particular, personal loss—of status, of income, of identity, of aesthetic worlds. The *Tribune* article broke from the dominant discourse by recognizing the agency of dholis. The reporter, Neeraj Bagga, remarked, "Though the dhol is an indispensable musical instrument during functions at any Punjabi household, very few have strived to know the condition of the dholwalas." The dholwalas (dholis) are shown to control their fate in one anecdote: "Audio cassettes earlier posed a threat, though dholis successfully overcame this challenge" (Bagga 2005). Thus particularized, we can better engage the author's claim that dholis are (were) facing "the toughest time ever." My own observation of Punjabi dholis for two decades, along with oral historiography that traces their development over a century, puts me in agreement: the lives of dholis, people who come from positions to which Indic society assigns the lowest status, *are* tough.

Still, I balked at the superlative "toughest" because I had also seen, through documenting the lives of senior players, that the previous half-century had afforded an overall improvement in the lives of their families. My dhol teacher, Garib Dass, had traversed a life trajectory that began as a nomad living in straw huts, later pulling a rickshaw and laboring in the fields, and ended with a career of prestigious work, fame, and travel to a dozen countries. Garib Dass said that he owed all his good fortune to dhol. His career as a dholi made possible experiences that were not available to his ancestors. Yet now I see that the uplifting he and other senior players had experienced in the twentieth century dovetailed with the depression noted in the *Tribune*. By the beginning of the second decade of this century, Garib Dass (1939–2010) and most other dholis of his generation had either died or hung up their dhols. The succeeding generation was earning diminishing returns from their investment in dhol. The stock of dhol was still rising. But an inverse relationship had begun between dholis' ability to earn two square meals and the love for their instrument in the world. Hindsight thus compels me to admit that the *Tribune* report correctly identified a trend of "tough[est] times" brewing beneath the intoxicating excitement for Punjabi music in the early years of the twenty-first century.

Nevertheless, at this point, still farther down the road, I believe the cause of those tough times was not so simple as was suggested—and that is why I missed the signs. Bagga's interviewee, dholi Mukhtiar Singh, decried the threat that DJs posed to dholis' livelihood: "It is not always possible to beat the machine." Competing technology does affect the market of all musicians to some degree, but its ability to account for "toughest times" is insufficient. Bagga himself noted that dholis had earlier overcome the competition from recorded audiocassettes and, Mukhtiar Singh's complaint notwithstanding, alternative technologies have not made dholis redundant. Those among the broad sample of dholis with whom I worked did not lament technology putting them out of work to any extraordinary degree. On the contrary, dholis, among all the traditional musicians, have been the most resilient professionals. In the last decade, dholis have added the job of DJ to their résumés. Even when prerecorded music is used at a function, dholis are hired to play along with the recording—such is the enduring value of live dhol. Dholis have taken to become recording artists as well. Playing dhol was far from a dying practice in 2005, and the *Tribune* itself stated, "About 2,000 families [in Amritsar's dholi neighborhood] depend on dhol to earn their livelihood." *Two thousand* families in just one city? Struggling or not, this number, if it is accurate, sounds incredible; I could scarcely imagine two *hundred*. Whatever the actual figure, it is quite high. In fact, in India at that time there were likely many more dholis than ever in history, and the number of people who play dhol since, on a global scale, has only increased.

I have found, alternatively, that dholis complain that the public does not or cannot appreciate real dhol. They have been compelled to change what they play and how they play to cater to audiences' taste and knowledge, which signals a change—many dholis would say for the worse—to "the dhol tradition." A more recently published piece, revisiting the theme of struggling dholis, corroborates my finding. Paraphrasing the Patiala dholi Mahinder, the authors write, "The dhol may still be famous, but people do not have the patience to distinguish the finely nuanced performance of the ustad [dhol master]" (Saini and Khanna 2019). Yet, as in the earlier *Tribune* article, the authors ultimately turn to the threat of competition—citing a local market flooded by immigrant Rajasthani dholis who work for low wages—to highlight Punjabi dholis' despair. I am again skeptical of market competition as the sole explanation for the decline. It is not as significant that the immigrants work for less as it is that they are unfamiliar with Punjab's dhol traditions. Laments about DJs at functions, similarly, are less about a concern for the live drummer being put out of work and more about what the acceptance of prerecorded music signals about the aesthetic environment. The dholis' root predicament is related to how dholis and their traditions are situated in relation to their audiences and society. The threat they face is not a simple economic one (e.g., a rendering obsolete, by technology, of practice) but rather an existential one (a rendering extinct of meanings and aesthetics).

One might ask how it is that dhol players' numbers are increasing if they are doing so poorly. Although the strands of causality are inseparable, we can identify some dynamics. First, there is the dynamic of supply and demand. As the number of dholis increases, creating ever more competition for a share of the market, the circumstances of individual dholis become poorer. Dholis become a dime a dozen and victims of the success of the group. This circumstance, however, raises the more intriguing question of why individuals would adopt or continue the profession of dholi in an increasingly competitive market. To understand the motivations for being a dholi—why play dhol?—we will need to consider the social-identity positions of the ethnic groups from which dholis come.

A second dynamic, which one can discern in dholis' statements, is the balance between quantity and quality. If the quantity of dhol playing increases, its quality is presumed to decrease. Indeed, more than outside forces like technology, dholis tend to identify the threat to their practice as *other dholis'* practices. By "quality," we need not only consider whether the playing is more or less competent. We may also consider how what dholis do resonates meaningfully within the culture of their communities. I allude here to meanings of dhol playing as established historically and within cultural frameworks that predate the changes of the twenty-first century. What dholis do—the dhol tradition(s)—has undergone changes that create the perception of a decline in such meaningful playing. And so, despite more dhol playing and players, dholis feel demoralized through perceiving a sort of spiritual decline in their lifework.

A third dynamic: consider the composition of individuals who make up the increase in dhol players. In the last decade, the greatest increase has occurred in the sector of lay players. It is a sector that exists outside Punjab's traditional, rural society. Understand that, in the historical context of the last few centuries, "hereditary" and "professional" have been nearly synonymous. To be a professional dholi meant that one was born into a kin-community of players or some other limited community that links genetic descent with a service profession. Therefore, playing dhol was a birthright and ingrained with social identity. This formulation binds dholis to their profession, regardless of market considerations. There is a feeling of compulsion to carry on one's historical practices despite economic disincentives, such is the value of the identity one gains from one's inherited path. This means that changes to dhol tradition are felt not just economically and aesthetically but also at the deepest level of self.

The current picture of dhol, that of abundant production on the visage while producers quietly suffer within, reflects that of twenty-first-century Punjabi society at large. In the popular imagination, Punjab represents abundance; its fruits are plentiful and its people live largely and passionately. Such is the picture of Punjab on its face. Yet Punjab, too, was a victim of its own success as the famed breadbasket of India. Having put all their [bread] in one basket, Punjab's most representative agents, its farmers, ever compelled to choose quantity over quality, push onward toward despair. Life in Punjabi communities outside Punjab, for those fortunate enough to emigrate, offers some escape but also a misleading impression that Punjabis as a whole are doing as well as the national stereotypes say. It is not that there are no successes to celebrate along with the troubles. Rather, what calls my attention to this story is that the trouble for the unfortunate is masked by the untroubled vision of the fortunate few.

In this work, I seek to uncover why, despite the popularity of dhol and the numerical flourishing of dhol players, the dholis' communities and traditional values are in trouble. I observe that the pursuit of a Punjabi national identity—one that aids Punjabis in large-scale political representation and in maintaining historical consciousness during times of change—leads modern Punjabis to make particular economic, social, and artistic choices. A casualty of this pursuit and concomitant choices has been the disenfranchisement of dholis despite the significance of dhol to that very Punjabi national identity.

The masking of these issues, that which hides them from casual observation, derives from the illusion created by separating dhol from dholi. The latter evokes a delicate world, rife with anxiety about the appropriateness of musical performance, notions of ethnic hierarchies, and class prejudices. But the former invites less hesitation to engage. Let the drum be beaten, full steam ahead, in all the corners of Punjab's representation! The problem is that the identity of the typical dholi does not correlate with the identity of the typical Punjabi presented in grand narratives. Yet the dhol instrument, despite being historically the purview of seemingly atypical Punjabis, is a multivalent sign—it can represent different things to different people. When released from its inconvenient association with marginalized people, the dhol provides an effective representative of values sought by the mainstream. This brings us to the overarching theme addressed by this book: a conflict between how dhol represents broad Punjabi identity and how it represents the specific identities of its historical players. On one level are the dholis, who correspond to a variety of marginalized sociocultural identities. On another level, we find subscribers to the idea of a national Punjabi identity that claims dhol, by proxy, as a product of Punjab. A clash between differently lived realities is emerging as the nation takes cultural ownership of the professionals' instrument. To gain economic and cultural capital, many dholis choose to follow suit in separating dhol from their identities. In doing so, they betray the values of their communities and, in the long run, undermine their own vitality.

DHOL IN THE PUBLIC SOUNDSCAPE: TWO VIGNETTES

Before outlining the social and political matrix in which drummers exist, we may preview the types of spaces where dhol might be encountered and through which we may understand it as valuable to the experience of Punjabi social life. In early twenty-first-century Indian Punjab, the time and place most central to this book, dhol was ubiquitous in the soundscape of major public events. The two vignettes that follow introduce some sites of play—one urban and more scripted, the other rural and more spontaneous. A common thread between them is the role of drummers to concretize the perception of an event or public ritual.

October 30, 2004

A Zonal Youth Festival, in which students from area colleges compete in the arts of Punjab, is being held at the Sector-10 DAV College in East Punjab's capital city, Chandigarh (audiovisual example 1). Since the mid-twentieth century, such youth festivals have been target venues for staged performances of heritage. They have also served tangentially to employ, through institutional patronage, alienated practitioners of the arts. On this last day of the festival, music and dance performances take place in the auditorium. In front of a raised stage sits a panel of judges from the educational and political sectors. The audience of hundreds is composed of students from area colleges and members of the public who were privileged to receive passes. Most of the seats are full throughout the day and, during the evening's much-awaited bhangra competition, there will be standing room only.

During the morning, students showcase their skills on designated folk instruments such as the bowed lute, *sārangī*, the earthen pot idiophone, *ghaṛā*, and the double fipple flute, *algozā*. Indeed, there are entry categories for all the prominent instruments except for the dhol. Several of the student competitors are accompanied, however, by professional dholis hired for the festival. For example, a young man who showcases his skill with the percussive tongs, *cimṭā*, is accompanied by dholi Bachan Ram. Like Bachan Ram, most of the dholis employed belong to an extended family belonging to the ethnic community known as Bazigar.

The significance of this community's involvement becomes apparent in the afternoon when the program shifts to a dance competition between groups presenting less familiar forms: *Malvaī giddhā*, *sammī*, *jhummar*, and *ḍanḍās*. Though competitions in the famous bhangra dance have long been the highlight of youth festivals, recently there has been an effort to recognize other dances through a separate competition. Notably, all these dances save *Malvaī giddhā*—more a recitation of poetry than a structured dance—carry some association with so-called tribal people. *Sammī*, *jhummar*, and *ḍanḍās* are best remembered by the tribal Bazigar people, whose families originated on the opposite side of the Punjab region. Thus, although dholis of several ethnic backgrounds form the accompanists to the long-established stage bhangra, it is primarily the Bazigar dholis who are competent in working with these other dances. And because a community of Bazigar dholis is concentrated in the Chandigarh area, the location of this festival offers an opportunity to see diverse stagings of these dances.

Each staging reflects a different, still-evolving school of practice in the process of remembering and converting the participatory genres into folklorized presentations.[2] All the presentations reflect, in various proportions, a choreography set by each group's coach (an adult hired by a college) or its accompanying dholi. Indeed, it is evident that the dholis, who control the shifting rhythms that coordinate dancers, have had significant input, as it is only they who have full knowledge of the rhythmic dimension. While the coaches worked only prior to the performance, the dholis are on stage shaping the performances in real time with a broad palette of rhythmic patterns and tempi. Standing on one side of the stage, each dholi is the leader of a battery of accompanying musicians. The dholis' authorial role is most evident in the case of the last dance, the stick dance, *ḍanḍās*, accompanied by senior dholi Mali Ram. This genre has rarely appeared in such competitions, for knowledge of it is exclusively the purview of Mali Ram's kin. Mali Ram's authoritative posture and blasé demeanor, his choice of everyday rather than fancy dress, his lack of any showiness while, with minimal movement, he powerfully executes the beats—all these signs project security of ownership. The *ustād* (dhol master) takes a blessing from the stage and his dhol before he rolls up his sleeves, ready for business. In this context, *he is the boss.*

At times during the performances, the excited sounds from the audience echo in the auditorium at such volume as to threaten the continuity between aural and visual. It is the duty of the dholi on stage to maintain continuity despite these offstage distractions. Yet it is also the booming sound of dhol that prevents public noise from ever causing social awkwardness. The dhol, like a high-powered sound system, creates a space in which people are given voice and license to act with less restraint.

March 29, 2005

The village of Jarg, in the Ludhiana district, is the site of an annual fair (*melā*) in honor of Sitla Devi (audiovisual example 2). She is a goddess historically associated with aiding individuals afflicted with smallpox.[3] Despite the difficulty of reaching the remote village via potholed country roads, a sizable crowd has made it to this springtime festival, being one among several that dot the local Punjabi calendar. Residents of Jarg welcome visitors to the open area surrounding Sitla Devi's temple with free cups of sweetened water (*sharbat*). The pomp of the *melā* is made evident by a bagpipe and military drum band. The band has a Sikh name and presentation, its members are dressed in smart uniforms and march in formations. Meanwhile, devotees offer fried jaggery cakes (*gulgulā*) to the goddess. Some of these sweet treats end up in the hands of eccentric-looking men toting dhols, several of whom are encamped in the shade beneath trees. They are itinerant mystics, *faqīrs*, who travel a circuit of such festivals. The dhol is only one piece of their paraphernalia and they do not present themselves foremost as musicians. They spring into action as drummers at appropriate times, however.

A woman wearing a black suit has indicated her desire for possession by the goddess as she moves toward the temple. She is accompanied by one of the holy-man drummers, whose unshaven face, oversized turban, and prayer beads, as well as the cloths attached to his drum, mark him as a Shaikh. The woman's own dress signals her humility and temporary abandonment of social norms of modesty; she has dispensed with a veil (*cunnī*), allowing her body to be in full view and her tresses to flow unfettered. Fairgoers cannot resist watching her in silent curiosity. More dholis join in playing the ubiquitous rhythmic pattern known as *dhamāl*, which has deep associations with spirituality and puts bodies in a state to receive the holy spirit. The swaying movements of the woman's head indicate she has entered such a state and become the vehicle of the goddess. The Shaikh dholi plays dhamāl continuously with a disinterested look on his face, as if it is simply his function to beat the rhythm—one he performs automatically—to facilitate the woman's experience.

Another dholi, clean-shaven, has a playful, engaged look. He is Rafi, a Muslim hereditary professional musician from the so-called Mirasi community that resides in Jarg. It seems to me as if Rafi, an entertainer by trade, does not take the religious experience as seriously. He plays along for the enjoyment of making music and, perhaps, regards the spirit possession as merely a colorful aspect of such fairs. Rafi attempts to make eye contact with the Shaikh and ornaments his rhythm, to invite the Shaikh to create more aesthetic interest. The Shaikh, however, does not appear to notice; he is focused on his duty. The devotee eventually slows her gyrations and appears to regain ordinary consciousness. She composes herself and salutes the goddess by touching her forehead to the temple steps. Remaining in an ecstatic (*mast*) mood, the woman in black then moves in ways more conventionally recognized as dancing. Another woman and a young boy, emboldened by the opened space and lighter mood, join in. Rafi sees this as a setting appropriate to the secular dance rhythm *luḍḍī*. He again casts a glance at the Shaikh and plays a break (*toṛā*) in an attempt to shift to the new rhythm. The Shaikh does not follow Rafi's cue, and the two rhythmic patterns briefly clash before Rafi resigns himself to continue playing dhamāl. Rafi's interest in morphing the performance to a presentational display is indicated when he places his dhol on his head to play. The stunt adds more to the mirth of the *melā* than to its devotional aspect. Other dholis continue to articulate dhamāl in a simple form, seemingly oblivious to the more complex figures that Rafi is adding to the mix.

A short time later, Rafi's brother, Gaga, makes merry in the open space; the religious tone has shifted to secular fun. Gaga, who has accompanied college bhangra teams in the city of Ludhiana, is enjoining fairgoers—including the ethnographer—to dance in freestyle fashion. I hand my videocamera to a local fairgoer and the participation of a foreigner, perhaps, makes the impromptu dancing even more fun. Dance style ranges from idiosyncratic, naturalistic movements to established actions borrowed from staged bhangra routines. The dancing is accompanied by the celebratory rhythms *bhangṛā* and luḍḍī. The sacred (serious) space is never far, however. The local, impromptu videographer makes sure to include a glimpse of a shrine to the Sufi poet-saint, Baba Farid, which is incorporated into the same structure as the Sitla temple. The Mirasi family of Rafi and Gaga, not in contradiction to their efforts to create secular moods, are the shrine's caretakers. Nominally sacred and secular modalities thus alternate, through shifting sounds and modes of engagement. A Sufi (Muslim) shrine abutting a Hindu temple forms the center of a gathering that has both devotion and entertainment as its purpose, and which is attended by Muslim, Hindu, and Sikh Punjabis sharing behaviors and imbricated interpretations.

IDENTIFYING PUNJAB

We now shift from the intimate peek to the bird's-eye view to locate the area of the world that dholis call home. "Punjab" (*panjāb*) connotes a region in the northwestern part of South Asia. Locating Punjab in relation to people who identify with it, however, is a matter of locating both a geographical entity and an ideological space. Framing Punjab as an imagined entity or idea, Anjali Gera Roy has characterized it as "a geographical region, social construct and state of consciousness" (2014, 139). The Punjab of which people speak will be composed of some matrix of these intersecting dimensions, contoured by personal criteria of importance. This is a Punjab of feelings, values, and social networks, which is nevertheless anchored by the idea of a place: The Land of the Five Rivers.

To find Punjab in a way that respects its construction as both a geographic and a psychic entity, we must imagine the viewpoint of individuals. Imagine, for example, a "Non-resident Indian" (NRI) in the United Kingdom, a Sikh of Punjabi parentage, born in India but raised in England. The individual has returned to India twice in her life, once as a young child not long after the family emigrated and now again in adult life. Memories from the first visit, albeit hazy, include the rural atmosphere of her ancestral village (*pinḍ*). The experience was replete with smells of sugarcane juice boiling and the burning of refuse, with sounds of the incessant mating call of the cuckoo (*koil*), with sights of people sitting on their haunches, staring back at the visitor. On the second visit, this NRI is eager to engage with what she understands to be touchstones of Punjabi identity. The one must-do for the visit is to pay respect at Harimandir Sahib (the Golden Temple) in Amritsar, the foremost religious site of the Sikh community. The flight would have arrived in Delhi and the NRI would have traveled northwest along the main highway, the Grand Trunk Road. Crossing the border into the Punjab state, much signage appears in the Gurmukhi script, and people are taller and wear colorful turbans (*pagg*). Along the way, the visiting party stops to eat at a roadside diner (*ḍhābā*) and smiles at the charming sight of bearded men driving motorcycles while their wives ride sidesaddle elegantly behind them. The NRI visitor's *pinḍ* is in the Doaba area, in the center of the administrative state and not far from the Grand Trunk Road. During the visit, she takes in as many sights of local color as she happens on while generally seeking spaces that provide comforts like air-conditioning, cold soft drinks, and Wi-Fi access.

These personal experiences, however conventional, and the emotions connected to them most influence this hypothetical individual's definition of Punjab, a cluster of nodes—*pinḍ*, *ḍhābā*, *pagg*, Golden Temple, Grand Trunk Road, . . . the sound of dhol. The visitor would combine these perceptions with the rhetorical knowledge that Punjab identifies a rather small constituent state in India, adjacent to a state called Haryana that appears to be more or less the same culturally despite its signage in Hindi's Devanagari script. She would also be aware that rivers are an important reference point, dividing the region into areas with names like Majha, Malwa, and her very own Doaba, but she might have little sense of how the landscape of the Punjab region looks on the Pakistani side of the border or how its areas might be divided up there. The same would be generally true (in obverse) for someone with recent origins in the part of Punjab contained within Pakistan. In sum, each Punjabi defines Punjab in terms laden with attachment and personal identity first. Some of the objective facts pertinent to the region may be unknown, even irrelevant, to any individual Punjabi.

Punjab would seem to be an unproblematic geographic area of plains coursed through by the supposed eponymous five rivers (*panj-āb*) of the upper Indus (Sindh) system: Jehlum, Chenab, Ravi, Beas, and Satluj. Such a Punjab might be considered bound by topographic areas that include the Pothohar plateau in the northwest, the Himalayan foothills in the north, and the seasonal Ghaggar River in the east. The southern side includes semidesert areas. Topography, however, is not unproblematic. Historian J. S. Grewal notes that "there has been no unanimity among historians and other social scientists about the space called 'the Punjab'" (2004a, 1). Some contemporary residents, on the basis of culture, recognize differences that reduce the geographic range of Punjab. Southwestern areas, contained within Pakistani administrative boundaries *called* Punjab, include people who only loosely affiliate with "Punjab"; their most tangible basis for separation lies in the difference between their language, which they call Saraiki, and other Punjabi dialects. Similarly, residents of Rawalpindi (a city in Pakistan's Punjab province), wondered what I was doing on the Pothohar plateau asking about Punjabi stuff, which they attributed to the plains. In a reverse phenomenon of ownership, some consider topographically diverse areas (e.g., the southwestern portion of the Himachal Pradesh state) to be part of Punjab. The Punjabi-language poet Dhani Ram Chatrik, in his poem "Panjāb" (1931), begins by praising topographic diversity: "your climate, your fertile lands, rivers, *mountains* and plains" (my emphasis). This is a perspective that considers "Punjab" as broadly as possible. Either because these areas have been contained within historical political entities called Punjab or because of the presence of Punjabi people in those areas, they are considered to be homes to Punjabi culture. Hence, the apparent simplicity of a topographical definition gets complicated with the intersecting political and cultural-linguistic dimensions of Punjab.

The use of *Punjab* as a political designation began in the sixteenth century. As Grewal explains, the Mughal emperor Akbar enlarged the province of Lahore to encompass a region spanning five interfluvial areas (*doāb*) (2004a, 2), including a sixth river, the westernmost Indus. The Mughal elite first identified with the label "Punjab." By the eighteenth century, the common people of the area, consisting mostly of Muslims, had developed a Punjabi identity (12). The kingdom of Sikh ruler Maharaja Ranjit Singh (1799–1839), based in the former Mughal province of Lahore, was later declared to encompass "Punjab" at its center, along with surrounding areas (12). Ranjit Singh's representation helped to enfranchise the followers of the monotheistic Sikh religion born in this region in the sixteenth century. Sikhs continue to feel uniquely linked to Punjab, where they are most concentrated.

With the annexation of Punjabi lands by British India in 1849, a newly incorporated Punjab Province was extended to include areas as far east as the Yamuna River. This province remains the largest administrative region

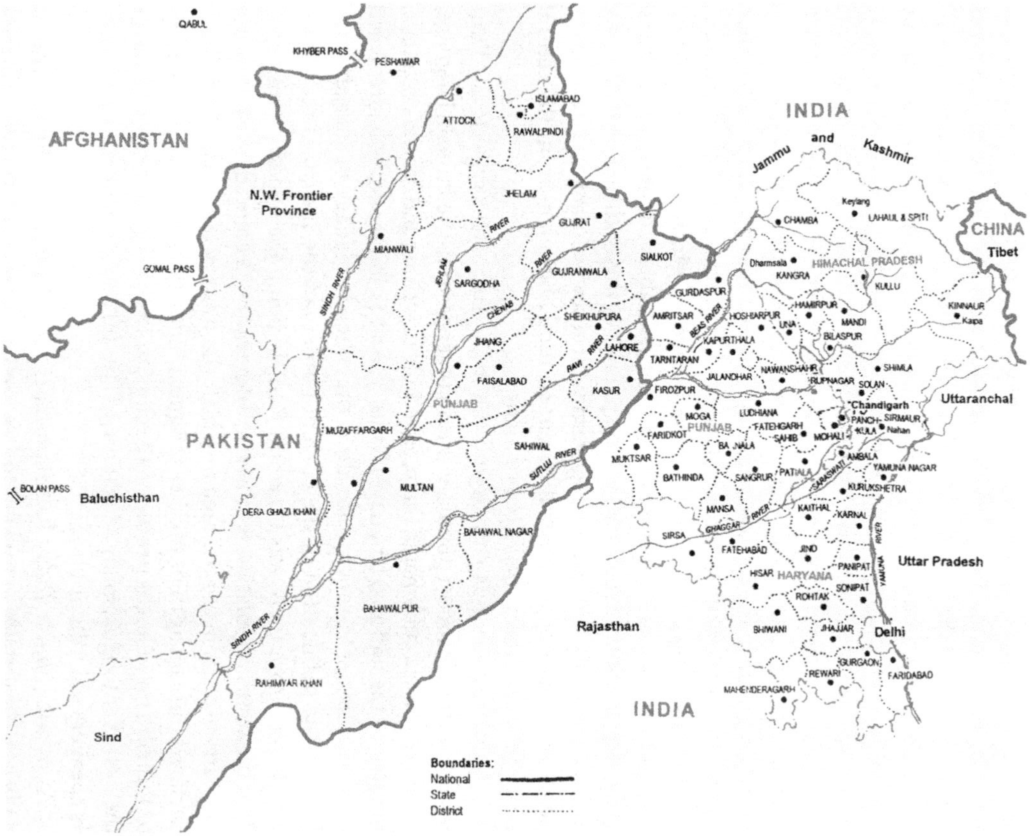

FIGURE 0.2 Administrative divisions of the Punjab region and surrounding areas, 2015. Courtesy Global Institute for Sikh Studies, New York.

in history known as Punjab. Lasting until independence in 1947, the Punjab Province stretched from Sindh in the southwest, nearly to Peshawar in the northwest, close to Kashmir in the northeast, and Delhi in the southeast. The center of its aesthetic culture and language remained Lahore, on the Ravi River in the area known as Majha.

Currently, two political units take the name of Punjab: a province of Pakistan and a constituent state of India (Figure 0.2). Because the sense of Punjab as a single geographical region is retained, these two administrative entities may be distinguished, respectively, as "West" or "Pakistani" Punjab and "East" or "Indian" Punjab. The most extensive ethnographic site for the present work was the Indian Punjab state, having an area of 32,000 square miles (about the size of the US state of Maine). The state's population at last census was around 28 million; the Pakistani province, in comparison, has roughly 110 million inhabitants.[4] These dimensions are relevant to a past-looking narrative of Punjabi identity that imagines Punjab in its largest geographic terms, a place roughly coterminous with the erstwhile British Indian Punjab Province. In terms of broad religious communities, Sikhs (58%) and Hindus (38%) dominate in the Indian state's population. Muslims comprise less than 2 percent, a smaller minority than that found in other states of northern India and in stark contrast to the colonial province, in which Muslims made up the majority. India's Punjab state exerts considerable economic and cultural influence despite its small size, yet the politics of this Sikh-majority state are often at odds with India's central government and what many Sikhs especially perceive as the Punjab state's different cultural alignment from the central government's Hindu-majority population.

The politics of language are significant in Punjab matrices. Pakistan's Punjab province is the most populous one in that country. The Punjabi language, however, is often sublimated there, especially in writing and official discourse, in favor of the national language, Urdu. The situation is somewhat reversed on the Indian side, where Punjabi is the official language of Punjab state. Indeed, the delineation of the current borders of the Indian Punjab state, which date from 1966, was based on Punjabi being the majority language.[5] That the state's population is majority-Sikh was not a coincidence but rather due largely to its being the area in which the most people—chiefly Sikhs—declared Punjabi as their mother tongue. Linguistic politics connects Sikhs to Punjabi, for whereas people of all religions in the region speak Punjabi as their mother tongue, many Muslims and Hindus choose to identify *politically* as speakers of Urdu or Hindi.

As of 2004, *India Today* had repeatedly scored Punjab at the top end of its list of "best states" in which to live, on the basis of a level of prosperity reflected in agricultural production, the consumer market, and investments (Saran 2004, 20–21). By 2018, Punjab had fallen to number 15 with respect to economy but regained (after a drop) the top place for agriculture ("India Today State of the States" 2018). Yet, despite its reputation for prosperity, the Indian Punjab has been wracked by demoralizing social crises in recent decades. One concerns the aftereffects of the Green Revolution. Beginning in the 1960s, agricultural production increased through the adoption of modern farming technologies, synthetic fertilizers, pesticides, and high-yielding seed varieties. As part of this change, Punjabi farmers moved toward monoculture, focused on intensive production of two seasonal crops: rice and wheat. The prosperity of the Green Revolution was exhausted by the 1980s, when the cost of production started to increase and productivity waned (Gill 2005, 226). Ecologically, overexploitation of water resources led to a falling water table, and overexploitation of the soil led to lower fertility (ibid., 229). Homogeneity put farmers at greater risk in the event of periodic failure of crops (ibid., 226). Trapped by debt, farmers were left with no choice but to continue the exploitation of resources and technologies with greater intensity. Small farmers, who made up nearly half of Punjab's agriculturalists in the early 1990s, were hit the hardest (ibid.). The concomitant economic distress, as Gill explains, is most responsible for the alarming increase in farmer suicides (235)—a prominent social issue of twenty-first-century Punjab.

A more recently rooted crisis in Indian Punjabi society is substance addiction. Indian Punjab lies at a crossroads of the drug trade, especially for opiates smuggled across the border from Pakistan (Chand 2016, 119). A study conducted in 2005 found that heroin was the drug most commonly abused, followed by opium (Ambedkar et al. 2016, 2). It estimated 860,000 users of opioids in the state, among whom at least nearly 175,000 were addicts (ibid., 3–4). In 2018 Rahul Bedi suggested that more than two-thirds of Punjabi households had one drug addict in the family. Moreover, the prevalence of injection among users increased the number of HIV-infected individuals (Chand 2016, 120). Opioid abuse was secondary to the most abused substance, alcohol. Punjab state is a middling consumer of alcohol in comparison with other states in India, but the country's alcohol consumption is on the rise, having more than doubled between 2005 and 2016 (Chauhan 2018), and Punjab is among the top states (more than 10%) for alcohol abuse (Ministry of Social Justice and Empowerment 2018, 3). The substance-abuse issues intersect with the issue of distress of indebted farmers, belying the traditional image of Punjab as home to hale and hearty, wealthy, and jolly agriculturalists. The agricultural crisis, while centered on farmers, affects all classes of a society where agriculture makes up the largest economic sector. The substance-abuse crisis particularly affects the lower socioeconomic classes, of which dholis are a part.

Just as "Punjab," a land of ever-shifting borders, took some time to emerge as a geographic construct, the notion of a Punjabi identity was not evident from early times. Significant ground for the concept had been laid through the development of Punjabi vernacular literature starting in the seventeenth century (Grewal 1999, 45). But an explicit notion, Grewal argues, emerged only in the late eighteenth century, when written references began to be made to a Punjabi language and Punjabi people (Grewal 2004b, 13). By the early nineteenth century, consciousness of Punjabi identity was being expressed widely. After independence, the Indian Punjab state was, on one hand, an economically exceptional one whose people were represented as hardworking, healthy, and proud to move the Indian republic forward. On the other hand, it was partitioned from cultural heritage sealed off in Pakistan, a country with which India was in conflict. The folklorization of bhangra can be seen as part of postcolonial elites' recovery of a distinctive cultural identity. It helped cultural nationalists to construct a historically rooted yet fresh practice of embodying Punjabiness in this changed demographic and cultural environment. Notably, while dhol had been a feature of everyday Punjabi life since at least the eighteenth century, the proliferation of bhangra as a sign of modern (East) Punjabi identity connected dhol to its expression.

Whereas "Punjabi" functions as a cultural identity based on region, the degree to which it corresponds to an identity based on ethnicity is a question that this book explores through focus on the lives of peoples of Punjab origin who are pushed to the margins. The question is aggravated most prominently by a tendency to privilege a particular ethnic group, the Jatt, as the group most synonymous with Punjabi identity. The Jatt were a pastoral tribal people with origins in Central Asia who settled in Punjab and whose lifestyle, by the sixteenth century, had transformed into an agricultural one (Habib 2005, 66–68). As one of the well-established ethnicities of the region, they have greatly influenced cultural values. As a result especially of their role as landowners in a region where agriculture has been of great economic importance, Jatts, who also are the largest ethnic group, have become representative of Punjabi culture. It is telling that, in the seventeenth century, the language of the Sikh Gurus was described by a Persian-language author as "the language of the Jats of Punjab" (Grewal 2004a, 11)—even though the Gurus themselves were not Jatts. Further, when one combines ethnic and religious identity, one finds Jatt Sikhs occupy a perceived center, in international and mainstream Punjabi discourse, of the (India-based) Punjabi identity. Anthropologist Nicola Mooney has explored the intersection of both normative Jatt and Sikh identities, theorizing that Jatt Sikhs often participate in a "rural imaginary," a framework in which they imagine themselves as "central arbiter of [Punjab's] predominantly village-based culture" (2013, 279). It is not that Jatt Sikhs believe they are the only people with a claim to Punjabi identity. Rather, Jatt Sikh claims to Punjabi identity are unimpeachable, and they appear to be the group that most consistently and most exclusively identifies with Punjab.

Tension between majority and minority ethnic groups over how they enjoy representation within a cultural landscape is not unique to Punjab. What must be noted here, however, is the way that the idea of a cultural region, as opposed to a sovereign state, defines Punjabi identity (Gera Roy 2014, 139). This phenomenon has implications for how minority peoples, whom we might naively ascribe to the Punjab region, negotiate their position in relation to the identity. Within the borders of a state (by which I mean country, e.g., the Republic of India), there is the possibility of validating all culture as "national" culture and all inhabitants as "citizens" of the state. As Baumann (1999) articulates, such aspirations conflict with the history of many states' bases in *nations*—groups of people perceiving themselves as a people with a shared heritage—which gives rise to dominant ethnic groups and cultural formations within a state. We may consider a state as the administrative unit circumscribing place, with which there is the interplay of nation, a unit circumscribing people. In the case of Punjabi identity, because there are (at least) two countries involved, it is preferable to consider a region as circumscribing a place. Participants in the Punjabi identity concept, moreover, may define Punjab not as an exact geography but rather as the region where Punjabi culture is present. What an individual perceives as outside the preferred cultural formation may be marked as outside the Punjabi region. Marginalized cultural formations in place, therefore, cannot appeal to a state to validate their inclusion in a commonwealth. They *can* appeal to a nation, but their incorporation means adopting the nation's culture. This book explores how the identities of marginalized peoples of Punjab can find representation in definitions of Punjabi that conceive a dominant cultural formation—a national culture—as its basis. It queries where dholis fit when their defining art form is included while their ethnic identities are more or less excluded from the national identity.

"Punjabi" is in demand as an identity construct that gives coherence to a visible global community, yet, in local conversations, its parameters are contested.[6] Issues revolve around tensions endemic to cultural identification in an environment of major divisions and disparities. The fault lines include citizenship, ethnicity, class, language, religious affiliation, and gender. As a cultural identification, "Punjabi" is practiced differently by individuals according both to their personal experience and to their membership in a matrix of various other identities. To these other identities they apportion investment differently, according to the advantages or disadvantages membership provides. Such is to be expected. What this book addresses in terms of a crisis of identity for dholis relates, however, to great disparities in advantage between their and others' identity matrices. For them, that which is ostensibly a position of agreement and unification—Punjab identity—becomes not only a site of contestation but also alienation.

PUNJABI MUSIC, MUSICIANS, AND DHOLIS

Outlining the borders of Punjabi music proves as challenging as locating Punjab itself. Whose Punjabi music do we mean? Garib Dass, for years, led me to believe or to think that *he* believed that a certain dance action belonged to the distant past. When I discovered, through independent evidence, that the action was created in the 1950s, I presented the information to Garib Dass. He confirmed it to be true and that he had known it to be all along. Had I known this at an earlier stage, it would have detracted from the clarity of the schema he had chosen by which to best make me understand at that time. Perhaps more important, that dance action, irrespective of its history, had been subsumed in a category of traditional that was most relevant to the representation he wished to convey. Garib Dass was not educating me about Punjabi music as some objective phenomenon but rather about *his* Punjabi music.

True representations are never practical, and so a practical orientation to Punjabi music—as might be expected by readers of this introductory chapter—must always be, to some degree, untrue. The Ghanaian highlife musician Nana Ampadu, recognizing the impossibility of conveying his art in brief to a documentary filmmaker, said, "If I say I will tell you where *highlife* started, then it means I am going to lie" (quoted in Agawu 2003, xiv). The misrepresentation inherent to all simple representations includes the speaker's necessary choice of categories, the speaker's simplified taxonomy of the phenomenon, which prompts the listener to adopt these categories at the outset of the journey toward knowing it. The schema one presents, intended to aid the listener's temporary understanding, is never as complex as the speaker knows it to be. Such is my dilemma in introducing "the music of Punjab." The rationale of my taxonomy is to present a structure that I have deduced from empirical data in the form of observations of what Punjabi people said about the phenomena and how they acted about them. To the extent that I "lie," I intend to facilitate a provisional understanding of the truth as further data and analyses appear in subsequent chapters.

My (mis)representation of Punjabi music encourages readers to note its potential differences, ontologically, from what I assume to be a familiar lens of globalized modern (European origin) music. The move is deliberately discursive to thwart the habit of thinking of music as an object defined by Western notions of sound art or else by broad axiomatic criteria (e.g., Blacking's "humanly organized sound," 1973, 3). Following the intellectual shift to treating musical activity through an active verb, "musicking" (Small 1998), I consider music in terms emphasizing action over product. One's world of what may expediently (untruthfully) be called music is best understood not as an assemblage of products but rather of culturally circumscribed fields of relationships between social actors and the meanings of their actions. Most important, in my view, is to break down musical activity in terms of the people involved (how they are situated in the social fabric) and what these people intend to do by their musicking. A given, culturally salient ontology of music will include numerous and not inherently related practices, which, however, may be read against social structure and, indeed, contribute to producing it (Seeger 1983).

We may begin to distinguish value metrics of musicking using Turino's *fields* model (2008). According to Bourdieu, the social world may be divided into social fields—"multi-dimensional space(s) of positions" (1985, 724), which are, as Turino elucidates, "defined by the purpose and goals of the activity as well as the values, power relations, and types of *capital* . . . determining the role relationships, social positioning, and status of actors and activities within the field" (2008, 26). Turino adapts this notion to theorize functionally distinct (albeit not exclusive) musicking fields, three of which are most relevant to Punjab. In *participatory* musicking, no distinction is made between artists and audience; the aim is to involve a maximum number of people in performing. In *presentational* musicking, an artist furnishes a performance for a discrete audience. And in the field that Turino calls *high fidelity*, recorded performances closely resemble the sounds of live performance while an audience (listeners to the recording) experience it at a later time (ibid.). This model helps us see beyond formal genre categories to what may be operatively important in the musicking experience. For example, the singing by Punjabi women at gatherings in the home preceding weddings customarily inhabits the participatory field. What happens, however, when the same genre is put into the presentational field, in the context of a performance on stage for a college audience in a youth festival? The performers may polish their sounds to shape a product intended to entertain their audience, shifting the function from its prior purpose of creating an auspicious matrimonial environment to entertainment, competition, or appreciation of heritage. The genre has also been distributed on recordings, the high-fidelity field, in which case it is likely to include instrumental sounds that would not be present in domestic gatherings. Used to evoke memories or as a learning aid, the high-fidelity performance somewhat misrepresents the sound of the domestic gatherings, at the same time not disturbing the idea that these *could* be live (and thus reasonably authentic) performances. Thus, we see what might be called more or less the same genre, when analyzed in terms of the form of the musical object, operating in three different matrices of value and social relationships.

I aim to see Punjabi social action through a musical lens, which cannot be accomplished by lumping all things called music together or by categorizing genres alone. My schema, therefore, identifies idiosyncratic fields that represent the intersections of social and material dimensions salient to the Punjab context. The schema does not describe music per se but rather a wider encompassing world of performance that includes sound, motion, and drama. It proceeds from the observation that such performance in Punjab is a strongly *marked* activity. Audiences/participants often vigorously ascribe limitations to and make judgments about performances on the basis of the social position of actors, their understood intent in acting, and the context of their act. I believe the comparatively high level of tension over the propriety of performance relates to the apparent fact that, unlike the modern Western concept of music that ascribes to it a default positive value, music in Punjabi society is treated as potentially dubious.[7]

To clarify what I mean by a marked activity, I offer the simile of a strongly marked activity in American society: sex. Whereas the sexual act itself remains the same, variations in actors, intent, and context with respect to gender, age, social relationship, privacy, religious ritual, and monetary exchange are salient factors having the potential to affect how Americans perceive the act's appropriateness and value. Broaching the subject of sex in American cultural discourse has the great potential of producing a feeling of tension, as discussants look beyond the generic category of sex and seek to locate the specific sexual act's propriety by asking who, why, where, and when. Until these questions are answered and the individual can place the act as one of a certain type, the prospect of sex is marked by tension. Likewise, to relieve the tension surrounding performance—an engagement with others through the body not entirely dissimilar to sex—acts of performance in Punjab are compartmentalized by the established norms that govern their value.

In what I call the Amateur Field, most sonic performance comes under the rubric of singing. It tends to be a ritualistic or an otherwise sharply context-limited recitation of texts. Playing of instruments is limited to a few, usually percussive, that are coded as domestic implements or easy to play. Women are the dominant actors in the field, and most of their performances coincide with ceremonial occasions. An example would be the singing of *ghoṛī*, a song in praise of a groom by a group of his relatives in his home during the weeks leading up to his wedding.[8] This type of performance is for oneself and the collective community in which one resides; it is "private." It is of a participatory nature and inclusion in the performance requires little or no formal training.

Within the Professional Field, performance is typically presentational. The material includes that which is called *sangīt*—the Punjabi term used to translate the English *music*. Sangīt strongly connotes the incorporation of melodic instruments. An example is the ballad, including *vār* (heroic tales) and *qissā* (love epics). Ballads have been sung for rural audiences in the bardic *ḍhāḍī* genre by performers like Sharif Idu (1939–2020), to the accompaniment of *sārangī* and hourglass drum, *ḍhaḍḍ*.[9] To perform difficult repertoire, characterized by complex texts and instrumental and vocal executions requiring rigorous cultivation, the performers are highly trained. As professionals, performers first and foremost do the act for payment. An added implication is that, because they depend on it for a living, payment is not just a feature but rather it is their priority. In diametric opposition to the Amateur Field, the Professional Field is dominated by men. Morcom observes that women in north India who performed in front of men tend to be viewed erotically, regardless of the nature of their performance (2013, 6). The same is generally true for Punjab, with the effect that women are strongly discouraged from performing within the Professional Field because of its usually public and mixed-gender audience. That such performances are not only before male-inclusive audiences but also done for payment puts them adjacent to prostitution, and the tension elicited when women perform in the Professional Field is so great as to form perhaps the firmest boundary between it and the Amateur Field. Yet the other great boundary between Amateur and Professional is ethnicity. Professional performance is considered to be labor purchased by others, and so its performers possess the low social status ascribed to service providers. Accordingly, they belong to specific ethnic communities that assert a hereditary birthright to a monopoly on paid performance.[10]

In Punjabi society, the landowners—comprising higher-status ethnic communities—were historically the patrons of musicians, and they have maintained a distance from professional musical practice. A government report from 1904 noted, moreover, that agriculturalists in Punjab, busy with work all day, had little time to listen to music outside the slow rainy season. What little musical entertainment they encountered might consist of the aforementioned ballads sung by "itinerant singers (*Mirasis* or *dhadis*)" (Punjab Government 2002 [1907], 102). In the late nineteenth century, most of the players of musical instruments were, in another author's observation, "Mírásis, Jogis, or *faqirs*" (Ibbetson 1995 [1883], 234). Traditional Punjabi society has reserved two appropriate social backgrounds for musicians, one conventional, the other exceptional. Musicians come either from a qualifying ethnic community or else live virtually outside the rules of society—as a *jogī* or *faqīr* (ascetics on a spiritual path who live unorthodox lifestyles and renounce social norms). Of the conventional, which we may call performer communities, some are associated primarily with music while others are those in which musical performance may occur though it does not have a strong bearing on the group's identity. Performer communities exist in contrast to the majority of Punjabi ethnic communities, who, aside from a stock of roles now supplied in the music industry, implicitly or explicitly reject public performance as socially appropriate behavior.

The apparent contradiction between the low social status of musicians such as these and the high value of the art they produce were noted early by Merriam (1964, 137–38). Schofield analyzed this issue as it presented among Professional Field performers during India's Mughal era. Such musicians, Schofield writes, could occupy a space of "social liminality" that granted them the "unusual cultural sanction to cross ordinarily strict boundaries that are of significance to a particular society" (Brown 2007a, 6). Although professional musicians were of lower rank because of their status as service providers, they could be granted "institutionally liminal status" (Brown 2007b, 20). Patrons offered respect to the performers temporarily in specific institutional contexts in which the performers' product was valued, such as a concert in a royal court. Disagreeing with Bourdieu, Schofield believes that cultural capital is not limited to elites but that lower-status individuals, too, may use cultural capital to improve their status (ibid., 32–33). Such an opportunity, however, is limited to those institutionally liminal spaces. Moreover, patrons may push back against performers' efforts to improve their status, leading to sanctioning or labeling them as deviant to reinforce their low rank (35).

The Amateur and Professional Fields reflect customary distinctions of preindustrial Punjab that appear to roughly bifurcate women's and men's performances. The Professional Field, however, in excluding all but certain proscribed ethnic groups, actually leaves out men of most ethnicities. Therefore, whereas women may appear to be subordinated to the position of performing only nonprofessionally, men of mainstream ethnicities are the demographic most estranged from musical performance of any sort. To be sure, the same demographic enjoys the most privileges in Punjabi society, and so it is a matter of interest that its musical privileges are limited. Perhaps it is a dubious privilege that women at large can lead the least prestigious songs or that the lowest-status ethnic groups are ascribed the role of musician in place of other opportunities, which reveals much about the value of musicking. One can begin to imagine the tensions generated as, in a changing society, mainstream men claim their privilege to do anything they choose, women seek access to professional musicking, and low-status ethnicities seek to break into nontraditional work.

An alternative space of performance, the Sacred Field, allows for temporary socially sanctioned transgression of the norms constraining the everyday ritual- and entertainment-oriented acts performed in other fields. My use of *sacred* is not to suggest a fundamental dichotomy between sacred and secular music such as Kalra (2015) argues vigorously against and as my earlier vignette, of the Jarg *melā*, belies. It is to acknowledge a flexible distinction, made evident through the social actors involved, between the intent of performances. I do not claim that performers of sacred music genres act differently from performers of secular music but rather that performers, by their very acts, may intend to create sacred space. We may invoke Turner, who notes that liminal phenomena blend lowliness and sacredness (1966, 96). His idea of *communitas*, the feeling of "even communion of equal individuals" (96), suggests that the sacredness of a space may be attributed to the dissolution of institutionalized norms and power structures (128). As in Schofield's concept of institutionally liminal status, performers here occupy a low status at the same time as they garner high respect, and the apparent ambiguity contributes to a sense of their being "outside the system" (Brown 2007b, 36). The Sacred Field is, however, distinct both from the "nonmusician" form of outsider status in the Amateur Field and the socially marginalized form of outsider status in the Professional Field.

Whereas the Amateur Field corresponds to singing as ritual and performance in the Professional Field is music as entertainment, performance in the Sacred Field constitutes a third category: devotion. Its perceived spiritual nature and devotional function are paramount. As a matter of cultural policy on devotion—a space of liberation from man-made laws—actors in this field may not be limited by gender, class, or ethnicity. Sacred Field actors may earn money, but because of the intent of their work, doing so does not injure their social status. Performance is thus open to those who are excluded socially from the conventional performer identities as long as their acts are oriented toward devotion. One may take, for example, the Jatt Sikh performer Sohan Singh Seetal (1909–1998). Though not coming from a hereditary musician family, Seetal obtained training from a Mirasi, forming a troupe for the *ḍhāḍī* genre in the late 1920s (Nijhawan 2006, 85). As Nijhawan explains, Seetal rejected the existing, nominally secular form of *ḍhāḍī* music. He thought instead of the genre as a form of *kīrtan*, a term that refers to devotional praise in the Sikh tradition (86). When, half a century later, women broke the barrier to performance of *ḍhāḍī* music, performers like Pawandeep Kaur similarly considered their performances to be acts of religious piety (43).

With modern Punjab came the Art Field. It is shaped by the belief that music can (or should) exist without a necessary attachment to social function. It is the notion of art in an absolute sense. Central to the field is the broadly established Hindustani music or so-called classical music of north India, several *gharānās* (stylistic lineages) of which developed in Punjab.[11] Its sonic forms are distinguished by adherence to a systematic theory of *rāg* (melodic mode) and *tāl* (metric mode). Before the twentieth century, Hindustani music was the exclusive purview of ethnically distinct performers operating in the Professional Field. The transposition of the notion of absolute art from European classical music to this elite genre of India arguably engendered Hindustani music's introduction to a new social field.[12]

In the Art Field, where actors perform for art's sake, performance is open to individuals without the same exclusion and judgment that accompany performance in the Professional Field. It is the prioritization of creating art, not mired in the profane business of pursuing monetary income, that distinguishes the Art Field from the Professional, and in this respect, the Art Field parallels the Sacred. Kalra cites a performer of Sikh *kīrtan* (devotional singing) who evoked a sense of the transcendental that he likened to "classical" music (2015, 44). Kalra's insight that Indian "classical" music—which I would call Hindustani music situated in the Art Field—includes an ethos of sacrality is apropos. In distinguishing the Sacred Field from the Art Field, my emphases are their perceived intents (one for devotion, the other for art's sake) and the markedly different social contexts in which their performances typically occur. Moreover, although both fields offer alternatives to the structures established by the Amateur and Professional Fields, the Sacred Field may be considered the older alternative, while the Art Field emerged in the colonial era.

With the advent of mass media, still another field emerged: the Mediated Field. It is characterized by media's ability to spatially separate a performance from an audience. The indirect nature of a mediated performance, whether prerecorded or remotely broadcast, removes the requirement for performers to be *in the presence of* their audience. Because the anxiety surrounding performance has much to do with norms of propriety about who may perform in the same space as who, media's separation of space or time allows the subversion of prior norms. Further, through mediation, aspects of performers' personal identities may be hidden. Consequently, the norms enforced by traditional performance customs in Punjab have been challenged and their restrictions have deteriorated in the increasingly mediated musical landscape.

Dhol playing appears to occur in most of these fields although is not a genre central to any of them. Perhaps most strongly determinant with respect to dhol's field is the fact that, notwithstanding the many lay women who have taken up the dhol in recent decades (mostly outside Punjab), professional dholis are exclusively male.[13] This, along with the customary restriction of dhol playing to proscribed ethnic communities who depend on income from playing, aligns it with the Professional Field. Yet, being percussion, dhol falls short of the ideal concept of sangīt, central to the Professional Field, which favors melodic instruments. Indeed, dhol playing is not normally labeled as sangīt or music; it is, simply, "dhol." Unlike a tabla solo by maestro Zakir Hussain, dhol is not usually intended for appreciative listening but rather a background element of the everyday soundscape. And, although this aligns dhol with the Amateur Field, the players stand outside its center in terms of gender position. Dhol performances occur in the Sacred Field in the form of men acting with devotional intent. The dhol is used, too, to contribute sound to performances of the Mediated Field, in which case, wrapped into an ensemble including tonal instruments, "music" is produced. Individual dholis may also give incidental performances in the mode of the Art Field, liminally producing something akin to the sangīt produced by Zakir Hussain's tabla. Finally, as dhol playing (particularly in the diaspora) becomes dislodged from its gender- and ethnicity-based norms of participation and is played for private enjoyment, its mode of performance occupies a sort of new Amateur Field. I suggest that the spread of dhol across fields lends to a perception that dhol as a genre is everywhere, and at the same time dhol playing's unique social dimensions lack clarification for observers unfamiliar with dholis' values and intentions. By this I mean to say that the Amateur, Professional, and Art Fields clarify the place of performers of *ghoṛī*, *ḍhāḍī*, and Hindustani music to a greater degree, whereas dhol players, merely accommodated by habitual categories, are liable to be misplaced. There is dissonance, moreover, between how dhol players situate themselves and how casual observers haphazardly situate them.

Dhol playing articulates a unique space of social relationships and, I believe, despite performers' accommodation within more prominent field constructs, constitutes its own field. I will call this the Dhol World, wherein actors' goals, values, and positions are in alignment with a structure established generationally by dholis and to which dholis ascribe a sort of native environment for dhol performance. While now present in many spaces, dhol players are frequently foreign to them, causing them to experience estrangement. The feeling of loss of identity, to which I attribute contemporary dholis' "tough times," is connected to the disintegration of their native Dhol World.

THESIS: NATIONAL IDENTITY COMES AT THE EXPENSE OF THE MARGINALIZED

I began this introduction with the recognition that something is amiss among Punjab's dholis—something more complex than the familiar tale of fading preindustrial traditions. Dhol playing, indeed, remains, for all intents and purposes, a type of traditional art that modern society has not obliterated. Noting the continual growth in the number of dhol players—both from the ranks of hereditary-professional families and laypeople—I then offered two vignettes to show the primacy of dhol and ubiquity of dholis in public life. That was probably why I had been slow to pinpoint the feeling of despair among traditional dholis. It is difficult, indeed, to objectively argue a net loss to the art of dhol. For, although older players lament the forgetting of pieces of repertoire and habits of practice, as we will see, in other cases, new rhythms and contexts for play have enriched the dhol traditions. The sense of loss, less tangibly, comes from the perception that there is something less special about dhol. To play dhol means less, or more precisely, it less resonates the significance understood by natives of the Dhol World. Dholis have valued dhol as a means of structuring distinctive identities. As dhol loses its power to do that for them, all while it has gained power to articulate a less differentiated Punjabi identity, the dholis' identity concept disintegrates. This deteriorating sense of self is no small loss for a marginalized people who derive little other compensation. The popularity of their instrument, though earlier a means of expanded career opportunities, offers them diminishing returns. It is toward locating this specialness, ultimately, that I problematized "Punjab" and "Punjabi music." Dholis *are* Punjabi (they belong to Punjab and Punjabi culture) and dhol *does* belong to Punjabi music. Dholis' sense of place, however, and dhol's position within Punjabi music are alternative, minoritarian ontologies. Already difficult to parse within dominant perspectives, shrinking representation for these ontologies is a cause for remorse.

The topic of dhol is valuable for uncovering subaltern Punjabi ontologies because entering the musicians' world means crossing fault lines within Punjabi identity. In particular, it exposes those created by ethnicity (and by extension, social class), which are often neglected in discourse about Punjabi identity. I surmise the reason is the unsavoriness of the subject, being linked to the disparities of castelike hierarchy. Overidentification with a caste—read as an exclusive ethnic group situated in a power relationship with others—is taboo among the more privileged classes from which representative mouthpieces for Punjabi culture tend to come. Yet, even when the floor is open to consider the broad difference between majority and minority peoples in

Punjabi society, discussion tends to obscure the particular group and individual identities. A simple dichotomy reveals only a set of others, effectively lumping them rather than making their identities visible.

Dhol is an insightful topic because it offers rich examples of how minoritarian ontologies are finely articulated. For subaltern Punjabis, identification is a daily, embodied practice of subtle gestures, the contours of which are easily missed by those who look only for the broad strokes of citizenship, religion, and language. Dhol playing is a site of negotiating identities based on these ontologies. Its examination allows us to consider those small gestures through which difference is constructed between people within the Punjabi population. It reveals friction between the various marginalized ethnic groups of which dholis are a part, as well as between dholis as an occupational class and the broader Punjabi-identifying community.

The key issue that draws my attention is what I have characterized as an existential threat to the identities of dholis: the foreclosure of their complex identities by the incorporation of the dhol into a generic Punjabi identity. The fact was brought into relief for me after comparing the practice of dhol outside Punjab, by nouveau enthusiasts, to dhol playing in traditional spheres of Punjab, by individuals from generational lineages. In the former context, dhol playing appeared to lose richness in its aesthetic dimension, surrounding ritual and rules of practice that were meaningful to individuals in the latter context. The repertoire shrank drastically and awareness of one style versus another style of play decreased. Players neglected behaviors that are important to the traditional players' identity. The behaviors in question ranged from minor issues, such as wearing or holding the dhol in an incorrect way, to major issues, such as using the instrument to draw focus to oneself rather than humbly supporting another focus of attention. In the extreme, dhol in the diaspora represented Punjabi culture first and foremost, such that what one played or how one played mattered less *as long as dhol was played.*

The trajectory had its genesis in the middle of the twentieth century, when the phenomenal success of folkloric bhangra as the de-facto national dance of (Indian) Punjab began to poise dhol as a sonic marker of a broadly Punjabi identity. Although the job of accompanying presentations of bhangra in Punjab has remained in the hands of professional dholis (synonymous with hereditary specialists), the significant change of the past two decades has been the acceptance of others as players of dhol. In the first decade of the twenty-first century, I would have said that mainstream Punjabis, as compared with an earlier awareness, were less aware of the specific ethnic identities of dholis than they were of their being of another class. In the second decade, it was possible to see dhol playing as unattached to class. The adoption of dhol in the diaspora by many heritage-hungry lay individuals contributed to this change. Before the 2010s, that phenomenon was isolated from happenings in Punjab—effectively, two separate worlds having different rules—but then the nontraditional players came to interact more with the hereditary professionals and social barriers broke down.

Dhol playing has headed down a path similar to that which Neuman (1990) describes as set on by Hindustani music a century ago, wherein the bourgeoisie came to partake in a formerly exclusive tradition. In a recent work, Katz (2017) reevaluated the process addressed by Neuman, with more attention to effects experienced by hereditary musicians. Until at least the late nineteenth century, nearly all practitioners of Hindustani music were Muslims, whereas today Hindus predominate. Katz outlines the explanation that access to the tradition was democratized when it was nationalized and, consequently, made available to the bourgeoisie (7). In that narrative, Bhatkhande's reforms to the music's theory helped to modernize its study in academic institutions accessible to the middle class, creating an alternative place and method of acquisition to the family-based master-disciple practice of hereditary professionals (133). Contributing to reformed views on cultural ownership, institutions such as the All India College of Music emphasized Hindustani music's place along a continuity of Indian music since antiquity. This opened conceptual space for Hindus to be included in a broadly Indian heritage rather than one belonging to specific (Muslim) families of recent centuries (109). Another narrative, Katz explains, celebrates the ability of Muslim hereditary musicians in the tradition to adapt to and evolve with these changes (10). Katz concludes that both these perspectives—one that emphasizes the co-opting of hereditary musicians' art and the other that gives the musicians more agency—are complementary. Yet, because the net result has been a marginalization of the hereditary performers and a decline of the intensive, one-on-one method of transmission (that, arguably, is the essence of the tradition), Katz chooses to focus on noncelebratory dimensions of change (ibid.).

How should we treat the changes to the Dhol World as its performers travel this path? The effect on their lives reflects a paradox inherent to the dissolution of caste-based social structure in South Asia. Insofar as hierarchy, discrimination, and immobility are embedded in its practice, the disintegration of caste-based society would seem critical to the cause of social justice. Still, the caste-based organization is not without certain privileges or rights for even the lowest groups and it provides some minimal protection of their economic survival. The rights are birthrights, the virtual guarantee that individuals may exclusively pursue the means to survival that society has assigned them. Communities developed, under the hereditary system, to make the most of the structure of interdependence, of dual-sided restriction-monopoly. Successive generations within families established strategies and came to depend on them. What happens to those people in the most disadvantageous socioeconomic positions when the system is dissolved? The theoretical opportunity for low groups to assume different social roles is not supported by a foundation of education, wealth, and land ownership. Such groups still deal with the social discrimination of caste even if state policy prohibits it. In the microcosm of dholis, the change to a postcaste structure poses challenges not only to their economic situation—which, yes, they may weather through new strategies—but also to their identity. The rule of hereditary occupation gave them not only a form of modest economic security but also pride in a cultural identity: *We, alone, know how to do this; others do not.*

A Punjabi figure of speech reflects the sentiment that one does what one can with the hand one has been dealt: *gaḷ piā ḍhol vajāuṇā*—Beat that dhol which hangs from your neck. Read in the context of the caste-based social structure, the dhol in this metaphor represents more than a situation that one incidentally finds oneself in. The dhol has been hung from birth; it is part of one's inborn identity, one's *dharma*. Garib Dass spoke of his *dharma*, his duty determined by his place in the cyclic rebirth of humanity. He said dhol was his *gurū*, the spiritual leader that instructs and leads one on one's path. For him, the Punjabi figure of speech was eerily literal. How then does a hereditary dholi reconcile his identity as a true follower of dhol as a spiritual position, a path, against an economic landscape that pressures him to follow other paths and a social zeitgeist that suggests others not born to the position are equally entitled to it? The traditional dhol-playing communities have had few other professions to fall back on and fewer that offer a similar exclusivity of identity. While upper-class Punjabis had the option of more comfortable lives, the dholis suffered the stigma associated with the profession. In exchange, they possessed the exclusive right to practice it. The dhol traditions, therefore, are most reasonably possessed by *their* people. It is a sign of their fatalism, and perhaps a customary resignation to the will of the upper classes, that traditional dholis voice as little resentment as they do toward the people arguably expropriating this emblem of identity. Is there any justice in the logic of now considering dhol to be a generically Punjabi tradition when, for most of history, only a small slice of Punjabis had a hand in developing it? Although we will note dholis' adaptation to market changes and celebrate the successes of extraordinary players, let us not fail to register their communities' losses beyond the economic. We owe it to the hereditary dholis, the creators and longtime caretakers of these traditions, to do more than note the inevitable changes, to consider how individuals have been affected, and to empathize with their lament.

This book argues, through the example of dhol's appropriation, that the empowerment gained by bolstering Punjabi identity in the global arena comes at the expense of people on Punjab's margins. Advancing such an argument does not suggest that dhol does not or should not represent Punjabi identity. It does, to spectacular success. Nor does it exclude the possibility of dholis benefiting from hitching their wagon to the Punjabi identity construct. On balance, however, the dholis have had to sacrifice more. Their sacrifice remains paradoxical—service to a cause that does not center them—and it cannot be ignored in hopes of simplifying the tale of Punjabis' journey to becoming a globally recognizable nation. This book seeks to show that dhol serves as something to represent Punjabi identity, but it does not serve in that capacity to represent all Punjabis equally. Dholis have been the architects of cultural touchstones (dhol and dance) on which consolidating a global Punjabi identity has been possible. Dhol traditions did not grow on their own from the soil of the land of Punjab. Someone cultivated them, and to them full credit has long been due. At this juncture in the story of Punjabis, explicit recognition of them is an ethical imperative. I hope that readers might extrapolate from this case to think about how the pursuit of overly essentialized collective identities, intended to serve in global contexts, can operate at the expense of and by further marginalization of people in local contexts. In short, the tale of dhol cautions us to consider the ethical dimensions of identity politics.

ORGANIZATION OF THIS VOLUME

Chapter 1 elaborates on the contexts of Punjabi identification among which dhol is situated. It explains that modern Punjabi identity concepts owe much to the idea of Punjabis as a (trans)nation shaped through migration. Movement of population has contributed to the diversity of Punjabi culture. The political situation of individuals, however, often suggests they strategically minimize that diversity. Punjabi cultural nationalism as a strategy for political recognition necessitates privileging selective markers of Punjabiness. The vision of Punjabi national unity, while loath to emphasize ethnic and class divisions, arguably neglects the perspectives of Punjabis who find themselves in subordinate social positions from falling on the wrong side of those divisions. This perspective sets the stage to think about the meaning of dhol when performed *as representative of* Punjabi identity and the lack of representation for dholis' identities in that vision.

Chapter 2 introduces the material object (the dhol drum), the sound forms played on it (dhol as genre), and contexts in which the sounds are given meaning. These all contribute to making the dhol a uniquely resonant emblem, both of Punjabi culture and of the identities of dholis. While many barrel drums are dispersed across Eurasia, and some of them also go by the name of *ḍhol* (or a similar term), the dhol of Punjab can be recognized particularly through unique habits or customs in how players approach playing it. This book lacks the space to describe dhol repertoire in detail, but an exposition of common sonic structures is offered to supply points of reference to understand players' aesthetic and practical values. The sonic structures correspond to various types of events, which may be categorized broadly in terms of such functions as signaling, organizing, and marking. Chapter 2 concludes by framing a broad distinction between the application of dhol to practical forms of communication and more purely aesthetic (ambiguous, nonreferential; Cross 2003, 24) performances. One will see in subsequent chapters that dholis' identities are located in reference to these points of distinction.

Chapters 3 and 4 outline the ethnic groups to which professional dholis belonged during the first decade of the twenty-first century. Each had its unique path for dhol playing, served different local markets, and supplied different services according to idiosyncratic methods. Chapter 3 introduces each group and representative individuals. The chapter omits the Bazigar community, whose dholis were especially significant in supporting twentieth-century Indian Punjab's folkloric programming. Chapter 4, therefore, presents the Bazigars with some depth. Complementing modern ethnographic writing on similarly situated communities elsewhere in South Asia (Agrawal 2004; Berland 1982; Fiol 2010), these expositions form the book's core contribution to general knowledge about people who are usually invisible in writing about Punjab. Chapter 4 includes a biographical sketch of an individual dholi, Garib Dass, situating him among a local tribe and illustrating the journey undertaken to become a leading figure.

Chapter 5 turns away from dholis' identities as ethnic group members in order to see both the unifying and dividing traits within their occupational group. It focuses on the metrics of professional status, habits of training, and performance style. Enculturation into particular ways of becoming and being a professional is key to what sets off "dholis" as a group that has a claim to this label and as distinct from laypeople who play dhol ("dhol players"). The discussion then returns to parsing the professional dhol-playing body to make visible the subtler ways that dholis mark their identities at both ethnic group and individual levels. Choices in aesthetics, methods, and materials of constructing instruments, playing technique, knowledge transmission, and repertoire, along with beliefs of what it means to play dhol, are among the ways they realize explicit and implicit boundaries.

Dhol playing in the diaspora is a relatively recent affair, dating back about half a century yet gaining prevalence only in the past two decades. Chapter 6 offers observations of the diaspora across time. The narrative moves from the immigrant pioneers to the growth of local lay players and to the recent increase in visits and residencies of dholis from Punjab. The advent of dhol playing in the diaspora opened the door for dhol to be played by large numbers of people outside the ethnic communities and life experiences of the traditional dholis. The chapter illustrates how being a dhol player differs in contexts outside Punjab and notes effects of dhol activities in the diaspora on current dhol traditions.

For the final chapter, I return to Punjab to take stock after a 12-year absence. Punjabi dholis in 2019 had incorporated adaptations to a changed market and the requirements of a new generation. The institution of master and disciple, while still relevant in concept, had deteriorated in practice. Individuals embodying the older model and maintaining the traditional values of an *ustād* had exited the stage. Gone was much of the strict discipline those figures enforced, along with the virtual borders of dholi identity that their rules created. The situation was exacerbated by a gutting of the middle-aged generation's vitality from the oversaturation of the market, existential despair, and poor health. There was a consequent disconnection between the youngest generation and the oldest. Hereditary dholis from younger generations had, on one side, acquired new freedom to explore means of income through their inherited knowledge while, on the other side, they lacked advising from elders. Also, developments in the diaspora had fed back to the homeland and gained enough critical mass to raise concern for the coherence of the Dhol World. Dhol's function as representing Punjabi identity grew to serve people in the diaspora, where there was most call for thinking about being Punjabi. Young professionals in Punjab got caught up in this trend and sought to present dhol-centered performances rather than serving a traditional supporting role.

Movement of the dhol to the visual center increased players' visibility in one sense. Yet in clashing with values of the Dhol World, popular recognition worked at the expense of undermining the preferred identity that older players felt to be slipping away. Such was the fragile ecosystem of the Dhol World that injuries to one part of the system threatened the sustainability of all. Whether the current situation proves ultimately to be a decline, a transition, or a new beginning can be known only in future hindsight. After the next 12 or 24 years, what will have become of Punjab's dholis?

1 THE SHORT END OF THE STICK

Strategies of Identification

The trope of land resounds in discourse about Punjab. *Land* is the literal and metaphorical terra firma that anchors the identity group *Punjabi* and makes the concept of Punjabi culture possible. Concerning economics, land is the source of Punjab's archetypal wealth, its agricultural produce. Concerning politics, land figures in the disputes over national borders. And concerning ethnicity, land resonates with the identity of the most powerful citizenry, the land *owners*. It puts farmers like the Jatt at the center of any form of Punjabi identity that prioritizes land as its basis. Punjabis of this class, even when situated outside Punjab, remain tethered to the land of Punjab. Their families retain ownership of ancestral land. Land is a Jatt's inheritance and it is said that for a Jatt to sell his [*sic*] land is a sin.

Despite the *firmness* that one might associate with this land, Punjab is also much associated with travel and migration. The Punjabi Canadian poet Ajmer Rode writes, "*Panjāb des de pairīṅ cakkar*"—"There's rambling in the foot of the land of Punjab." The association between Punjab and population movement would be formed through specific incidents and patterns of migration during the modern era. This is not to say, however, that Punjab has become any kind of Shanghai or New York. Punjabi society is yet characterized by parochial and rustic ways. Its diversity comes in spatial variety, exemplified by the adage that one encounters a new dialect with each river one crosses. This sentiment coexists, however, with the perception that, rather than a multicultural society, Punjab comprises a (mono)cultural region. Perhaps the reason we so often hear about migration in conversations about Punjab is that those people most inclined to talk about "Punjab" are those who have experienced migration. The very idea of a Punjab entity whose existence supplants both local formations and the influences of encompassing sovereign states (i.e., Pakistan, India) asks one to suspend the reality of always living in a politically, socially, and culturally particular space. To suspend this reality is easier for individuals whose life trajectories occasion them to experience living in multiple spaces and to configure salient differences as those occuring between a broader region and places outside that region. Thus, Punjab's existence as a coherent concept scales to Punjabis' mobility; its unity appears more as one zooms out. In this chapter, I emphasize movement and positioning in relation to Punjabi spaces. I argue that a "national" Punjabi identity exists precisely because of migration and I illustrate how that identity interacts with other, locally constituted, identities.

Punjabis' individual identities are matrices that include belonging to an envisioned cultural region (Punjab) along with any number of other intersecting dimensions of identity. To be, for example, a male-identifying Punjabi or a female-identifying Punjabi is surely different. Does one start with the idea of one's connection to Punjab in both cases, only after distinguishing male versus female? Or does the gender identity come prior to Punjabi? Both orderings occur in individuals' situational practices of identification. Yet the identifications we often encounter in salient *group* representations are not so freely multidirectional and some orderings predominate. The Punjabi national identity construct is characterized by such a predominant ordering wherein types of citizenship, religious affiliation, gender, and ethnicity are prioritized after satisfying the ostensibly primary aspect, belonging to the Punjab region. As the Punjabi national identity comes to be represented as coterminous with Punjabi identity, it forecloses other orderings. Individual Punjabi identities have more or less power of expression and representation in relation to how closely their matrices align with Punjabi national identity.

Movement is significant to this process. Punjabis who travel and take up residence in cosmopolitan spaces are the privileged actors who most advance and formulate the picture of Punjabi national identity. Movement by the ethnic and class demographics represented by dholis has not been as frequent nor has it taken the same shape. The example of dholis is thus an acute case of the phenomenon wherein smaller communities' and individuals' particular identities—the orderings they prioritize—are minimized or erased by a national one. While dhol becomes ever more deeply inscribed as a sign of Punjabi identity, and as more Punjabis are compelled to adopt the national matrix, we must ask: *whose* Punjabi identity is this?

IDENTITY, CULTURE, ETHNICITY, AND NATION

Before proceeding further, I must specify my usage of four recurring analytical concepts: identity, culture, ethnicity, and nation. Each refers to a phenomenon that is theoretically amorphous while, in practical deployment, recognizes patterns in the behaviors of individuals situated in society. Turino provides the helpful idea of *habits* to negotiate the dual need for theoretical fluidity and practical ascription of categories. Habits may be defined as behaviors, inclusive of action and thought, that tend to be repeated. Their repetition suggests stability while the notion of tendency, rather than fixity, allows for thinking about such behavior as mutable (2008, 95). Turino grounds the discussion of habits of identification in the concept of *self*, defined as "a body plus the total sets of habits specific to an individual that develop through the ongoing interchange of the individual with her physical and social surroundings" (ibid.).

Identity may then be defined as the *representation* of the self, in dialectic fashion, by both the self and others (Turino 2008, 102). Whereas the self is the totality of habits and the body, identification entails a partial selection of habits and bodily attributes that are used for representation. Which aspects of the self are selected depends on what is relevant to foreground in a given situation (103).

Culture, which is separate from the body, comprises habits shared among individuals (Turino 2008, 95). Because borders of culture are indefinable, the use of *cultures* to denote bounded entities is theoretically incongruous despite its currency in colloquial discourse. Turino rectifies this issue through use of the adjectival form, *cultural* (109). When the need presents itself to affix broad, pervasive patterns of shared habits to groups of people who share a majority of them, we may refer to *cultural formations* (112).

Whereas cultural formation, based on a cluster of shared habits, gives virtual shape to culture, *ethnicity* gives shape to a group of people on the basis of social boundaries. According to Barth, ethnicity is based on neither biological descent nor shared culture but rather the construction of boundaries that persist despite changes to the gene pool and cultural characteristics (1998, 9–11). Observed shared characteristics (biological, cultural) within an ethnic group are the result of the inclusion-exclusion dialectic that accompanies social organization into such groups (11). Ultimately, ethnicity is manifested in the dynamic ascriptions of classification of a basic identity by which actors "categorize themselves and others for the purposes of interaction" (13–14). Shared characteristics serve to articulate the ethnic identity, rather than constituting the ethnic group as such. As in Turino's emphasis on a selection of traits in identification, it is not the sharing of traits in sum that mark the ethnic groups' delineation of boundaries but only those traits that are taken to be significant. Amplifying significant points of affiliation and difference, as through the use of emblems, aids the maintenance of boundaries. Barth notes that in the South Asian caste system, boundaries between castes reflect ethnic boundaries (28). It is with this rationale that I shall treat castes and similar groupings in Punjab as *ethnic communities.*

Nation is a term I use in deliberate distinction from state. A *state* is defined as a sovereign territory with a centralized government within which membership is based on a system of citizenship (Baumann 1999, 30). By contrast, when I employ the term *nation*, I am referring to an entity lacking a sovereign territory and centralized government, for which ethnicity operates as the basis of membership. A nation is a people. The challenge here is to distinguish nation, insofar as it is formulated through the phenomenon of ethnicity, from ethnic group. I consider nation to be a superethnic group that subsumes salient divisions of (smaller) ethnic groups. As Baumann puts it, "The nation is . . . both postethnic, in that it denies the salience of old ethnic distinctions and portrays these as a matter of a dim and distant prestate past, and superethnic, in that it portrays the nation as a new and bigger kind of ethnos" (ibid., 31). I use *nation* to accommodate the perception that Punjabis, in total, are a people independent from (or indeed without) a state. While acknowledging the problematic nature of this concept of nation, I have adopted it precisely to highlight the issue at play: the ascription of national identity is ultimately arbitrary. At what level of ethnic division is it to be based? A nation must justify the grouping on the basis of some natural inclusion of what it deems to be significant attributes while ignoring others. In the case of a Punjab nation, ties to the land must be part of it. Yet, since there is no Punjab state (country) to confer Punjabi citizenship, and since there must be an ethnic basis, not all who happen to be located in Punjab can be Punjabi in the national sense, or at least not equally so. A broad cultural formation must also be sought to give representational coherence to the nation. *Cultural nationalism* is the ideology that serves to delineate a nation through the selective identification of shared culture.

Hutchinson explains cultural nationalism as a response to crises of identity and purpose (1987, 3). Its goals reflect the distinction between nation and state, where the nation's idiosyncratic traits are considered to be and respected as natural, while the state's supposedly arbitrary policies are accidental (13). Cultural nationalists, therefore, do not aim to achieve and support a state as political nationalists but rather strive for moral regeneration of the national community (9). Historical memory is important to cultural nationalists (29), as revival of and education in common heritage contribute to the myth of the nation. For this reason, scholars and artists play key roles in cultural nationalist movements, for they are responsible for creating historicist ideology and cultural institutions (9).

To summarize, identity is the phenomenon whereby individuals represent themselves and are represented by others through selected traits of the self.

Types of identity include cultural, where recognition is based on a surfeit of shared habits, and ethnic, where recognition is based on signification of customary social boundaries. Ethnic groups, while tending to share cultural formations and draw on their signs to signify their boundaries, are not coterminous with them. A larger grouping of people based on a social us-versus-them dialectic is a nation. Just as ethnic groups select from traits taken to be significant to construct the boundary between us and them, the nation does so in such a way as to include multiple smaller groups in its fold by emphasizing some traits shared between them. In the case of the Punjabi nation, origin in the Punjab region is the foundational shared trait. Cultural nationalism additionally prescribes a broad cultural network as the nation's shared trait in preference to sharing membership in a political state. The formulation reconfigures ethnic boundaries and downplays cultural diversity to unify the idea of the nation and, in the process, minimizes or erases other ethnic and cultural identities.

DIVIDED PUNJAB

Cultural nationalists promote the idea of Undivided Punjab, a Punjab as it was before the region's division between Pakistan and India and in which different faith communities coexist(ed) in harmony. Their vision gives the impression that Punjabis are one people and that the unfortunate rifts—which active remembering of shared heritage shall overcome—lie with capricious boundaries created by states and religions. At the heart of this book's subject is a conflict between a modern vision of Punjabi people's cultural unity and the past—signifying lived reality of traditional dholis within a society sharply divided by ethnicity and class. The trouble for cultural nationalists is that to discuss such divisions disintegrates their picture of social unity. The trouble for dholis is that ignoring ethnicity and class does nothing to elucidate their continuing lived reality.

Talking about musicians—not music, but *musicians*—compels us to talk about ethnicity, class, and a construct that lies at their intersection, caste. As Sherinian points out, by ignoring caste, which remains an operative construct despite its fluidity, we risk ignoring the relationship between social identities and music (2014, 15). Caste is a sensitive topic for Punjabis, however, and more so, I observe, among the higher socioeconomic classes. Middle- and upper-class individuals, who associate freely with people of other castes within their same class, follow the conviction that caste does not matter, as it were, because it *should not* matter. The difference they experience, between themselves and people of the lower classes, appears precisely as a *class* difference. This appearance belies the recognition that class differences largely correspond to caste differences. To be clear, it is the implied hierarchical dimension of caste that makes its consideration most distasteful. Thus, discourse from the perspective of upper classes neglects caste as ethnicity (or ethnicity, as such, at all). Punjabis occupying the lower classes most acutely feel caste's effects and, in reverse fashion, project caste onto the difference between themselves and higher classes. While the upper classes talk about their Punjabi identity, the lower classes talk about their ethnic identities. Yet, for lower-class individuals, who tend to be most conscious of communal identity, hierarchies are not the focus but rather particular group identities in distinction from others. Their communities function like extended family units in which members focus energy on helping their closest kin to survive. Because those with fewer economic choices must rely on their (ethnic) community in this way, they in turn fight for its distinction to the same degree as one would fight for the ownership of one's property. One cannot appreciate what is at stake for musical property without acknowledging the preeminent importance of ethnic community for the economically disadvantaged.

In discussing Punjabi society, the familiar term *caste* has some utility in reference to the phenomenon of ethnic communities being ascribed social statuses. In reference to *groups of people*, however (as opposed to the phenomenon that ascribes their relationships in society), more useful is a native term, *qaum*. A qaum, as I reasoned earlier with provisional reference to caste, may be considered as an ethnic group on the basis that its people draw a boundary between theirs and other such groups. Differentiation between qaums is reinforced through endogamy, identification with select professional and cultural practices, and, to a greater or lesser degree, social segregation.

While this all corresponds to some of the connotations when speaking of a caste, *qaum* avoids certain popular associations with the former. First, because in Punjabi history the ethnic communities, qaums, have been dynamic, use of the term avoids the notion evoked by *caste* of a set of fixed groups. Second, while hierarchical relationships between ethnic communities are important for the analysis of Punjabi society, use of the word *caste* risks readers transposing familiar hierarchical structures gleaned elsewhere in South Asia to Punjab. In Punjab, the ethnic communities do not relate hierarchically on the basis of an ancient Hindu schema that supposes, for example, that the priestly caste (in Punjabi, *Bāhmaṇ*) resides at the top of a celestial order. In rural Punjab, landowning farmers, though they toil with their hands, are situated as the highest-status group. Departure from familiar hierarchies might be explained by the fact that, although the phenomenon of caste is seen to have emerged in the subcontinent along with the diverse beliefs collectively known as Hinduism, in Punjab it encompasses a substantial number of individuals of other religious faiths. Both Islamic and Sikh theology reject the notion of caste. Still, the practices that realize qaum differentiation also exist among these religious groups (I. Singh 1977, 79; Jalal 1995, 216), as do prejudices between communities.[1]

Third, whereas popular discourse on castes tends to emphasize occupational exclusivity, and even though that phenomenon is characteristic of many qaums, a more salient basis for the cohesion of qaum is kinship. It is organized into an endogamous set of exogamous clans that supports economic objectives. Although a qaum's occupational specialty may be more or less exclusive with respect to other qaums, in all cases kinship regulates sustainability by nurturing members' career development and keeping those outside the kin network from oversaturating the local markets for an occupational service. I must reiterate, however, that neither ancestry nor occupational specialty can be considered the *defining basis* of qaum. People related by kin may split into new qaums, the ultimate basis of which is the socially constructed recognition of group identities, ethnicity. We will see in Chapter 3 how a kin-related people previously known as Dum have shed that identity and reformed under such separate qaum identities as Jogi and Mahasha, as well as how previously unrelated people came under the label of Bharai.

A final reason for using qaum is to include a continuum (see Jalal 1995) of different types of ethnic community formations. At one end of the continuum is that type best evoked by *caste*—ideally, one of numerous closely interdependent groups assumed to perform particular, complementary functions in a social network (on this point, see Leach 1962, 5). Yet also well represented in Punjab, at the other end of the continuum, is a type called "tribe," *kabīlā*. It may be defined ideally as a larger-scale, independent group of individuals who believe they are descended from a common ancestor and who, at some point, occupied common territory.[2] Within a tribe, the occupational choices of members are relatively flexible, as are their social roles. Punjab's so-called tribal peoples, *kabāilī lok*, now live amid the larger society of complementary occupational groups, though in the past many lived peripatetic lifestyles, which remains a component of their identity.[3] Characteristics of tribes have included unorthodox religious beliefs (often propitiating deities particular to the tribe), idiosyncratic rituals, and an independent court of elders with proprietary justice proceedings (Thind 1996, 42). The historical tribal groups existed outside "society," and so their occupational practices, while intended to support themselves, were not integrated precisely into the caste network. Now that most tribes are participants in the social mainstream, it does not pay to overdistinguish ethnic community types along the continuum, and *qaum* accommodates all of them. Nevertheless, some value in retaining some distinction of caste versus tribe lies in the fact that tribes retain a sense of themselves as historical outsiders.

According to the social paradigm of qaum, an individual's situation in his or her community has a bearing on a great many aspects of life. The tendency to marry only within and to associate mainly with others of the same qaum is strong, and many qaums possess a more-or-less distinct combination of lifeways, habits, religious beliefs, and dialect (Juergensmeyer 2004, 44). Such a close relationship between culture and ethnicity is not unique to Punjab, yet the relative exclusivity of social spheres engendered by the prejudices and class status hierarchies that come with the caste construct suggests that, in comparison with some other parts of the world, Punjab is less united as a broad cultural formation and more a collection of subcultural formations.

The placement of qaums through occupation in the economic system maps to class inequities. Punjab's agricultural economy has engendered a basic class structure of a feudal type. A village is divided into a class of landlords (*zimīndār*) and a class of service providers employed by them (Ahmad 1977, 73). The socioeconomic system, *jajmānī*, articulates a codependent relationship between patrons (*jajmān*) and clients (*kammī*).[4] In this arrangement, the landowning patrons historically supported the service providers in exchange for their goods and services. Their support came, most significantly, through sharing a portion of their harvest but also might come through housing, gifts or cash, and privileges. The families of such patrons and their patronized, within a given village, maintained their mutual arrangement through successive generations. The Jatt were the archetype of the landowners. In Jatt tradition, land ownership is passed down through patriarchal lineage. Through this practice, the exchange of land ownership is minimized, and, because the landless have few opportunities to acquire land, the feudal structure tends to be preserved to this day.

The professional performer communities fall within the class of service providers who remain dependent on the landowners and others in control of financial capital even if, at present, they are paid in cash and not strictly retained by landowning families. The vast majority of professional musicians are not only members of the service class but are also members of those qaums that form a subclass of society known officially as the Scheduled Castes and politically as Dalits. This subclass has its basis in peoples historically known as outcastes and comprising those who were situated outside of mainstream society. Being marginalized as untouchables (ritually polluted) has meant not only (ongoing) stigmatization in social interactions but also physical marginalization, where Scheduled Caste communities typically live segregated from or outside the settlement of mainstream communities.

Though the origin of so-called untouchable communities is a matter of conjecture that I cannot resolve here, it is nonetheless relevant to gain a sense of what historical narratives say insofar as they contextualize the histories of the communities that I will describe. According to a popular theory, such communities derive from the contact between the ancient Indo-Aryan-speaking newcomers and earlier inhabitants of the subcontinent. The *Ṛg Ved* indicates that although such distinct native tribes existed as the Dāsa, Dasiyu, and Paṇi, the Indo-Aryans regarded these people as a single mass that represented "forces of darkness" (Grewal 2004b, 37). The canonical Hindu treatise *Mānava Dharma Shāstra* (c. 200 BCE-200 CE) described a fourfold class or *varṇa* system (Grewal 2004b, 108). No mention was made, however, of the doubtless large numbers of individuals engaged in the least desirable work that was not covered by those four classes. Much later, however, the eleventh-century Persian visitor al-Biruni took note of people "outside" the scope of the class system (al-Biruni 2000 [1910], 101–102). Being carrion-eaters or having such professions as executioner or musician earned them a reputation as polluting to those within the system, and they were obligated to live outside village walls (Grewal 2004b, 141).

The outcaste class of society included not only menial workers but also the independent tribes. Nineteenth-century British administrators designated some of the latter as the Criminal Tribes, as much on the basis of the reported practices of theft as on suspicions inspired by their itinerancy, private dialects, and unorthodox lifestyles. Such tribes were identified for the purpose of monitoring in the Criminal Tribes Act of 1871 until it was repealed in 1952 (Schwarz 2010, 2). Other tribes were labeled as the Gypsy Tribes. These, which did not carry the criminal stigma, were known for their entertaining performances and received their designation by analogy to the lifestyles of the Rom-Sinti "Gypsies" of Europe.

Early-twentieth-century efforts to uplift the status of marginalized peoples included campaigns to change attitudes to them. Bhimrao Ramji Ambedkar was instrumental in lobbying for the creation of separate electorates and reservations for outcastes. In 1935, in the Government of India Act, the term "Scheduled Caste" was coined in reference to any community that was included in the list ("schedule") of those eligible for affirmative action programs (Kamble 1982, 31). The Constitution of India (first ratified in 1949) states, in Article 341, that "The President may with respect to any State . . . specify the castes, races, or tribes . . . deemed to be Scheduled Castes in relation to that State" (Government of India 2007, 210–211). The list of communities, first published in 1936, is thus particular to each constituent state. It is periodically modified, but it essentially includes all those castes once treated as untouchable, as well as formerly itinerant tribes of like social predicament. Accordingly, "Scheduled Caste," tends to be treated conversationally as a euphemism for outcaste.

Aiming for empowerment, the catchall term *Dalit* ("downtrodden"), has been propagated since the 1970s as a self-chosen alternative. Many individuals from these communities have yet to identify with the Dalit label, however, and "Scheduled Castes" remains the most politically versatile term. "Scheduled Castes" arguably undermines the political unity offered by "Dalits," but it more accurately reveals their disunity. For within the Scheduled Caste population itself, distinctions of rank between communities are made (Moffatt 1975, 117). Furthermore, the political struggle under the rubric of Dalits is apt, with some irony, to marginalize all but the most numerous communities among the Scheduled Castes. Just two communities, Chamars and Sweepers, make up three-quarters of the Scheduled Caste population while three dozen much smaller communities make up the remaining quarter (Ram 2017, 51). Dalit as a movement dominated by majority-minority groups adds yet another layer to the alienation of diverse Punjabi minority peoples that the bureaucratic category of Scheduled Castes causes.

In the 2011 census, India had a Scheduled Caste population of some 200 million (out of a total population of around 1.2 billon) or 16.6 percent of the total. The state of Punjab had the densest population of Scheduled Caste persons in the nation, numbering more than eight million or about 32 percent of the population (Census of India 2013). Thirty-nine communities are registered as Scheduled Castes in the Indian state. In some villages of Punjab, Scheduled Caste persons make up more than half the population; their numbers may be as high as 75 percent in the rural sector (Ram 2017, 45). Intermarriage between members of different Scheduled Castes is still considered taboo (ibid., 50). Such significant numbers and persistent social structures mean that issues of caste, and the divisions they engender, are pointed in Punjab.

PUNJABIS ON THE MOVE

Estimated conservatively, Punjabis number around two million outside Punjab (Thandi 2015, 235). As early as the 1980s, it was suggested that more than a third of some Punjabi villages had emigrated abroad (Dusenbery 1989, 1–2). Every resident of Punjab has some relative or acquaintance who has emigrated, and families depend on the remittances sent home by those working abroad. Yet these facts and figures mainly impress the idea of Punjabis as a nation with a significant global network. One needs a clearer picture of the ethnoscape in these movements. In developing this picture, we can see how the multiple migrations of Punjabi people reconstituted Punjab's social divisions through the very fact that movement does not affect all people equally.

Punjab's fame, influence, and overall notability as a site of cultural history owe something to its being a site of population movements. From the so-called Indo-Aryans (people of the *Ṛg Ved*, from circa 1500 BCE) to Alexander the Great's invasion (fourth century BCE) to the Greek rule (second century BCE) to the Ghaznavids of Afghanistan (eleventh century CE) to the Mughals (sixteenth century CE), one sees Punjab's history characterized by migrations of people.[5] This is partly attributable to Punjab's location forming the vestibule to the subcontinent; Punjab is supposed to be the brackish region between the Indian hinterland and the sea of outsiders. Yet, although the arrival of newcomers forms the focus of Punjab's originary narrative, and current discussions note, for example, changing demographics from the influx of labor from other states in India, I suggest that movement *into* Punjab is less significant to the story of modern Punjabi identity that frames the present issues of cultural production. More significant is movement out of and across the region.

When new settlers came, when new cultural formations were introduced, where did the locals "go"? My question implies that prior residents did not always remain in place. One instance of displacement with relevance to modern Punjab's cultural history concerns tribes that roamed western Punjab in the nineteenth century. The settled residents called them Jangli (*jānglī*) peoples, referring to the sparsely populated, arid *jangal* (jungle) areas they inhabited (Harkirat Singh 1995, 118). People of this origin themselves used the term without derogation to refer collectively to the qaums with whom they shared a lifestyle. Jangli peoples sustained themselves on the milk and meat of their herd livestock, the grazing of which kept them regularly on the move. They lived clustered in temporary thatched huts (*jhuggī*). Living separated from the agricultural qaums in population centers, Jangli peoples practiced a culture apart. Their society's tone was distinct from that of the mainstream in being more egalitarian and, arguably, more practical-minded than propriety-driven. An observer of Janglis in the early twentieth century described the status of men and women as more equal than in his society and found that the custom of *pardah* (veiling or segregation of women) was unknown (Harjit Singh 1949, 25). Sometimes women were more numerous than men in wedding processions (usually the purview of men in mainstream society), and relations between the sexes were less restrictive (Daler 1954, 189).

In 1885 the British Indian government began a project building an irrigation canal to bring the interfluvial jungle areas under cultivation. The completion of the Lower Chenab Canal in 1892, which brought water to the Sandal Bar, was a milestone in this engineering project (Darling 1947, 113). Before the British quit India, nine "canal colonies" had been created (Ali 1988, 8). To do so, previously uncultivated lands were claimed by the state without recognition of the Janglis' grazing grounds (Ali 1997, 342). The government gave incentives to farmers drawn largely from eastern Punjab to settle and cultivate plots there (Darling 1947, 115–117). The activities brought Jangli culture in regular contact with that of the colonists. Punjabis from the cultural "center," both from the western and eastern sides of the province, gained exposure to music and dance of marginal tribal communities.

Aesthetic culture of the margins became more deeply entwined with the Punjabi body politic after one of the most traumatic events of modern South Asian history and its largest rapid migration. This event was Partition, the 1947 division of the region between the newly independent republics of Pakistan and India. Being determined with an eye to divvying up districts according to either a Muslim or Hindu majority population (Sikhs were not a majority in any district), a new international border was drawn through the Punjab province. Many Muslims sought residence in the Islamic Republic of Pakistan and most Hindus and Sikhs from the western side of Punjab left for India. The resultant population exchange of about twelve million people (Kirpal Singh 1972, 132) and the bitterness and bloodshed that ensued remain in Punjabis' memories as a profound physical and spiritual uprooting. Each of today's "two Punjabs," however, is not merely a side of the previous Punjab region. Rather, the sifting of population according to faith communities effected an enormous reorganization of culture. For example, many varieties of musical specialists were Muslim and, because these individuals concentrated in Pakistani Punjab, they left Indian Punjabis without access to their cultural knowledge. The Partition's movements also sent cultural forms from western Punjab to the east, as canal colonists of the Sikh community, originally from the east, returned to their ancestral lands. The famous bhangra dance, based in areas of current Pakistan, was reinvented as the state folkloric dance in the east through this movement.

Patterned migration from region to globally dispersed metropoles created a Punjabi diaspora. In charting this movement, we may notice, as did economist Shinder Thandi, both push and pull factors inspiring migration (2015, 236). We may also understand the circumstances that would make migration possible or impossible. Intensification of emigration began with the advent of the British Empire in Punjab. Being the front line against neighboring states to the northwest, Punjab was strategically important. The annexation of the Punjab Province to British India in 1849 connected Punjab with far-reaching processes of the empire (Tatla 2004, 47). The late nineteenth century in Punjab was marked by poor economic conditions, famines, droughts, epidemics, and a population explosion (Jensen 1988, 24)—push factors. Families encouraged emigration by some of their members as a defensive strategy to ease the strain locally. Punjabi employees of the government had occasion to be sent to other locations within the British Empire. Punjabis were especially important to the empire in other regions for food production and for security (Tatla 2004, 49), and opportunities in such regions constituted pull factors.

It was the recruitment of Punjabis into the military services that first instituted a global diaspora (Axel 2001, 64). In the late nineteenth and early twentieth centuries, the British Indian Army drew greatly on Punjabi Jatt Sikhs for its ranks (Tatla 2004, 49). The British always had some interest to protect somewhere in the world, and their notion that various Punjabi communities constituted "martial races," along with Punjabis' reputation for loyalty (e.g., during the 1857 Sepoy Mutiny) made some Punjabis—Sikhs in particular—highly desirable for these assignments. Through these posts, Punjabi men established a network, from Punjab to Calcutta, Burma, Singapore, Hong Kong, and eventually Canada (Dusenbery 1989, 4–6). The networks opened channels for migration to seek other forms of work, and Punjabis' status as subjects of the Crown made emigration possible. Some were employed to work on the Ugandan Railways project and for associated services in East Africa (Tatla 2004, 53–54). From 1903 on, Punjabis began work on the Western Pacific Railroad and in lumbering on the western coast of Canada. Before the Immigration Act of 1917 barred immigrants from British India, several thousand Punjabi men from among this network were able to gain entry to the western United States to work in agriculture and other manual labor (Leonard 1992, 24–32). Overseas migration ramped up in the postcolonial period. From the 1950s, men went to labor in factories in the United Kingdom. The United States, after lifting its ban on immigration from Asia in 1965, gave preference to highly educated individuals in needed professions. What is to be noted is that conditions and feasibility of movement for different types of Punjabis resulted in Punjabi diaspora communities whose composition does not mirror society in Punjab.

MOVEMENT, IDENTITY, AND MUSIC'S ROLE

Discussions of Punjabi diaspora communities frequently land on questions of change to, maintenance of, or negotiation of identity by Punjabis situated outside Punjab. My inquiry, however, takes a different form: how has movement of Punjabi people within, away from, and back to the Punjab home region shaped the very identity of "Punjabi"? Rather than assume a prior "Punjabi" identity was endemic to the residents of Punjab, an "original" form that underwent change for emigrants, I argue that migration has been the impetus for constructing what is now known as Punjabi identity. A secondary question, then, is how that Punjabi identity has been constituted, through this process, with respect to the cultural and ethnic diversity of Punjabi people. As noted, the notion of successive waves of invaders, passing travelers, and settlers entering Punjab as the primary land route into India and contributing to developing "rich" Punjabi culture, has long been part of narratives.[6] In spite of this, and as if the historical cultural interaction contributed only to forming preindustrial Punjabi culture, in the modern era, cosmopolitan Punjabis have favored a strategic essentialist outlook that minimizes cultural diversity. This section considers how movements of people interact with Punjabi identities and individuals' choices of whether to present their group as uniform or diverse.

Migration necessarily affects one's identity. Shifting away from home and encountering others provokes consciousness of aspects of one's identity. Imagine, for example, refugees at the time of Partition who found themselves in camps. They would have searched and sifted among the masses for people with whom they could identify, seeking familiarity in communication and practice. In the process, they would have come to know different peoples with whom they would not previously had contact. They would notice the otherness of strangers and, perhaps for the first time, need to articulate aspects of their identities that they once took for granted. To see the process at work, I offer a sketch of an analysis of Punjabi popular music's development, across space, as a site for development of Punjabi identity.[7]

When commercial production of sound recordings in Punjab began in the 1930s, performers were not articulating Punjabi identity in broad terms. Punjabis in local villages had no particular reason to declare their Punjabiness, for the proverbial fish has no reason to contemplate the water in which it swims. Identification occurred along lines of gender, class, qaum, and so forth, along with areal differences (e.g., Majha versus Malwa). The vernacular music that made up the material of early recordings consisted of ballads performed by hereditary specialists. Drawn from a tradition of oral literature, the ballads contained themes with which many listeners in the greater Punjabi cultural region could identify. Yet they were not about being Punjabi.

By the 1960s, however, a revival "folk music" emerged on commercial recordings that glorified the Punjab region. Although the ballads were likely material for the earliest recordings, being among few extant types of standalone music in a presentational format, their rustic, old-fashioned style and timbre were less palatable to the urban, genteel audiences that would come to constitute the record-buying public. Consequently, the epic ballads were superseded by lighter songs that could better fit the short, recorded format and be presented with the novel instrumentation used for film songs. These short-format popular songs consisted either of traditional songs recontextualized as entertainment listening items (i.e., as opposed to being embedded in ritual, life events, or dance) or newly written paeans to Punjabi identity. The appeal of this genre lay most, I suggest, in its signification of "Punjab" for people distanced from Punjab by geography or, as it were, by modernity. Punjabis living in urban areas did not experience traditional songs, as their ancestors may have, in the context of village-based life events, but they could enjoy the memory of those songs in the high-fidelity field. Punjabis who had left the region—fish out of water—came to contemplate their difference, their Punjabi identity. One of the prominent artists in this revival music, Surinder Kaur, had worked as a singer in the Bombay film industry before locating in Delhi—both being big cities outside Punjab. The songs she sang represented Punjab within the broader context of the Republic of India. For Punjabis disconnected from local or rural spaces, such songs reaffirmed their sense of Punjabi identity among (and distinct from) other regional identities.

A similar process next played out on an international scale. Popular musical style was Westernized through adopting such elements as so-called disco rhythm—that is to say, rhythm associated with spaces conducive to dancing to recorded music. Before the 1960s, Punjabi music operated according to the logic that songs or music for listening (cerebral) and rhythms for dancing (corporeal) were exclusive of one another. Traditional Punjabi group dancing was facilitated by the sound of percussion, like dhol, and its accompanying sung texts consisted more of "verses" (e.g., *bolī*) as opposed to "songs" (*gīt*). The notion of collapsing song music and dance, such that a concert performance becomes a space for dance and, moreover, *individual* dance, was adopted first by diaspora Punjabis in the West. Punjabi British musicians started forming bands to perform at weddings as early as the 1960s, before the genre developed through such activities and became known as bhangra music and appreciated more widely in the 1980s (Banerji and Baumann 1990, 142–143).

Punjabis in diaspora were keenly aware of their cultural difference within host societies, but in the initial decades surprisingly little reference was made to Punjabi identity in this music's lyrics. Rather, simply continuing the traditional tropes of earlier established Punjabi songs was, in itself, the gesture of identity affirmation. By the 1990s, however, the gap between Punjab and wherever one was—geographically *and* culturally—had become a prominent, explicit theme in diaspora Punjabi popular music. Moreover, a discourse about the music also emerged.[8] An idea among some diaspora Punjabis was that they inhabited two competing identities (Asian and British) that needed reconciliation. The issue was worked out sonically, aided by music production's move away from live bands and toward the studio-based methods of sampling and multitracking. Producers juxtaposed fragments of traditional-sounding Punjabi music—the full expressions of which had not been easily reproduced in their entirety in the diaspora—with contemporary, globalized dance genres like reggae and house. The process lent itself particularly to the juxtaposition of disparate elements. For one to truly perceive juxtaposition, certain elements must be clearly marked or recognizable; the more distinct the elements combined, the more dramatic the juxtaposition. Remixes of this sort depend on essentialized or sharply indexical musical features. In the mix, what was "traditional" or "Punjabi" became essentialized. Whereas earlier products of Punjabi diaspora musicians were no less Punjabi, so to speak, this newer music called attention to its Punjabiness, its distinctive differences.

Still newer Punjabi popular music, of the twenty-first century, is less reductive. Rather than individuals feeling caught between Punjabi and (for example) British, there now exists support for being a sort of "global Punjabi citizen." In turn, elements in the music hardly need marking as Western (different), for they are part and parcel of the contemporary sound. Established as part of a decades-long development, they are capable of representing Punjabiness, too. Nevertheless, recent music's palette of timbres and stock of musical forms constitute a distinctive sound such that even when the lyrics do not sing the praises or lament the hardships of being Punjabi, it is difficult for the hearer not to be aware of the music's Punjabi identity. What is important here is how the development of Punjabi popular music, in its earlier stages, raised the awareness of identity as a regional, then a global, people united by their Punjab origin. Popular (mediated) music is one of the most powerful media by means of which, using Benedict Anderson's (1991) formulation, Punjabis imagine belonging to a community, most of whose members one will never meet but which, one supposes, are like oneself.[9] My emphasis here is on mass media's effect of allowing Punjabis to imagine a broad Punjabi community. Movement provides occasion to reflect on and to consolidate one's sense of identity and to do so in broad terms of essential difference between Punjabis and non-Punjabis. Media support such an identity by supplying themes and productive gestures that resonate with individuals in the position of migrant.

As exemplified by developments in Punjabi popular music, in order to have a flourishing awareness of Punjabi national identity, the condition was that people move outside Punjab. Movement away from the center encourages individuals' seeing themselves as part of a wider category of distinction, in this case, the Punjabi nation. Yet, if we also accept the premise that individuals composing this movement are of a particular set and likely to extrapolate their characteristics to the vision of the nation, then we can suppose the group identity best represents them, the migrants. A Punjabi national identity, constructed through such a process and supported by its media, represents these actors (expatriates and cosmopolitans) more accurately than it represents people located within Punjab's local or traditional spaces.

THE COMPOSITION OF PUNJABI IDENTITY

To see the minority cultural formations with which this book about musicians is concerned, we must open the floor to identities alternative to the ones prominently represented in Indian Punjabi mainstream visual media, bhangra music, and diaspora communities' public-relations presentations. Less popular representations tend to occur only between members of local Punjabi society, in the space that Herzfeld (2005) calls "cultural intimacy."[10] Herzfeld reasons that official narratives are not entirely the result of top-down forces such as pressure from the state, but that there is also "uncoerced enthusiasm" among individuals to participate in the narratives of imagined community (2005, 5). We cannot solely blame media, for instance, for promoting selective images of Punjabi culture. Rather, even those people at the bottom of the social order voluntarily support official narratives that protect some of their interests. Generally speaking, because uniformity is a strategy of defense—for example, of one's family honor within the village, of Punjab state's place within the Indian republic, of Punjabi immigrants among national others—one has to dig deliberately to excavate the diversity in Punjabi identity. When we do so, we meet resistance from both the more and the less powerful.

One of the characteristics of Punjabi national identity, and one that reflects the composition of the diaspora (migrants), is the central position enjoyed by Sikhs. If one considers the broad tract of land that Punjabi nationalists would like us to call the Punjab region, the Sikh population comes a distant third to Muslims and Hindus. Yet, as explained earlier, Sikhs' identification with the Punjabi language led to their becoming the majority in the current Punjab *state* of India. As a result, when one travels to the state, the one administratively labeled Punjab, one experiences something of the effect of entering "the land of the Sikhs." Equally important, many see the Punjabi diaspora as a Sikh diaspora. We must, however, see beyond the habitual representation of the Sikh community and the diaspora as Punjab, lest the traditional dholis—few of whom are Sikh or reside in the diaspora—get pushed outside the frame.

In contrast to the official and commercial discourses that reinforce this conflated representation, critical scholarship in Punjab studies has seen a trend of antiessentialism. Oberoi challenges the seemingly unified front of what now is supposed to constitute the Sikh Tradition. According to Oberoi, "there was immense diversity within Sikh society for much of the nineteenth century" (1994, 24). He traces the current atmosphere of perceived uniformity to the so-called Singh Sabha movement that began at the end of the nineteenth century, which "began to view the multiplicity in Sikh identity with great suspicion and hostility" (25). Characterizing the dominant discourse of Sikhism as being both extremely essentialized and destructive to the recognition of minority Sikh identities, Oberoi observes, "A new cultural elite aggressively usurped the right to represent others within this singular tradition. Its ethnocentric logic subsumed other identities and dissolved alternative ideals . . . under a monolithic, codified and closed culture" (25). Gera Roy transposes the argument about Sikhs and their tradition to the situation of the Jatt ethnic group in relation to bhangra music: "The *jat* caste's domination of Bhangra production leads to a 'new form of tyranny' through which Bhangra is not only appropriated as *jat* music but *jat* culture essentialized as Panjabi" (2010, 236). These writers argue for seeing diversity in Punjabi society, but in doing so they become positioned at political odds with essentialists.

Another example related to Sikh identity illustrates the stakes in the conflict between identity representations emphasizing uniformity and those emphasizing diversity. Axel (2001) discusses the Punjabi diaspora as a site for promoters of the proposed Sikh state, Khalistan. The movement for Khalistan, a lingering issue since before Indian independence, gained momentum in the 1980s, at times taking the form of terrorist activities. The conflict came to a head in 1984 with the storming of the Harimandir Sahib in Amritsar by an Indian government perceived as Hindu to ferret out a group of agitators. Previously, only a slice of Sikhs supported the movement for Khalistan, this assault waged at—effectively, on—the holiest of Sikh sites was tantamount to an assault on Sikhs at large. One reaction to it was the assassination of Indian prime minister Indira Gandhi by two of her Sikh bodyguards, inspiring, in turn, riots against Sikhs in India (Grewal 1998, 227–229). Many Sikhs emigrated from India to escape a diffuse climate of persecution and to envision their autonomy in new lands. After these traumatic, formative events, Axel explains, "Diasporic supporters of Khalistan began to understand the Sikhs to be a nation" (2001, 5). The shared experience of the events of 1984 bind Sikhs together in a sense of nationhood regardless of where individuals fall on the issue of Khalistan, as the following anecdote will illustrate.

In Surrey, British Columbia, at the 2019 celebration of the holiday of Visakhi, I observed a surprising number of displays, floats, speakers, and performers advocating for Khalistan. The event commemorates the 1699 formation of the core Sikh community, Khalsa. In attendance were roughly half a million participants, most of whom appeared to be Sikh. The central fixture of the annual event is a *nagar kīrtan*, a procession through the streets of the Sikh holy scripture, Sri Guru Granth Sahib. Veneration of the holy text, which since the 1699 Visakhi has been considered to be the divine Guru in book form, is something that unites all Sikhs. Visakhi is a time with significance for Punjabis of all creeds, being the traditional seasonal marker of the culmination of the spring (wheat) harvest and, in effect, the "agricultural new year." Yet there is no mistaking current Visakhi celebrations in the diaspora as anything other than Sikh events. A non-Sikh Canadian whom I encountered crudely referred to it as "the orange parade" (in reference to the preponderance of items colored saffron, the symbolic color of the Khalsa). From the perspective of non-Punjabi Canadians, Visakhi, indeed, is a holiday belonging to the Sikhs. And insofar as the event centers on a *nagar kīrtan* organized by the local gurdwara (Sikh temple), Sikhs have a valid claim to understanding the event as theirs. The Khalsa represents the idealized core of the practicing Sikh community and so, although not all Sikhs choose to practice so as to be included in the Khalsa identity, it provides the firm center around which an identifiable Sikh community coheres. Most Sikhs do not, on the other hand, advocate for Khalistan. Nevertheless, the supporters of Khalistan aid in making possible a strong show of representation, a great "orange parade" of hundreds of thousands showing the presence of Sikhs in British Columbia. Khalistanis want a state, the ultimate expression of the sovereignty of a Sikh (political) nation. Other Sikhs may be content with just a Sikh nation in the form of a global community among whom to belong, but they benefit from the strong show of nationalism that the Khalistanis' struggle entails.

Recall the antiessentialist position of Punjab studies scholars. In their view, the model of a group with an exclusive core cannot be accepted. In the view of Khalistanis, by contrast, "the proposition of a closed group—a people with a destiny—represents the only possibility for survival" (Axel 2001, 7). The former view, emphasizing diversity and fluidity, threatens the cohesion of the group, which, in the latter view, is maintained by strict adherence to rules of inclusion and exclusion in order to form a powerful force. Scholars and Khalistanis (to create a selective dichotomy) represent opposite ends of a spectrum, somewhere between which sit (rhetorically) typical Sikhs. "Typical" Sikhs resist total essentialization, yet they gain nothing from dismantling group identity entirely. A similar argument can be made for the group identity of Punjabi. Jatt culture, that of the dominant ethnic group, may be understood as noncoterminous with Punjabi culture, but, as with the Khalsa for Sikhs, the benefit of upholding a concept of Punjabi cultural national identity warrants accepting Jatt culture as its core.

The above cases show, however, that different group members are required to strategize at different levels. When critiquing unbalanced power in a village in Punjab, the dominant Jatts make an easy target. They control the land and, among other forms of control, give or revoke permission to low-caste people to use that land for their morning toilet. Their faces are seen, their ways most celebrated in media. Jatts reside, literally, at the center of village life. In that place, it may appear an injustice for Jatt culture to dominate, even stand in for, Punjabi culture, for it would appear to crowd out cultural identities of the Punjabis living in the margins. Two variations in scenario, however, suggest that we not end our analysis here, satisfied in having found the villain.

First, consider a change of actor. In the vicinity of that same village is a clan of drummers who are marginalized in relation to Jatts. To be sure, they are getting the short end of the stick. To partake of the benefits of Punjabi national identity, they have to concede that it represents Jatt culture better than their own. The drummers gain in some respects by hitching their wagon to Punjabi identity even if it manifests here through Jatt culture. In living this strategy, the drummers may choose to adopt values more typical of Jatts to fit into what stands as Punjabi culture—that which can appear to override qaum-class-difference and unite the Jatt and the drummer. This is the same logic by which a Sikh happily settled in Canada may not completely disavow local Khalistan activists, though it is unlikely Khalistan would have a Tim Horton's.

Consider, second, a change in place that shifts the Jatt from the center to the margins. A Jatt in Los Angeles finds himself in a marginal position relative to the wider society. He is now a minority, despite the power he enjoys within the Punjabi community.[11] Just as the village drummers strategically identify from the margins, the Jatt can sublimate his particular identity and hitch his wagon to an American identity. The Jatt in Los Angeles may alternately choose another strategy, which is to find strength in the numbers of the group in which he dominates: Punjabis. In this place, it makes sense for the Jatt to subscribe to Punjabi identity and to welcome all Punjabi ethnic groups under the umbrella. This is not to say, however, that the Jatt in diaspora welcomes emphasis on diversity if it goes as far as to threaten the cohesion of the support group. When we encounter a Jatt in diaspora playing dhol, how do we see it? Should we emphasize that an individual from the dominant group of the Punjabi community has appropriated the cultural property of minorities? Or should we see his dhol playing as a gesture to represent the Punjabi "national" culture, which is his salient distinction from mainstream America?[12] The interpretation must vary with place. What can be said with consistency, however, is that the Jatt has, in net sum, a greater number of choices. By contrast, in no place outside his immediate qaum can the drummer choose to drive the oxcart.

PUNJABI CULTURAL NATIONALISM AND THE ISSUE OF MINORITIES

Within the more accessible spheres of Punjabis—among the middle class, in the diaspora, in academe, in mass media—I observe a discourse about Punjabi culture that is congruent with the ideology of cultural nationalism. This ideology is characterized by the belief that Punjabis constitute a nation of people joined by fundamental cultural similarities, and that, further, takes explicit pride in this nation and aims to promote its interests and to spread its culture. It assumes that Punjabi things are inherently valuable, and so ascribes positive assessment to any (celebratory) engagement with Punjabi things. In this frame, Punjabi culture and identity are strategically essentialized for the sake of unity. There are well-founded defensive reasons for this essentialization. Among the more Westernized, urban, or middle-class communities within Punjab, a sense of disconnectedness from historical consciousness of pre-Partition Punjab prompts rallying to preserve some semblance of the past. In the wider nations of India and Pakistan (yet for different reasons), Punjabis may struggle to have their political voices heard. And, in the diaspora, Punjabi communities rally for representation among a non-Punjabi majority population. Representation, period, becomes more important than representation with nuance, for nuance ultimately leads to individualism and the collapse of grand ideas. Hence, value is placed on a unified view of Punjabi culture, not just in South Asia but also globally.

Punjabi cultural nationalist discourse often invokes Partition, for the resulting trauma to the Punjabi body politic, more than the colonialism that preceded it, makes up its originary narrative. The grand division figures, at times poetically, in service of uniting sentiment to support national identity. Such sentiment is epitomized by twentieth-century Punjabi poet Amrita

Pritam's clever reference to the eighteenth-century poet Varis Shah in the wake of Partition: "Today I call upon Varis Shah: Speak, from beyond the grave!" Pritam called on Shah to heal the nation, so to speak. The audience understands that Pritam, an Indian Sikh calling on a Muslim of "Pakistan," Shah, is a gesture that transcends religion and politics. Shah addressed the Punjabi nation in its language—a unifying element. In his celebrated telling of the tragic-romantic story of the lovers Hir and Ranjha, Shah spoke about what are seen to be universally Punjabi conflicts. He now represents a pre-Partition unifying figure. Just as the estrangement of Hir from Ranjha was an unbearable separation, Pritam suggests, Punjabis post-Partition were going through an even more violent separation from each other. "Once a single daughter of Punjab [Hir] wept; you wrote lamentation upon lamentation / Today, *millions* of them weep" (Pritam 2006, 78). One cannot, however, assume that all Punjabis feel unified by the calamity of Partition, nor did the event affect all in the same way. Partition may have strengthened bonds between people and their own groups, but the bond is not necessarily with Punjabis at large. Indeed, Partition cannot be assumed to have divided a unified Punjabi people by splitting their land. The violence that took place at the time revealed divisions between residents of the Punjab region, and the theory of manufactured difference—from, for example, a British policy of "divide and conquer"—is inadequate to wholly explain such differences. Thus, Punjabi nationalists invoke Partition as something that unites Punjabis in a common experience of uprootedness while Partition's events also remind us of the social differences in Punjab.

Punjabi cultural nationalism emphasizes healing the divisions of religion and state origin. It can be observed, for instance, that Punjabis of Pakistan origin and those of India origin often operate in distinct spheres even within diaspora locales despite their geographic proximity and presumed cultural similarity. Viewing the division as tragic, Punjabi nationalists encourage cooperation and mutual appreciation between Pakistanis and Indians, and between Muslims, Sikhs, and Hindus. They support the dissolution of boundaries implied by such divisions. At the same time, however, they draw a boundary around the Punjabi nation. It is as if to say, "Let's forget our differences and remember we are all Punjabis" while simultaneously saying "Punjabis are different from others by virtue of these ways that make Punjabis the same as each other." The approach asserts the moral value of inclusivity while allowing the individual to practice exclusivity, according to one's interpretation of Punjabi culture, to aid a coherent sense of identity. Still, as Baumann observes, nationalism privileges the ideology of certain actors while disadvantaging others (1999, 39). Even while good Punjabi nationalists work to include Pakistani Punjabis, one finds that Punjabis of Indian origin predominate in their discourse. One may observe a lesser interest in Punjabi nationalism in Pakistan, where Punjabi cultural identity, connected with vernacular culture and assigned a lower status, is sublimated in favor of the state (Pakistani) identity. The opposite is the case in India, where regional, vernacular culture is more greatly celebrated and where many choose to see themselves as Punjabis first and Indians second.

As it plays out across the demographics of class, Punjabi cultural nationalism requires certain groups of Punjabi origin to sublimate their particular identities more than others do. Indeed, class positionality makes all the difference in shaping perspective. Punjabi nationalists tend to come from the position of the center of a Punjabi culture construct, from which position it may be difficult to see that what appears to be good for all is, more accurately, mostly good for them. Their position is comparable to those critically called "white liberals" in US political discourse. Such liberals are "well-intentioned"; they support the rights of all, inclusive of minority groups, and hold to a position of antiracism that derives from the idea that race should not matter. They stand in opposition to political conservatives, among whom they locate the forces of division—the analogs in Punjabi context being religious fundamentalists, Indian and Pakistani nationalists, and Khalistanis. People of color and other critics of white liberals, however, express frustration at white liberals' inadequate recognition of the practical realities of minority groups' identities and class positionality. The logic of Punjabi cultural nationalism—an ingredient of a "Jatt liberal" politics—accepts minority people as part of the fabric of a broad Punjabi cultural formation while doing little to combat their marginalization.

My work with marginalized members of Punjabi society has forced me to question the unified view of Punjabi people in both liberal and conservative formulations to stake out a third position. I find that, in their own spheres, marginalized people express less sentiment for Punjabis as a nation and more advocacy for the interests of the smaller groups to which they belong. Their position challenges any presumption of Punjabi nationalists that minority groups would like to be included in their vision of Punjabi culture. It may appear that I am identifying the problem to be that minority groups are unfairly marginalized within the concept of Punjabi culture, on one hand, while on the other hand suggesting that these groups not be considered as part of Punjabi culture at all. There is no contradiction if one considers the situation from the perspective of the minority groups. Minority groups want to be included, strategically, for the situational benefits gained from connecting to the operating Punjabi culture construct. Yet, in that they want to represent themselves and to be understood, it is preferable to be considered outside the framework of Punjabi culture insofar as the latter must necessarily marginalize them. They do not want to be seen as outside Punjabi culture, to the extent that the idea of Punjabi culture exists. They are better off, rather, if the idea of Punjabi culture did not exist. Much has been made of the identity struggle of Punjabis in the diaspora to exist "between" cultural formations. Minority groups in Punjab live that struggle without leaving home.

2 DHOL MANIFESTED

Body, Sound, and Structure

In light of the potential for Punjab and Punjabi culture to be divided in so many ways, is there any representative thing that unites Punjabis as a nation? Religion, citizenship, and language, all located on political fault lines, prove inadequate. Symbols of these things, like flags or literary works, are limited accordingly. Is dhol the answer? When I first traveled to Punjab in 2000, I noticed the pervasiveness of dhol in public life. On my latest visit, the sound of dhol continued to echo across the landscape. Perhaps it is so that when I hear dhol, I feel that I am in Punjab. Stokes discusses how one's sense of place is informed by music: "The musical event . . . evokes and organises collective memories and present experiences of place with an intensity, power and simplicity unmatched by any other social activity" (1994, 3). Music is a means through which people recognize not only place but also identity connected with place (5).

With such thoughts in mind, in previous work, I argued that dhol now functions to represent Punjabi cultural identity (Schreffler 2010). I followed Turner's idea that, in a set of rituals, one finds a nucleus of dominant signs in a central position that "are characterized by extreme multivocality" (1973, 1101). Transposing the idea from ritual to identification, I concluded that dhol occupies a central position in the signification of Punjabi identity, where a cluster of signs work together to deepen its power. Dhol is polysemic—it signifies in multiple ways—partly from its nature as a musical instrument, a sounding body. It has a physical form, makes a sound, and conveys abstract messages (created through organizing its sound habitually into certain patterns). It is a sign complex with rich potential to affect those who engage it, on multiple levels.

A framework for interpreting such signs is provided by Peirce, who classifies signification in terms of how a sign relates to that for which it stands, its object (1932, 2: 143—144). In Peirce's schema, *icon* refers to a relation of resemblance. A drawing of a dhol, for instance, can be called an icon in that it directly represents an object (dhol). Next, the term *index* denotes a sign having a relationship of natural association with an object and that indicates it. In this fashion, the sound of dhol (for example) indicates a dhol (even if one does not see it). Though an index is not as direct in its representation as an icon, the natural relationship between an index and its object makes it more direct of a sign than the third type, *symbol*. Symbol, an abstract sign, refers to a sign whose relationship to an object is mediated by convention. The word *ḍhol*, for example, represents a drum only through agreement that in a particular system (i.e., Punjabi language) a verbal sound (or writing) stands for an object.

To elaborate: signifying as icons and indices are the dhol's object form, its sound, and the rhythmic patterns played on it. Its large, rotund size, a form replete with decoration and brandished prominently in a crowd by a mobile player in a standing position, make it a distinguished item in the visual experience of events that it accompanies. The sight of a dhol, therefore, points to such events. The drum is a metonym of activities that feature it, especially the folkloric dance, bhangra. The dhol's sound is an index of the instrument, distinctive in its timbre. The rhythmic patterns played on the dhol also index the function that the drum is accompanying. In the traditional system, one applies patterns exclusively to assigned activities, and to hear a given rhythmic pattern is to know a particular activity is happening.

Because a symbol is an indirect, abstract type of sign, it is more complicated to demonstrate dhol acting as a symbol. One short argument might be that the sound of a dhol represents an experience (i.e., of hearing a dhol played in Punjabi contexts) and that that experience of being within a Punjabi milieu approximates the abstract quality Punjabiness. A longer argument might work down a semiotic chain, from the sound of dhol (an index) to the dhol-object, from the dhol-object (as index) to bhangra dance, from bhangra dance to the image of particular dancing bodies used to represent the Punjabi body politic, and from there to the essence, Punjabiness. An image of the dhol drum then might be worked into a logo as a symbol of Punjab. A less complicated dhol-related symbol is the name of the instrument, a word. As with most words, it stands for something (a drum) through conventional agreement. The same sign—the word /ḍhol/, a homonym—also represents the Punjabi concept of a male beloved from whom one has been separated. This term is a trope in love songs of longing, in songs sung during group dances (in the presence of the dhol drum), and in romantic legends. Theoretically, two meanings of /ḍhol/—"drum" and "beloved"—may become conflated, and effects are created by the sign transfer to the other object. Thus, I have suggested (2010) that the drum has the power to evoke those feelings of longing related to separation. While dhol signifies, in the first order, Punjabiness and Punjabi identity, it may, in the second order, simultaneously signify feelings of longing that deepen the effect of its first order of signification.

Because numerous things that dhol signifies relate to Punjabi identity—from bhangra dance to the feeling of longing associated with songs of separation—it works as a multifaceted *emblem*. Singer discusses emblems, from a Peircean perspective, as sign complexes that combine icons, indices, and symbols (1984, 106). More precisely, emblems are symbols that depend on icons and indices in their makeup. As the US flag is a symbol of the United States, its fifty stars are iconic of the number of states. Musical instruments from the harp of Ireland to the great pipes of Scotland and the steel drum of Trinidad have been used as emblems of a people or a country. In their resonant contexts, such instruments are not ordinary signs but carry overtones of historical depth and sentimental import. Emblems may encompass a national or cultural identity because they cover many bases, functioning as symbols of the abstract political or ethnic unit and individuals' deeply felt emotions. Musical instruments, through their iconicity (read, immediacy) and their conciseness—they represent music and yet are easier to manipulate visually—are effective emblems.

Hence, dhol does not refer to Punjab in the form of a cold symbol. It is something, above all, endearing to Punjabis. People are conscious of its affective mystique. The idea of dhol as an iconic heartbeat of Punjabis is a common one, as in Nahar Singh's statement, "On the rhythm of dhol, all Punjabis' hearts beat as one" (1988, 35). A similar sentiment was expressed to me by a member of the Gill Band in Hoshiarpur who said that dhol was so powerful because it has a direct connection to the heart.[1] As support for his statement, the musician claimed that his 6-year-old son did not respond to recorded music on disc, yet whenever live dhol was beaten, the boy responded to it "automatically." It is among such ideas that the importance of dhol as a *sonic* sign is apparent. Other emblems, while also complex signs, may not have such immediacy. Dhol's beat can be *felt* immediately, as a heartbeat, as a powerful sound, at the same time as its visual presence leads one down the chain of cultural associations. Although, theoretically, all people might feel this heartbeat, the fact that it is supposed to be Punjabis' heart reflects dhol-sound's reference to a specific shared experience. Qureshi (1997) theorizes the efficacy of sound in facilitating feelings of shared experience, wherein its physical sensation in the body creates an experiential bond between listeners. With the enormous group of more than 100 million Punjabis having few unifying signs outside the land of origin, one thing they share is the experience of being in the same space with the sound of dhol and *feeling*—something—at the same time.

This chapter sketches the physical and acoustic dimensions of the emblem, dhol. It introduces the material form of the instrument, its manner of play, the sound forms created with it, and their place in cultural contexts. The introduction will provide a background for discussing, in subsequent chapters, the ways that dhol fills a role both as a resonant emblem of Punjabi culture and as a means of identification for its players.

BODY AND SOUL

After years engaging dhol as a sort of guiding star in the Punjabi cultural galaxy, I realized how much I had become acculturated to Punjabis' anthropomorphizing of the instrument. I had come to feel, like these Punjabis, a *soul* in "Dhol." When I was in a room with a dhol, the instrument felt like the vessel of a being in the room, as the Hindu faithful perceive a religious icon. Garib Dass felt a similar regard for all instruments. When he stayed with me in the United States, we practiced in a room that contained numerous instruments. Whenever we entered that room, turning on the light and thus revealing the instruments, Garib Dass would smile and intone, *jai ho!*—"Praise be!" "Dhol" has certain iconic "human" features. Dhol's barrel shape maps to a human torso. The "belly" (*kukkh*) of Dhol is periodically filled with nourishment in the form of a spice and oil mixture, *masālā*, which is reasoned to keep the individual warm (in the Ayurvedic medicinal sense) while also improving his voice (*avāz*). When at rest, Dhol should be seated on a chair or bed, rather than on the floor. He sits with his bottom side (the bass drumhead) below and his head (the treble drumhead) above. The drumsticks, Garib Dass instructed, should not be left resting on Dhol's head. Before playing, one salutes Dhol with a brief, private prayer[2] and before a performance, participants touch Dhol to receive his blessing as they would touch the feet of a respected elder. All dhols are clothed with tassels or pom-poms (*phuhmmaṇ*) attached to the rings for tightening the rope lacing used to adjust the pitch of the drumheads. Before playing, dholis adjust the position of the pom-poms in an act described as "dressing," just as they "undress" Dhol after his performance. Garib Dass was sensitive to the treatment of Dhol, as one would care for a family member. Damages to Dhol's body are treated by the application of "bandages" (*paṭṭī*), rather than discarding the instrument or replacing it with a new one. Garib Dass's dhols were thus family members for life; years after the master's death, his grandsons still maintained his dhols with ever more bandages. Should Dhol become broken beyond repair—having "died" in a sense—he is sent off in proper ritual fashion. Like the cremated bones of a deceased loved one, Dhol is gathered up in a cloth and taken to a river. Dhol is saluted and immersed in the water to be washed away. Neglect of this personage—treating him as a mundane object—is unacceptable.

I share these details to convey how important the dhol is to its historical caretakers, the dholis. Beliefs about and practices of the instrument are among that which constitutes the dholis' identity. An affront to dholi identity is experienced as the instrument finds its way into the hands of ever more players—who cannot be expected to have acculturated to the same values. What would Garib Dass, who lovingly maintained just two dhols throughout his career, make of the current trade of dhols among diaspora enthusiasts who acquire and resell dhols like automobiles? Such a volume of instruments now exists in suburban residences in North America. In another decade, will these be tucked away in the corner of a garage, used as garden planters, or become firewood? Like the careful regulation of dhol players through the *ustād* system (Chapter 5), a conservative sort of family planning had once limited the number of dhols brought into the world. After all, the dhols were family members who have to be cared for.

LINEAGE

The dhol drum, while strongly signifying Punjab today, simultaneously feels elemental to world music generally, as it sits within a long and expansive lineage. Many double-headed barrel-drum forms are dispersed across Eurasia, and some of them also go by the name of dhol (or a similar term). In this organography, the Punjabi iteration has its distinctive place.[3]

The antecedent to the term *ḍhol* was likely the Persian *dohol*. It is reasonable to conclude (e.g., Dick 1984, 91; Dick and Dournon 1984, 560) that the Persian-type double-sided drum, introduced to South Asia with the Delhi Sultanate as early as the thirteenth century, provided the model in form as well. Amir Khusro made mention of "duhlak" (an instrument of women) during the Khilji dynasty (early fourteenth century) (Sarmadee 1975, 258). The *duhul* (the Persian term rendered in Indic orthography) was well established in Emperor Akbar's court (late sixteenth century). The *Āʾīn-i-Akbarī* describes Akbar's *naqqārah khānah* or *ṭabl khānah*, "house of drums," which included four *duhuls* (Abul-Fazl 1872, 46; 1873, 51). The drum ensemble, a feature of Islamic rule, belonged to and articulated the sphere of power connected with the military might and sovereignty of rulers.

In the greater Punjab region, I find no literary evidence of the precise term *ḍhol* before the seventeenth century, though at the onset of that century there is reference to an instrument with that name. In the legend of *Hīr* as composed by Damodar Gulati, circa 1600—1615, the pomp of a wedding procession is described as including dhol paired with a double-reed pipe (*sarnāī*).[4] This civilian usage of the instrument, however, is overshadowed in the contemporary literature by continual reference to military applications. In the Sikh text *Dasam Granth*, circa 1690s, in the "Chanḍī dī Vār" composition that narrates a clash of heavenly adversaries, the dhol is mentioned several times among instruments spurring on the battle.[5]

In the mid-eighteenth century, we see the dramatic emergence of the dhol as a high-profile object that had secured a place in everyday Punjabi life. In Varis Shah's *Hīr*, composed circa 1766, the dhol is mentioned seven times. Shah mentions the instrument not only in actual playing context (e.g., during marriage festivities) but also in metaphor and proverbial expressions.[6] Though double-headed drums already existed in India, the occurrence in *Hīr* was a distinct cultural manifestation of the instrument type, having its own contexts and customary uses.

THE MATERIAL OBJECT

The early twenty-first-century[7] Indian Punjabi dhol has a barrel shape, measuring on average 25 inches long and 12 inches wide at both ends. Its body is carved from a tree trunk, the woods being selected for their hardness; harder wood is thought to produce a better tone. The most common woods from which dhols are carved are mango (*amb*, *Mangifera indica*) and Indian rosewood (*ṭāhlī*, *Dalbergia sissoo*). The latter—the state tree of Punjab—is considered to be of higher quality and, along with its greater availability than other high-quality materials, means it is used for the majority of instruments.[8]

In India, dhol bodies are rarely manufactured in Punjab, which in part can be explained by the paucity of trees in the state. Earlier, suppliers of dhol bodies were located near forests in Jammu and Kashmir, but in recent decades manufacture in that region has declined. In the 2000s, a guild of Muslim craftsmen in the city of Amroha (Uttar Pradesh), known for its woodworking industry, assumed the place of dhol suppliers. Supplying many forms of drums throughout north India, the craftsmen from Amroha make periodic trips to Punjab to sell their wares during festival days. If dholis want to purchase new dhols, they generally either make a journey to the Jammu area or wait for a visit from Amroha craftsmen. Because of dholis' conservative attitude toward acquiring dhols, there is no significant market for ready-made dhols in shops, which, furthermore, cannot be trusted to furnish instruments assembled to professional specifications. Dholis, instead, complete their own instruments after the wholesale purchase of bare bodies, doing so also being more economical. Other work that dholis may assign to others before their work on the instrument is the installation of a system of tightening hooks and bolts at one or both ends. The bolt system has replaced the traditional rope-lacing method for attaching and tuning drumheads. Because of their convenience, bolts have been adopted by a majority of Indian dholis.

Dholis' own work on a dhol begins with sanding the wood and treating it with the application of mustard oil. The oil also adds color to the instrument, a rich, dark shade being preferred. The aforementioned *masālā* is next spread throughout the inside of the body.

Dholis with the ability to do so then fabricate the drumheads from goatskin. One drumhead (*puṛā*) is thin and the other is thick, to create contrasting treble and bass heads. In the 1990s, the brass band industry introduced prefabricated drumheads made of "plastic" (polyester). Though widely considered inferior in tone, synthetic drumheads' imperviousness to changes in weather, their low cost, and the convenience of purchasing them (i.e., rather than constructing one's own, from hide) has led to their wide adoption. Because the thinner, treble goatskin heads of a dhol are most susceptible to puncture and weather-induced variations of pitch, many dholis choose to use plastic drumheads for that side of the dhol only and to retain goatskin heads, for their preferred tone, on the bass side.[9]

Drumheads are next attached to a dhol either with rope, the aforementioned system of nuts and bolts, or a combination of both. Even in the case of using bolts on both sides of the instrument, rope lacing is applied as a matter of tradition, though it has ceased to function in its purpose for tightening and adjusting the pitch of the drumheads. Although attitudes to the importance of tuning vary among players, it usually is not intended to be as precise as one finds in the case of drums like the tabla. The bass head of the dhol needs only to be set to vibrate deeply. Nor is the treble head usually required to have any particular pitch; rather, it is "tuned to itself," so that it "sounds good." This means having a sufficiently bright and "clear" sound, defined as having its overtones in consonance with one another.

Because one usually plays the dhol in a standing position, dholis have to make a shoulder strap, often from a dense cotton belt material (*nuār*) used for rural applications. The final touch is to beautify the dhol with the addition of homemade *phuhmmaṇ*, which Indian dholis make from yarn, whereas Pakistani dholis retain an older style of tassels made of leather.

Professional dholis also craft their own drumsticks, the design of which makes up one of the unique features of Punjabi dhol playing. The contrasting shapes and materials of the two sticks suit the respective drumhead each is used to strike. The bass head is struck with a bent wooden beater called *ḍaggā*. Regional variations in ḍaggā shape notwithstanding, the most common shapes are designed to be beaten on their side, not on the apex of their bend. The treble head is hit with a thin stick or flexible switch called *chaṭī*, *chaṛī*, or *tīhlī*.

The dhol may be distinguished in form—though better so in function and cultural significance—from the drum called *ḍholkī* (less often, *ḍholak*). Adding the diminutive affix /-kī/ to /ḍhol/ yields "small dhol," and the ḍholkī is indeed a similarly shaped yet smaller instrument. The ḍholkī, however, is always played with bare hands on both sides and often in a seated position. It is not adorned with *phuhmmaṇ*, nor is it revered through ritual gestures such as those offered to the dhol. The dhol is a loud instrument, beaten in "outdoor" contexts such as dance or contexts that tend to convey power and a masculine ethos. The Punjabi dhol is, customarily speaking, played exclusively by men. By contrast, the ḍholkī is considered a domestic instrument in Punjab, of the home and available to the layperson. It is thought better suited to accompany "indoor" music and contexts where a softer volume is required, as when singing amateur songs or hymns. Most significant, in consonance with its feminine-gendered name, the ḍholkī is often played by women. Indeed, though both sexes play the ḍholkī frequently, it is one of few instruments traditionally ascribed to women.[10] Whereas the terms *ḍhol* and *ḍholkī* (*ḍholak*) have been conflated in other parts of India, in Punjab they refer to different instruments that occupy distinct social fields.

PHYSICAL APPROACHES

Unlike many north Indian instruments, one most often stands while playing the dhol. This reflects the instrument's role as an "outdoor" instrument, or, at least, one not rooted to a stage, for one may move about while playing. It also reflects the notion that although the dhol is a sound instrument, it is not properly an instrument of music. Music (sangīt), formulated as that which is actively listened to for aesthetic enjoyment, is more often enjoyed seated. While standing to play, a dholi wears the instrument by means of its strap. Wearing the strap hanging from the shoulder of the treble-side hand is traditionally considered proper. A second way, allowing the strap to cross one's back and pass over the shoulder of the bass-side hand, allows the drum to stay more securely in position, and doing so is useful if the player is required to walk while playing. Despite this advantage, few professionals in Punjab wear the strap across their backs, and they criticize wearing the instrument like this as a sign of amateurism.

The two different sticks are used to strike the dhol in different ways. The *ḍaggā* is grasped like a hammer yet strikes the drumhead through rotation of the forearm. One can distinguish an "open" (resonant) stroke (the default stroke in the notations herein) and a "closed" (dampened) stroke. The *chaṭī* is grasped in a more relaxed manner, with the thumb placed on one side of the stick while the other fingers are splayed out on the other. Most often, the *chaṭī* is held so that the index finger is closest to the end of the stick, with the bulk of the stick's length extending out past the little finger. The angle of the *chaṭī* is roughly perpendicular to the arm and the forearm rotates to achieve the stroke. Some dholis grasp the *chaṭī* with a sort of reverse grip, where the little finger is closest to its end. This technique is often stigmatized as the mark of an ill-trained dholi, despite the fact that some very technically proficient players have employed it.[11] Sometimes, when a dholi wants to imply other dholis are less skilled, they attribute the reverse *chaṭī* grip to them, even when in fact those dholis do not use that technique.[12]

A number of other techniques are used to strike the dhol to provide timbral contrast or for effect. Contrasts are created on the treble side by striking the head at different angles, in different places between the center and edge of the head, or with "open" and "closed" strokes. Such contrasts are more important in the playing style of some dholis than in the style of others, for whom the default clear and open stroke nearer the edge of the head is primary. Tonal contrast on the bass head can be achieved by tapping the head with the bend of the ḍaggā. More gimmicky stick techniques involve hitting the dhol somewhere other than the membrane of the drumheads. In the dhol tradition of the marginal area of southwestern Punjab, hitting the rim of the bass head is actually a standard technique, especially in jhummar dance rhythms. In the mainstream area of play, this technique has been adopted in a newly created (late-twentieth-century) rhythm called *bhalvāṇī* (see the later discussion and Figure 2.17, where such strokes are indicated by a ▲ notehead). A showy version of this rhythm emphasizes the gimmick by striking the center of the dhol's body, rather than the rim.

Besides playing with sticks, the flesh of the hand is used to various degrees. For special effect, the ḍaggā may be dispensed with altogether in favor of the bare hand. One might slap the head, tap with the fingertips (*thāp*), or press the skin with the heel of one's hand to modulate pitch. In stick-play, the fingertips, while still managing to hold the ḍaggā, are also used in specific ways. Dholis stop the sound of the bass head from ringing at times that are specific and consistent, either by placing the hand on the head or by brushing the fingertips in an upward stroke across the surface of the drumhead, which may add a perceptible glide up in pitch. The notation in the figures, for simplicity, represents all these gestures with a single notehead shape (■).

SONIC STRUCTURES

Dhol's two heads provide the means of creating distinctive sonic forms through the sharp differentiation between their pitches. Most dhol playing consists of units of conventional rhythmic patterns distinguished through high-low pitch contrast and the sequence of strokes within a cycle of time. A construct known to Punjabi dholis as *tāl* refers to such a rhythmic-timbral pattern, which the player repeats indefinitely. Dhol players gloss *tāl*, in English, simply as "rhythm." It is important to understand, however, that *tāl*, which is more specific than the general meaning of English *rhythm*, does not correspond to what is known as *tāl* in Hindustani classical music. The latter is more akin to meter—that is, a regular pattern of emphases that structure pulse. The classical concept of *tāl* constitutes a set of underlying (theoretical) metric criteria that may be fulfilled using any number of rhythmic patterns manifested in a given performance. Classical musicians do recognize specifically identified conventional or model rhythmic patterns, bound by the metrical rule structure of a given *tāl*, which they call *ṭhekā*. In performance, however, they are not bound to indefinite repetition of these patterns; indeed, variation of rhythm is expected in a classical performance. By contrast, dhol playing is expected to maintain a more or less fixed pattern, akin to Arab music's concept of rhythmic mode (*īqā'*). A dhol *tāl*, while its abstract, underlying structure may be analyzed, is not conceived as a potentiality; it is a concrete, clichéd utterance. To resummarize the distinction, classical *tāl* identifies a framework that suggests potential patterns of sound whereas, in dhol terminology, *tāl* identifies a prescribed pattern of sound.[13] This is not to say that dhol *tāl* patterns are immutable; they may vary from player to player (or, more commonly, between communities or regions). Rather, an individual player maintains his own sense of a specific pattern that is linked to a *tāl* identity.[14] The specific pattern a dholi plays constitutes the message, the communicative content of dhol playing. To bring the idea into focus, it may be helpful to think of classical music and dhol playing as products of distinctly different underlying intents. Whereas classical music intends to forefront imagination and beauty through sonic structure, dhol playing structures sound with the intention of communicating more directly and specifically.

Dhol playing places so much emphasis on the specific pattern, the voiced message, that the more abstract grammatical structure, meter, may suffer some ambiguity in its perception. While in the early stages of documenting dhol rhythms, I was sometimes challenged to identify the meter of dholis' performances, particularly in my initial attempts to transcribe them. My thought process, rooted in the formal study of Western music and prior exposure to classical tabla, began by trying to identify the meter. I would then proceed to situate the rhythmic events—the drum strokes—along the graph of the meter, which I presumed could be divided into pulses and subpulses. What I came to discover was that, in some performances, some drum strokes did not align precisely with subdivided time points in the (projected) metrical graph. This violated my basic conception of meter, something that is not only cyclic but also composed of (and divisible into) a set of evenly spaced pulses.

My first breakthrough in knowing dhol playing more authentically came while learning to play the instrument. It happened during a rare moment when Garib Dass guided me to practice a *tāl*, *bhangṛā*, beginning at a slower and proceeding to a faster tempo. On this occasion, I observed that the timing of Garib Dass's strokes, in relation to my theorized time points, changed as the tempo varied. The effect was akin to *swing* in jazz, wherein the metrical construct of eighth notes is realized differently according to tempo. At slower tempi, "swing" eighths approximate a compound subdivision of a beat, whereas at faster tempi they approximate a simple ("straight") subdivision. In the practice session, as tempo varied, some rhythmic events remained anchored to precise time points within a cycle and others changed their position. Specifically, while Garib Dass played bhangṛā (see Figure 2.10), the first of each pair of treble strokes occurred precisely on the beat, regardless of tempo. The second of each pair, however, which was structurally off beat, varied in its timing between the third part of a triplet and the fourth part of a quadruplet. After this experience, I came to understand that as long as a long-short relationship was articulated, it mattered little exactly how much time transpired between the first and second stroke of the pair. More pointedly: the exact timing did not change the content of the message one was articulating.

A second breakthrough came as I observed young children from dholi families beginning to learn dhol. Though the youngsters often failed to perform in meter, their attempts were nonetheless praised if they managed to execute the strokes in proper sequence. Much as developing children attempt to put together sentences through successive speech sounds, the young dhol learners aimed to construct the message inherent to a *tāl* identity. With time and greater facility, they could execute the successive pattern of strokes in the required time framework of a cycle, where the start of each iteration of the cycle must occur at regular intervals.

Yet a third breakthrough came after I learned to play well enough to execute the rhythm without actively thinking about what I was meant to do. In an experience similar to what Rice went through in acquiring the cognitive categories to understand ornamentation in Bulgarian piping (1994, 64–86), I had earlier learned to process the rhythm dhamāl by breaking apart the pattern. I listened to my recordings and transcribed the rhythmic "lines" of the treble and bass parts separately. This I did even though my teacher never played the lines separately and neither did native learners employ such a process. In the rendition of dhamāl that my teacher and some others played, captured reasonably well by the notation in Figure 2.1, doing so was easy enough; the two lines mapped well to a simple metrical representation. I learned to perform each line separately and then reconstituted the rhythm, through practice, by juxtaposing the two lines' patterns in the manner of a drum-kit player learning a new rhythm from a score. I thus acquired the ability to perform the rhythm. While I played it, I gave some thought to how the parts fit together and, to some extent, visualized the parts as they appeared situated along my mental graph. During one particular playing session *alone*, however, I played dhamāl over and over, until the body movements were so familiar that I was no longer focused on thinking *about* the rhythm as I played. Dhamāl is a rhythm used to facilitate trance states—a use to which I had often heard it put—and, as I played it continuously, my mind went to thinking about things other than the rhythm. This appears to have loosened my mind's attachment to the rhythm as a sound structure to be performed. Perhaps, as I lessened my focus on placing my rhythm into the matrix of temporal boxes, my body also loosened. At some point, I realized that I was producing a sound I had heard before. It was not a sound possessed of the sort of "clear diction" that Garib Dass happened to employ when he articulated the rhythm, but it was the sound I had heard at other times among dholis of Punjab, a sort of casual speech. It was not that I had merely become more fluent in speaking the language of dhol so much as that it had become second nature. My epiphany was that I had been hearing this "accent" of dhol playing without realizing it existed. It was dhamāl played with swing.[15] When hearing dhol like this before, I had not processed that it was different, much less had I tried to think about *how* it was different. Now I understood that in the process of expression while focused on the message, variable by-products of sound, the "surface structures" of Blacking (1971) were created unconsciously by the body. After that, I could hear dhol rhythms better, discerning the "deep structure" generating the utterances. This all led to the conclusion that traditional dholis, to the degree that they have not been exposed to classical music theory, do not operate within a cognitive matrix of finely subdivided meter. Rather, they aim to articulate the message in the rhythms holistically and they hang them on the highest-tier structural points of a cycle, its start and its halfway position.[16]

This discussion of dhol "accent," addressing the variability with which different players articulate the message to express a metamessage (about identity), takes us into the metaphysical topics I wish to postpone exploring until Chapter 5. Staying for the moment focused on the physical sound object, then, it remains to address variety in the structure of rhythms. We can begin by registering that variety is an aspect of dhol that was not emphasized. Such was particularly true of individual variation, the demonstration of which is far more important to classical musicians than to dholis, as the former prioritize creativity. Dholis emphasize more the *accuracy* of what is played to produce the optimal communicative effect. Nevertheless, one sees variety in the form of *variants* of the rhythms. The variants are like dialect differences such that dholis of different geographic regions, qaums, or stylistic lineages may play different versions (variants) of a rhythm. Such variants, however, are recognized as the same *tāl* identity.

Nor is embellishment necessarily important in dhol playing—with a caveat. When dholis step out of their primary mode to engage in aesthetic presentational (i.e., "classical") playing, embellishment is essential to demonstrate their skill and, precisely, to offer something out of the ordinary. The degree of embellishment is meaningful in terms of what it says about the player and the context. Most contexts do not call for much (or any) embellishment, and I would go as far as to say that embellishing figures were borrowed from classical music and are essentially foreign to native dhol tradition. Embellishment takes a few similar forms whose roughly applied names are often confounded, likely a result of a weak custom among dholis of verbalizing what they do. One form is *tirakaṭ*, a brief, dense rhythmic figure that sets up an approaching emphasized beat.[17] Longer sequences (a full cycle or more) of such dense patterning are sometimes called *laggī*,[18] though untutored dholis may just as well use the same name, *tirakaṭ*. Similar again to *laggī* is a form of embellishment Indian dholis call *ḍabal* (from the English word, *double*). Loosely identified, it might refer to any way of making a texture more complex or denser, nearly or completely synonymous with *laggī*. All these embellishments have correspondences in classical theory. Native to the Dhol World is a second referent of *ḍabal* (also called *mel* by Pakistani dholis). It consists of a second part intended, when multiple dholis are playing

FIGURE 2.1 *Dhamāl* rhythm (common variant).

FIGURE 2.2 *Ḍabal* of *dhamāl* (Garib Dass, Chandigarh).

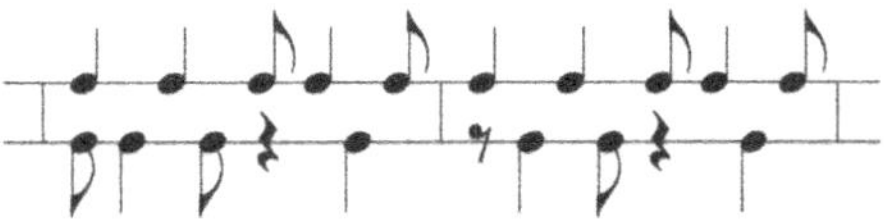

together, to overlay and complement the main (first) part. Such a double is a specific, conventional pattern—a secondary *tāl*. Each *tāl* identity, more or less, has, in theory, its corresponding elaborating second part. Contemporary India's dholis, however, have a very partial knowledge of the various double patterns.[19] For a sense of the nature of *ḍabal* patterns, one may compare the main pattern of dhamāl (Figure 2.1) to its *ḍabal* pattern (Figure 2.2).

Dhol performances are punctuated by figures that mark the beginning and end of bouts of playing *tāl*. The name of such a figure, *toṛā*, translates as "break." To begin or end a performance or to shift gears to a different rhythm, accompanied dance step, or song section within a performance, one must play a *toṛā*. A *toṛā* sets the tempo of the *tāl* that is to follow. *Toṛās* are drawn from a body of variations on a few conventional structures (e.g., Figure 2.11). Which *toṛā* a dholi plays is determined by the rationale that certain *toṛās* are fitting to certain genera of *tāl*, according to practical consensus or individual preference. As one might recognize the style of a writer by her punctuation, one might know something about a dholi from his *toṛās*.

MESSAGES IN CONTEXT

In 2018 I chatted with Muhammad Boota, a dholi from Pakistan, in his Coney Island home. We talked about many details of dhol playing's practical aspects and his family's history in the tradition. At one point, Boota appeared eager to make a point, which he clearly believed was important to understand lest all the specifics lose their contextual framework. Boota, in a manner not unlike an anthropologist, was considering a big question: what was the *aim* of dhol playing? An outsider such as myself might suggest several possible answers. They range from the mundanely economical—"Dhol playing is a means of income for financially challenged, low-status individuals"—to the abstractly metaphysical—"Dhol playing situates social actors in distinctive roles among the play of local and global perceptions of identity." Boota, however, had in mind the sound of dhol and the function of that sound: "Dhol is a message (*sneha*)." He elaborated that dhol communicates various messages, of joy and sadness, about birth, weddings, and worship. Referring to the time of his youth in Pakistan in the decades after Partition, Boota noted that dhol was played at mosques on Sabbath days, sounding the message that it was time to pray. He remembered as well that if a child was born in some house, dholis would go to play there and sound a congratulatory message. The era has changed, however, he said. Now we have telephone, television, e-mail, and text messages. Many messages of dhol, he lamented, have been forgotten with the passing of generations.

Boota's lament came from the position of the diaspora, in the isolated setting of the Pakistani Punjabi community of New York to which he had emigrated decades prior. In the intervening years, dhol had developed to serve a limited function: to lend an air of joyous exuberance to South Asian weddings and similar events. Despite this, Boota, uniquely among dholis in the diaspora, had kept up the practice of delivering one of the forgotten messages. Each year, during Ramadan, he would rise before dawn and go to the center of Brooklyn's Pakistani neighborhood. Walking through the streets, he played dhol to wake fellow Muslims so they might have their breakfasts before the daily fast. Yet though from Boota's vantage he was one of the last of the traditional dholis, it would not be accurate to say that the diverse communicative functions of dhol are lost. Back in Punjab, they are alive.

As the following sketch of dhol's cultural applications will show, communication is at the heart of a full complement of dhol-playing activities. Through its loud voice, the dhol transmits a nonverbal message that lets people in on the intent, mood, and content of a social event. Dhol sound is a code that signals, announces, marks, and organizes what is (or will be) happening.

As an instrument of pragmatic communication, the powerful dhol was once used to send signals over a distance. Mention was made in the colonial era of a pattern for calling a crowd (Harjit Singh 1949, 31). In recent practice, such signals, *sadd* ("call"), are practically obsolete, but some individuals remember them. Mali Ram remembered a *sadd* to scare off a tiger that comes in the vicinity of a settlement. Garib Dass demonstrated a *sadd* to bring someone home, a Morse code—like, unmetered stream of alternating long and short strokes. I heard a simple *sadd* calling the participants to dance when dholi Lacchman Singh brought together villagers to begin jhummar (audiovisual example 3). Garib Dass retained this traditional gesture even in staged performances of bhangra dance when, before a section displaying jhummar actions, he would tap the ḍaggā repeatedly before initiating a *toṛā*. Broadly speaking, the playing of dhol could be said always to be a call to attention. It attracts a gathering of people and communicates that something is happening. I had once suggested to Garib Dass that I might practice the dhol in the forest, so as not to disturb the cohabitants of my residence. The ustād warned that my plan was not feasible, as the sound would inadvertently call people to me.

Besides the targeted signaling associated with *sadd*, dhol sound in its predominant form, cycles of *tāl*, announces present or forthcoming events. At least until the end of the twentieth century, dholis of Lahore played during Ramadan to mark the time when the fast may be broken (Wolf 2000, 281). In India, I observed a newer such use of dhol, in political campaigning. Dholis came to congregate at city hall on days when politicians were going to formally announce their candidacy, whence they were hired by candidates to drum them in. More traditional forms of advertising matched the event to a conventionally meaningful rhythm. I once saw a dholi going through the lanes of a village while playing a rhythm for wrestling. Although the drummer did not speak, his rhythm communicated that wrestling matches would be held the next day.

Dhol marks events that are part of the life cycle. It is not appropriate on all such occasions, however. Earlier in my discussion with him, Boota indicated marking the event of childbirth with dhol. In Punjabi, he used the word *baccā* for child, a grammatically masculine word which could be interpreted either as indicating a male child specifically or simply the use of the masculine as a default for a child of any gender. The custom in traditional Punjabi culture, however, has been to celebrate the birth of a son but to downplay the birth of a daughter. Moreover, the majority of life-cycle events for both females and males have tended to be marked intimately by women singing unaccompanied songs. The dhol is appropriate to the more particularly male-centric or else highly public events.

Weddings are the best-known life event marked by dhol. Nowadays, dhol is ubiquitous throughout the festive parts of urban weddings. In former practice, dhol chiefly figured in the *janj*, the procession of the groom's party (*barāt*) that accompanied the groom, on horseback, to the site of a wedding. Dholis in the procession played a specific rhythm matched to the occasion, utilizing both a main *tāl* and its *ḍabal* (Figure 2.3; audiovisual example 4). Although this rhythm was remembered by older dholis like Garib Dass and Muhammad Boota, the younger generations of dholis do not. Instead, the majority of Indian dholis play the common rhythms luḍḍī and bhangṛā to accompany the dancing now expected in these processions (audiovisual

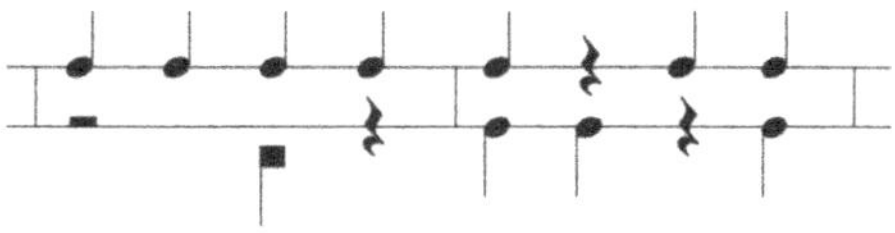

FIGURE 2.3 Wedding procession rhythm (Garib Dass, Chandigarh), with swing.

example 5). More often than not, a brass band is hired to play in the wedding procession and dholis are hired, separately, to play along with the band music. When this is the case, some of the tunes call for the dholi to play what they perceive as a Western popular dance rhythm they call "disco" (see Booth 1991, 64). To be sure, all within hearing distance would get the message that a wedding was in progress, but the specific drum code that once spoke "wedding" has ceased to be sounded.

Seasonal festivals, the most public occasions in Punjabi life, call for dhol to mark the event and create the atmosphere. Dholis are found among the mirth, playing informally. Because most festivals have a basis in some sacred rite, dhol also has specific application to processions that formally mark their religious dimension. The standard procession for Sikh holidays is *nagar kīrtan*, in which the holy scripture, Guru Granth Sahib, is brought through the streets, effectively giving the public an audience with what Sikhs consider both a sacred and a royal personage. The singing of hymns (*shabd kīrtan*) is the highest valued sound in *nagar kīrtan*, but dhol is an added feature that, through the solemn dhamāl rhythm, signifies the coming of royalty. The symbolism harks back to retinues of medieval rulers when the dhols filled the place of the regal kettledrum, *nagāṛā*.

Festival days are a pretext for asking for alms while playing dhol. Individual dholis engage in this activity haphazardly during the hustle and bustle of fairs, and they also do so methodically at festival times. For example, there are two annual festivals of "nine nights" or Navratri, during which the goddess Durga is worshipped. At this time, teams of dholis go door to door seeking offerings in the name of the goddess. Similarly, in the autumn, the period between Dussahira (the festival celebrating Lord Ram's victory over evil) and Divali (the festival of lights, marking Ram's return to the throne) is a general festive time during which people remain in a generous mood. Some destitute dhol players took to exploiting the mood by begging alms from businesses. The Lohri festival, mid-January, sends away the cold of the winter through a symbolic bonfire. During the days preceding Lohri, young children go from door to door, singing and requesting seasonal treats. Again, dholis go from door to door, playing and begging alms. After collecting treats and money, the dholis go home and enjoy their take with their families. In addition, dholis are called to play for dancing at celebrations that occur on the night of Lohri.

Another function of dhol is to motivate action. Antecedents to the modern dhol were described in the context of leading armies to battle in various Islamic empires, from Egypt to Persia (e.g., Farmer 2000). Such application to warfare, long obsolete, suggests a possible originary function alongside signaling and announcing. The Berber traveler Ibn Battuta described military music around Delhi in the early fourteenth century: drums were played at regular hours at army centers in peacetime, and during wartime when the army marched, entered battle, or won a battle (Husain 1976, 1). Though Ibn Battuta's Arabic text uses the word *ṭabl*, we might infer the word included the dhol-type drum in addition to kettledrums. The role of such drums, which continued during battles involving the emerging Sikh community of the seventeenth century, has already been noted. In the second half of the eighteenth century, though such warring had ceased, Varis Shah remembered the wartime association of dhol, metaphorically: "The dhols having been beaten, the assault should begin / Yet the vanguard moves not."[20] And in the colonial era, Harjit Singh (1949, 31) noted that Punjabis had dhol rhythms for marching to war and for attacking in battle, though they may have been remembered rather than contemporary phenomena.

The motivational function of dhol seems to have transferred, in peacetime and civilian life, to the agricultural fields, where dhol was played to accompany difficult or repetitious labor like digging and harvesting. In the 1920s drummers beat dhols behind teams of reapers as they progressed through the field at harvest time (Dhami 1996). Professor Rajpal Singh of Patiala remembered that, even up until the time of his youth (mid-twentieth century), dhol was used in India during reaping.[21] As Garib Dass recalled, rows of ten men cut the wheat with sickles, and each row was followed by two dholis.[22] The ustād remembered a rhythm specifically tied to this function, though few others remained who had any knowledge of it (audiovisual example 6). With harvesting now generally replaced by tractors, drum accompaniment to reaping is functionally obsolete.

Motivational dhol playing is far from passé, however, in that it inspires sportsmen, for whom a meaning akin to battle remains inscribed in its sound. The sporting application stretches back to Mughal times. An illustration from *Bābur Nāma*, circa 1591, depicts dhol-type drummers in boats accompanying a fishing expedition by the emperor.[23] In modern Punjab, dhol came to accompany competitive sports broadly, as it had accompanied wrestling since its importation by the Mughals in the sixteenth century.[24] Punjabis maintain a tradition of indigenous sports that they practice at rural fairs. Fencing or *gatkā*, once practiced with bamboo sticks, now takes the form of a wider set of martial arts that is practiced year-round by Sikhs, who use a variety of weapons holding significance for their military traditions (audiovisual example 7). The acrobatics and feats of physical prowess displayed by the Bazigars, *bāzī*, while not competitive, might be put in a similar category. The presence of dhol enhances all these activities—especially those requiring great strength or displaying impressive feats. Dhol playing attracts the audience while it inspires the contestants.

Wrestling, known by such terms as *bhalvānī*, *kushtī*, *ghol*, and *dangal*, is the Punjabi physical sport par excellence, and the *bhalvān* (wrestler) is a beloved figure in Punjabi culture. During bouts, the dholis play while pacing counterclockwise in a circle around the arena (Figure 2.4). The dhol accompaniment to wrestling differs from region to region within Punjab, making it an area rich in variety of rhythms (Figures 2.5, 2.6, and 2.7; audiovisual example 8). In the distant past, a single performance for wrestling employed several rhythms, arranged according to procedure. Recently, such structured performances are absent in Indian Punjab, and instead the dholis simply play whatever associated rhythms are in their repertoire. Wrestling's close cousin is a team sport reminiscent of war operations, *kabaḍḍī*. An offensive player, a "raider," seeks to score a point by entering the territory of the opposing team, touching an opponent, and then making it back to his own team's

FIGURE 2.4 Wrestling matches in the village of Dadu Majra, accompanied by dholi Sonu, 2001. Photo by the author.

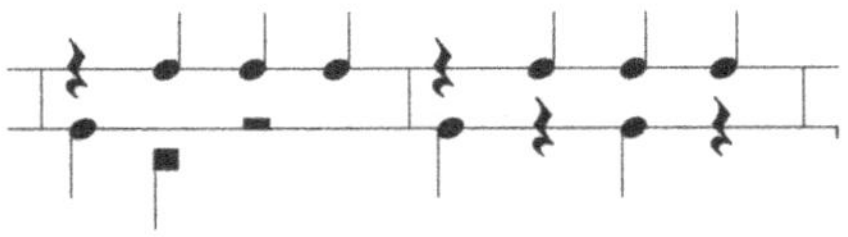

FIGURE 2.5 Wrestling rhythm (Sonu, Dadu Majra).

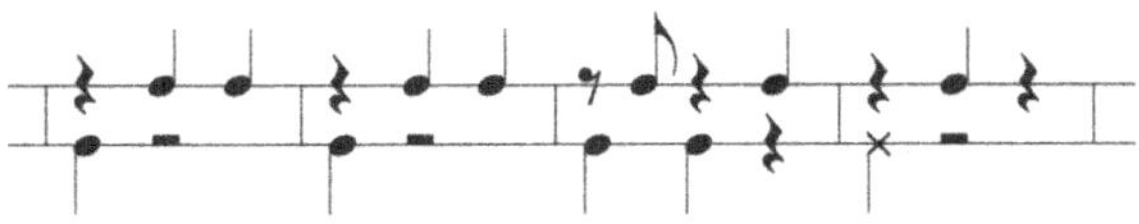

FIGURE 2.6 Wrestling rhythm (Mali Ram, New York).

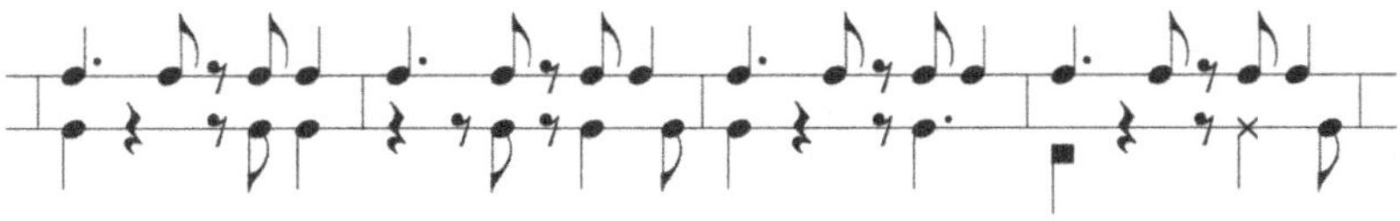

FIGURE 2.7 Wrestling rhythm (Garib Dass, Chandigarh).

territory without being tackled. As with wrestling, dholis circle the *kabaḍḍī* arena, playing one or another rhythm locally ascribed to the sport (Figure 2.8; audiovisual example 9).

Among dhol's most ubiquitous and deeply imbricated contexts are devotional ones. In such contexts, one can see several of the functions of dhol in effect. The sounds call devotees to practice. They make an event of their act of worship, especially at vernacular religious sites that are humble in construction and informal in their worship procedures. Moreover, dhol playing, often in rhythms conventionally signifying a specific deity or the spirit of a saint, marks the space as a special one belonging to the divine. This, however, is a public and political gesture in addition to being a sacred gesture. Recall that kettledrums and dhol-type drums of the *naqqārah khānah* once were conventional symbols of the power of local sovereigns in Mughal times. As Wade explains, the Mughals doled out standards and ceremonial drums as ensigns of power; those who possessed the right to have the drum played for them were particularly endowed (1986, 30). In modern Punjab, this same sense of power is lent to sacred persons and deities by drumming. Drumming tells all that in that place resides a seat of power, a celestial court (*darbār*).

FIGURE 2.8 *Kabaḍḍī* rhythm (Garib Dass, Chandigarh).

What dhol playing does most spectacularly at Sufi shrines (*dargāh*, *khānqāh*) is to facilitate inducement of trance and other altered states of mind. Sufi shrines are popular sites of worship for Punjabis of all creeds. The sainted dead, *pīr*, are believed to be capable of bestowing boons, for which devotees make offerings of cash, food, and sacrificed animals. Dholis congregate at Sufi shrines, where their playing is considered auspicious and for which they are rewarded with visitors' donations (audiovisual example 10). Sufi devotional practices include recitation or remembrance of the name of God, *zikr*. It involves synchronized, rhythmic, group recitation of the Name, along with bodily motions. The act of *zikr* may take the form of *samā'*, the spiritual listening to devotional music that can induce trance or lead to ecstasy (Qureshi 1986, 82).

At some shrines of Punjab, devotees (*murīd*) and dervishes (*malang*) pay homage to the saint through participating in a *samā'* practice known as dhamāl. Starting slowly, the dancers revolve faster until they reach a mystical state (*hāl*). The goal is to induce trance (*samādhī*) and ecstasy (*mastī*). Dhamāl is performed on Thursday evenings (the eve of the Muslim Sabbath) at certain shrines and on the *'urs* (death anniversary) of saints. Drumming is essential to the practice. The rhythm most often selected by Punjabi dholis is the one widely known as dhamāl, alternatively as *naubat* or, with personalized endearment, as *bābā jī dī tāl* ("the sainted father's rhythm").[25] Even at shrines that do not host dhamāl, as in the case of mixed-denominational sites in Indian Punjab, I saw people go into a personal trance. Speaking of the experience as a Hindu, Garib Dass explained that when dhol is played at a shrine, the soul of the saint comes out of its tomb and enters receptive people.[26] Such an interpretation reveals the importance of the specific code emitted by the dhol, for the intention is not to whip the devotee into a frenzy with undistinguished sound but rather more precisely to call the spirit by playing its tune.

This nominally Muslim paradigm of worship through unification of body and spirit is not limited to Sufi shrines. It exists, too, at nominally Hindu places. In the recent past, dholis used to play for devotees visiting temples of the Mother Goddess (*mātā jī*, in various incarnations), which are numerous in the mountains skirting Punjab. While people sat in vigil (*caunkī*) at temples, they jerked their heads in trance to the goddess's particular rhythm, *mātā dī caunkī*.[27] The Jogi dholis around Jammu would play for devotions at the temple of Vaishno Devi. Recalling this former practice, a senior member of the community, Bal Kishan, boasted knowledge of four rhythms meant for the goddess;[28] even Garib Dass's clan, far from the abode of Vaishno Devi, could play one of them (audiovisual example 11). The Mother Goddess was not the only spiritual figure with her own rhythm. Various particular rhythms for propitiating saints, including Gugga Pir and Sakhi Sarvar, were known to players whose focus was the devotional application of dhol (audiovisual example 12). It is important to note, however, that most traditional dholis I met in the 2000s gave no indication that they knew such particular rhythms, and it is safe to assume that most dhol players in the world at present have no notion that individual rhythms for saints and deities exist. It is notable, too, that older professionals like Bal Kishan and Garib Dass wanted it known that *they* knew. For those who lack knowledge of the particular rhythms, dhamāl has developed into a sort of all-purpose rhythm for religious applications.

DANCE ACCOMPANIMENT

The sound of dhol unites Punjabi bodies in the communal experience of dance. The traditional dance genres of Punjab were of a group type, usually involving a ring of dancers who moved counterclockwise in a circle while uniformly performing a limited set of actions. Nearly all such dances in which men participated were accompanied by dhol with specific rhythms for each dance. Many dances did not survive the changes of Partition intact. Nevertheless, dance performance in Indian Punjab has developed into a preferred vehicle to represent the region's heritage. The development has meant much creation of new dance elements and dhol repertoire. As a result, dance accompaniment has become the field, at least in India, for the most diverse array of new sonic structures for dhol.

Bhangṛā is the best-known term associated with Punjabi dance, and forms associated with it have provided the model for the similar development of other dance genres. In my historical review of bhangra, I circumscribe three broadly distinguishable dance-centered phenomena (Schreffler 2013). Moving chronologically, the first to develop was a participatory dance of agriculturalists that was practiced perhaps no earlier than the final decades of the nineteenth century and which effectively disappeared after Partition. It was current in a limited area at the center of Punjab and only during a specific time of the year, the spring wheat-harvesting season. Male farmers danced bhangra informally in the evenings after each day of reaping and more formally at fairs in celebration of Visakhi (Punjab Government (1990 [1921], 71). Bouts of vigorous, intoxicated dancing by the men were broken up by the declamation of short verses. Only the dancing was accompanied by dhol, played by the same village professionals who used to provide motivation during the harvesting. The original rhythm called bhangṛā was moderately fast, with a galloping quality created by a rippling stream of treble strokes (Figure 2.9; audiovisual example 13).

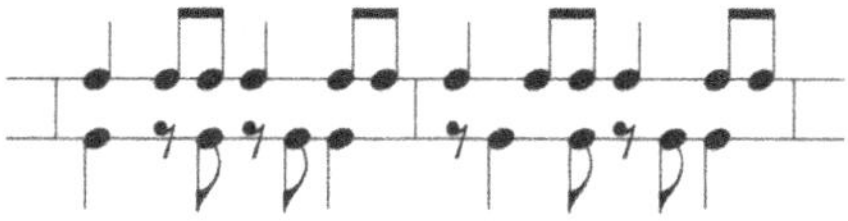

FIGURE 2.9 Original-style *bhangṛā* rhythm (Garib Dass, Chandigarh).

In a second theater of development, bhangra emerged as a presentational dance of postindependence India. While the chaos and uprooting of communities during Partition was one cause for the discontinuation of the participatory bhangra dance, a simpler explanation is the fact that little of the area in which that dance was practiced was contained in East Punjab. So, while some migrants to the India side remembered it, after Partition, practically no context or place remained for it to flourish. What developed, instead, was a dance to mark state holidays and other contexts where conscious representation of Punjabi identity is desired. In the early 1950s, young men of the Deepak family, native to eastern Punjab's Malwa area—who had actually remigrated from a canal colony of western Punjab—teamed up with local college students and Bazigar refugees. The Bazigars were dholis and dancers; they contributed a broad knowledge of dances from the western areas.[29] The young men from agriculturalist classes (Kamboj and Jatt) brought an enthusiasm for maintaining heritage in a time of reform of the state. Their project to revive folk dancing was subsequently patronized by a local raja of the erstwhile princely states known as the Patiala and East Punjab States Union (PEPSU).

The collective envisioned a dance medley, an amalgamation that, within the compass of one routine, displayed glimpses of various Punjabi genres. On the occasion of their first officially sponsored presentation, the raja declared the dance to be "our state dance" and "our dance of Punjab."[30] The PEPSU-sponsored troupe and additional forces were consequently invited by the Ministry of Defense to perform at the Republic Day festivities in New Delhi on January 26, 1954. The annual Republic Day parade, replete with displays of military might and national symbols, features contributions from each state in India. Framed in this context, the 1954 Republic Day parade performance—which was billed as bhangra for the occasion—both exposed the nation at large to a particular representation of Punjabi dance and helped codify it as *the* popular image of dancing Punjabis. Films featured this reimagined bhangra in subsequent years, and colleges developed programs to cultivate it among students as a healthy and patriotic engagement with their heritage.

From that time, presentations under the rubric of bhangra have undergone continual development and periodic codification. Although bhangra presentations are ubiquitous on any occasion where Punjabi identity ought to be represented, in the day to day, they are most cultivated within educational institutions. Colleges and universities, in particular, have maintained teams whose grandest outlet is in intercollegiate competitions during youth festivals each autumn. They are important for the form of bhangra, for they have provided the stage on which new additions have been introduced, popularized, and canonized.

Whereas the historical form of bhangra, like other participatory dances, dwelt on one or two characteristic rhythms, the stage dance honors variety as its aesthetic. By the mid-1980s, the typical presentation of folkloric bhangra had come to include a dizzying array of steps and corresponding rhythms, crunched into a timeframe of just 10 minutes—the time limit in youth festival competitions. Moving in synchronization, the performers are coordinated from action to action, moving smoothly and without pause. The dholi must rapidly shift among a set of more than 20 rhythms on cue and match each action. A few of them may be enumerated.

The bhangṛā rhythm, though prominent, does not make up the majority of play in folkloric bhangra dance. It has been simplified from its original form; the number of treble strokes is reduced so that it can be played at a faster tempo (Figure 2.10). Indeed, it is reserved for the fastest actions and climaxes, wherein the tempo reaches a maximum as the dancers move as vigorously as possible. The rhythm often functions as a double time in complement to the most common rhythm, a swinging rendition of *kahirvā*, which some call luḍḍī (Figure 2.12).[31] In this way, slower and faster actions are alternated to provide excitement and to manage the stamina of the performers.

While luḍḍī is undoubtedly the globally most-played rhythm on the Punjabi dhol today, and it is strongly associated with bhangra phenomena, there was an element of contrivance in its introduction. It owes its popularity to

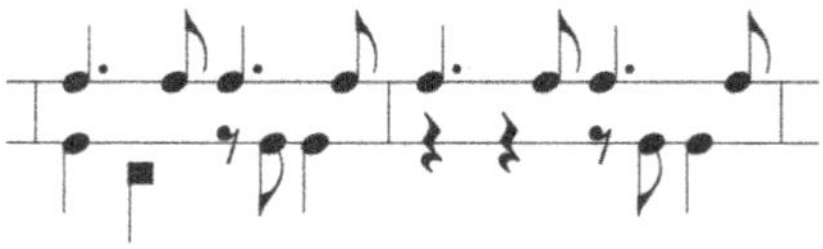

FIGURE 2.10 Stage-style *bhangṛā* rhythm (common variant).

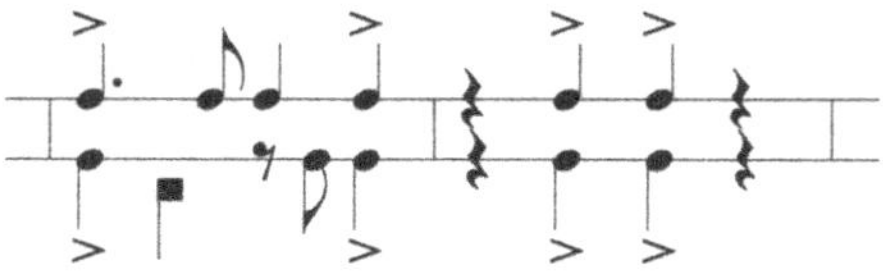

FIGURE 2.11 *Toṛā* for *bhangṛā* (Garib Dass, Chandigarh).

one of the PEPSU team's dancers, Balbir Singh Sekhon, who was then a student at Mohindra College in Patiala. A dance called luḍḍī was, and remains, practiced in various forms in the northwest of the Punjab region, yet its rhythm is different. One of luḍḍī dance's characteristic movements is hand clapping. Sekhon appears to have been inspired by this element of the luḍḍī dance, adapting it to a stylish step. Although set to the kahirvā-style rhythm of dhol, practitioners of folkloric bhangra began to call Sekhon's step luḍḍī, and so began the conflation of the terms.

In a most remarkable development, the redubbed luḍḍī rhythm went on to provide the base for variations in rhythm that dholis employed to match more newly developed actions. The paradigm was established after an event that occurred in 1971, when Punjab sent a bhangra team to perform at the Fourth International Folk Festival in Monastir, Tunisia. Each participating group in the festival was scheduled to perform for 45 minutes. Realizing that the current parade- and competition-oriented loop of bhangra was of insufficient length to sustain interest, the team padded their performance with new steps danced to variations on the luḍḍī rhythm. We can credit Lal Singh Bhatti, the sole accompanying dholi, for developing the rhythmic variations.[32] After the success of this performance, the team returned to introduce the expanded repertoire of steps. Dance steps in Punjabi are known as *cāls*, and so these new steps, created for the international tour, were referred to as the "international cāls." The modifier *international* was later dropped, and each of the new steps received specific titles, often incorporating the word cāl: "single" cāl, "double" cāl (twice as long as single), *hans* cāl (resembling a swan), *pakkha* cāl (making a fan action), and so forth. An example of such an action and its rhythmic variation is *tuṇkā* (Figure 2.13; audiovisual example 14), which means "jerk." The dancer sharply jerks one leg backward at a timed moment. The accompanying rhythm keeps time with the treble

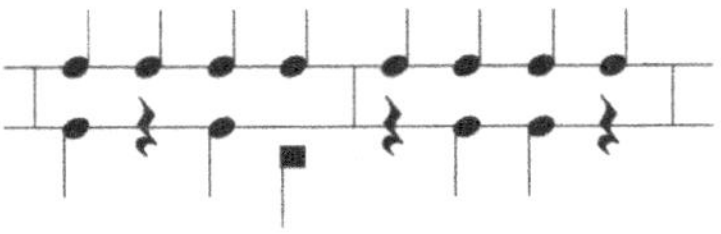

FIGURE 2.12 *Luḍḍī* rhythm (common variant), with swing.

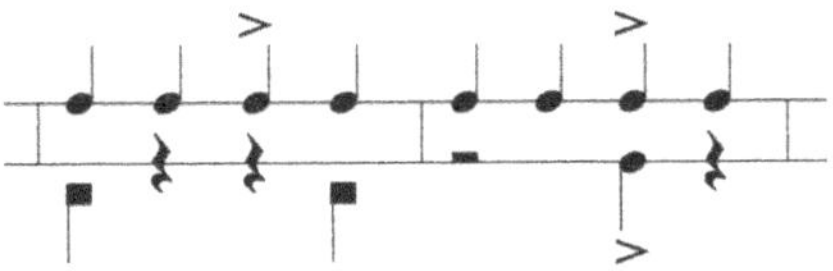

FIGURE 2.13 *Tuṇkā* rhythm (Garib Dass, Chandigarh).

strokes of luḍḍī and sounds a heavy bass stroke on beat eight, the time of the leg jerk. In a final twist, the general form of rhythm that accompanies all these steps—kahirvā or luḍḍī—has become known to diaspora-based dhol players by the name of *cāl*.

Diverse rhythms in folkloric bhangra serve to match actions that represent particular dances—real or imagined—as well as actions developed to accompany popular songs and to evoke cultural practices. In the category of particular dances, the true luḍḍī dance is displayed accompanied by its actual rhythm (Figure 2.14). Carrying an association with the Multan area (southwestern Punjab region), it goes by a name with a disambiguating modifier: *Multānī luḍḍī*. The same genus of rhythm accompanies an action, *paṭhāṇīā*, intended to evoke dancing of the Pathan (Pushtun) people in northwest Punjab. An action intended to represent the historical bhangra of the Sialkot area, in which the dancers balance on one leg, has been dubbed *siālkoṭī* and receives a unique rhythm (Figure 2.15; audiovisual example 15). The jhummar and *sammī* dances (discussed later) are thematized in folkloric bhangra, with varying accuracy with respect to their original forms. Because only a few dholis have had experience with the historical forms of these dances, many have inherited the need to present them as part of established routine without knowing their historical rhythmic accompaniment. The situation has led to much inconsistency with respect to the rhythms they employ, which have been developed among the dholis of different qaums and localities.

Unlike the participatory bhangra, folkloric bhangra is performed to a regular sequence of songs and other sung verse throughout the dance. An example of a song-based action and rhythm is *mirzā*. *Mirzā-Sāhibāṅ* is one of the well-known love epics of Punjab, and the singing of its verses (e.g., in the version by the poet Pilu) is a standard item in the repertoire of ballad singers. The *ḍhāḍī* bards in particular are known for their singing of the

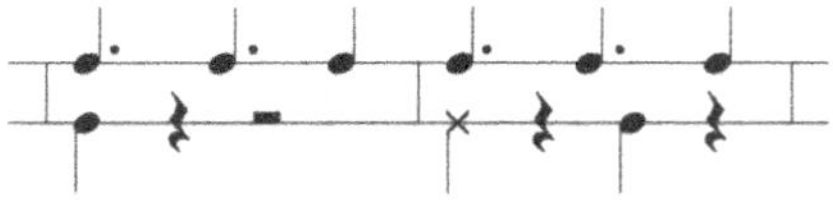

FIGURE 2.14 *Multānī luḍḍī* rhythm (Ramesh Chand, Dharival).

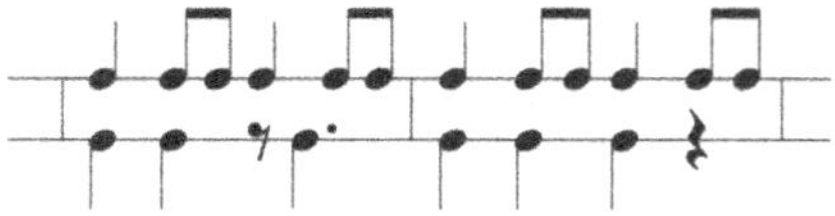

FIGURE 2.15 *Siālkoṭī* rhythm (Garib Dass, Chandigarh).

Mirzā-Sāhibāṅ epic set to a melody in a 14-beat meter, which they accompany on the small hourglass drum, *ḍhaḍḍ*. The introduction of verses from *Mirzā-Sāhibāṅ* to bhangra meant adapting their meter to the dhol, and the resultant *mirzā* rhythm is an outlier among the predominantly duple rhythms of the dance. Moreover, the asymmetrical meter inspires some dholis to treat it with classical embellishment, as in the *laggī* gesture seen at the end of Figure 2.16 (audiovisual example 16).

Bhangra presentations evoke such aspects of Punjabi culture as Sufi devotion and the wrestling arena, in the form of whirling and macho high-stepping, which are accompanied by variations on dhamāl rhythm. In the 1980s, a new step was developed to represent wrestling, bhalvāṇī, which involves the characteristic wrestler's gesture of challenge by slapping one's thigh. A unique rhythm created for the action includes the unusual gesture of rapping the rim of the drumhead or the body of the dhol with the ḍaggā (Figure 2.17).

In bhangra's third theater, the diaspora, we see a popular heritage dance that finds expression through a combination of the participatory, presentational, and high-fidelity fields. By the late twentieth century, staged presentations of bhangra dance had occurred in most of the diaspora nations with sizable Punjabi communities yet, until relatively recently, the form of such presentations had not developed in step with the folkloric bhangra of India. The largest bloc of dance groups was based in Canada and the United States, where competitions and participating teams make up the so-called North American Bhangra Circuit. From the 1990s, most North American universities with significant South Asian populations have formed bhangra teams, competitive or otherwise. The phenomenon expanded to other countries,

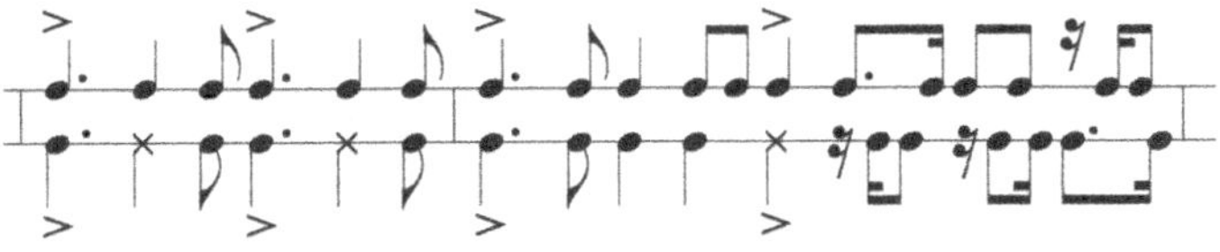

FIGURE 2.16 *Mirzā* rhythm (Kaku Ram, Jalandhar).

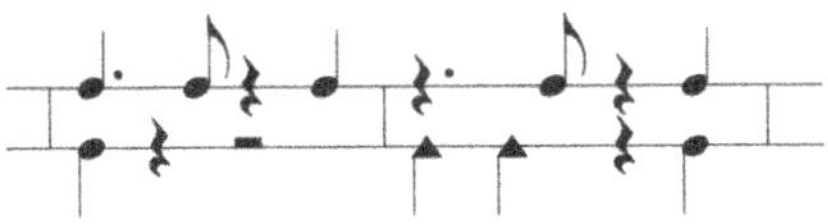

FIGURE 2.17 *Bhalvāṇī* or "*ṭikā-ṭik*" rhythm (Mahindar, Chak Khiva).

too, but aspects that make this theater of bhangra most unique are best seen in the North American version.

Developed largely by young diaspora-born people from images in popular media, diaspora bhangra dance followed the emergence of bhangra as a category of popular music. Since the late 1950s, cinematic *melā* scenes depicting country fairs had been marrying bhangra-like dance to popular music (i.e., film songs). The scenes created juxtapositions that did not exist in real life, for example, musical ensembles playing to accompany dancing in a field or women dancing with men. The diaspora dance had its base in the continuation of the cinematic *melā* phenomenon, as in music videos for the "bhangra songs" of the 1980s and 1990s. Pockets of activity in the vein of folkloric bhangra existed, but most developers of diaspora bhangra did not have access to them. More typically, the dancer-choreographers were students acting through such outlets as campus-based South Asian identity organizations and performing in cultural shows. The precedent, in cultural shows, was pantomimes of Bollywood dance to recorded film music; in the earliest cases of diaspora bhangra, the music was simply changed to Punjabi popular music. What made this form of coordinated, staged dance fundamentally different from folkloric bhangra was its prerecorded soundtrack. Without a dholi to coordinate the complex sequence of conventional actions and to supply their particular rhythms, diaspora bhangra could not replicate folkloric bhangra. The vast majority of recorded bhangra music tracks was set to the luḍḍī rhythm, compelling dancers to limit their actions to those that fit the rhythm, undifferentiated. When, on occasion, an intrepid performer of dhol was invited to play along with these performances, he would be limited to playing the luḍḍī rhythm, which, for many, became synonymous with bhangra.

The diaspora bhangra network was already enormous by the time, in the mid-2000s, video sharing sites like *YouTube* made it possible for diaspora bhangra dancers to study the folkloric bhangra presentations current in India. The videos initiated a trend toward imitating the folkloric bhangra, seeking training in its forms, and going "live"—performing to the accompaniment of a dhol. Yet the hybrid character of diaspora bhangra was already broadly established and the attractive "traditional" quality of "live bhangra" was of limited appeal. Interest in the sort of cultural purity that folkloric bhangra offers did not displace the interest in incorporating inspiration from hip-hop and R&B dancing and staying ahead of the competition through innovation. The luḍḍī rhythm has proven to work well for both Punjabi and hip-hop-style dancing, and well-mixed tracks of continuous rhythm are more pleasurable, for many, than the erratic shifts of folkloric bhangra's dhol.

Not just bhangra but most of Punjab's other dances have been folklorized in some form or another. Their histories are too lengthy to narrate here; we may note a few that correspond to unique dhol repertoires. Dances called jhummar were practiced, before Partition, in areas to the west and southwest of bhangra's area. More popular than the original bhangra in its day, they continue at community functions in Pakistan. Yet jhummar, too, underwent a patchy process of revival in Indian Punjab, marked by tension between who was choreographing it most authentically and who aimed to merely create a choreography serving as placeholder for the name and the vague memories it conjured (Schreffler 2014). Though regional historical variations of jhummar abound (Figure 2.18; audiovisual example 17), along with newly fashioned rhythms to serve the staged dance, all offer an alternative in tone to the bhangṛā rhythm. Perhaps reflecting the disposition or environment of the people from whose areas they come, they are lighter, soberer.

To the east of bhangra's historic area, comprising most of the Indian side and especially in the Malwa area, Punjabis practice *giddhā* in distinct female and male forms.[33] It has been maintained in offstage versions and adapted to onstage versions. Giddhā is only nominally a dance, for it does not conform to the usual paradigm of a group moving in a circle to the beat of the drum. Moreover, although the other dances include sung verse between or in addition to dance-play, in giddhā the recitation of verse is central. It is based on the singing or chanting of a simple couplet form, arranged in sets called *bolīāṅ* (audiovisual example 18). Dancing in a traditional giddhā performance is rather haphazard and incidental to the versification, though stage presentations have emphasized the dancing aspect. Dhol had no place in traditional giddhā, but the requirements of the stage have called for hiring dholis to coordinate and, indeed, to choreograph such presentations.[34] This use of the dhol replaces the hand-clapping accompaniment in the women's form and the amateur *ḍholkī* playing of the men's form. Being a relatively new and unorthodox practice, dhol accompaniment to stage giddhā varies among players. The methodology entails translating grooves as might be played on the *ḍholkī* to comparable dhol rhythms. For slower tempos, this means the luḍḍī rhythm. For faster tempos, dholis play a galloping rhythm

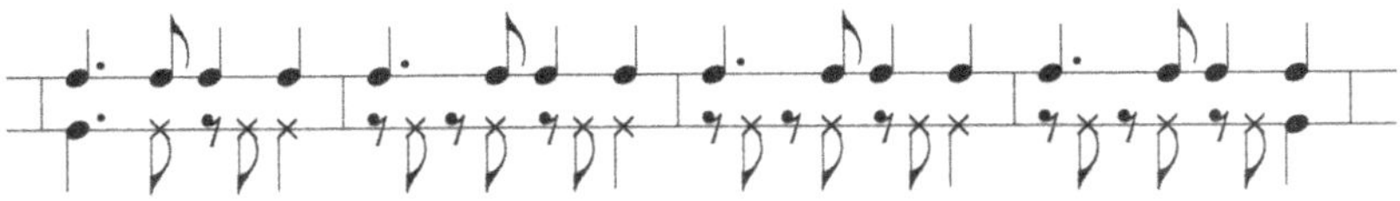

FIGURE 2.18 *Jhummar* rhythm (Garib Dass, Chandigarh).

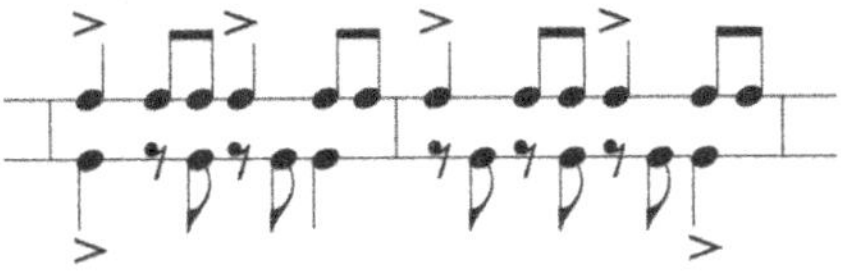

FIGURE 2.19 *Lahariā* rhythm (Garib Dass, Santa Barbara).

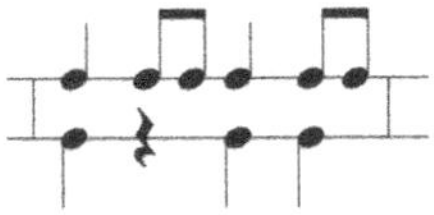

FIGURE 2.20 Men's *giddhā* rhythm (Des Raj, Chandigarh).

called *lahirīā* ("rippler") (Figure 2.19). Some dholis take their cue from the *ḍholkī* accompaniment played by the male troupes of giddhā performers that converge on country fairs (Figure 2.20).

MUSIC

We turn last to the application of dhol playing qua "music." One of the contexts for dhol as a type of sangīt is *mahifal*, a cordial gathering that includes poetic recitation, singing, or courtly music for the purpose of artistic appreciation. The term is used by dholis to refer to any scenario in which dhol playing is consumed for its aesthetic properties. Such scenarios, however, are rare and incidental, for they are outside the scope of the dholi's usual service-providing functions. A mahifal atmosphere may occur when several dholis, meeting under the common circumstance of employment, pass the downtime by sharing their playing with each other and attending friends. In these circumstances, one would not play the run-of-the-mill functional rhythms but rather rhythms coded as more aesthetic that come from the classical repertoire. Further, dholis in a mahifal context use the everyday rhythms as a base for improvisation and skillful elaboration.

Dholis with an inclination to classical style have maintained a repertoire of classical rhythms or, indeed, *tāl* in the art-music sense. Among those that I have heard dholis adapt were *dādrā, tinn tāl, ektāl, rūpak, dīpcandī,* and *ārācautāl*. Contemporary Pakistani dholis who place a greater value on art forms might play structured sets of rhythms. For instance, to demonstrate his art for me, Saghir Ali played a rehearsed 12-minute-long suite. He was accompanied by a second dhol, a double-reed pipe (*shahnāī*) that maintained a repeating reference-point melody (*lahirā*), and an electronic drone generator. The suite began with *tinn tāl* in slow and fast tempi, worked through a variety of other *tāls* in 10, 12, and seven beats, and finished, to bring it to a climax, with an accelerating bhangṛā rhythm (audiovisual example 19). As in Hindustani music performances, mahifal-type dhol performances sometimes take the form of a duet, *jugalbandī*. As one dholi supplies the referential, basic *tāl*, the other is given the creative freedom to play elaborating rhythmic compositions.

Dhol playing also becomes "music" in the context of orchestras, multi-instrument ensembles that accompany popular songs. Before the late twentieth century, orchestras called for *ḍholkī*, tabla, or both, those being the membranophones having the subtlety and softer volume required for such indoor music. Dhol playing, which is associated with loud, "outdoor" sound, was not deemed appropriate to accompany song. The emerging symbolic import of dhol, however, has since made it attractive to include in the accompaniment of commercial songs when sound reinforcement is adequate.

THE SONIC LANDSCAPE, TRANSFORMED

The sonic landscape of Punjab, in which dhol figures so prominently, has undergone many changes since Partition. The causes of the changes to dhol's sonic output include, first, the languishing of local or preindustrial cultural practices and the concurrent development of performing arts to serve modern, nationalized representations of Punjabi identity. A second, resultant, cause is the ever-growing iconicity of the dhol. Third, economic concerns—the constantly shifting strategies of dholis to optimize their earning potential—have a bearing on where dholis focus their efforts. All these causes have some root in the dynamics of movement discussed in Chapter 1.

We have seen that, before Partition, dhol was played to serve functions on particular occasions, to communicate information about events, to mark spaces, to motivate and coordinate action, and to facilitate devotional experiences. The sonic structures of dhol playing developed to serve these direct applications. They consisted of repetitions of rhythmic patterns that constituted codes that conveyed clear messages. The primacy of the code encouraged the development of many specific codes to match the different events. The subsequent obsolescence or modern adaptation of some of the cultural practices in which dhol had figured led to the obsolescence and subsequent forgetting of dhol codes. After Partition, new practices emerged for the dhol, but the creation of new codes did not keep pace. Instead, dholis often applied old codes to the new functions. The best example is dhamāl rhythm, which, because it is applicable to many devotional and sporting contexts, can serve for all of them in place of more specific rhythms. The great exception to this trend has been the folkloric dance stage, where the creative endeavor of choreographing new dance necessitated creating new dhol repertoire too. Moreover, the demand for folkloric dance presentations, with ever more variety, increased the need for dholis, and the vigorous use of folkloric dance to represent Punjabi identity since that time has meant that dhol, on balance, is heard more than ever.

Yet the proliferation of dhol through folkloric dance and, later, through popular music evoking the dance, has a double effect on dhol's sonic structures. Whereas folkloric dances gave dholis new repertoire, the economic opportunities they offered suggested that dholis put all their eggs in one basket. Increasingly, with each new generation of players, the repertory of staged bhangra rhythms threatens to encompass the entire dhol repertory, such that dhol repertoire exclusive to other contexts is neglected. Moreover, a tendency has arisen to view modern bhangra as a sort of encyclopedia of examples of Punjabi cultural forms. Professional dance accompanists are compelled to adopt whatever form of rhythm has been institutionalized within the stage routines, as narrow or, in some cases, as historically erroneous as they might be. An example is jhummar dance, whose historical variations in movement and rhythm are many. When exhibiting a "jhummar" sequence within folkloric bhangra, one adopts one of a few jhummar rhythms that one has come to learn as appropriate for that context, and, through that process, it becomes *the* jhummar rhythm. A consequence has been a graying out of the diversity of jhummar rhythms.

Consider again the way displacement and migration have disrupted Punjabis' sense of place. After Partition, dholis from different locales, representing effectively different dhol traditions, were thrown together in Indian Punjab. Just as the historic site for Visakhi-time bhangra dancing was partitioned off, so too were innumerable sites for dhol playing. Dholis refocused their practice on available work in the new political state. They acquired unfamiliar repertoire, often imperfectly, from other communities' performances and adapted their style to contemporary taste. Yet, as subsequent generations of Indian dholis were reoriented to a new sense of place, the movement of dhol outside Punjab again displaced it from locally established practice. As dhol approaches being everywhere, it becomes less rooted in place and more something that creates a diffuse feeling of Punjabi space.

The dramatically increased profile of dhol as an icon of "Punjabi" space means a greater call for dhol and a greater demand for dholis. Yet it also means that the specific communicative functions of dhol, conveying direct messages, might be less important than the oblique messages it conveys as a "Punjabi" sound. Specifically, such messages may include fun or optimism, strength or power, and masculinity, yet all factor into the broader metamessage, Punjabiness. In the gloomiest scenario, what is played on the dhol—its sonic structures—matters less than the fact that dhol is simply played, rendering the dhol's sound as indexical *noise*. Dholis attuned to the narrow demands of the market find little advantage in cultivating a repertoire beyond the most common and versatile rhythms. Three rhythms, luḍḍī, bhangṛā, and dhamāl, do the work for many of the past functions of dhol while meeting the general threshold for indexical sound. The situation is not as dire within Punjab, yet, in the diaspora, where the value on iconicity is arguably greater and contexts for dhol are less diverse, the range of sound is quite narrow.

In conclusion, the dhol traditions are unusual in that, while many past performing traditions have been reduced to a few knowledgeable practitioners in the twentieth century, dholis have thrived. But the price paid for the flourishing of the dholi profession has been a wholesale change in the sonic landscape. Attuned to these sound-shifts, older dholis no longer recognize *their* Punjab in what they hear. One will note, however, that many of the structures exemplified in this chapter were the creation of those very dholis in the process of furnishing material for a market that supported their unprecedented economic prosperity. Like the enthusiastic farmers of the Green Revolution, dholis have been participants in their own loss. Political and economic conditions outside their control—Partition, nationalism, and the global market for human capital—set the conditions under which they were compelled to participate in changes to their sonically informed feeling of place. The absurdity of questioning their willingness to participate in this process characterizes the complex timbre of the dholis' lament.

3 ASKING RUDE QUESTIONS

Dholi Ethnicity

To meet a traditional dholi is to come face-to-face with the marked "ethnic" of Punjabi society. For mainstream Punjabis, dholis register as local Others who disrupt the uniform cultural atmosphere that the former imagine to predominate in a landlocked, peasant society. Dhol playing has been linked for centuries to ethnic minority identities. At the same time, the precise identities of dholis have been opaque to outsiders because social interactions with their communities have been few and their representation in mainstream discourse has been slight. A barrier to dhol being fully absorbed as a piece of generalized (majority-favoring) Punjabi culture has thus been the unclear, yet always other, nature of the identities of the dholis. I emphasize that this is a face-to-face matter. The difference in who dholis are, in contrast with who other Punjabis are, is most palpable in their presence. And nowhere is the distinctiveness of dholis' ethnic identities as noticeable as when one meets dholis on their home turf, in the neighborhoods, markets, and settlements where they reside. It is only recently, through the process of being mediated, whether through the visual, auditory, or narrative discourse, that dholis' divergent ethnic identities are minimized, partitioned, or omitted sufficiently to imagine dhol independent of ethnicity.

To traditional dholis, ethnic identity matters greatly, so its erasure or ambiguation through mediation is a cause for no small concern. Yet the situation is not simply one of mediators ignoring the otherness of dholis. Even sympathetic mediators, while acknowledging the difference of dholis, are challenged by the lack of knowledge to give it accurate representation. Whether the aim is to disregard or to acknowledge, the subject is troubled by an anxiety that accompanies it, and the seeking of knowledge is hindered by an essential issue of discomfort: *it is rude to ask*. Talking about ethnic identity, which so often maps to hierarchical relationships in the caste system, evokes historical and ongoing relationships of dominance and subjugation and provokes concomitant feelings of shame in people on both sides of the relationship. Laying bare individuals' histories within this system of relationships may be considered an interrogation of their actions or an unwanted outing of their identity in an environment where, to minimize repercussions and to maximize social mobility, the relationship is thought better left vague.

Integral to these dynamics is the fact that patrons of folklorized performing arts, generally of a higher social class, are less comfortable around dholis. And yet the case of contemporary dholis as visible culture-bearers presents a different scenario than that encountered in typical cases of interaction between social classes. The upper classes have socially prescribed ways of interacting with the lower classes, born of the fact that the latter provide services to the former. Exchanges tend to be formal and not longer than necessary. Interactions, made awkward by the gulf in wealth and social mobility, are relieved by gestures of generosity or magnanimity by the upper-class client and above-and-beyond service or gratitude of the lower-class service provider. This model of interaction works to describe cases such as when the trash collector daily comes knocking at the door. And it has applied when, in the past, dholis of the villages came to beat their drums on special occasions and were rewarded by their clients. Dholis of the current era, however, often blend into the middle-class spaces of folklorized performance. These spaces place dholis as the odd men out within, rather than at the margins of, spaces dominated by majority groups. So, while dholis remain separate in their everyday social lives, they are sometimes poised in their professional lives as coworkers.

Through the first decade of the 2000s, dholis could be described as service providers working in the midst of the upper classes. It was often a thrill for the dholis who had achieved such positions to be in these upwardly mobile scenarios, rubbing elbows with "big people." The exhilaration of being a part of such scenes, indeed, had an inspiriting effect on the dhol-playing community at large. Dholis did retain their identity as outsiders and practiced the conventions of service providers interacting with clients. They did so, however, without needing to articulate, to their audiences or their copresenters, their specific ethnic identities. As a result, when I entered the field at the millennium, I found no one available among middle-class interlocutors to give such information about dholis. In the search for information, the only recourse was to ask dholis directly, "What is your community?" Such a question did not usually—and perhaps could not—receive a straight answer. My fate was to wander through every district of India's Punjab, meeting dholis, asking rude questions, and getting ambiguous answers.

To elaborate: traditional dholis belong to the unlanded or the service class, and they descend from Punjab's lowest-status ethnic communities, all of which are identified under the rubrics of Scheduled Castes or Other Backward Classes.[1] These categories are meant to aid through identifying, yet discomfort on the part of the upper classes and embarrassment among the lower classes often means a reluctance to identify through labeling. The basic fact that the dhol-playing communities come from this sector of society thus remains, at best, implicit in discourse. There is little chance that dholis' even more particular ethnic identities will be recognized. Few authors, out of the many producing books on folk music or folk dance, have ventured to state the ethnic affiliations of dholis. Nahar Singh, a folklorist writing in Punjabi, is one of these few, and he notes that the dholi for past social dances was usually a village's "Bharai, Mir, or Dum" or "Dum, Jogi, Shekh, or Bharai" (1988, 69; 37). Even these references, however, receive no explanation—and not because the labels would be self-evident to the average reader. I once visited the local Scheduled Caste Development Office, the government body designed to serve the interests of these groups. All the groups named by Nahar Singh appear in the schedules. None of the officers, however, had any more than passing knowledge of the groups mentioned, and about some they had no clue.[2] Scheduled Castes and Backward Classes, indeed, are minorities within the society's minority sector. Even when minority identity is made most explicit politically, in the movement for Dalit rights, the dholi communities' specific identities are buried behind more populous and familiar Dalit ethnicities.

Lack of clarity about ethnic identity also exists among the dholis' neighbors and within the self-segregating dhol-playing population at large. Garib Dass, of the Bazigar people, once told me that his ustād was a member of the "Jogi," who are "Hindus and Muslims." He went on to say that Jogis were "Mirasis," and they were also called "Shaikh." I expressed puzzlement at what sounded like numerous ambiguities and contradictions in this explanation. Garib Dass, dropping his initial authoritative voice (which is expected of a teacher), admitted that he never *asked* his teacher what his ethnic affiliations were.[3] His explanation was that one does not ask one's teacher *anything*, out of "fear." By engaging in this discussion of Garib Dass's ustād's ethnicity, I was being inappropriately bold in relation to my own. I felt a mixture of embarrassment and gratitude to him for overlooking this breach of the relationship. In such discussions with dholis, however, after the rudeness and embarrassment of the question were absorbed by both parties, the drummers were often interested to share more. They indicated that they had never spoken with anyone who cared to know about their qaum, and began to speak with pride and hope for its recognition.

Conversations with a (foreign) scholar in which dholis are keen on sharing stories of their communities do not, however, indicate a breakthrough toward dholis sharing their ethnic identities with their Punjabi neighbors. When performing for the general public, in which case dholis are situationally engaged in the representation of Punjabiness, it remains risky to raise the specter of ethnicity or call attention to difference. Onstage, they are simply Punjabis whose difference is minimized. Offstage, when interacting with upper-class patrons, economic reality dictates that working dholis maintain their idealized role of cheerful service providers—implicitly different, yet not engaging others in the details of who they are. Resigned not to be known to society, the desire for recognition I found expressed by dholis was thus contextually limited. In some cases, they desired to be recognized among the dhol-playing community at large, their professional peers, in terms of their qaum's skill, special style, or historical influence. In other cases, they had cautious dreams of their people being known generally in society (or in the historical record) while not wanting to rock the boat in their professional life. Having their praises sung by a foreign academic is different from attracting publicity in Punjab, and so the present discussion is an exceptional, safe space to introduce the people behind the stage personae. The final tragic dimension of this exercise is that not only did the acquisition of information entail asking rude questions but also the presentation of it—the appearance of putting people in boxes, as it were—inescapably entailed the feeling of being rude. I am mindful both of dholis' desires to be known and the simultaneous anxiety that accompanies it.

It is within this discursive context of anxiety, of attempting to increase representation while that representation lays bare people's sensitivities to socially ascribed hierarchy, that this chapter offers ethnographic sketches of dholi communities. The rationale, of course, is that representation is important, even crucial, for the survival of these communities. The dholis' identities, indeed, cannot be fit into neat boxes. Nevertheless, through a dialog between outsider and insider perspectives, we can begin to recognize the particular social group frameworks in which dholis negotiate their still more particular personal identities. For each qaum, I begin with a discussion of the nature of its formation and history. Then I map the major sites of that qaum's dhol-playing population. I proceed to acquaint the reader with some of the individual players I found at those sites. This presentation, voiced in the past tense, will give a sense of the lifestyles and attitudes that exemplified membership in each dholi community as I observed it principally during the 2000s.[4]

I use "dholi communities" to refer to those qaums that possess a dhol *paramparā*—a tradition. A dhol tradition or paramparā can be understood as a collective heritage, sharply determined through birth and daily life circumstances that belongs to a qaum. It carries the connotation of a professional practice that has been passed on by numerous players through at least two generations. In identifying traditional dholis, I consider members of these qaums as the individuals entitled to the label.

DOM GROUPS

Dom (*ḍom*) is an ethnic term found widely in South Asia.[5] The historical presence of people labeled as such, over a large area and practicing diverse professions, has suggested to writers that they once constituted a nation whose residence predated the postulated in-migration of the Indo-Aryan-speaking peoples associated with the Vedas.[6] In recent centuries of South Asian history, one sees people connected to the Dom label framed as ethnic Others, positioned outside the incorporated caste society while participating in economic relationships. Dom communities have practiced such professions as scavenger, executioner, basket maker, musician, blacksmith, leatherworker, weaver—in short, occupations considered menial. The colonial writer Baines wrote, "in the Gangetic region there were functions which even the scavenger caste would not undertake, there being the Ḍōm at hand to perform them. Here, then, is found a caste which, if not at the bottom of the social scale, is, at least, not far from it" (1912, 84). Contemporary Punjabi informants corroborated this perception. Fraught by tensions of status and insider-outsider dialectics, the term *Dom* is now often considered derogatory.[7] Dum (*ḍūm*), the Punjabi version of the name, though it appears in official documents (e.g., K. Singh 1998, 4: 863), is not a preferred term of public identification.

These terms are provisionally useful for historical discussion, however, seeing that communities referred to as Dom have long been connected with musical performance in some fashion. The Persian scholar al-Biruni (early eleventh century) noted that Dom were among those people whose occupation was to sing and play a lute (2000 [1910], 101–102). A contemporary of al-Biruni, Gardizi, noted a class of people he called Dunbi. He described them as dark-complexioned "players on stringed instruments and dancers" who occupied an untouchable class of society (Minorsky 1964, 202–203). In Punjab since the nineteenth century, Dum were best known as hereditary musicians, bards, and genealogists. A related ethnic group were the Dumna (*ḍūmnā*), found mostly in the hills and northern areas, whose traditional occupation was work in cane and bamboo (see also Rose 1911, 250). They were still linked through social relationships to the Dum musician community; the terms Dum and Dumna both appear on the same line in the list of Scheduled Castes for Punjab (India). At the time of research, the people of apparent Dum origin who specialized in dhol or music affiliated with one of three qaums: Jogi, Mahasha, and Mirasi.

The Jogi (*jogī*), a Hindu community, were known as gurūs both in musical arts and religious life. Their name, which appears to have been adopted in the modern era, made for some confusion stemming from the fact that *jogī* has been applied to various types of individuals without ethnic denotation. In its most formal sense, *jogī* (or *yogī*) refers to ascetics of Hindu orders such as that of Gorakh Nath. By the nineteenth century, *jogī* had also come to be used in an informal, generic sense for any sort of devotee, indoctrinated or not, who follows his path in a heterodox way, wandering and living off the charity of others. A *jogī* of this category may be of any faith and, in this sense, *jogī* overlaps colloquially with *faqīr*—formally, a mendicant-ascetic in Indo-Islamic traditions. Thus, in the popular sense, *jogī*s are variously romantically and derogatorily described as mystics, mendicants, or quacks, Hindu or Muslim, who render specialized parareligious services. In premodern society, *jogī*s or *faqīr*s began to describe a liminal category of individuals known among public music makers.[8] Dholis from the Jogi qaum of Punjab said their ancestors were once expert at singing ballads. In this way, we might speculate the transformation, through equivocation, of a regional Punjabi Dum community into Jogi because of the image their activities suggested. Jogis were based in the hill regions on the northern side of Punjab, rich in powerful Hindu sites (chiefly, the Vaishno Devi temple), where the Dum had been facilitators at ritual in temples and homes. The role would have made Jogi a more respectful term than one with the low-status connotations of Dum.

Jammu district, adjacent to Punjab, was a center for the Jogi community. While passing through the area, I saw Jogi clan names like Balgotra and Dalgotra on the signs of businesses. Dholis from the community were scattered throughout the surrounding villages. One was Madan Lal Balgotra, in the village of Purkhu. He and his son, Rinku, headed up the Panjabi Dhol Party, which played for wedding functions, village dancing, and devotional vigils at Hindu temples. In addition to the dhol, they played *bīn*, a small double-reed pipe. Madan Lal's family had reportedly "always" followed the professional dhol line, although his youngest son was considering going into the furniture-making business. Theirs was a village-based dholi family of the older model, who did not get outside the area often to play.

The urban dholi community of Jammu, in touch with contemporary trends, was concentrated in the Nayi Basti section of Jammu Cantonment.

They occupied a *ḍholī galī* (dhol player alley), a strip market along a street that contained many small offices from which one could hire dhol services. This particular *galī* began to form circa 1952 with the in-migration of dholis from villages.[9] Before 1947, the dholis played for weddings only occasionally. They mostly played for wrestling and prayer offerings. One of the dholis, senior master Bal Kishan (Figure 3.1), told how his people used to sing and play all sorts of instruments. His skills extended to the tabla and *pakhāvaj* drums, and, like other dholis in the area, *bīn*. Bal Kishan also supplied dhols, the instruments constructed from trees in Jammu's nearby forests being highly prized. Bal Kishan emphasized the value of learning a repertoire of Hindustani music. In this vein, he stated that if one first learns to speak the *bol*s (representative vocables) of a rhythm, then playing would come easily. It was striking how religious-minded Bal Kishan's family appeared to be, both in habits and manner of speech. Bal Kishan had perhaps the loftiest spiritual

FIGURE 3.1 Bal Kishan outside his office in Jammu Cantonment, 2005. Photo by the author.

attitude of any dholi I met. This attitude, which reflected the notion that his local community was associated with the performance of religious ritual, suggested the perception of a higher social status than dholis from the Punjab plains. Moreover, in his conversations, Bal Kishan never used the word *Jogi*. Instead, he referred to his people as *ustād lok* ("teacher people"), reinforcing the inadequacy of both the euphemistic *Jogi* and the vulgar *Dum*.

In Punjab's nearby district of Gurdaspur were Jogi dholis including, in Dharival, one of the twentieth century's celebrated masters, a migrant from Sialkot named Milkhi Ram (d. 2002). Milkhi Ram's son, Ramesh Chand, was carrying on the duty he inherited from his father of being the dholi for bhangra dancer-educator Harbhajan Singh. Ramesh embraced the Jogi label and tied it, along with the dhol, to Hindu icons like the monastic order of Gorakh Nath and the *ḍamrū*—the hourglass-shaped rattle drum considered to be Lord Shiv's instrument.[10]

In Ludhiana city, the dholis were predominantly of Jogi background. Their influence on the contemporary scene was great because, unlike the dholis in most cities, those from centrally located Ludhiana were called all over Punjab to play. The city had its own *galī*, which was founded by the famous Jogi dholi, the late Munshi Ram. Munshi came along with his father, dholi Nanak Chand, from Gujrat at the time of Partition.[11] The tradition continued with Munshi's son, the late Madan Lal, throughout the 1990s. He was the main accompanist for the performing troupe of popular dancer-singer Pammi Bai. When I first visited the *galī*, the torch had recently been passed to Madan Lal's son, Ravi Kumar, known as "Dana." Dana introduced a virtuosic style of play, replete with original use of unorthodox figures and reinterpretations of the basic rhythms, inspired by the artful style of his grandfather Munshi Ram—who was also his teacher. Ludhiana was also home to Jogis who had migrated from Sialkot. Notable among them was Sewa Ram, a sixth-generation of dholis, who distinguished himself as a builder of dhols. The Ludhiana *galī*, however, was primarily a place of more practical business. The dholis' offices there booked dhol and wedding band services. One office belonged to Madan Lal's younger brother, Surindar Kumar Chindu, who, in addition to dhol, played trumpet in a band he led. The prestigious work of accompanying college dance teams in Ludhiana had its leadership in Janak Raj (b.c. 1950). A student of Munshi Ram, Janak Raj had regular duties with Punjab Agricultural University, while his older brother, Des Raj, accompanied GGN Khalsa College through the 1980s and 1990s. In the 2000s, Des Raj's son, Satpal Bovi, had taken over his father's duties. The same generation of Jogis included excellent bhangra team accompanists (brothers) Ravi Kumar and Ramesh Kumar ("Meshi").

In terms of geographical distribution, I observed that a strip of the Jogi community ran down from the ancestral area of north-central Punjab (Gujrat—Sialkot—Jammu) southeast to Ambala. The senior masters in the latter city were the brothers Gulzar, Mahindar Singh, and Janak Raj. Although the dholi scene in Ambala (in the state of Haryana) was minimal, being further from jobs in Punjab, they still formed part of the Jogi brotherhood—the players being maternal nephews of Bal Kishan of Jammu.

Another dholi group of Dum origin was the Mahasha (*mahāshā*), an urban community that originated around Lahore and Sialkot. In the Mahasha story, one sees the ongoing development of new qaums. Recall that Dum and Dumna are closely related communities; their work and kin relationships had at one time overlapped, with the most visible distinction being that Dumna better identifies workers in reed material. The Arya Samaj movement provided an opportunity for the Dumna to raise their status. Arya Samaj was a Hindu reform movement that resonated in the Punjab of the later nineteenth century, at a time when a decreasing population of Hindus worried some in that religious community. To revive the strength of the community, they thought, Hindu practice should be brought in line to conform with modern ideas (Jones 1976, 32). The Arya Samaj attempted to highlight the rational, scientific aspects of faith as contained in the Vedas, which were looked to as representing a Golden Age before the faith was allegedly corrupted by excessive ritual (Banga 1996, 27). The Arya Samaj movement offered to incorporate outcastes and converts to other faiths—who were the nominally Hindu population being "lost" to the Sikh, Muslim, and Christian communities—back into the Hindu fold. Such individuals were invited to rejoin it or "reconvert" via a ritual of purification (*shuddhī*; Jones 1989, 100–101). The movement had established a headquarters in Lahore by 1877. Local members of the Dumna community availed themselves of the reconversion opportunity en masse, whereby they were newly dubbed Mahasha (K. Singh 1999, 510). With this virtual rebirth, many gave up the stigmatized professions of cane work and scavenging. The abandonment of low-status work and the reinvention by renaming contributed to erasing the memory of their previous status. Indeed, while the Mahasha were still regarded as outcastes by some, most contemporary Punjabis had forgotten that the Mahasha were once Dum.[12] One of the "clean" occupations that the Mahasha could do was to run shops. "Mahasha," which smacks of flattering or euphemistic address for a Hindu shopkeeper, ambiguated their historical ethnic affiliation. Mahashas had no lack of pride in their identity, as long as it is clear that they were Mahasha. A Mahasha man in Jalandhar, for instance, rhetorically distanced himself from cane workers (presumably of Dumna background) whom we encountered in his neighborhood.[13] Despite past alliances, the Mahasha were also considered distinct from the Jogi. The Jogi community was slow to recognize the label Mahasha. Several times I found Jogis calling their cousins Bhanjra (an alternate term for Dumna); one Jogi of Jammu was highly amused by my use of the term Mahasha.[14]

The largest Mahasha dholi community was in Amritsar, where the historic dholi neighborhood lay near Sultanwind Gate. Inside this gate to the Old City was a long *galī* where the more established dholis had their offices (Figure 0.1). Outside the gate, the less fortunate dholis, those without offices, congregated. Their dhols were hung on the gate's outer wall as a way of advertising their services. Across the street, even more destitute or junior dholis sat on the sidewalk, idly tapping on their dhols as vehicular traffic went by. The economic and living conditions of these dholis were very poor.

In one of the alleys off the main strip was the home of a family of dholis so renowned that they required no office. The late dhol master Ghuggi, originally from Sialkot, was remembered as one of the greatest dholis of Punjab. As an example of his legend, one of his disciples, Garib Dass, narrated an anecdote from the master's career. Ghuggi participated in a dhol competition in Ludhiana, along with other masters of the day. At one point in the event, Ghuggi was engaged in an improvisation on a classical *tāl*, *ektālā*. Instead of the typical brief statement, the master played figure after figure of embellishment, seeming as though he would never play the concluding phrase (*tihāī*) or come back to the first beat (*sam*) of the regular pattern. During these meanderings, he had tucked his ḍaggā behind his neck in his shirt collar and played with his bare hand in a nuanced fashion. The audience members were shouting in amazement, "Come back, Ghuggi! Enough! Mercy, mercy!" It was some time before the "dove" came back down to earth.[15] The agent of Ghuggi's unfortunate downfall, like that of many dholis', was alcohol. His disciple said that the master would never play the dhol having drunk liquor (which can be construed to constitute a form of disrespect to the instrument). A coartist alleged, however, that he would drink and play alternately; in effect, he was drinking "all the time."[16] Ghuggi was also reported to have been in the habit of smoking a marijuana joint before playing. Marijuana is said to belong to Shiv, and smoking it would imbue the master with the fiery power of the deity.[17] Ghuggi accompanied the bhangra dancers at Khalsa College in the late 1950s before that sort of work became prestigious. According to the telling of one of his sons, Chabli Nath, Prime Minister Jawaharlal Nehru himself gave Ghuggi the title of Punjab Champion in 1957.[18] This is how he, already deceased, was remembered in the 2000s, though the influence of his family was not strong. Ghuggi's dholi son, Bhula Nath (Pappu), had also died young from complications related to overdrinking. The tradition was being carried on in Ghuggi's lineage by grandson Chuch Mahi. Educated, professional, and smartly dressed, he was making a lucrative income through work at local schools like Khalsa College, DAV College, Hindu College, and Guru Nanak Dev University.

The other giant of Amritsar's Mahasha dholi community was Harbans Lal Jogi (b.c. 1932–1933). When I first met him in 2006, somewhat by accident, I was surprised to find him still living. He attributed his longevity to his healthy lifestyle, which contrasted with that of his friend and contemporary, Ghuggi. Harbans Lal firmly abstained from alcohol. He resided away from the dholi neighborhood, outside its downtrodden atmosphere. Even his adopted name, "Jogi," suggested identification with another community, which, perhaps, represented to him a set of lofty ideals. Harbans Lal was born in Lahore, near Tixali Gate. He remembered going to watch aesthetic performances of great dholis in Lahore before migrating to Amritsar in his teens. In post-Partition India, Harbans Lal established himself among an elite class of dhol "artists." In a 1960 competition—probably the same one in which Ghuggi had soared in the sky—Harbans Lal, too, competed against the likes of Jogi masters Nanak Chand, Munshi Ram, and Milkhi Ram. Harbans Lal took first place (Ghuggi took second).[19] Harbans Lal followed an uncommon aesthetic by which he approached the dhol like the classical tabla. In performances, he would recite the *bol* patterns first and then play the rhythms precisely. His sons and grandsons, therefore—Harbans Lal was proud of this—did not take up the dhol but rather the tabla. Harbans Lal devalued the regular dholi's work of weddings and bhangra accompaniment, and he is the only notable Indian dholi of whom I have heard who did not make an income in these ways. He suggested, indeed, that playing for bhangra was a cheap way to make a living, and he objected to the notion of making money from art. True artists were the people he respected, for whom he reserved the term *kasbī*, and among whom he included, by implication, himself.[20] Although he said that he was the greatest dholi in Punjab, he somehow managed to say it in the humblest of ways. His legacy is his influence as a teacher of dholis who sought to add "art" to their playing.

One of the leaders of the Amritsar dholi neighborhood in those days was Harbans Lal's student, Tilak Raj (b.c. 1946). Although he had his own office in the alley (Figure 3.2), he lamented that while dholis in other cities had gained some material comforts, those in Amritsar remained poor. His relatives made ends meet in a variety of ways, in which one could still see the old Dumna profession of cane work. On one visit, for example, Tilak Raj's father, retired dholi Mela Ram, was working with his wife splitting cane and making the hoop frames used to construct drumheads.

FIGURE 3.2 Tilak Raj (left) and family at his office in Amritsar, 2005. Photo by the author.

The next largest Mahasha dholi community was in Jalandhar, where many of the families had come from Sialkot. They brought with them a brass band tradition. Not only did most dholis' offices double as band headquarters, but also the dholis had skills on band instruments. Wedding services and similar functions were, therefore, their main employment, and a few families offering dance team accompaniment stood out among them. The dhol scene in Jalandhar was developed largely by Charan Das (b.c. 1933), who came from a village not far away. Charan Das's master was Nikka Ram of Amritsar, brother of Ghuggi. Like other dholis of the day, Charan Das found opportunities to play at New Delhi's Republic Day events for several years in a row in the early 1970s. Charan Das appeared in several films, including *Jija Ji* (1961) and *Batwara* (1983). Perhaps his most lasting legacy was playing for DAV College (Jalandhar) for 25 years. In 2004, retired from playing dhol, Charan Das lamented the current trend of dancing not to live dhol but to prerecorded music.[21]

The next generation of Mahasha dholis in Jalandhar was represented by Harbans Lal "Kaku." He was inspired to follow a musical path by his maternal grandfather, who was a player of *nagāṛā* and *shahnāī* in royal courts.[22] Kaku began playing dhol in 1969 and became the disciple of Sohan Lal.[23] In his example, we see some changes in a dholi's work from the time of Charan Das. Like Charan Das, Kaku gained success by standing out among the local dholis as an accompanist to bhangra teams; his influential incumbency at Jalandhar's Khalsa College lasted from 1979 to 1998. In contrast to Charan Das, Kaku's success was not marked by performances for national events and leaders but rather by his going abroad 14–15 times. Kaku was retired in 2004 when I first visited his home, comfortable and off the track of a dholi ghetto, in contrast to his brother-in-law's, Tilak Raj's, in Amritsar. Wary of the pitfalls of alcoholism in the community, Kaku said that he had abstained from drink for more than two decades. Kaku's three sons were all enterprising dholis too. One son, Jolly Bawa, had taken over playing for Khalsa College. The youngest son, Manish, had been on tour with pop singer Gurdas Mann. Dholis in Jalandhar often got such opportunities. They were fashionable young men, enjoying a time and place in which a dholi with connections had many chances to earn, and sometimes live glamorously too.

The more typical Mahasha dholis of Jalandhar were located in an area radiating from Purani Kotwali Bazaar, which contains wall-to-wall band shops on both sides of the street. Among these dholis was Kala Takhi, who spent his days in a band office along a strip in Ashok Nagar. He occupied the office, for booking Bharat Band, with his three dhol-playing brothers, Channa, Pammi, and Sonu of the Bhatti clan.

Though nowhere as established as in Amritsar and Jalandhar—the biggest urban centers—Mahasha dholis were found in and around other cities. In more remote Bathinda, the originators of the scene were two brothers, Kartar Singh and Babbu Ram, who had learned from a Muslim who migrated to Pakistan in 1947.[24] Many dholis congregated by the rail line, near a Sufi shrine at which they would gather to play. In the absence of offices, they hung their dhols from trees to advertise. The Bathinda dholis played along with bhangra but in their ranks were no dedicated university bhangra accompanists. The closest market for that work was Patiala, though that, community leader Vishnu said, was usually taken by locals to that city. In fact, in Patiala, the community of Mahasha dholis also had relatively little to do with college bhangra. Their shops and roadside shacks were scattered in the city in areas such as Tripuri. The older generation included master Bishan. One of his disciples, Noora, was a nephew of Kaku of Jalandhar. The donation bag that Noora had ingeniously attached to one of his dhols indicated that his work came from weddings. Indeed, with other communities vying for dhol work in the heritage-oriented city of Patiala, local Mahasha dholis were scarcely seen outside the wedding season.

Since medieval times, a central position in the concept of professional musician in north India has been occupied by people called Mirasi (*mirāsī*). Though properly an occupational label, "Mirasi" has also been used, by outsiders and insiders alike, with the intent of identifying one or more qaums. Insiders variably accept or reject the Mirasi label if and when it suits them; the term has meaning for identity only in context, as when in dialog with others' perceptions. For outsiders, "Mirasi" is an attempt to give shape to communities whose boundaries are most recognizable through occupation. The term appears to derive from the Arabic *mīrāth*, "inheritance," which may refer to the hereditary nature of their profession, the maintenance of heritage, or the inheritance of the client families whom they serve (Chaturvedi and Singh 2000, 51).

Historical discourse suggests that the so-called Mirasi communities—they are better referred to in the plural—emerged from the Dom. Not only were the professions of local Punjabi Dum and Mirasi identical in past accounts, but also the terms have been treated as synonymous, even up to the present day. Guru Nanak's minstrel companion, Bhai Mardana, was said to have been a Mirasi, according to Bhai Gurdas (early seventeenth century) (Var 11:13, 2009 [1610s–1620s], 565). Brothers Satta and Rai Balvand, who worked as minstrels in the courts of Guru Nanak's successors, were said to have come from the Dum community (*Sri Guru Granth Sahib*, 966). By the end of the nineteenth century, however, the erstwhile Mirasi people had ceased to identify with and even looked down on those who might be called Dum (Rose 1914, 106). The dissociation with Dum identity was aided by a change of religion, for "Mirasi" connoted a Muslim identity. Parallel to the Dom-based Hindu identities (Jogi, Mahasha), the term "Mirasi" may have once offered a noble title to replace the lowly Dum. By the late twentieth century, however, the name Mirasi had acquired connotations of contempt (Lybarger 2011, 97; Nayyar 2000, 763). In my locally situated experience, those called Mirasis in Indian Punjab were not generally bothered by the term, though they were receptive to flattering alternatives like the fancy Arabic term *Mīr ʻālam* ("lord of the world"), or to be addressed as *mīr* ("chief"). Like other communities in this chapter, they accepted the expedient outsider term, perhaps because their nuanced identities were too complicated to present with practical coherence.

Some steps can be taken, however, to bring nuance to distinguishing the communities lumped under "Mirasi." Lybarger (2011) offers an analysis, based in Pakistan, of the major classificatory schemes in print. My analysis, based on field data from India, finds that contemporary Mirasis in the Malerkotla area (the major concentration) distinguished three endogamous groups within a larger Mirasi community. The first were the Mardana (*mardānā*), who served the Jatt and other land-owning communities. Their name is a reference to the aforementioned Bhai Mardana (1516–1591), about which iconographic evidence tells us he played a version of the plucked lute the *rabāb*. One from this community asserted that Bhai Mardana's actual name should be parsed as "Mīr Dānā," and that the specific name for his community was, indeed Rababi (i.e., players of *rabāb*).[25] The Mardana Mirasis had historically been singers and players of *rabāb* and *sārangī* (bowed lute) and, before the mid-twentieth century, professional performers of Sikh hymns, *shabd kīrtan*. They felt pride in having been connected to Sikh traditions, with which they were intimately familiar and through which association (with the dominant religious community in that area) they held status.

Another Mirasi group was the Bhand (*bhanḍ*), who served the Valmiki and Mazhbi communities (the sweeper qaum, below). They specialized in a comedy act consisting of a straight man who receives wacky retorts to questions that he puts to a funny man. The performers dressed in exaggerated bumpkin attire. Whenever the funny man made a clownish remark, the straight man slapped the other's hand with a piece of rolled-up leather (*camoṭā*). The sound of this constant slapping—analogous to the slapstick—gave a rhythm to the routine. In the traditional context, such duos or trios entertained at childbirth and wedding celebrations. In the *Ā'īn-i-Akbarī* (late sixteenth century), people called Bhand were noted for playing *duhul* and cymbals (Abul-Fazl 1894, 257), but I cannot confirm a connection between these people and contemporary Bhands.

A third group of Mirasis was the Naqqalia (*naqqalīā*). They specialized in family troupes of performers called *naqqāl*, which included dramatists, comedians, singers, instrumentalists, and female impersonators (*nacār*). Their art was called *naqal* ("imitation" or "mimicry") and was in essence a variety show of traditional dramatic tales, comedic skits, songs and *qavvālī*, and *kathak*-style dance.

Being professionals, the Mirasi's attitude to payment was one of entitlement for services, both musical and nonmusical, that they provided. Both women and men of the Mirasis served patrons in the role of intermediary (*lāgī*), for which they were entitled to customary dues. In a wedding, for instance, the family's Mirasis would be the one to hand *shagan* (monetary donations) to the groom. They were also the genealogists and praise singers who were expected to extol the virtues of an individual's family line. The Mirasi—taken again in the broad, occupational sense—could be found as players on just about any instrument and as singers of any entertainment genre of song. Mirasis had been major players in the development of Hindustani music (Neuman 1990, 102). Any Mirasi might play the dhol. And yet, Mirasis generally had skills at performing on many instruments, such that the specific identity "dholi" was relatively weak. Mirasis were more interested in boasting of their multifarious skills in the art of music (generally) than to front dhol playing as a singular profession. Moreover, *qavvālī* and Hindustani music remained more important cultural symbols to Mirasis than dhol. Nonetheless, I found that many of the oldest dhol masters from Hindu communities living through the late twentieth century had learned from Mirasis.

Being a Muslim community, most Mirasis left East Punjab during the Partition. Some stayed behind and remained attached to their substantial patrons. They were most densely populated in the districts of Ludhiana, Sangrur, and Patiala, the areas closest to the princely states that remained autonomous after 1947. More significant, they are close to Malerkotla, the only city in Punjab to have a majority Muslim population. Also located in Malerkotla, the shrine of Baba Haider Shaikh provided focus as one of the important Sufi shrines in East Punjab.

A variety of Mirasi dholis were regular performers in Malerkotla. For instance, there was Faqir Ali (Figure 3.3), the son of Sadhu Khan, the leader of a *naqqāl* party who belonged to the Patiala vocal *gharānā* of Barkat Ali. This multigenerational Naqqalia tradition was passed from Husain Bakhsh to his son, Nigahi Bakhsh, who performed in the court of the Maharaja of Patiala, Bhupinder Singh. Nigahi had three sons, all of whom also had royal patrons. Among them was Lahauri Khan, and one of his sons was Sadhu Khan. Sadhu was born into a village of the Sangrur district in 1933. After spending time in the Matoi refugee camp at the time of Partition, Sadhu's family decided not to go to Pakistan but to settle in Malerkotla (Thuhi 2017, 99). The Naqqalia Mirasi dholis at Haider Shaikh, though practicing a less prestigious musical tradition than others in their family, were nonetheless proud of their lineage and enjoyed a sort of home-team privilege in Malerkotla. They viewed themselves as savvier than the "outsider" dholis who also found employment at the shrine and dismissed them.[26]

Another set of Mirasi dholis in the rural areas around Malerkotla were Mardanas. One who came regularly to Haider Shaikh on Thursday evenings was Muhammad Shukardin, alias Billa. I first met Billa at a country fair, where he was showing off to a crowd. He was playing fast figures on the dhol while

FIGURE 3.3 Faqir Ali at the shrine of Haider Shaikh, Malerkotla, 2005. Photo by the author.

balancing it on his head. Afterward, he sat down next to me, gazing with his exotic green eyes, and asked *me* straightaway, "What is your qaum?" We were all, in some sense, outsiders from diverse ethnic communities. Billa and his younger brothers, Gaga and Rafi, belonged to the village of Jarg, about 10 kilometers from Malerkotla. They were the sons of Sher Khan of the Pabbi clan, a cousin of the noted singer and recording artist Muhammad Siddiq. The family enjoyed a respected status in their village, and they mingled with the local Jatts. Their house was modest, but it was located, notably, among the homes of landowner families, and they even had a servant boy from Bihar. Sher Khan and his sons were caretakers of the local shrine to Baba Farid. Professionally, they were experts in many types of music. Billa was the leader of the Billa Brass Band, a tradition started by his father, who played clarinet and saxophone. Band instruments adorned the walls of their home's main bedroom. Most family members were adept at singing in a classical style and at playing the harmonium. All the men in the family could play dhol to some degree. Their playing tended to be informed by their experience with drumming in classical music. The star dholi among them was young Gaga. Gaga could not stay on a rhythm for long without jazzing it up with many ornamental gestures. He attacked the dhol like a lion devouring its prey, letting loose bombastic streams of fills without inhibition (audiovisual example 20).

BHARAI

In the picture of Punjabi drummers that belongs to the historical rural imaginary, the "other" drummers—those not of the Dom class—came from the Bharai (*bharāī*) community. Whereas the Dom-based musicians occupied a clearly marked outcaste group situated among a hierarchy more pronounced in urban centers, Bharai performed dhol without the same social stigma in the rural landscape. By the same token, Dom-based musicians were purveyors of sophistication in music, providers of sangīt; we have seen that playing dhol was not necessarily their preferred occupation. Bharai, by contrast, were seen as "folk" musicians and the dhol, in particular, was their instrument. The position of Bharai as the proverbial village drummers has since disintegrated, however, and neither the Bharai nor their drumming pedigree is well known to people in the current era.

The Bharai's identity is linked to the twelfth-century saint, Sakhi Sarvar Sultan, a personage revered by many in the Punjab region. Hazrat Sakhi Sarvar, also known as La'alanvala Sarkar (lord of the rubies) and Lakhdata Pir (saint who gives in millions), is a giver of sons. The saint is also worshipped to protect animals and children from disease (Bhatti 2000, 90). Worshippers come from all classes and religions. According to oral hagiography, the saint, birth-name Sayyid Ahmad, was a descendant of the Prophet Muhammad who came from Baghdad and settled in Shahkot, Punjab (Temple 1977 [1884, 1885], 1: 66). As part of his spiritual development, Ahmad journeyed throughout the region. It is said that in village Dhaunkal (near Wazirabad) he performed the miracle of creating a water well by striking his staff on the ground (Rose 1919, 566). Ahmad gained many followers, for which his relatives became jealous and tried to kill him (ibid., 567). He then fled to the barren and inaccessible location of Nigaha at the edge of Balochistan. The remote shrine at Nigaha, commemorating Sakhi Sarvar, became a site of annual pilgrimage for followers. Before Partition, pilgrims came all the way from the eastern side of Punjab—an epic journey. The pilgrims formed encampments along established routes (ibid., 570), arriving for the annual fair held in honor of Sakhi Sarvar's *'urs*. In this subculture, the Bharai were Sakhi Sarvar's special devotees.

Origin tales of the Bharai suggest that they did not come from any one qaum but rather formed out of devotees drawn from several. One legend offers an origin story for the Bharai as musicians. When Sarvar was being married, the Mirasi meant to act as *lāgī* showed up late for the wedding. As a further slight, the Mirasi rejected Sarvar's modest offering of a piece of cloth. Thus spurned, Sarvar gave the cloth to a Jatt companion, Shaikh Budda. Declaring that he did not need a Mirasi, Sarvar instructed Shaikh Budda to tie the cloth around his head as a badge of honor and to play the dhol (Rose 1911, 85). Henceforth, non-Mirasi individuals, known as Bharai, acted in service to the saint's worship as priests, drummers, and guides. In Rose's estimation, the Bharai community of the time (late nineteenth century) formed a loose occupational group composed of various castes (ibid., 86). Bharai clan names given by my informants included Dhillon, Chima, Tinda, Grewal, Gill, Brar, and Baraich—several of which correspond to Jatt names. (This does not necessarily denote their belonging to Jatt families, as many of these names have been adopted by families from low-status qaums.) A Pakistani Bharai interviewee traced his ancestry to the warrior tribe Janjua.[27] The Bharai are sometimes confused with the Mirasi by laypeople (from their musical occupation), but the above origin story highlights their identity as an alternative to Mirasi labor. More important, the Bharais I interviewed were clear about their separate identity. By the same token, Mirasis distanced themselves from and felt superior to the Bharai. A Mirasi argument was that the Bharai lower themselves by doing work other than music and by using music for begging (Nayyar 2000, 768). The term "Bharai" is yet another one imposed by outsiders, and the community, finding it inadequate, preferred the ennobling title of "Shaikh." Yet *Shaikh* is ambiguous, having been applied to so many individuals (including Mirasis), which leads to confusion in the historical record and among commentators.[28]

The traditional duty of Bharais was to guide pilgrims to Nigaha. During the treks, Bharais led the singing of songs and dancing in praise of Sakhi Sarvar. They also led devotees on shorter trips to local shrines or festivals and begged for offerings on holy days. While playing the dhol, a small troupe of Bharais would enter a neighborhood or village carrying several items of distinct paraphernalia. The first was a long bamboo pole on which were tied colorful strips of cloth or veils (*dupaṭṭā*). Women offered the cloths to give thanks for boons granted, like the birth or marriage of a son (Rose 1911, 86; Faruqi et al. 1989, 35). The pole, representing a bridegroom (Bhatti 2000, 128), was emblematic of the worship of Sakhi Sarvar and carried as one bears a flag in a parade (Darshan 1996, 35). Another piece of paraphernalia was a leather satchel worn around the neck, in which to receive offerings from devotees. The last piece of paraphernalia was the dhol itself, another emblem of the Bharai.

When not leading the worship of Sakhi Sarvar, Bharais had other duties. Among them was the general role of village drummer, to play dhol at the time of reaping the harvest, for bhangra dance, and during wrestling matches. Like the Jogis of Jammu, Bharais accompanied their drumming with *bīn* or (as it was also called) *ṭoṭā*.[29] In the absence of the Nai (barber) community, Bharais performed circumcisions.[30] A unique activity of Bharais was to sing lullabies, *lorī*, to children. Once or twice a year, the Bharais of a village went to the homes where a son was recently born (N. Kaur 1999, 29). The main singer of the group took the child on his lap or sat the child on the dhol (Darshan 1996, 45). The Bharais' sounds were a blessing on the child and the house. The content of the *lorī*s, while addressing the child, simultaneously praised Sakhi Sarvar and, when sung in other contexts, were hymns to the saint.

In the contemporary East Punjab of my research, the Bharai community was small. I found them only in Malerkotla and its surrounding villages. They estimated their size to be about 100 households in the city, with a few in each surrounding village.[31] Although there is a specific Sakhi Sarvar shrine in Malerkotla, its popularity had been overshadowed by the shrine of Haider Shaikh. Indeed, now that the historical worship places of Sakhi Sarvar were cut off from Punjabis in the east, Haider Shaikh seemed to have transmuted into a form of Sakhi Sarvar. Iconography of the two saints was confounded.[32] That this site had already become an important place for the Bharai, to which they led devotees, was noted as early as 1960 (Gurdit Singh 1960, 205). In 2004–2005, a Bharai in uncommonly old-fashioned garb sometimes haunted Haider Shaikh's shrine. Bearded and beggarly, draped in blue clothes, he carried a dhol wrapped in cloth. His name was Muhammad Sabi and he came from a village in Fatehgarh Sahib district. Haider Shaikh was only one of the many sites he visited. Sabi was proud to be the possessor of knowledge and a way of life he believed others had forgotten. For instance, he asserted that other dholis at Haider Shaikh (i.e., Mirasis) played the wrong rhythms for propitiating the saint.[33] His playing was as much visual as aural. Each time he struck with his drumsticks he raised his arms high in the air. His dhol was obsessively decorated, almost beyond the point of functionality (audiovisual example 21).

A more typical contemporary lifestyle for Bharais was that of the Dhillon family, proprietors of a musical instrument shop in the city center (Figure 3.4).

FIGURE 3.4 Akhtar Dhillon (right) and his nephew, Sultan, at his shop in Malerkotla, 2005. Photo by the author.

The shop specialized in supplying instruments to order, including dhols, smaller folk instruments, band instruments, and kettledrums for gurdwaras. Akhtar Dhillon (b.c. 1958) was the senior figure. Back in his village, Akhtar had learned to play the marching-band side drum. His teacher was a Mirasi who, "although he was illiterate," was capable of playing all sorts of classical *tāls* on the instrument.[34] Shortly after his family moved to the city in the early 1980s, Akhtar saw one of his cousins play a bit of dhol. It seemed to him that he could easily transfer his rhythmic knowledge to that instrument, and around 1985 he began playing dhol in earnest. His dhol instruction, too, did not come from within his qaum but rather from *ustād-lok*—Mirasis. The use of the appellation *ustād* for Mirasis here seems to acknowledge their musical (technical) knowledge. In painting a picture of dholis in Lahore, Wolf indicates the other side of the relationship: technically proficient dholis had disdain for the allegedly simple playing of Bharais (Wolf 2014, 29–30). A statement that Akhtar Dhillon made to me years later revealed mixed feelings, however. He dismissed the Mirasi dholis at Haider Shaikh, saying they were "just Mirasi . . . they get 10 rupees here and there for playing at the shrine."[35] Dhillon simultaneously rejected the image of the traditional professional musician, bound to eke out a living, while reserving admiration for musical art.

In describing his people to the outsider, Dhillon first called them "Muslim Jatt," with emphasis on "Muslim." However, once the façade was no longer needed, he shifted to "Shaikh," and lastly to the more specific "Bharai." Yet, as his foremost identification with the Muslim community indicated, he wished to make a distinction between his social circle who lived a modern lifestyle and the stereotypical image of Bharais. While speaking to Dhillon once about the Bharai community, the *faqīr*-like Muhammad Sabi walked into his shop. As he approached, Dhillon said, "Now *here* is a Bharai." After that traditional specimen of Bharai left, Dhillon explained that Islam teaches one should work to earn one's money, never beg.[36] His attitude was similar to that taken by Mirasis to Bharais, whom they consider beggars. As comembers of the Muslim community, indeed, Mirasis and Bharais might share the same values about musical practice, yet their membership in different qaums suggests that they articulate the values differently.

In light of this, for Bharais like Dhillon, the status of dhol in relation to their contemporary identity was tenuous. Dhillon, his sons, and nephews all played dhol, although Dhillon's own father did not play. Their association with dhol was secondary to other interests. Despite this, Dhillon said that for the Bharai to play dhol was in their blood. It follows, said he, that in every Bharai family there were at least a few dholis.[37] At the same time, he downplayed the importance of dhol to the Bharai identity. Dhillon maintained that, even before Partition, Bharais did all sorts of work and that nowadays he and his sons were actually among *few* that play dhol in the area.[38] The issue seems to be in how the dhol is used, to what artistic and financial ends. The dhol playing of the Dhillon family, rather than begging at shrines, was oriented to the staged bhangra repertoire. In 2005 Akhtar Dhillon's nephew, Sultan, was studying to get his bachelor's degree at the Government College in Malerkotla. Meanwhile, he was accompanying the college dance teams—prestigious work. Paradoxically, Sultan cited his identity as Bharai as a way to establish some authority in relationship to dhol. According to him, the work of Bharais "*from the beginning*" was to play dhol at Haider Shaikh's shrine.[39]

A Pakistani Bharai immigrant to the United States, dholi Muhammad Boota, reflected an identification similar to that of the Dhillons of India. He said that his family were Shaikh but, more important, they were Muslim—though they remember their ancestors were Hindu. Boota acknowledged his people's historical connection to Sakhi Sarvar but distanced himself from the business of saints in general as if it were not the proper Muslim thing to do. So, while he also knew his people were connected with the label of "Bharai," that identity was not at present important. Even without the legacy stigma of untouchability that troubles the identity of the Dom-related communities, the Bharai, imagined to be lowly drummers, have preferred to hitch their identity to a better wagon.

LESS-ESTABLISHED COMMUNITIES

The prevalence of the Dom-related qaums and the Bharai in historical discourse suggests that they occupied the ethnic positions most central to the identity of dholi at least until Partition. Dom-related qaums have occupied, in addition, a privileged position with respect to the identity of professional musician in general, among which the ability to play dhol is included, although Bharai had historically a more specific tie to dhol. In constructing the idea of "traditional" dhol-playing communities, I have labeled as such those groups in which dhol playing has been passed on, as a profession, by numerous players through at least two generations. Under the "traditional" designation I include, therefore, in addition to the well-established Dom-related qaums and the Bharai, those communities having shorter or less-recognized dhol traditions. We might call them less-established communities.

The Bazigar community, who will be discussed in Chapter 4, were competitors with the well-established groups during the latter part of the colonial era. They were, however, an itinerant tribal community situated outside the framework of mainstream society, and their identity as dholis was overshadowed by their other identities or else overlooked. By the early twenty-first century, other groups had established or were beginning to establish dhol traditions. All were low-status communities, more or less invisible socially, who operated in more local or culturally narrower contexts and whose identities as dholis had not emerged among the increasingly gray landscape of the profession.

The most problematic ethnographic label in this topic is "Chuhra" (*cūhṛā*). Unlike vulgar terms that are not the preference of insiders or that fail to capture their nuanced identity, it is a term that is offensive,[40] while at the same time it does correspond well to a long-established identity group. Further, this community is perhaps the most visible of those discussed in this chapter. The group's hereditary and, ultimately, defiling occupations were "sweeping and scavenging," including the removal of dead animals and waste. Yet such was the stigma of this work that the workers' own name became a term of abuse. To discuss them collectively and historically, I will substitute the English gloss, "Sweeper." Sweepers are found throughout India where, along with the Chamar, they make up the majority of the population of the erstwhile untouchables or, in affirmative parlance, Dalits.[41] In the nineteenth century, many Sweepers converted to Sikhism and Islam to escape their restricted status in the Hindu caste system. After conversion, they were known as Mazhbi (*mazhbī*) and Musalli (*musallī*), respectively. Although these groups subscribe to different labels based on their religious affinities, all emerged from one *ethnic* community. Indeed, the Sweeper-based groups tend to have more in common, socially, with analogous groups of different religions than with other qaums. Arguably, the Sweepers have retained their own distinct lifestyle, rituals, language, and deities. Their status as outcastes, living on the margins of village life and severely restricted in their interactions with other classes, has engendered these idiosyncrasies.

In East Punjab, Hindus of Sweeper background find empowerment in identifying with the term *Valmīkī* (or *Balmīkī*), after Valmik, their patron saint and the poet of the epic *Rāmāyaṇa*, who was supposed to be of this community. Although they are employed in a range of occupations, they remain associated with cleaning tasks. For example, anthropologist Ronki Ram found that Valmiki continued to predominate in the work of cleaning latrines (2017, 52). Yet Valmiki also are involved in a range of musical activities, both for devotion and as a source of income. For instance, an account from a Hoshiarpur village in the 1920s relates that it was the Sweeper's job to walk through the streets while beating a *daff* (frame drum) to announce coming events (Dhami 1996, 55). A recent author states, "Practically, all the members of the marriage band parties are Balmikis" (Puri 2004a, 9).

One could see the Sweeper's music most distinctly in the worship of the religious figure Gugga Pir. Gugga was a Rajput believed to have lived during the mid-twelfth century (Rose 1919, 171) in the barren northern borderlands of Rajasthan known as the Bagar area. His legend starts with a king, Jevar, and his queen, Bachal, who are without children (Rose 1919, 172–182; Temple 1977 [1884, 1885], 1: 122–209). They are visited by the *jogī* Gorakh Nath, from whom Bachal asks the boon of a son. Being finicky about to whom he gives his blessings, the great *jogī* refuses the queen. Queen Bachal goes on to ask the deity Bhagvan for a son. Bhagvan shakes some of the dirt from his head and gives this to Bachal, who gives birth to an heir to the throne, Gugga. Gugga passes an unusual childhood during which he displays a unique power over snakes. As Gugga matures and awaits the day he will become king, his half-brothers grow jealous of his property. One day, while out hunting with Gugga, the brothers try to kill the prince. Gugga gets the best of them and returns home with their heads. Queen Bachal is not pleased by the sight, and she banishes her son. Upset by his mother's rejection, Gugga requests that Mother Earth swallow him up. In a twist, Mother Earth refuses to do so because, as a Hindu, Gugga may only be cremated, not buried. To get around this technicality, Gugga converts to Islam, after which Mother Earth consents to swallow both him and his horse. Because of this, devotees consider Gugga to be the ruler of all things beneath the earth.

Around Gugga's grave was erected a shrine in the form of a Muslim *mazār* (mausoleum). Known in Rajasthani dialect as *Gogā Meṛī*, it lay in the middle of a desert in Hanumangarh district. From the original grave, dirt was taken by followers and brought back to their local communities to establish smaller shrines, *māṛī*.[42] The center of each Gugga *māṛī* contained a mausoleum that housed a marble tomb draped by cloths with Muslim motifs. (While no one was buried in these tombs, they contained dirt taken from Rajasthan.) Devotees entered the inner sanctum, touched their foreheads to the ground (*mathā ṭekṇā*) before the saint/tomb, and made offerings. The devotees then took *parshād* (consecrated food) from the officiant and circumambulated the tomb before exiting. On Thursday evenings (following Sufi custom), devotees paid their respects to Gugga, greeted their brethren with *jai ho!* ("hallelujah," a Hindu slogan), and sat in observance on the ground outside. At sunset, one or more dholis would play. Devotees arrived over time and sat for about 2 hours, when concluding rituals were performed by the priests. These might be more or less elaborate, but usually included a *havan* (sacrificial fire) and an *ārtī*: praise of the divine spirit through ringing of bells and making of clamor, accompanied by drawing the spirit's blessings out through the medium of a lamp.

During the monsoon season, corresponding to the native months of Saun and Bhadon (July–September), Gugga was worshipped by Punjabis of all qaums and, indeed, religions. This is the season when snakes are most active, and the belief was that appeasement of Gugga protected one from snakes and cured one of their bites (Rose 1919, 171). Others came to Gugga requesting the boon of a son. Sweepers were especially linked to his worship and the maintenance of related traditions and made up the most of Gugga's dedicated devotees, *bhagats*.

Small groups of *bhagats* formed processions during the daytime in the monsoon season. The *bhagats* carried with them the emblem of Gugga, a long bamboo pole (*chaṛī*) topped with a sort of broom of peacock feathers. As Bhatti explains it, the pole, which resembles a broomstick, represented spiritual purification (2000, 76). One could see the iconicity between the broom and the Sweepers who carried it. The pole was also an icon of Gugga himself. The *bhagat* who carried the pole received special honor. He was called the *ghoṛī* ("mare") and represented Gugga's steed. The *ghoṛī* wore a leather harness across his back and shoulders, with a pouch in front in which to place the end of the weighty pole. The procession of *bhagats* move from door to door seeking offerings. Some gave alms, while some women gave cloths to be tied to the *chaṛī*, as with the pole of the Bharai. On the way, the devotees sang songs in praise of Gugga, *sohlā*.[43] I believe that with the absence of Bharai in East Punjab since Partition, the worship of Gugga was following the pattern of Sakhi Sarvar.[44] Indeed, in former times, it was the duty of Bharai to lead women to the annual fair in honor of Gugga Pir in the village of Chappar (Gurdit Singh 1960, 205), but by this century Sweepers had taken over this function.

Gugga Naumi, the saint's birthday and annual festival, was celebrated with fairs at Gugga *māṛī*s on the ninth day of Bhadon (late August). Gugga's worship began on the preceding evening. The devotees gathered at the *māṛī*, where they went through the usual Thursday night routine but in a more festive atmosphere with more intensive rituals. The rituals might include the head priest of the *māṛī* going into a trance, during which he beat himself with a set of iron chains—part of the paraphernalia of Gugga (Bedi 1991, 1255). At each stage of the ritual, dhol was played by members of the Valmiki community. The day of Gugga Naumi was marked by a few distinct features. One was *miṭṭī kaḍḍhṇā*, the scooping of dirt. Devotees scooped the earth with both hands seven times to honor Gugga and receive his protection from snakes. Another custom was to "feed" snakes by pouring diluted milk (*kaccī lassī*) into their holes in the ground. Yet another custom was to eat *sevīāṅ*, a milk-based pudding made with vermicelli. The wormlike *sevīāṅ* provided another evocation of snakes. Finally, it was the duty of the *bhagat*s of local *māṛī*s to make a pilgrimage to the main shrine in Rajasthan. They brought along the emblem pole and took blessings at various sites significant to the Gugga story and Gorakh Nath. At each place of obeisance, the pole was dipped and waved as if it were a devotee prostrating himself. In this way, the *bhagat*s renewed the connection between the main shrine and their satellite shrine, and pilgrims accumulated spiritual merit (audiovisual example 22).[45]

The bards of Gugga also belonged to Sweeper communities. These musicians were specially engaged to perform on Thursday nights and the holidays during the festival season when, over the course of many nights, they recited episodes from the tale of Gugga. The instruments used were *sārangī* and *ḍaurū*. The latter is a medium-sized hourglass-shaped, variable-tension drum with two heads, only one of which is beaten. Closely resembling another Punjabi drum, *ḍhaḍḍ*, the *ḍaurū* is larger and beaten with a small stick, and its drumheads are larger in diameter than the length of its body. Its hourglass form is iconic of the *ḍamrū* of Lord Shiv. Players of *ḍaurū* also beat time and signaled when the emblem pole was carried in procession. When visiting Goga Meri in Rajasthan, *ḍaurū*-playing bards were hired by pilgrims on site from among a pool of itinerant musicians. Whereas *ḍaurū* was the original instrument for these activities, it had lately been replaced in Punjab by the louder dhol.

Activities of Valmiki dholis were closely connected with the worship of Gugga. Their dhol tradition had developed relatively isolated from related circles; they tended to be unaware of other traditions and fixed in their ideas about how and when dhol should be played. Their activities revolved around the site of the *māṛī*, which provided a central gathering point (Figure 3.5). In its functional aspects, their knowledge included what to play at ritual moments. On Thursday nights, the dholis received offerings from the devotees at the *māṛī*. In village Dadu Majra in the 2000s, Valmiki dholis also played for wrestling matches; the other drummers in that area—Bazigars, who earned a living especially as dance accompanists—could not be bothered to do that work. Valmiki dholis had to gain other employment because dhol was only a supplement to income; it was first and foremost part of their religious life. So, although some families of Valmiki had been playing dhol for a few generations, it was not considered to be one of their traditional occupations. For instance, the father of Bhagat Gulab Singh, leader of Dadu Majra Colony's erstwhile Gugga *māṛī*,[46] had played dhol, yet not "professionally," and Gulab Singh himself took no interest in learning. His father's playing was "just for fun" at family functions and there had been no tradition in the family earlier.[47] Gulab Singh's brother, Shamsher Singh, worked as a housekeeper in Chandigarh's Mountview Hotel and none from that side of the family had knowledge of dhol. In contrast, Gulab Singh's brother-in-law, Tara Chand,

FIGURE 3.5 Valmiki dholis of Dadu Majra Colony, 2004, including, clockwise from left, Ustad Kala, young Kala, Ustad Puran, Ustad Tara Chand, young Gaurav, and Sonu. Photo by the author.

was part of a young tradition of dhol playing that began with his father, a soldier. Tara Chand's family had migrated from Rawalpindi (Pakistan) and he began to learn dhol when he was 10 years old. Tara's premier student was Puran, who already had students of his own. And Tara Chand's son, Sonu, was one of the most active Valmiki dholis of Dadu Majra. Sonu's son, Kala, had been playing dhol since he was 5 years old and could keep up with his father and grandfather when I met him at age 9. So begins a tradition.

Most of the Sweeper dholis in East Punjab belonged to the Valmiki community, but Sikh Sweepers, the Mazhbi, also played dhol. The community still had close ties with the Hindu Valmiki, and their social position had not improved much; they are recognized as a Scheduled Caste in Punjab state. In this sense, although the Mazhbi are a Sikh community—a religious population from which few traditional dholis come—as a low-caste group, dhol was considered to be within their purview, especially when avoiding identification with the Professional Field. Mazhbi players used the dhol to play at shrines for offerings. Balbir Singh of the village of Ladda (Sangrur district), whom I met at Haider Shaikh's shrine, wandered to various shrines and festivals around Punjab and as far away as Kashmir. His teacher did the same, traveling to the Goga Meri in Rajasthan and as far as Bihar state. Balbir said that, although technically he was a Mazhbi, as a Sikh he did not believe in caste. His occupation? "The work of God."[48] What the Sweeper group of dhol-playing communities had in common, indeed, was a focus on religiosity when playing dhol.

Yet another less-established community challenged ascribed ethnic labels. Among those dholis I will group as Sain (*sāīṅ*), most were descended from the Muslim Sweeper community who called themselves Shaikh—not to be confused with the Bharai community. One thing that unified them was their Muslim faith; beyond that, the nomenclature served, once again, to negotiate the low-status identity of marginalized people. Like the Hindu term *jogī*, *shaikh* is a term of variable usage carrying ambiguous associations with both religiosity and nobility.[49] Here, "Shaikh" was an ennobling alternative to Musalli, the original rebranding of Sweeper converts to Islam. With time, "Musalli" was understood by cynics as little more than a euphemism for "Chuhra," and in recent decades it has taken on its own overtones of derision (Salim 2004, 160). In the continued struggle for dignity, "Shaikh" was adopted by a great number of Muslim artisan and similarly ranked qaums, including the Musalli.[50]

With respect to their playing, the Musalli imbued *Shaikh* with one of its earlier, Arabic connotations: a leader in Sufi worship. Musalli-turned-Shaikhs served as facilitators in reaching union with the Divine. Still, these Shaikhs, while predominant, made up only part of an umbrella category that we might call "Sain" dholis. As evidence that the Sain community is ethnically heterogeneous, we read in Wolf's account of Pakistani dholi Niamat Ali, who came from a family of Bazigars who converted to Islam at the time of Partition (2014, 25). His father took up dhol late in life and subsequently taught it to Niamat's cousin—thence the entry of the family into a paramparā.

Dholis of this group were a distinctly Pakistani phenomenon. In styling themselves as Sain, they adopted the image of a *faqīr*, for which *sāīṅ* is a respectful form of address. More precisely, these individuals appeared as *malang*, ascetics who live at shrines or wander according to their patron saint's commands while living off charity.[51] The stereotypical image of the wandering *faqīr* was not germane, for they were typically householders. More accurately, their distinguishing trait as veritable *faqīrs* could be considered their unorthodox appearance and their manner of religious devotion. In appearance, they cultivated overgrown locks, donned long robes, and adorned their fingers with rings—all symbolic gestures to evoke femininity within the heterodox religious metaphor of devotee as a female lover of God. In method, Sain dholis performed at shrines of saints, albeit not exclusively. Dholis from these ranks in Lahore also were hired for weddings and similar functions (Wolf 2014, 25). In my observations, whereas dholis from most communities might play at shrines, their communities regarded the role as a low-prestige resort in lieu of other options, whereas Sains preferred to embrace it as part of their identity. Further, the Sain dholis' performances were motivated less for the financial gain of offerings and more for the sake of artistic ideals and (incongruously, in their special context) prestige. Their playing was, in addition to having spiritual import, meant to be heard and appreciated. Sain dholis, indeed, played for ritual functions, namely the inducement of trance, dance, and *mastī*. I suggest, however, that for a good percentage of Sain dholis, religious devotion in this manner also provided an excuse to step outside their expected social role as nonmusician service worker. The identity of Sain offset the stigma associated with practicing music as a profession.

Among the most famous of the Sain dholis was Lahore's Zulfikar Ali (b.c. 1961), known better as Pappu Sain. His tradition began with his father and uncle (Wolf 2014, 154), who at that point were the only players in this Musalli family. Pappu's father, known as Luddan Sain, learned from a hereditary musician friend, Mian Qadir Bakhsh Hussain; Pappu later became a disciple of Qadir Bakhsh (ibid.). Before Partition, Luddan Sain played at shrines in a classical style. Pappu made the fascinating claim that it was his father (albeit standing on the shoulders of other giants) who made dhol popular in Lahore, and he was the person who introduced the now-ubiquitous dhamāl rhythm (ibid.). Pappu learned tabla from his father and teacher, transferred his tabla playing style to the dhol, and began playing regularly at the shrines of two of Lahore's saints, Madho Lal Hussain and Shah Jamal. As Wolf relates, in the late 1990s, students from the National College of Arts made it popular to hang out and listen to Pappu Sain at the shrines (2006, 253). By the time I saw Pappu at Shah Jamal's shrine in 2001, a large number of foreign hippie types were in attendance. They sat listening attentively, perhaps attracted as much to the hypnotic music as to the freely flowing hashish that could be consumed anonymously in the dark performance space below the shrine. Sain-type dholis often perform in pairs, one dholi playing the base rhythm while the other improvises or plays a complementary pattern. Pappu's partner on that night in 2001 was his disciple, a mute dholi nicknamed Gunga Sain (d. 2021). The two drummers began their performance in an improvisatory way, playing complementary, soloistic patterns of classical tabla style: dynamic explosions, various beat subdivisions, *tihāīs*, dramatic crescendos, and glides. This was the aesthetic part of the performance. At its conclusion, Pappu began prodding audience members out of the way to clear a dance area. From then on, for the devotional part of the event, Pappu led dancers in high-stepping, head-bobbing, and fast, whirling movements designed to embody the spirit. His characteristic feat was to whirl around while playing the dhol. In the performance, one could see the dual emphases of Sain dholis. One was the commitment to the idea of being a vessel for the spirit and to facilitate the spirit's habitation of others. Pappu expressed the idea that his talent, indeed, came from a mystical source (Wolf 2014, 155). By contrast, dholis of Mirasi, Bharai, and other communities at the Sufi shrine of Haider Shaikh (in India) provided the service of moving the spirit within others while remaining aloof from the experience themselves. Moreover, a Mirasi's talent came from his birthright and upbringing in a guild of professionals. The Sain dholi's second emphasis, on virtuosity and classical figures, contrasted with the approach of other dholis in devotional contexts. The latter subscribed to the idea of playing a simple rhythm that contains a straightforward message, to call the spirit, and which was certainly not something that they would expect an audience to consume as art—not even as art that inspires contemplation of the Divine.

Another dholi of the Sain type was Saghir Ali Khan (b.c. 1968) of Jhelum. He and his brother had been engaged as cultural ambassadors by Pakistan's National Council of Arts. In this capacity, they had performed for heads of state. In 2006, when I met the brothers, their photos graced the national folklife museum, Lok Virsa in Islamabad. Since first going abroad in 1998, Saghir Ali had been to Holland, China, Japan, Qatar, Turkey, and India. In this context we see dhol playing recognized again as an artistic product, such that national agencies would be proud to have it represent Pakistan. Saghir Ali first learned from his father, but his formal master was a Mirasi, Gulam Haider. In the teacher's photograph, which hung on the wall of Saghir Ali's office, I could discern changes from the master's generation to Saghir's generation. In brief, the master and his dhol looked like a dholi of any community one finds now in India. Like other Sain dholis, but unlike his master, Saghir and company wore their dhols in a new style and used new types of sticks, all of which served their new style of playing. Their entire style of performance approached that of a concert of light Hindustani music. While we discussed a currently popular dhol rhythm of India, it seemed to me that Saghir missed the significance of the rhythm, which was its novelty and popular success. He dismissed it as "too easy; for kids." Then he played a set of lightning-fast strokes. "See, now, *that* is difficult!"[52]

Sain dholis differed from those of other communities studied insofar as they were predominantly located in Pakistan. Though the past social status of the community was comparable to the Valmiki's, more recently some Sains were using dhol as a tool for raising their social status. They did this by circumventing the stigma placed on the profession of dhol playing while embracing the locally situated respect-gaining enterprises of religious devotion and art. It is important to understand that their Pakistani context differed much from the Indian context. In India, dance accompaniment provided the best chance for prestige and only the least skilled dholis were relegated, as it were, to playing at shrines. Conversely, in the Islamic Republic of Pakistan, folkloric dances were held in lower regard and Sufi shrines, on the precedent of genres like *qavvālī*, were perceived as sites where fine art could flourish. Sain dholis had developed a niche in their own political context.

Some qaums had only recently initiated a dhol paramparā. One was the formerly itinerant tribal people, Sansi (*sānsī* or *sainsī*). Numbering 122,000 in Punjab (India) in the most recent census, the ongoing separation of the Sansi tribes from mainstream society is shown by their unique dialect.[53] The Criminal Tribes Act of 1871 stigmatized the Sansis as incorrigible thieves. According to the act, the Sansis and similar tribes were forbidden to travel beyond village boundaries without special permission, and the wandering Sansis were forced to settle down (Sewa Singh 2015, 17). Although the Sansis were unjustly branded as a criminal tribe, mainstream Punjabis' stereotyped association of this community with theft has some basis in reality. In a biographical profile of Natha Singh, a Sansi who was born around 1921, the subject testified to his community's former practice of small-scale theft of grain, cotton, and fuel. Indeed, Natha Singh characterized his community as experts in stealing from farmers. Women stole from shops or in buses, and men looted trucks (McCord 1996, 5; Sewa Singh 2015, 30–32). In my interactions with Sansis in Dadu Majra Colony, I found them suspicious of outsiders. They protected their living quarters from neighboring communities' intrusions by means of sentries, who intercepted would-be visitors and grilled them with repeated questions of "Who are you and what is your business here?" Their closest neighbors, the Bazigars, would point out instances of Sansi's petty theft, and one informant directed my gaze to a Sansi who was bringing a cargo of illicit liquor into the settlement.

As with most tribes, however, the characteristic employment that the lay public associated with Sansis was not their main means of sustenance. Sansis had traditionally raised buffaloes, goats, sheep, and donkeys. Some kept hounds for hunting. Others made and sold brooms. Sansi women made and sold grass winnowing baskets and strainers (S. Bedi 1971, 13). In the villages, Sansis were engaged in agricultural labor and buffalo herding for others (McCord 1996, 5). Colonial ethnography states that Sansis had also been hereditary genealogists and bards to some Jatt clans of Punjab (Rose 1914, 362). Musical activities of the Sansis were formerly connected with busking. Natha Singh recounted how Sansi women used to sing and solicit donations, especially at wedding parties. Some men of his community formed a small musical band, which consisted of flute, cymbals, *daff*, and "dhol" (possibly *ḍholkī*). The band played at weddings, death ceremonies, and Lohri celebrations for the lay community (McCord 1996, 4).

In the 2000s, Sansis were a minor community in dhol playing and were just starting to enter the profession in some locales. In recent years, seeing the employment opportunities for dholis, Sansi men have begun to learn and to earn. In the mid-1990s, Bazigar dholi Prem Chand began teaching Sansi youths to play dhol for a fee. Some Bazigars protested at the time, objecting to the fact that Prem would teach their community's craft to these people whom they considered unsavory. They remarked with vindication that once the Sansi students began earning money playing dhol, they considered their lessons to be finished and ceased to pay tribute to the teacher. Raju of Dadu Majra Colony was representative of a handful of young Sansis who had started the trend in that area. Before this time, Sansis of Raju's local community had no dhol tradition, but now the knowledge was spreading between cousins. Besides keeping goats, the local Sansi's primary occupation was to supply mares for weddings. The decision to learn dhol was an ingenious economic move in this respect. In addition to a horse, there is one more special thing needed by modern urban wedding celebrations: dhol. This way, the Sansis could supply both items as a package deal.

Dakaunt (*ḍakaunt*) was another new community whose members had taken up dhol in patches. The community, which is listed among the Other Backward Classes of Punjab state, has received scant mention in the historical record. A mid-nineteenth-century source described them as "A caste of Brahmans who consider themselves able to bear the calamity of *jabbardán* and therefore do not hesitate to receive it" (Newton 1854, 213). The *jabbardán* is an offering one makes when under a bad astrological sign in hopes to avert a disaster by transferring it to the receiver (a Dakaunt in this case) (ibid., 183). At the time of my research, members of this community were known best—by sight, but not by name—as solicitors who took collections for the deity Shani Dev on Saturdays. Shani Dev, associated with the planet Saturn, is purported to have a malevolent influence on those born under its sign. Dakaunts offered their service to people to propitiate the god and thereby save themselves from Saturn's negative effects. In particular, Saturdays were considered inauspicious days for travel. Considering the high rate of accidents on Indian roads, the worship of Shani Dev had been popularized as a way of protecting travelers. Dakaunt alms collectors, men dressed in white with turbans, approached individuals in the market, or else in their vehicles at railroad crossings and busy intersections, and presented them with a bucket or platter containing an image of the deity. The superstitious donated coins or mustard oil, but others dismissed them as run-of-the-mill beggars. Dakaunt were especially dense in some villages surrounding Patiala and Rajpura. One village, Jainagar Rurki (Patiala district), was home to about 300 Dakaunt men who bused to Patiala city each Saturday morning and earned a living collecting for Shani Dev (Gurvinder Kaur 2002). Besides this activity, Dakaunts performed agricultural labor and other occupations available to lower classes. Some had chosen to augment their income by playing dhol, though this phenomenon was largely restricted to Patiala.[54] As in the case of the Sansi dholis near Chandigarh, the phenomenon of Dakaunt dholis was enabled by instruction from local Bazigar teachers like Biru Ram.

The Rai Sikh (*rāe sikkh*) are a Scheduled Caste of agriculturalists. Their ancestors were members of the itinerant tribe called Mahtam who converted to Sikhism. This historical tribal identity makes them distinct from Jatt Sikhs or Mazhbi Sikhs. As in the case of the latter, the Rai Sikh's religious identity is shared by privileged groups and adheres to a philosophy that rejects caste hierarchy, belying their low social status. Rai Sikhs are well represented in Indian Punjab's dry Fazilka and Firozpur districts and the border areas of Rajasthan. An interviewee from the community claimed that Rai Sikhs and, to a lesser extent, the closely allied Kamboj, made up over 90 percent of the population in that region.[55] A significant portion of the Rai Sikh population there migrated from the southern *bār* (interfluvial) areas of western Punjab.

Before Partition, the jungle environment that the *bār*-living Rai Sikh populated was bereft of dholis from settled communities. Instead, accompanists for the community's dances, chiefly jhummar, were Bazigars. The Rai Sikhs themselves had no tradition of dhol. In the post-Partition era, however, some Rai Sikhs, their community transplanted east of the Ravi River, took up dhol. These individuals were atypical dhol players in that they were also farmers. Playing the dhol was mainly a pastime, yet even playing as a pastime was unusual for other Punjabi farming communities. It was probably a shortage of professional dholis in the area that prompted them to play for themselves. Moreover, being of a Scheduled Caste, Rai Sikhs were, in a sense, "permitted" to adopt the instrument without the blow to status that Jatt farmers might receive.

This emerging paramparā was isolated from dhol trends developing in the population centers of the middle of the state. In 2005 Jangvir, a Rai Sikh from the village of Tahliwala, was one of the regular dholis for the famous family-based jhummar troupe started by the late dance master Pokhar Singh. The notable position allowed Jangvir to stand out from the crowd; locals said that Tahliwala seemed to have "one dholi for every household." On the eastern bank of the Ravi, at the border with Pakistan, in a village called Chak Khiva, I met dholi Lacchman Singh (Figure 3.6). He had just come from working in the fields. His technique was unorthodox, yet he was respected, not as someone pretending to be an artist but rather for his value to the community as a repository of cultural knowledge. Lacchman had around twenty-five students from the village in 2005. The playing of his students was, expectedly, informed by the traditions of southern Punjab, with its influence in turn from Sindh-Rajasthan. Both their method of playing and the construction of their instruments corresponded to current regional ones in Pakistan and were different from those developed elsewhere in the Indian state.

The youngest paramparā was emerging within the Chamar (*camār*) community. Traditionally associated with leatherworking, the group makes up the largest Scheduled Caste community. In the early twentieth century, the Chamar made great strides in income level and education. Following a successful religious reform movement, *Ādi Dharm*,[56] some Chamar redubbed themselves *Ādi Dharmī* in distinction from mainstream Hindus. Others, revering the fourth Sikh Guru, Ram Das, and Ravidas, a Chamar *bhaktī* poet of the fifteenth century whose verses were enshrined in Sikh scripture, began to call themselves, respectively, *Rāmdāsīā* and *Ravīdāsīā*. The latter two are now Chamar subgroups that have established themselves as distinct from the

FIGURE 3.6 Lacchman Singh on his property, village of Chak Khiva, 2005. Photo by the author.

mainstream Sikh fold. Despite the historical stigma attached to their status, or perhaps rather because of the community's numerical strength and success in establishing their political rights, the label Chamar is often asserted as empowering, rather than degrading, at least when used by group-members.

A noted arts administrator stated in 1992 that "Ramdasia have also begun to know dhol" (Bhag Singh 1992, 67). I observed Ravidasia dholis in a holiday procession for Ravidas (audiovisual example 23). Elsewhere, in performances of *nacār*, a music and dance presentation that centers playful female impersonators, the troupe (including dholis) was made up of Chamars. One interesting Chamar exponent of dhol was Jagdish Yamla (d. 2005) of Ludhiana, one of the sons of the famous singer Lal Chand Yamla Jatt. Following in his father's vein, Jagdish had started out singing and playing *tūmbī*, going on to play other instruments like the harmonium, tabla, and *ḍholkī*.[57] Although musical practice had stretched back at least to his grandfather, Jagdish was the first in his family to play dhol,[58] which he had being doing for a decade. When I met Jagdish in 2005, he showed me recent photos of himself posing with a dhol, and, before he died soon after, he was exploring the options of promoting his services as a professional dholi. His two sons had already attained great skill on the dhol as well, and it looked as if the family was on its way to developing a dhol paramparā.

• • •

This chapter has introduced the social environment and ethnic identities of the diverse dhol-playing qaums, along with representative personalities. The emphasis has been on gaining an understanding of who they are (or were) within the broader field of Punjabi identity and to situate their areas of activity within the Punjab region. We can begin to see, also, how they situate their particular identities as dholis among the wider pool of Punjabi dhol professionals. A fuller exposition of these particularities—how these people approach dhol playing to situate themselves—is a subject of Chapter 5.

4 A PORTRAIT OF A DHOLI AND HIS COMMUNITY

Ustad-ji was born sometime in 1939. Well, thereabouts. Of the day he was uncertain, and his passport gave a different year. His place of birth was somewhere near the village of Dochok, in the Kirana Bar, between the Jehlum and Chenab rivers, close to Phalia, in the south of the Gujrat district (now district Mandi Bahauddin), Punjab Province, Undivided India (now Pakistan). The exact place, too, was unclear, and not only because the political borders were redrawn, the names of places changed, and the individual forever separated from the possibility of returning to it. The Bazigar community into which Ustad-ji was born was at that time itinerant; the nominal village of birth does not represent a true home. Even the individual's name lacked fixity. A few days after birth, his father gave him the name Vilayati—"foreigner." "In those days, people like my father did not know any better." They gave children any name they felt like without first consulting a Hindu priest. Around the age of 5, Vilayati started to have health problems, some unremitting illness. His parents took him to a priest who, looking at his astrological charts, declared that Vilayati had been named incorrectly. The *panḍat* bade the parents to rename the child Garibu—"impoverished one." Some days after the name change, Garibu's condition improved. Although he never used his family name as a means of public identification, there was one thing that was certain from the beginning: he belonged to the Vartia clan of the Khari tribe of the Bazigar people.

From his earliest years, Garib Dass—the formal name adopted by Ustad-ji when he became an adult urban dweller—embodied an identity that was more fluid than the typical Punjabi portrayed in mainstream narratives. The archetypal Punjabi is connected to the land, at least in the case of the privileged male majority-ethnicity subject. The history of patriarchy and feudalism suggests that women and most minorities are connected by proxy through those with whom they marry or to whom they provide services. In all cases, the remembered birthplace, actually or euphemistically a village, one's *piṇḍ*, gives them an identity of belonging to somewhere in the landscape of Punjab. New acquaintances ask each other, "What is your *piṇḍ*?" Such villages, stars in the constellation that is Punjabi society, provide a connection to events in the long history of the region. Most Punjabis trace their lineages to a remote time, the length of which further validates their enfranchisement in the Punjab story. The archetypal Punjabi is also born into the identity of a religious community and receives his name through the customs of that religion. In the case of Garib Dass, however, the incidental *piṇḍ* was not only vague in memory but also unremarkable in legend. It was a new place, formed on the ground of a space off the historical map. The name Dochok (*do-cak*) translates as "Villa 2," indicating that it was a numbered settlement in a canal colony. The community to which Garib Dass was born had religious beliefs as much as any other, yet they inhabited a cultural space outside the dominant religious institutions. Theirs was an identity unincorporated into the dominant discourse of Punjabi identity. And yet Garib Dass's people, travelers by definition, know Punjab with a breadth of perspective that exceeds that of Punjabis tied to a village. Their story is unimpeachably a Punjabi story. Although in so many ways these people occupy a position opposite to that of the representative social subject, they are not less Punjabi but rather the obverse face to the normative one. A complete picture of Punjabi culture calls for understanding people such as the Bazigars.

The previous chapter highlighted ethnic diversity within the broader occupational group of traditional dholis. Such a broad view, however, could survey only the particular histories and life experiences of each community and a few of its members. It was not possible, indeed, to conduct intensive research on all the communities, and so by way of compromise, this chapter offers details for a selected group for its focus, the Bazigars. The Bazigars do not represent all dholis, but their story is valuable as an illustration of how a small minority group of Punjab married its identity to dhol playing. Before folkloric bhangra became a major source of employment for drummers, the Bazigars were marginal among the occupational group. Subsequently, dhol playing became one of the Bazigars' staple bread-winning activities and they came to make up the majority of players in some areas of Indian Punjab. The stories of Bazigar dholis illustrate the development of the dhol's identity from a proscribed minority instrument to an emblem of the Punjabi people insofar as their activities were entwined with folklorization. A deeper view of the phenomenon can be obtained through a portrait of the individual player, Garib Dass. His life story tells the tale of a dholi who crossed spatial, class, and financial frontiers. The example of Garib Dass is both representative and exceptional. His biography provides information on the life experience of a Bazigar community member, giving specificity to generalizations about the culture in which his path was shaped. Concurrently, Garib Dass's career follows the spectacular rise of that cream of dholis who might be referred to as key figures who shaped dhol's development.[1]

HISTORY OF THE BAZIGARS AND THEIR STATUS IN PUNJABI SOCIETY

The Bazigars suffer the double bind common to Punjab's ethnic minorities. The majority, on one hand, imagines them one-dimensionally and fancifully. On the other, the Bazigars are not seen at all as a community but rather as disconnected, faceless practitioners of a profession. In this limited view, the label confirms the contents, which, in turn, confirm the label. The term *bāzīgar* glosses as "someone connected with *bāzī*." Punjabi *bāzī* translates generally as "play," in the sense of gaming or sporting, yet the word has additional, special denotations, as in this case. People unfamiliar with the specific genre of Bazigar performance that goes by this name, venturing to rationalize *bāzīgar* through a familiar meaning, connected the root /bāzī/ to *kalābāzī*, "acrobatics." They, therefore, conceived Bazigars as acrobats. This was fair only to the extent that acrobatics was a skill in which some Bazigars excelled. Insiders to the community, however, understood bāzī to cover a broader field of play comprising any number of entertaining performances based on physical acts. More important, bāzī was only one aspect of the community's identity. The performance of bāzī had practically died out by the 2000s, and if one thing then distinguished the public profile of Bazigars, it was dhol. Facing the double bind, however, Bazigars were resigned to bāzī being that feature by which outsiders distinguished them, and they accepted a name that they, in fact, did not call themselves. Speaking among themselves, they call their people Goaar. Yet, as always, such groups must act strategically. When operating outside the Goaar community, outside their own language, to accept "Bazigar"—to refrain from asserting their unfamiliar autonym—is to reserve some modicum of representation. For that reason, Bazigar is also used here advisedly.

The view from the inside, however, reveals a more complex situation than a people mislabeled and essentialized by their neighbors. The people ascribed the label "Bazigar" are not a singular qaum. Indeed, *both* "Bazigar" and "Goaar," being outsider and insider umbrella terms, encompass multiple endogamous tribes. Three were based in western Punjab before migrating eastward during Partition: the Panjabias, the Kharis, and the Ravis. Another tribe, already belonging to the east, is referred to by western Punjabi Goaars as "Desi Bazigar."[2] This last is an outsider term—of some Goaar tribes for another—which simply indicates that the tribe is native (*desī*) to the eastern area, whereas the western Goaar tribes were immigrants to that area. It emblematizes western Goaars' own limited knowledge of the eastern Goaars, belying the notion of a unified Bazigar/Goaar community. Garib Dass asserted that the tribes were distinct "from the beginning."[3] In my conversations with Bazigars of various tribes, members showed almost as much disinterest in other Bazigar tribes as they did in any other qaum. Nonetheless, when viewing them all from the outside perspective, significant shared characteristics and clan names make it not unreasonable to retain the idea of a set of related Goaar/Bazigar people.

Origin stories for the Bazigars resemble those of other historically peripatetic tribes of north India.[4] Bazigars claim to have once belonged to a community of Rajputs from Rajasthan (Thind 1996, 31; K. Singh 1999, 196). Some stated that the specific region of origin was the Marvar area of western Rajasthan (Ibbetson 1995 [1883], 288). According to some tales, they occupied that barren area after being unseated from elsewhere, for example, as a result of the Hindu community's conflicts with Mughal forces (Deb 1987, 17, 22; K. Singh 1998, 4: 340). Garib Dass ascribed his people's origins to the Rajput Bajwa clan of Punjab.[5] Note that in contrast to many Indian communities that place their origins in antiquity, Bazigars' apocryphal narratives set their origin in the medieval period. Oral history and genealogy suggest an even later origin, however. A twentieth-century sociological study of Bazigars reported that the community had spread through northwest India only in the previous two centuries (Deb 1987, 10); that is, they originated in the late eighteenth century. Bazigars openly stated to me that their younger adults represented only the seventh generation of their people. This is supported by the genealogy of Garib Dass's clan, which suggests that the clan's patriarch, Bhagu, was born around the late eighteenth century. By the late nineteenth century, Bazigars were recognized as an autonomous and nomadic tribe of entertainers among those the colonial ethnographer Ibbetson classified as "Gipsy Tribes" (1995 [1883], 285).

By the early twentieth century, some of the western Punjab–based Bazigars started to settle down, especially in the districts Shekhupura and Sialkot (Deb 1987, 10). Causes for the location would have included the restructuring of western Punjab for the canal colonies project (from the 1880s) and the government's restrictions on the mobility of "vagrant" communities. During the Partition, many of these Bazigars (who identified as Hindus), migrated to the Republic of India. Like other refugees without ancestral land in the east, they were first situated in camps. In the 1950s and 1960s, some were resettled in colonies or on common village land (Deb 1987, 11).

This period of the Bazigars' history, however, contradicts the simple narrative of Partition as a time when all Hindu residents of western Punjab, then becoming Pakistan, rushed to India in 1947. From the Bazigars' position at the margins of society, the decision to migrate at that moment was neither so obvious nor so feasible as it was for others. Some Bazigars remained in Pakistan, not necessarily a conscious decision despite the opportunity to evacuate (Ravinder Kaur 2008, 293). It seems, rather, that some were confused about what was going on politically among the mainstream population and consequently failed to emigrate in time. Garib Dass heard tales that Bazigars who remained in Pakistan were subject to forced conversions to Islam. The experiences of his relatives lent authority to the matter. In 1960 some Bazigar bands that had been "stuck" in Pakistan, including Garib Dass's (second) wife's community, decided to surreptitiously cross the border into India. They obtained the services of a man at the border of Rajasthan who would help them across. Weighing the risk, some ultimately decided to stay behind, while some 400 families committed to the plan. They arrived at the specified crossing late one night carrying minimal baggage. As the families crossed, no one said a word, and their animals' mouths were bound shut. The Bazigar party had been told to expect a landowner in Rajasthan who would give them work when they arrived. Once they did arrive in Rajasthan, however, they were unable to find work with anyone. By selling off some animals, they got their first Indian cash currency. According to the account, the group roamed through the districts Firozpur and Amritsar of Punjab, but they remained without work and were starving. Having finally come to Delhi and without a place to stay, a man who worked for the railroad helped to smuggle them in empty storage cars of a train. Families from the group disembarked at various places along the rail line, where they reunited with relatives who had migrated in 1947.[6]

The once-itinerant Bazigars of western Punjab underwent a wholesale transformation into a stationary people of India. In the 2000s one could still see Bazigars living in temporary huts along roadsides, outside the main population settlements. Most, however, lived in government-sponsored housing projects or segregated wards in suburban areas. In the Indian Punjab state, Bazigars were most heavily concentrated in the districts of Patiala, Firozpur, Sangrur, Bathinda, Gurdaspur, and Faridkot (Deb 1987, 13; K. Singh 1998, 4: 341). In the last census, their population in the state was estimated at 241,000.[7]

Although the Bazigars were becoming more and more integrated into mainstream society, their past and their status as relative newcomers to (settled) village life made their position in Indian society both ambiguous and marginal. The Criminal Tribes Act did not include the Bazigars among its notified groups (Thind 1996, 54), but they were nevertheless confounded with these groups and vulnerable to similar prejudice. In 1960, after the act was repealed yet while itinerant people were still stigmatized, it was reported that the Bazigars "obtained a writ from the court declaring that they cannot be categorized among the ex-criminal tribes" (Biswas 1960, 2). The Bazigars *were*, however, included among the Scheduled Castes in Punjab. Perhaps not understanding that the caste schedule is, technically, a bureaucratic classification, Garib Dass asserted that the Bazigars were "not *really* a Scheduled Caste."[8] The issue of course is that a Scheduled Caste, while ostensibly defined merely as one eligible for benefits, carries with it a stigma of presumed untouchability. Indeed, in the 1980s, the usual government initiatives designed to assist Scheduled Castes were found to have little effect on the Bazigars because of the community's own assumptions that they were not a Scheduled Caste. Confusion stemmed from the fact that, in comparison with some other Scheduled Castes, Bazigar were not as separated socially from upper castes (Deb 1987, 11). A survey in two villages in 1970 indicated that, in the caste hierarchy, people ranked Bazigars above potters, oil pressers, Ramdasias, and Mazhbis (Harjinder Singh 1977, 86). Furthermore, Bazigars were reported to perceive themselves as having a high social rank, such that they themselves did not accept food from "untouchable" communities (K. Singh 1998, 4: 340).

GOAAR CULTURAL IDENTITY

Features of the Goaar lifestyle have contributed to shaping their identity as a distinct people. Chief among such features is their language, which they call *goāroṅ ri bolī* (audiovisual example 24). Although it has much in common with Punjabi and Rajasthani, *goāroṅ ri bolī* is not mutually intelligible with them and thus may be considered a distinct language unique to the Goaars. In addition, Goaars have a secret language, entirely unrelated to Punjabi, which they call Pārsī or Pashto. They use it to elude comprehension by outsiders.[9]

The historical Goaar tribes had a set protocol for traveling and earning. Garib Dass's Khari Bazigar tribe, for example, before Partition roamed in a band of about forty households. They had no fixed migration, though they might return to the same spot if it was a good one. Each family traveled with its livestock (camels, goats, and donkeys), from which they derived milk and meat and which hauled their belongings. They stopped to camp for one month or more (sometimes up to a year) in an open space outside a village or town. Bazigar dwellings, called *sirkī dī jhuggī*, were temporary huts made of reed grass and tree branches. Once arrived at a new location, men from the group went to notify the nearby landowners—in whose fields they had set up camp—of their presence. They asked to be hired to do agricultural labor. This protocol underscores the point that many itinerant communities, whatever the special professions with which they were associated, also depended on agricultural work. In addition to earning through employment, the Bazigars subsisted in various ways. Women fashioned objects out of grass, straw, and reed (e.g., breadbaskets, *canger*) to sell door to door. Bazigars used dogs to hunt game, including jackal, hedgehog, deer, and rabbit, in the forests. They raised goats and camels for sale.[10]

During the Bazigars' stay at a camp, the local villagers would come to know of their presence. They would invite the Bazigars to engage in sports, at which they excelled, like kabaḍḍī and wrestling. Bazigar performers found additional earning opportunities through performances of music, dance, and dhol. The activity in which they uniquely specialized, of course, was bāzī, and the Bazigars' presence meant a chance for villages to organize bāzī performances. In exchange for the performances, the villagers would pool their resources to present the Bazigars with gifts of cash, food, and clothing. Bazigars also performed for tips at homes where an engagement or wedding was taking place (Thind 1996, 32). The tribe would map out groups of villages and assign them to specific clans (Kumar 2002; K. Singh 1999, 200). The status of clans within the larger community was proportional with the number of villages to which a clan could claim rights. Such performance rights were viewed as wealth and, in marriage arrangements, the rights to particular villages formed part of the dowry (Sumbly 2007).

A classic bāzī performance, exhibited exclusively by men, consisted of a variety of physical feats—of strength, balance, agility, and courage. It included acrobatics, contortions, dangerous stunts, and lifting or pulling heavy objects in unusual ways. The performance was accompanied by the beating of dhols to call attention to the event and to enhance the excitement. Bazigars have rarely performed bāzī in recent decades, except for a few groups for special exhibition purposes. It was reported in 2002 that only six families in Punjab were performing bāzī (Kumar 2002). When I saw a group perform in a parade in Jalandhar in November 2004, it seemed many spectators did not know who they were. The parading group, from the Lalka clan near Phagwara, was picked up in 1985 by the North Zone Cultural Centre, under whose patronage they had been supported to continue the art in heritage-presentation contexts (audiovisual example 25).

One might assume that Punjabi popular dances were of a wholly participatory nature before Partition, but professionals also presented them for discrete audiences.[11] Bazigars danced professionally for weddings of the landed classes. In the post-Partition era, their expertise in dance placed them in demand for staging folkloric dance. The Bazigars also maintained participatory dance practices within their community, even while they faded in the mainstream cultural landscape. Figure 4.1 shows an impromptu jhummar dance performed, as remembered from a former time, at a Bazigar wedding. The participants, dholis Garib Dass (left) and Prem Chand and dancers Sardari Lal (left) and Jagat Ram, struck up the dance during some downtime in the proceedings. They considered this form of jhummar, never performed on stage, to be a distinctly Bazigar style (audiovisual example 26).

We have already seen that it was Bazigar refugees who provided the know-how to the ensemble of dancers who first folklorized bhangra in the 1950s. Bazigar input was responsible, indeed, for the fact that the stage form was not exclusive to traditional bhangra steps but rather included glimpses of various Punjabi dance forms. In those early years, the influence of Bazigars on bhangra was most obvious in the bāzī-like stunts employed by the PEPSU team. The team's cameo performance in the film *Naya Daur* (1957) is full of tumbling, along with their signature stunt of one man standing on

FIGURE 4.1 Bazigar-style *jhummar* dancing at a family wedding in Balachaur, 2005. Photo by the author.

a pot balanced atop another man's head.[12] Further development of bhangra, including the addition of yet newer rhythms and actions, occurred especially through the work of Bazigar dholis.

The Bazigar influence on dance was even more concentrated in the case of dances whose folklorization followed. Jhummar was revived for the stage from several lineages of practice, in each of which Bazigars had some hand (Schreffler 2014). The Bazigar influence was nearly exclusive on the *sammī* dance. In the Sandal Bar area, where Bazigars were predominant as performing artists, the *sammī* dance had existed as women's counterpart to jhummar. Recalling this heritage, a performance of *sammī* by Bazigar women was first staged near Chandigarh in the late 1960s.[13] After that time, however, Bazigar women were never to publicly perform *sammī* again because the tribe did not feel comfortable with their women performing.[14] A dance presentation called *sammī* was later developed, however, for lay Punjabi women dancers. Its most authoritative performances were directed by a handful of Bazigar dholis of Chandigarh and Patiala areas (see Schreffler 2012a).

Songs of the Bazigars consisted of both mainstream songs they brought with them from western Punjab and unique songs in the Goaar language. The last named were more or less endangered genres performed only in the intimate setting of local Bazigar communities. Still, some Bazigar performers were distinguished in the public sphere of musical and dramatic arts. Whereas before Partition certain genres were associated with Muslim professionals, in post-Partition East Punjab, Bazigars stepped into those roles. For instance, a few Bazigars carried on the tradition of professional ballad singing with plucked lute, what Thuhi (2002) calls *tūmbe-algoze dī gāikī*. Bazigar Sudagar Ram, originally from the Gujrat district, was a disciple of the famous (non-Bazigar) Nawab Ghumar (Thuhi 2002, 55). After Partition, Sudagar Ram settled in the district of Kurukshetra, where he passed the tradition to his Bazigar disciple, Jagat Ram Lalka (Thuhi 2002, 56–57). In the 2000s, one could hear Lalka give performances in which he included a distinctive form of the *māhīā* song genre that was connected with Bazigar culture (Schreffler 2011, 243–245). Famous among the *algozā* players was Mangal Singh Sunami (1931–2002) of the Panjabia tribe, who was a member of the PEPSU bhangra team.

Another performing art that some Bazigars adopted was *naqal*, the rural theatrical art previously associated with a community of Mirasis. A troupe of *naqqāl*s operating in the Chandigarh area in recent decades came from the Khari Bazigar (Chowdhry 2011).[15] Their leader, Prem Chand, was a student of Chajju, one of the *naqqāl*s in the court of the Maharaja of Patiala.[16] Prem's group, which included several other members of the Vartia clan, acted out dramas like *Hīr-Rānjhā* and *Kīma-Malkī*. One of their star members was Mundri Lal (d. 2018), whose routine included a feminine style of dance in which, donning *ghungrū* (bells) on his ankles and twirling a veil coquettishly, he performed steps from *kathak* dance and card tricks.

Playing dhol has had an auxiliary place in the Bazigar lifestyle for as long as anyone can remember. After Partition, each generation brought more specialists. The change began with the success of Bhana Ram (c. 1906–1999) of the Valjot clan of the Panjabia tribe (Figure 4.2). Bhana Ram belonged to the subdistrict of Nankana Sahib of the district of Shekhupura where, before Partition, he was the disciple of a Mirasi, Muhammad Ali. At Partition, Bhana Ram went to the Jawaharnagar refugee camp in Ludhiana before being settled in the town of Sunam—the birthplace of the PEPSU bhangra team. As the dholi attached to that ensemble, he took part in national functions,

FIGURE 4.2 *Portrait of Shri Bhana Ram* by R. M. Singh, oil on canvas, 24″ × 18″ (courtesy R. M. Singh).

international delegations, and several films through the mid-1960s.[17] He achieved his accomplishments despite the fact that, as some contemporaries opined, he was not among the most technically proficient of dholis. Some said, with a hint of jealousy, that Bhana Ram was simply in the right place at right time. Nonetheless, for the model he created, he could be considered the godfather of modern bhangra dhol. Bhana Ram's only son to follow the profession was Bahadur Singh (c. 1942–2019) (Figure 4.3).

Bahadur Singh's brother-in-law, Biru Ram (c. 1931–2011), of the Vartia clan of the same tribe as Bhana Ram, migrated from the district of Lyallpur (Faislabad) (Figure 4.4). After the Jawaharnagar refugee camp, Biru Ram

FIGURE 4.3 Bahadur Singh at home, Sunam, 2005. Photo by the author.

ended up in the Bazigar ward outside Sanaur, near Patiala. He had also played for the PEPSU team on occasion, and, in the late 1950s and 1960s, he was a regular feature at many local colleges.[18] In 1960 he accompanied the second-generation bhangra team led by Master Harbhajan Singh at Republic Day in New Delhi. Biru made his last appearance at Republic Day in the 1970s, during which it became apparent that he could not keep up technically with some of the younger dholis. Biru continued to play for and advise college dance teams, however, to which he contributed much unique knowledge that he had received from the older generation of his community. In this way, Biru established the Bazigar niche of working with students. So it was that Sunam and Patiala were the starting places for the modern Bazigar dholi community. In consequence of the activities of these pioneers, Bazigars became the dholis of choice for college and bhangra presentations in Punjab state's heritage center, Patiala.

FIGURE 4.4 Biru Ram and son, Manak Raj, at home, Sanaur, 2005. Photo by the author.

FIGURE 4.5 Bazigar dholis (from left, Shivcharan, Vijay, and name unknown) waiting for roadside clients in Mohali, 2004. Photo by the author.

In their business strategies during the period of my research, Bazigars relied largely on word of mouth and long-established relationships with college personnel and government officers. Some advertised by displaying their dhols outdoors so as to be seen from the road. The visual of the instrument precluded any need for text announcing their services. Bazigar dholis of Mohali (greater Chandigarh) had a unique method of advertising their services in the 2000s. They arranged themselves and their instruments in a row along the steel barrier on the side of the main road that demarcated the border between Mohali and Chandigarh. On the waist-high barrier and nearby stones were painted their names and phone numbers. It was possible with this arrangement for motorists to drive alongside and book dhol services directly from the windows of their cars (Figure 4.5). Most of the dholis were enterprising village youths who, armed with a nice shirt, a mobile phone, and a drum, were determined to make dhol into their sole career.

THE LIFE AND CAREER OF A DHOL MASTER

Dhol master Garib Dass represents what could be called the second generation of post-Partition professional dholis. The first generation, such as Bhana Ram, were those whose careers began before the Partition and found themselves in a position to be the incumbent leaders in the transitional period. The second generation were their successors, who reaped the benefit of status-raising opportunities and, through them, shaped new paradigms. A flourishing dhol scene was not achieved, however, without much struggle. Before even more opportunities were opened to a broader pool of second-generation dholis, pivotal artists had to establish new models and networks. We see a dramatic arc in the story of Garib Dass, beginning from a position where dhol was not a viable focus to the position where playing dhol professionally was an obvious career choice for his descendants.

Garib Dass characterized his people during his childhood as *jānglī*—denizens in the wild. They roamed intermittently from place to place, perhaps ten miles at a time. When packing up to move, the family's frame cots were overturned and loaded on its camels first, then the rest of its belongings. Little Garibu was loaded last, atop a camel or a donkey. The Bazigar children made a game of running between the legs of camels while their fellow nomads, Baloch camel drivers, herded them in long caravans. Young Garibu's father would flip him over and lift him high above his head to prepare him for learning bāzī. Such were the lives of traveling entertainers.

In 1947, when Garibu was 8 years old, his group migrated across the new border near Amritsar. They were first placed in the refugee camp at Kurukshetra to await resettlement. About a year later, Garibu's family settled in the village of Sialva Majri (district of Ropar, about 10 kilometers from Chandigarh). Still a child, Garibu began working for a landowner by doing labor in the fields and grazing buffaloes.

Meanwhile, Garibu's personal interests grew. Prior to his generation, dhol playing was not a prominent profession in his family. His eldest cousin Mangat Ram, however, was already playing dhol and, inspired by him, Garibu began drumming "on tin cans in the alley." By 1954 (at the age of 15–16), he was playing dhol, picking up what he could from cousins. In the beginning, Garibu played dhol for wrestling and *kabaḍḍī* matches, and at the local Gugga *māṛī*. One of his first regularly paying jobs was to make announcements to advertise for the traveling cinema. The film screenings happened in makeshift theaters in small roadside towns like Kurali and Kharar. Garibu's dhol was part of a band of young men—one wearing a sign, another clashing cymbals—whose task it was to go on foot between villages and announce the screenings. Garibu also took an interest in wrestling, and in his late teens, he trained as a wrestler. At that time, he had the image of a peacock tattooed onto his thigh (a popular choice of wrestlers) and pulled bullock carts (a competitive feat of strength).

In 1955, as the staged form of bhangra was beginning to develop, Garibu received his first job accompanying this art form at Panjab University's College of Education in Chandigarh's Sector 20. Garibu came on foot each day from the village to prepare what he described as a very simple choreography. Next, in 1957, he worked with schoolmaster Surjit Mann at the Khalsa School in Kurali. He admitted that he did not know many rhythms at that time. Soon after, Garibu moved on to accompanying bhangra at the erstwhile Government College in Chandigarh's Sector 23, where he met then-student Mahinder Singh and the two built a beneficial relationship for the theatrical arts scene in the city. Garibu soon married, but his wife died of illness a few years later (1964) and he was left alone with a 2-year-old son. Not yet able to rely on dhol for a living, Garibu supplemented his income by pulling a rickshaw, laundering clothes, and performing field labor at harvest times. The situation compelled him to move back to the life of living in thatched huts on the outskirts of the city, where he remained during the formative years of his career.

Garibu's male cousins and brothers were also developing into artists of various sorts. The aforementioned cousin, Mangat Ram (c. 1917–2009), had learned dhol before Partition from a Jogi master named Ali Mohammad. By the time I met Mangat Ram in the early 2000s, he had given up playing dhol because of his advanced age and illness, but his son Dev Raj was one of Chandigarh's most active professionals. Mangat Ram's brothers (Garibu's cousins) became musicians, too. The second-born, Prem Chand (1940–2011), gained a reputation as a hustler, and in this manner secured the position of dhol accompanist and choreographer in various influential positions. His three sons, Naseeb Singh, Ramesh Kumar, and Sewa Singh, would go on to become leading dholis in the Chandigarh area. Prem was also the leader of the community's *naqqāl* party. Yet another cousin on this side of the family, Ujagar, was a tabla player. The youngest of these cousins was Mali Ram (b. 1945), who began playing dhol in 1968 (Jaimalvala 2008). Garibu's own brothers could play a bit of dhol—most Bazigar men had at least some proficiency—but did not make it their profession. Eldest brother Sardari Lal (c. 1925–2007) was a dancer; at the age of 80, as I observed, he still found the energy to dance jhummar at weddings. Garibu's other brother, Pathani Ram, trained as a youth in bāzī. He also danced as a *nacār*, a female impersonator, in the clan's *naqqāl* group. Such was the arc of Pathani's career that, by the 2000s, he had become the *pradhān* (one of the high governing members) of the *panchāyat* (tribal council) for all the Khari Bazigar.

Garibu got his artistic break in 1965 when he met Professor Saroop Singh of Panjab University's Evening College. Saroop Singh told me that he was riding his bicycle when he saw Garibu, then in his mid-20s, walking with his dhol along the road. He had earlier seen Garibu performing *Rāmlīlā* (drama of Lord Ram's life) with the *naqqāl* group. The professor stopped and invited Garibu to Chandigarh to play for his college's nascent bhangra team.[19] Garibu played for Evening College for a decade, during which its team came in first at annual competitions. Garibu became "Garib Dass"—a professional dholi in Chandigarh, Indian Punjab's newly established capital city.

The next career stage was to become attached to leadership. In 1967, during the shooting of the film *Heer Ranjha* (1970), Garib Dass met the first-generation dhol master Ghuggi. Placing a modest offering of *laḍḍū* (sweetmeats) at Ghuggi's feet, Garib Dass requested and was awarded discipleship from the master. Garib Dass would then make regular trips to Amritsar to serve his gurū, bringing him gifts of meat and liquor and massaging his legs in the typical behavior of a disciple. Garib Dass also considered himself to have gained a gurū in dance. This was Sardar Bhag Singh, a government culture minister who, as it happens, was an immigrant from the northwestern area of Punjab who had a wealth of knowledge about traditional dance. Through such connections, Garib Dass was poised to become ingratiated with the top-tier artistic and institutional leadership developing the folkloric bhangra genre. He would go on to make his own contributions to the college-style bhangra that, by the 1980s, had taken a standardized form. Garib Dass boasted that, in those days, every team in the area feared him. If they found out one of his teams was in a competition, they just left! He even triumphed against a team accompanied by his master, Ghuggi. The master was pleased with the upset, however, saying that it was good for one's disciple to be successful.

In 1970, as part of a stable of artists organized and mentored by Bhag Singh, Garib Dass gave his first New Delhi Republic Day performance of bhangra, which received the national dance award. He subsequently appeared in the Republic Day festivities seven more times. At his last appearance in 1986, the number of dholis in attendance had swelled to some three dozen. Garib Dass's group from Punjab was competing with a team of drummers from the southern Indian state of Kerala. The challenge was to play a rhythm that the other team would not comprehend. Garib Dass stepped forward and played a 21-count *tāl* and a 16-count *tāl* in which the *sam* (first beat of the cycle) and its anacrusis were deemphasized; both stumped the Kerala group. During this period, Garib Dass also traveled to Bombay for seven years consecutively, often with Bhag Singh's group, to play for Visakhi and Lohri festivals. Indeed, he gave performances in many states throughout India: Himachal Pradesh, Kashmir, Maharashtra, Bihar, Orissa, Assam, Tamil Nadu, and Kerala. The result meant much intranational exchange. Garib Dass was both an ambassador for Punjab and the recipient of broad experience with the country's representative traditions. Such cultural exchange gave Garib Dass and similar figures a special identity by which they proudly distinguished themselves in their craft. For example, an unorthodox way of playing the dhol solely on the treble head with two *chaṭīs* (Figure 4.6), which he sometimes exhibited

FIGURE 4.6 Garib Dass exhibiting the "Kerala" technique for a university audience in Santa Barbara, California, 2003. Photo by the author.

in solo performances, was something he attributed to his exposure to drummers in Kerala.

With the increase in prestige, Garib Dass could round out his profile with other types of opportunities. Playing with a band behind a star singer in concerts, now considered glamorous by the younger generations of dholis, was an employment not yet developed during Garib Dass's time. He believed he was one of the first dholis to do that sort of work, as when he played with Indian bhangra music pioneer Gurdas Mann in Bombay around the time of Mann's first hit, "Dil da Mamla Hai" (1980). He was even asked to stay in Bombay to work in the film-music recording industry, but he declined, preferring the cultural scene in Punjab. Garib Dass did, however, have onscreen cameos in films, including *Sat Sri Akal* (1977) and *Jatt Punjabi* (1979).

Garib Dass's career reached the next level through international work. His first such work occurred at a Punjabi conference in Bangkok in 1983, shortly followed by a trip to Singapore. He remembered his shock and disgust when seeing the street foods in Thailand, which appeared so strange to him. He laughed thinking about the routine of him and fellow traveling artists from Punjab when they returned from trips abroad: immediately on arriving back at the Delhi airport, they stuffed themselves with the Punjabi food staple, *roṭī*. The experience abroad that Garib Dass was most fond of was his stay in Canada for 6 months during the 1986 World Exposition in Vancouver. Indeed, this prestigious and remarkably long trip was the crucial event in solidifying his international artist credentials. Being at a time when few dholis had traveled to North America, his visit had a lasting impact on the history of dhol in the diaspora. The following year he was invited back to Canada for performances in Vancouver, Surrey, Toronto, and Calgary, and three more times thereafter (1990, 1998, 1999). The master filled three passport books with visas from more than a dozen countries, the last of which, perhaps most glamorously, was the United States (2003, 2007). This activity is all the more remarkable because Garib Dass did not speak any non-Indian languages, nor had he ever learned to read. Such global travel, carried on with bravery, was in accord with an idealized adventurous image of the modern Punjabi subject. Yet Garib Dass, a Bazigar who spent his childhood dodging camels and his youth pulling a rickshaw, had not the typical profile of such modern, globe-trotting Punjabi entrepreneurs. Dhol, one might say, was the vehicle that carried him to these places and the propulsion was the wave of Punjabi cultural pride that crescendoed at the end of the twentieth century.

Professional success meant that by the 1980s Garib Dass's family could move into *pakkā* (brick) housing. They eventually settled down in Dadu Majra Colony (DMC), a ghetto peripheral to the city of Chandigarh. Like other low-rent housing colonies, DMC was home to the poorest of local residents. They included, along with Bazigars, marginalized Dalit communities like the Valmikis and the Sansis, each more or less segregated into ethnic-specific wards. On one side of the colony, the smell of the city dump pestered the inhabitants and the opposite side faced Chandigarh's Sector 38-West, a place for affordable middle-class housing. In clear view from Garib Dass's home and in contrast to the relative squalor of the colony, Sector 38-West also represented hopeful aspirations for Garib Dass that he would pursue the remainder of his life.

Indeed, a traditional dholi's career was not about pursuing personal glory but rather support of his family and local community. Garib Dass's achievements improved the financial status of his family and put his heirs in a position to make their living through music rather than hard labor. So, by the time Garib Dass's youngest son Des Raj came of age, playing dhol was a career option from the start. Garib Dass began teaching Des Raj in 1986 after returning from Canada and then brought him to Jogi master Janak Raj of Ludhiana to become a disciple. Des Raj gained experience in teaching bhangra and giddha dance to college groups. In the 2000s, following the path blazed by his father, Des Raj was being invited annually to Canada, where he accompanied popular singers like Hans Raj Hans and Babbu Mann. Notably, unlike those from prior generations, Des Raj graduated from high school. This was a source of pride for his parents, who valued education yet had not themselves had the opportunity to receive it.

All Garib Dass's grandsons gained some facility with the dhol from an early age. The most advanced, Sunny and Honey, took advantage of the high demand for dholis to earn money and to acquire some youthful comforts, fashionable clothes, and audio-video systems. Sunny began accompanying his grandfather at performances in his mid-teens. After completing high school, he was earning enough money as a dholi to go directly into that profession, playing for indoor wedding parties. By the age of 5, Jass, Des Raj's elder son, could already play several rhythms quite well, and even the youngest grandson, Jasbir, had begun training with small sticks.

In his later years, satisfied with his reputation, the elder Garib Dass focused on less glamorous jobs that were to his liking while continuing to lay the foundation for following generations. Prestige had been a means to an end, but he maintained that a dholi must be prepared to humble himself to maintain a steady income. As a trusted quantity among Chandigarh's dholis, Garib Dass developed two niche skills in service of local institutions. The first was organizing large groups for performances at special functions, some of which called for large forces of coordinated dancers and musicians in heterogeneous routines. For example, at the 31st National Games (at Ludhiana in October 2001), Garib Dass led a group of seventy dholis. The second specialized skill was working with young children. He led summer-camp classes for youths and visited private schools for children from well-off families, whose parents valued having someone such as this to impart an awareness of history and heritage that the children might miss in their Western-influenced upbringing. It was while returning home on his bicycle from one of these sessions that Garib Dass was struck by a car and died from his injuries on November 17, 2010.

OUTLOOK

The recent stories of the Bazigars show the changes modernity brought to one Punjabi people. Some two centuries ago, this ethnic nation emerged at the margins of Punjabi historical space. They remained unincorporated in Punjabi mainstream society through the colonial era, developing original strategies for survival. If the profession through which outsiders identified them, bāzī, has been romanticized, in reality, they had to rely on sporadic migrant labor for their major sustenance. Nonetheless, they were uniquely engaged with performance arts—dhol, dance, theater, and music—across a broad area of the Punjab region. Instead of the fixed, interdependence model of providing services that characterized many minority groups, the Bazigars combined sporadic patronage with an independent tribal lifestyle.

The effect of the Partition on the Bazigars cannot be overstated. Although the same event uprooted millions of Punjabis of various communities, the case was extreme for the Bazigars in that the vast majority were displaced, which resulted in wholesale changes to their lifestyle. Weathering these changes, the Bazigars' flexibility was their strength. They adapted to new forms of patronage. New opportunities for performance in state-sponsored forms—especially folkloric dances and auxiliary representations of heritage to which they gave birth—presented a lucky break. The Bazigars successfully shifted their source of patronage from village communities to government and university programs by emphasizing their traditional knowledge of dhol and dance training. In these positions, Bazigar artists played a key role in transmitting historical western Punjabi forms in the eastern Punjab state on the Indian side. Bhangra, the most emblematic form of Punjabi performance today, would not exist without Bazigars.

Gradually with each generation, playing dhol became an escape from the drudgery and backbreaking labor of agricultural work. Garib Dass paved the way as a model dholi in his family, bringing them from a nomadic lifestyle to a sedentary one. All this has been working toward the aspirations of a contemporary Bazigar family: education, true independence, and ownership of property. Despite individual strides, the Bazigars as a whole remain in a marginalized social position. As their quality of life improves through integration into society, they lose some of the practices that made them distinct. Pride in their still-unique lifeways sustains them, however. Their identity is clear, even if it is unfamiliar to outsiders.

5 BECOMING AND BEING A DHOLI

Who are dhol players? The question always took some work to pose to my teachers. As important as *I* felt the question was, I was also aware of how puzzling it might seem. For professional players of the instrument, doing research *on* dhol was, understandably, an odd notion. They reasonably assumed that my interest was in learning to *play* dhol. Yet because I would clearly never become a *dholi*, and because, in their concept, the purpose of learning dhol is to become a dholi, the proposition was fundamentally absurd. When I clarified that I was interested in knowing *about* dhol, thoughts turned to the history of the instrument: "Where does dhol come from? What is its origin?" These, too, are reasonable questions, yet tangential to my interest. My anthropological lens motivated my interest in who, while regular people without such fixations might assume that the answer was obvious. Quite simply, those individuals who play dhol constitute who plays dhol. It seemed to be another absurdity, this time not of action but of inquiry. My question could be clarified by making it known that I was inquiring not (only) of individuals, but of groups—broader, sociocultural units. Is there some pattern, some larger grouping to those individuals who play dhol? Here, the answer, to many interlocutors, also appeared self-evident: Punjabis play dhol. Yet what I wanted to understand lay between the individual and the nation. Who *among* Punjabis, *typically*, plays dhol? The tautology of "dhol players play dhol," at worst, suggests that anyone might be a dholi, for it does not consider the factors that make some individuals more likely to play than others. As if we were to say that mail carriers deliver mail, it ignores the *cultural* significance of playing dhol (something that is less pronounced in delivering mail). At the other extreme, the idea that Punjabis play dhol gives some acknowledgment to culture. Yet this, too, is problematic, for it suggests that any Punjabi—any person supposed to embody Punjabi culture—might play dhol. The assertion behind my question then is that dhol players had a specific sociocultural identity. They were not just people who happened to play a particular instrument, nor was their cultural identity so diffuse that "Punjabi" captures who they were. To be a dhol player meant something specific within the Punjabi sociocultural system. Chapters 3 and 4 established a correlation between professional dholis and particular ethnic communities, which may be considered embodiments of subcultural formations within Punjabi society. The consistent patterns of belonging make clear that not just anyone plays dhol. Playing dhol may, by simple definition, make one a dhol player, but dhol players rarely exist without ethnic identity connotations. On the other hand, the identity of dhol player only *intersects* with ethnic identity. To belong to an ethnic group, for example, the Bazigars, is not coterminous with being a dholi. (Not all Bazigars are dhol players.)

This chapter aims to explore what it means, specifically, to be a dholi—a professional dholi, one who carries the identity of "dholi" in a way that is more meaningful than simply being an individual who has played dhol. I observe what commonalities of identity, *other than* the ethnic group membership already explored, make up that identity. What are the shared experiences, habits, and values that make up dholis' identities? It finds that the identity of "dholi," while greater than individual identity, is not monolithic. There is a common dholi identity, just as there is a common Punjabi identity. Within that, however, dholis distinguish their identities in particular ways. Perhaps initially confusing, the particular ways correlate again with ethnic group, for it is within the environment of these subcultural formations that the identities tend to be formed. Illustrated simply: it means something to be a Mahasha, Mirasi, Bazigar, and so on. It means something to be a dholi, irrespective of ethnic group affiliation. Yet it also means something to be a Mahasha dholi, a Mirasi dholi, or a Bazigar dholi.

The complexity of this situation indicates just how unlikely it is that, without analysis, dholis' specific identities can be recognized. In Chapter 3, I argued that, although those who come face-to-face with dholis recognize their ethnic otherness, as a class, recognition of their ethnic identities is hindered by general lack of knowledge about the qaums and the underlying issues of discomfort and propriety that obstruct that knowledge. How, then, can one hope to see dholis' more specific identities as dhol-playing members of those ethnic subcultures? The solution I offer is an analysis of data collected from a wide sample of dholis. I observed and interviewed dholis, from the remarkable to the ordinary, in every district of the Indian Punjab region and at multiple sites in the Pakistani province. Each dholi community practiced a different repertoire, played in a different style, and utilized different playing techniques. Dholis' work activities varied, along with their attitudes to that work and their future aspirations. Dholi communities' methods of learning differed, as did their habitual treatment of the instrument. They used different equipment and procured or constructed their instruments in different ways. And what each dholi said about himself—his values and his social role—distinguished him from or among other dhol players. Sometimes what a dholi did or said revealed a conscious decision to situate himself. At other times, his situation was an unconscious result of his local environment and his difference was evident only to the outsider who makes the comparative study. Speaking on religion in Punjab, Oberoi points out that, despite the appearance of discursively bounded religious communities, it was "a highly localized affair" (1994, 14). The same could be said for dhol, meaning that, although coherence in the present discussion practically demands I consider "the" dhol tradition of Punjab, dhol is, in reality, made up of numerous traditions.

PROFESSIONALISM

To be a dholi—to inhabit the identity—meant to be a professional.[1] The configuration here follows the idea, explained in the introductory chapter, that in the traditional cultural formation of Punjab, being a musician and being a professional are mutually inclusive. Musicking in traditional Punjabi culture, in contrast to the modern West, did not confer value to an individual for its own sake. Perhaps there are people with an interest in unclogging drains, but are they really *plumbers* if they do not do it for a living? Looked at through this exaggerated analogy, it is clear why only the proscribed qaums with compelling reasons and inherited traditions pursued dhol, and why those from outside the community had little cause to play. Outstanding dholis could acquire a modest form of prestige in their careers, but playing dhol according to its traditional function—a service—was not prestigious in itself. It was not a talent one could add to one's résumé, as a successful lawyer might also note that she is an accomplished piano player. A musician was not merely a person who plays music, but one who plays music expressly to make a living. Their act of performing music was, furthermore, perceived by society to be tainted by the fact that they received payment in compensation. *Others* might find socially acceptable rationales for performing, including the creation of art and religious devotion. These rationales, which circumvented judgments placed on the act of performance *as a service*, effectively shielded their subjects from music's dubious connotations.[2] In contrast, from the perspective of professionals, who received negative judgment for their acts, nonprofessionals were outsiders. Professionals transformed social degradation into a badge of honor and exclusivity.

Being a professional musician, then, entailed the intersection of professional activity and particular biological descent. Dholis were at once an exclusive group and a proscribed group. They suffered as members of society's most marginalized communities. Individuals from other qaums were discouraged by society from playing dhol on penalty of lowering their status through association with outcastes and the degraded profession. The dholis' rare privilege as outcastes was thus to enjoy a monopoly on dhol playing as a means of bringing money into the household and the right to claim it as their inheritance and birthright. For those outside these communities, not only did playing bring the risk of association with a lowly activity but also it had no real *place*. It was unclogging drains on the weekend, for fun, unlikely even as a hobby. Within these dynamics, until recently it was considered rather nonsensical to play dhol as anything other than a professional trade, and only then if one's inherited social position was also of a low status.

Although one's birth conferred the right and potential to become a dholi, one was not born into the identity of dholi. Moreover, the degree to which one inhabited the identity of dholi might be thought of on a spectrum. In some of the qaums from which dholis came, a large percentage of males acquired some ability to play the dhol. Among them, those who occupied a more central position in the identity of dholi were the active professionals, earning their living primarily through dhol. Indeed, the market could not support all members of the community becoming professional dholis. So, just as the restriction of playing to certain qaums limited the number of potential dholis, standards within those ethnic communities further regulated their number and quality.[3] Concepts of what made the ideal dholi, in competence, professionalism, and ethics, could be understood less as artistic goals and more as a way of maximizing economic gain for the greatest number and, thus, ensuring the survival of the community. A qaum might be known as specialists in dhol, but the market could support only so many players. Moreover, although growing up in a dhol-playing qaum gave a natural advantage to would-be players, not all had the interest or aptitude in playing the instrument.

Working as a dholi was not a simple matter of personal career initiative. To be a professional dholi meant default membership in a guild of craftsmen whose interests all members worked to sustain. Family networks acted like companies whose dholi members worked in collaboration to provide labor to clients. So, for example, an individual dholi had to be willing to pass a job offer on to his relative and if too much work or commission went to one, the others grew sore. Likewise, if one performed poorly, his relatives ceased sending him to jobs, for his behavior reflected on the whole company. Dholis who did not keep up a professional demeanor lost access to quality work, and their families were neglected by the "company" when such members fell out of favor. Dholis with greater success tended to prioritize the well-being of their nuclear families if it was seen that other families in the community could not pull their weight. The uneven prospects for success made being a dholi a risky occupation, even despite the safety net of a community. Players were driven by hopes of better economic status gained by personal pluck, yet also dragged by competing responsibilities to qaum and family.

Simply living in the environment of these communities made dholis' lives hard. Uninspiring surroundings, social conflict, and erratic employment made dholis susceptible to alcohol abuse. Many shortened their careers or met a premature death from degraded health caused or exacerbated by drinking. The specter of alcohol was so ubiquitous that the topic emerged in most extended conversations I had with dholis. The specter might appear as a request I buy him alcohol, that I accompany him in drinking, or the simple statement—leaving me to guess his meaning—that he had not drunk for a given period of time. It also included, equally, statements against drinking. For drinking, by all accounts, was something deemed unprofessional. Dholis certified their professionalism by stating that they did not drink. Unfortunately, leaving aside practicing Muslims, many dholis who had reached middle age had, at one time or another, been in the habit of overdrinking, and those who said they did not drink were, in reality, struggling to abstain. In Chapter 3, I profiled Bal Kishan, a Jogi from Jammu whose lofty religious discourse made an impression on me in 2005. His assertion that he did not drink was part of that presentation of himself. Some years later, I was told by a dholi relative that Bal Kishan had died (prematurely). The relative, too old to mince words, did not hesitate to add that Bal Kishan "drank too much." I remarked that the Jammu master had told me he did not drink, to which the relative replied, "He was just handing you a line."[4] Two pieces of the dholi identity, being a man and living hard times, correlated to drinking. Yet being a professional, another part of the identity, discouraged it. Dholi identity thus faced a regular threat of demoralization.

TRAINING

We have seen that to be a dholi archetypically was to be, by birth, a man and a member of one of the dhol-playing qaums. By status, it meant to practice dhol professionally—to play the dhol as one's primary means of earning a living. Being even more of a dholi, as it were, scaled to one's success in earning a living through dhol so as to be more exclusively linked to the quality of professionalism. One did not become that sort of dholi through passive experience but through training and relationship. More precisely, one best attained dholi identity through association with a special kind of teacher, a master. Paradoxically, this path to being a dholi is, now, the one most accessible to outsiders to the dhol-playing qaums. We will see in subsequent chapters that most of such outsider players of dhol, who also resided outside Punjab, lacked even this criterion; they lacked formal teachers. In the recently developed landscape, however, many outsiders have been able to acquire formal teachers, and, through having undergone this process associated with becoming a dholi, they have become something like dholis. The irony is that they may never really become dholis as long as the definition includes the concepts of inheritance through blood and musical professionalism that are endemic to the culture. And yet, again, while men born into dhol-playing qaums are potential dholis by birthright, they too must go through a process.

The ideal dholi participated in the master-and-disciple system. In this arrangement, the master is called *gurū* or *ustād*.[5] The disciple is called *celā* or *shagird*. As my English word choices suggest, the connotation of these roles was different from teacher and student. The connotation of master and disciple best represents the formal relationship between two members of the guild. The master had an unequivocal position of power in the relationship. In addressing the comparable context of Hindustani tabla learning, Kippen describes the master-disciple exchange as asymmetrical, emphasizing that the perceived "omniscient masters" could not be questioned by their disciples (2008, 126). Thus, the master was not only someone with mastery of musical knowledge (a maestro) but also, in this relationship, he was the master of the disciple. The disciple was bonded to his master, his ustād. He was expected to serve (*sevā karnā*) and to pay tribute. The disciple's service, which might take innumerable forms, did not stop when instruction stopped; the disciple was expected to "remember" (verbally acknowledge and pay tribute to) the ustād for the rest of his life. It was taboo to put a monetary value on this relationship. All benefits of the relationship had to be negotiated implicitly in ways that did not involve cash payment but rather were remunerated through ongoing obligations. All this lent a seriousness to entering into a master-disciple relationship, which, in turn, validated the relationship's importance.

It follows that neither party treated the *ustād-shagird* relationship casually. They regarded it as proximate to a familial relationship, as between father and adopted son. As ustād Mali Ram put it, indeed, "The ustād loves his disciple more than he loves his own son."[6] When the disciple served the master, therefore, his service did not take any fixed fashion but rather transpired in the multifarious ways that a devoted child might serve his parent. He also had obligations to be a good citizen and to make his "father" proud. The disciple was expected to become a contributing member to the success of the guild as a whole. To fulfill his own "parental" obligations, the master had the duty to nurture the disciple beyond the narrow confines of providing instruction. He had to care for the welfare of the disciple, not only during the formative period but also in the disciple's future career. As a Punjabi father's duty is to get his son married, the master strove to see his disciple placed in a successful professional career. The master was expected not only to teach and guide but also to be a role model, to set an example. These were great responsibilities that yoked the two parties: the master had to maintain himself as an ideal example and the disciple to live up to the example. One can imagine the potential of the actions of either party to fall short of the ideal vision of the master-disciple relationship and the potential for tension when one party viewed the other as lapsing from his obligations. By the same token, the value placed on this relationship, and its proper realization, mapped to the moral standing of the guild of dholis and the communities they represented.

To elaborate on the master's role: because a master's disciples reflected on his and his family's reputation, he had a vested interest in both the disciple's fruitful development and his character. He had to choose carefully when accepting disciples, both to ensure that the disciple was likely to reflect well on him and because his careful nurturing represented a considerable investment. For the image of the master, the moral character of the disciple might, ultimately, be more important a consideration than his potential to perform skillfully. Garib Dass related that once a man asked to become his student, but the ustād had to ask him to go away, because he refused to teach the applicant until that man "took the badness from his heart." With respect to investment, because the master was not directly paid for lessons, he offered his time with the expectation that the return for the investment would be the overall success of the guild and the transmission of his legacy.

In the case of Garib Dass, I know of only one person whom he made his bona fide disciple: Gurvinder Kambo of the United Kingdom. Kambo was an unusual case, in that he was outside the community, and yet he proved to be a faithful transmitter of the master's legacy. Garib Dass found no one *in* his community that was eligible and did not deem the investment in disciples there worthwhile for the mere sake of having them.[7] Nevertheless, others have claimed Garib Dass to have been their master. One was Garib Dass's younger cousin, Mali Ram, who grew up alongside him and had, in those close quarters, learned from him.[8] Mali Ram had a successful career as a dholi, with numerous disciples of his own. He expressed that he and I, who both learned from Garib Dass, shared the relationship of *gurū-bhāī*, "brothers" of the same gurū. I cannot fault Mali Ram any more than I can fault myself in giving the impression that I am a student of Garib Dass and, in that modified sense, consider him to be my teacher.[9] The fact remains that Garib Dass, to my knowledge, never acknowledged Mali Ram to be his disciple. Garib Dass's standard for whom he embraced as disciple as opposed to whom he merely taught was high and reflected his effort to maintain the traditional principles of the master-disciple system.

The struggle of masters to maintain their ideals included facing judgments from others in society. For example, masters who appeared to have many disciples were viewed with suspicion. Cynical onlookers, doubting the multidisciple master's ability to fulfill the ideal obligations for so many, would suspect that the relationships were not true. Insofar as having disciples makes one a master and to be a master is a position of prestige, to claim one is a master of many disciples might be read as a bid to proclaim one's glory. Onlookers might also suspect that such masters were taking advantage of the service provided by their disciples. Mastership, in general, risked being judged as less than ideal if the ustād received gifts and cash from his disciples. Yet gifts were not uncommon, and accepting gifts was a temptation for many dholis living in strained economic circumstances.

In the above case of Garib Dass and his cousin, Mali Ram, such a perceived transgression appears to have been at the root of familial conflict. Garib Dass discouraged me from developing an acquaintance with Mali Ram. Although the underlying cause of the poor relationship and the conflicting claims of master and disciple status were never made explicit, I interpreted the reason to be Garib Dass's wish to disassociate with a person who did not represent his ideals for a dholi. On one occasion, Garib Dass alleged that Mali Ram received a gold bracelet from a disciple.[10] Bearing in mind that this was only one side of the account, nevertheless, the allegation was one point of conflict between the family members and, no doubt, a cause for the ambiguity in the status of master-disciple relationship between the two dholis. Further, Mali Ram was a dholi who proudly claimed to have many disciples.[11] In defense of Mali Ram, he also evinced an interest in maintaining good behavior as an ustād. For example, he related to me an account of his hazing a disciple, wherein he asked the person to perform the messy service of cleaning and prepping leather for drumheads.[12] In hearing this account, secondhand, from the perspective of the disciple, it seemed possible that the disciple's labor was being taken advantage of.[13] In Mali Ram's own telling, however, I interpreted the dholi's intention as testing the sincerity of the disciple, which was a common practice. Mali Ram showed me a video of another of his disciples, whom he praised and about whom he spoke with genuine nurturing concern. Garib Dass and Mali Ram took different approaches, one more conservative, the other more liberal, to the master-disciple concept. Dholis walked a fine line between maintaining their moral status through modeling idealized master behavior and taking needed advantage of their skills to increase their economic status.

Although the master-disciple system applied to most traditional paths to becoming a musician in north India, learning dhol happened differently in some ways than how one typically learned classical music.[14] The difference lay in the fact that most contemporary disciples of classical music were not expected to become professional musicians. The creation of art, more than earning a livelihood, was their priority. In the classical practice, a student's education customarily began with finding an ustād. The ustād might give the disciple his or her first exposure to their instrument, and he had a strong personal influence over how the disciple played. In contrast, in the dholis' practice, most learning took place through enculturation. Notable for its contrast to instruction in classical music, the method of verbal articulation of rhythms in vocables, *bol*, was infrequently and far less formally utilized for instruction in dhol.

Because most dholis came from dhol-playing qaums, they were around dhol from birth. Small boys experimented with playing, now and then gently guided by their father, brother, or an older cousin. Children were encouraged to play in the way an infant is encouraged to walk (audiovisual example 27). The developing child dholi might play in amateur situations, such as community festivals or at worship places. Eventually, the teenaged dholi was allowed to accompany an older relative on jobs, first to observe and carry gear and, later, to play along. When a minor function came up, the older mentor would recommend the boy. Yet this training while growing up preceded and may be distinguished from the sort of learning that came from an ustād. These facts underscore the idea that becoming a disciple to a master was not, as the surface appearance might suggest, the means through which a person learned to play dhol. Rather, it was that important relationship that, once formed, solidified one's status as a dholi. Knowing how to play dhol and being a dholi were different things.

It was not uncommon for a dholi to be in his 30s and well into a professional career before he found a master. Once taken on by a master, the disciple might have to serve him for some time before being taught anything related to dhol repertoire and technique. In fact, the master might teach little in technical knowledge, which the student had instead to get from observing the master whenever he got the opportunity. What the disciple learned from the master might come in several forms. A younger student would learn practical knowledge about being a dholi and moral lessons of character.[15] Indeed, in recalling what he learned from his master, Ghuggi, Garib Dass said he was given the message, "Never do bad works with the dhol. Never cheat anyone through the dhol, nor commit immoral acts in its presence." As Garib Dass relayed this to me, it was as if he was passing down this knowledge, to teach me similarly. He continued mediating the instruction of Ghuggi: "Son, don't do any thuggery or dishonorable deeds; don't lie. If you play the dhol with a true mind, God will cross you over to the eternal life."

An older student might learn, after repeated requests, specific techniques that he could not have learned through osmosis such as complicated classical figures. More enigmatically, he might earn the right to play items, which he essentially taught himself, with the privilege of saying he got them from his master. It was possible in all cases that the disciple learned little, especially if he had little face time with the master. The classical musical practice described by Neuman, wherein a disciple cohabited with the master's family and engaged in long practice sessions, did not apply. Consider again Garib Dass and his master Ghuggi, who lived in faraway Amritsar. We may understand that Garib Dass's opportunities to travel and meet the master were rather few. Masters were not teachers in the sense of instructors, rather they might be thought of as spiritual guides in the sense conveyed by the term *gurū*. The concept of gurū has clear religious overtones, being a spiritual leader. In all, having a master offered more symbolic social value than practical value. Just as, in Punjabi society, one should get married to "be complete," a fully formed "man," it was desirable for a dholi to have a master if he were to be realized. A further paradox is created by the struggle between ideal concept and situational practice. In reality, it was impractical for all dholis to have a master. So, despite the great value invested in the symbol of *ustādī* (the institution of ustād), practical needs might suggest that symbolic was, indeed, only symbolic. In some families obtaining a master was not essential. With the student already in his 30s or 40s, having already learned dhol from one's family or peers and earning an income, the formality of "marriage" to a master was skipped over.

The various dhol-playing qaums had different feelings about who a student should have as a master. In the Mirasi community, I found that the child was apprenticed to his father or an uncle, that is, someone within the immediate family. This arrangement brings into concordance the notion of transmission "from father to son." Jogis and Mahashas also tended to learn from someone at least in the extended family, although not typically from their fathers. An exception, Jogi Ramesh Chand, stated that his master was his father and that he would be master to his own son.[16] In some circles, becoming the disciple of one's father was considered quite improper. The child might be shown things initially by the parent, but he was to learn elsewhere if he was to be considered fully developed. Among the Bazigars, one never had his father as his master, though much informal learning was transmitted down zigzagged lines from uncles and older cousins. According to master Ghuggi's son, his Mahasha community also disallowed sons to become disciples of their fathers.[17] The case was the same in the Bharai family of Dhillon, and a published account corroborates the Bharai custom.[18] In these cases, the father might send the son outside the local community or even outside the ethnic community. Sending the child outside the qaum to learn from one of the traditional *ustād-lok* (e.g., Mirasi, Jogi) was a practical consideration, as they were masters who held status as the traditional musical maestros. But many dholis learned from non-*ustād-lok* such as Bazigars and Mahashas, too.

In these practices, we may again draw an analogy to the institution of (arranged) marriage. The disciple's father would usually approach the ustād—as the father of a bridegroom would do—and suggest the match for his son. If the prospective disciple's father was also a dholi, the prospective master would show deference to the father's eminence: "How could I become the master of *your* son?" The deference works both as a gesture of humility during the process of taking on a disciple and an excuse if the master does not want to accept the disciple. In a similar scenario, Garib Dass of the Bazigars related how a grandson of his Mahasha master once approached him to make him his master. In explaining his declining the invitation, Garib Dass offered the reasoning, "How could my ustād's grandson become my disciple?" In light of Garib Dass's aforementioned reticence to take on disciples, I suspect he was citing this unwritten rule as a respectful way to excuse himself. As was the case here and the case when Garib Dass became the disciple of Ghuggi, a person enamored by a particular master might approach the master on his own (i.e., without the intervention of an older relative). If the match was accepted, a formal initiation ceremony followed. The ceremony varied with the religious beliefs of the community of the master. In Hindu communities, it usually involved the master tying sacred thread (*maulī*) to the disciple's wrist and the disciple making an offering of sweets and cash to the master.[19]

On a Sunday morning in 2004, 8-year-old Gaurav Gill of the Valmiki became a disciple of master Puran. The ceremony, which lasted about 20 minutes, was performed at Gaurav's home. Puran's master, in turn, Tara Chand, was also present, along with Gaurav's parents, his grandmother, the family priest, another disciple of Puran, and I. A small, sacrificial fire of charcoal was made on the floor of the family's sitting room. Behind it was placed an image of the family deity. Master and disciple sat before the fire, their heads covered in piety. A platter nearby contained *kaṛāh parshād* (consecrated semolina pudding). Incense and a small oil lamp were burning. Some candy, also to serve as *parshād* (ritual food-offering, in general), was laid out on a strip of newspaper between the participants and the fire. A bottle of whiskey was placed in the same position, as Valmikis considered liquor to be a valid form of *parshād* as well. The ritual incorporated a *havan*, a sacrificial offering to a deity through fire. The priest began by saluting the fire. He made offerings into the fire of ghee, followed by hard candy (*patāsā*). He instructed the master to take some of the candy in his hands and to wave it over the fire in a circular motion. The pieces were then stuffed into the disciple's mouth. The priest continued, waving his empty hands over the flame and pressing them on the disciple's head. The boy's grandmother gave him the auspicious amount of 51 rupees, which he was instructed to put near the deity's image. Then the master waved his hands over the fire and placed them on the disciple's head. Gesturing to the master, the priest told Gaurav, the disciple, "This is your gurū-jī." Gesturing to the master's own master, he continued, "and this is your dādā gurū-jī, understand?"[20] After the *havan*, Gaurav gave a token gift of ten rupees and, in some cases, a piece of cloth, to each of his elders present. He took their blessings. Like many Punjabi religious rituals, this one was consummated by eating. The *parshād* was distributed among all present, but only after taking some outside, presumably across the way to offer at the Gugga shrine. Finally, the adults consumed salty snacks along with the whiskey.

AIMS OF DHOLIS: FUNCTION VERSUS ART?

In Chapter 2, I enumerated contexts for dhol playing and the sonic structures that accompanied the contexts. The close relationship between most of the forms and their application, along with the forms' minimal variation, suggests that dhol playing was, first and foremost, functional. One chooses a hammer or a wrench to do a job made for a hammer or a wrench. The user of such tools may get pleasure from their material beauty, but that beauty is secondary in value to their value as tools. Such is the nature of (most, historical) dhol playing. The beauty, the aesthetic satisfaction, it provides is found less in the (sonic) object itself and more in the elegance by which the tool—a *tāl*—fulfills its purpose. I am asserting here what I believe to be a reasonable distinction between the functional and the artistic, without denying the ability of functions to be performed artistically or of arts to serve a function. That which I rhetorically frame as sonic art indicates an orientation of the performer toward creating a product intended primarily for aesthetic consumption, whereas a performer with functional goals uses sound to organize daily life, to coordinate physical action, and to communicate in more mundane (direct) ways.

This distinction is not intended to excise aesthetic values from a discussion of dholis but, on the contrary, to locate them along the continuum of behaviors and to locate dholis among the kinds of Punjabi performers. There is art in dhol. Aesthetics are important, and differences in aesthetic values are indices of identity among dholis. How the playing of dholis is intended and received in relation to the poles of function and art is paramount to the understanding of their social identities. The point is all the more important because of the potential for the globally current ("Western," "modern") constructs of music and musician to obscure and confound how we might see dholis if we were to treat them generically as "players of a musical instrument."

Were dholis craftsmen who practiced a craft or were they artists who produced art? Whereas designating them as the latter seems to be an appealing gesture of validation, the evidence of their practices and of the motivations behind those practices suggests that, for most traditional dholis, the craftsman label is more appropriate. Most dholis played for the pragmatic reason of earning a livelihood. Dholis did create art in the broadest sense of aesthetic communication. What they did, however, was missing a criterion attached to the local cultural definition of art. Art in this definition, idealized, is beyond the social structure; it transcends mundane concerns. Dholis could rarely divorce their lives from such mundane concerns. Hence, my reservation about calling them artists does not deny them value; rather, it ensures we do not ignore their existential needs. When dholis' playing was portrayed as art, it was a strategy that temporarily pushed back against social reality. Some players used this strategy to alleviate the constraints on social identity and the status it ascribes. Some listeners used this strategy to remove the distaste of that social reality from the experience. Yet as long as dhol is tied to the notion of hereditary practice, an inborn trait, it cannot achieve the unattached status of idealized art. Dholis, like blacksmiths or cobblers, were craftsmen or artisan specialists with more or less attention to producing beauty within the limitations on their craft imposed by their social position. Most playing was designed by these artisans (dholis) to fulfill a practical or ritual function, through which the performers best negotiated their social value as individuals. Being an artist, while it provided temporary status, was less valuable for securing social capital.

When I refer to the aesthetic behavior of dholis, I refer to behavior motivated by the desire to achieve satisfaction of one's sense of "good effects." To locate this behavior, we can distinguish the less common motivation of producing art, wherein good effects manifest as beauty of form, from the motivation of practical efficacy. In the latter case, the good effects manifest as the dholi's success in correctly completing his function. Such aesthetic concerns had an ethical dimension, in that they related to how well a dholi executed his responsibility for his craft and fulfilled his charge as a service provider. Aesthetic concerns of this nature often related to the clarity and appropriateness of one's playing. Speaking of clarity, good effect was achieved when one's playing supported comprehension of the message. While articulating the basic message, dholis made aesthetic choices of how to shape musical texture. Such might take the form of timbral differentiation, achieved through decisions about where to strike the drum (on its treble or bass head or elsewhere, separately or in combination), how to strike the drum (e.g., with a closed or open sound), and the relative volume of strokes within a pattern.

To address the question of appropriateness, one might consider, for example, not only when dhol should be played (and, following, what should be played) but also when dhol should not be played. A pre-Partition account notes that there was a specific dhol rhythm meant to be played on occasions of grief or death (Harjit Singh 1949, 31). More recently, dholis in Multan (Pakistan) continued to play during the solemn month of Muharram (Wolf 2000, 104).[21] Muhammad Boota, a dholi from Pakistan, made several references to a rhythm played on the occasion of death. His tacit refusal to play it during our meeting made unambiguous its sorrowful association.[22] Nevertheless, I found that recent Indian dholis did not support the use of dhol to accompany sadness and thought that dhol was appropriate only on joyous occasions. I was at Garib Dass's home on Christmas and at one point Garib Dass instructed me to practice dhol. Before asking me to play, however, the master cautiously inquired whether Christmas (which, he admitted, was a holiday about which he knew little) was a happy occasion. He had seen images of the Crucifixion and, not knowing exactly how they related to Christmas, suspected that it might be a time of grief. He said that if Christmas was not a happy occasion, he would not compel me to play. On another occasion, I asked Garib Dass whether it was possible to play dhol at a funeral. Garib Dass explained that dhol was entirely inappropriate to play at a funeral, because it was a sad occasion. Playing the devil's advocate, I cited the fact that several dholis had played at the funeral of master Bhana Ram. Garib Dass reasoned that such an event was an exception in that Bhana Ram had lived a long and full life and that, moreover, he was a dholi. By way of another example, I expressed to a Valmiki priest my observation one day that the usual playing at his Gugga *māṛī* had ceased. The priest explained that a young girl in the neighborhood had recently died, and hence there was a temporary moratorium on dhol in that locality.[23] That there was no universal consensus about such behavior indicates that the decision of when to play is a matter of local or personal aesthetic values.

I have focused on the end of the continuum of dhol playing where art is subordinate to function and which best represents what I have been calling the Dhol World. Yet there were exceptional contexts, some of which I described in Chapter 2, when playing could be purely aesthetic. Such contexts, however, usually occurred outside professional situations, in the personal rather than the public sphere, when the dholi was free to play around. In a professional (public) context, too, an individual dholi might craft his performance in more subtle aesthetic ways, such as by including difficult ornamental fills. Such gestures, however, were likely to go unappreciated by almost anyone except other dholis. Indeed, on most occasions, they would go unnoticed, serving largely to occupy the player himself and to relieve the monotony of his task. In pitting function versus art, my point has not been to mutually exclude the two notions in the identity of dholis. Rather, it is to see that practical concerns took such precedence as to limit artistic expressions. Nonfunctional playing, which prioritizes beauty-centered art, was frowned on insofar as it appeared to weaken the prescribed effect of the playing. It came into conflict with the ethical values of the Dhol World that related to clarity and appropriateness. Balancing these concerns, for fulfilling one's expected functional purpose and offering artistic value, played out with respect to individual dhol players' identities insofar as they depended on strategizing their socioeconomic position.

STYLE AS ETHNIC AND PERSONAL IDENTITY

When I first visited the market of Jogi dholis in Ludhiana, the dholis in the first office asked me to demonstrate my playing, which I obliged before continuing our conversation. Afterward, I met dholi Ravi Malhotra in his office a few doors away. He had heard my earlier playing and asked where I was visiting from. When I told him I lived in Chandigarh, he said, with a feeling of validation, that he knew from my playing that someone from Chandigarh had come.[24] The Ludhiana dholis asserted that there was something distinctive as well in their style of playing but could not explain, merely referring to it as "special."

The ethnic lines along which dholis were divided socially in their practice of the profession were reinforced by and signified through the content of what they played, preferences about dhol construction, methods for going about their business, and countless other attitudes and practices. In many cases, attitudes and practices developed as a consequence of dholis' tendency to develop near exclusively within the subcultural formation of their particular communities. In their discourse, however, it emerged that they were not entirely unconscious of how they had been shaped by their cultural environment; they did not always assume that their way of dhol was *the* way. Many dholis were aware that something in their practices made their community of dholis different from others participating in the occupation. Ravi Malhotra's inference that I learned in Chandigarh correlated to the fact that a community of Bazigars (from whom I took my influence) dominated that city's dhol-playing population. In other words, Malhotra made a deduction about place that was based on a higher order of difference: ethnicity. If place-based trends were discernible, nevertheless playing diverged between dhol-playing qaums within the same place and converged between dholis of the same qaum across different places. Dholis spoke of how "we" do things, wherein "we" referred not to the local population of dholis, but to their qaum. The style I had played was a Bazigar style and the knowledge that Bazigar dholis were well represented in Chandigarh suggested the place. Such were the correlations between practice and qaum that not only can we say that a dholi's qaum was a passive influence on his practice, but also that dholis actively used their practice to represent their membership in a qaum.

Active signification of identity was not limited, however, to drawing lines at the ethnic-group level. Individual dholis also represented themselves in distinction from others in their qaum, in which case they spoke not of "we" but of "I." In doing so, they might associate with individual values shared by dholis belonging to other qaums, effectively transcending the lines of ethnicity. Thus, on one level, the differences that remained consistent within qaums made it possible to identify the qaum to which a dholi was likely to belong. At another level, the individual identification of dholis with moral or aesthetic values beyond his environment suggests another way of configuring traditions with respect to dhol. All this instantiates the richness of Punjab's dhol playing as a network of coexisting and ever-developing traditions at the intersections of place, practice-based ethnic identities, and value-based individual identities.

Malhotra's deduction of my origin, based on sound alone, shows the significance of stylistic differences in marking location-based, ethnic, and individual identity. How might we observe these differences? The phenomenon that I called swing (Chapter 2) was one aspect of playing that could mark style. Differences in swing between players, however, such as differences in accent between speakers, can be difficult to hear without practice in listening.[25] Other markers of difference manifested in the slight variants of a rhythm that different dholis played, yet analysis of these minutiae is beyond the limits of the present discussion. As a broadly accessible illustration of stylistic difference, therefore, we may consider degree of ornamentation as a marker of different dholis' identities.

Ornamentation style correlated with gestures of more or less aesthetic playing and what such gestures said about players' position in relation to the earlier-discussed poles of artistic and functional. In particular, large amounts of ornamentation correlated in sound to classical music and its association with the Art Field. In India, Mirasi dholis, drawing on the historical involvement with classical music in their community, tended to be most appreciative of such ornamental playing—though many a Mirasi serving in the humble role of shrine drummers played simply, too. Communities historically related to Mirasis, the Jogi and Mahasha, were the next most inclined toward classical figures. A Jogi from the Ludhiana group, Madan Lal, had an exceedingly ornamented playing style, and his son, Dana, played ornamental variations that were wholly original. The technical masters Ghuggi and Harbans Lal Jogi created a space for a similar ideal among some Mahasha dholis. Harbans Lal fell at the extreme of the spectrum, and cannot be considered entirely representative. He bragged that drummers in his family knew how to count *tāl* on their fingers in the manner of classical musicians, and he claimed that other dholis did not have that knowledge. More typical Mahasha dholis were less oriented to classical figures in their everyday playing, although, like the Jogi, they often broke up rhythms with ornamental fills. Kala Takhi of Jalandhar could hardly play a single cycle of rhythm without breaking it up with *tirakaṭs*. Harbans Lal Kaku, another distinguished Mahasha master, impressed on me that while plain, everyday playing was called for under normal circumstances, "Learning classical is essential." He offered two reasons. The first was that "After learning classical, folk is easy." The second reason was that if the dholi found himself at a mahifal, someone might ask him to play some classical *tāls*. "If you play *tinn tāl* [a classical tāl] it will seem that you've learned something, but if you play dhamāl [a folk rhythm], that is just child's play."[26]

By contrast, Bazigars believed that ornamentation dangerously obscured the efficacy of the rhythm, which should be articulated transparently. When I visited Mali Ram in his Queens, New York, home in 2018, the senior master felt no urge to perform with any ornamentation. He did, however, think it was important to show me rare rhythms, such as one for the Mother Goddess. He noted that people did not play that one anymore, and that, indeed, most did not know how. Thus, his emphasis was on knowledge of rhythms, not the ability to interpolate ornamental figures. He poked fun at Jogi dholis for playing too much classical. Lumping Mirasis in the same category, Mali Ram related an anecdote of a job he shared with a dholi of that community. He smiled mischievously as he relayed how he had quizzed the Mirasi, asking what other *tāls* he knew; the Mirasi did not know any. Articulating the same Bazigar position, Garib Dass characterized his playing style as "pure folk" (using the English words). He believed that the dhol tradition, a desī or "native" practice, had become muddled through the propagation of exterior musical material, citing for an example the possible influence of musicians of the Mumbai film-music studios. Like Mali Ram, he had anecdotes that supported his position. When he first went to Republic Day in New Delhi, among other dholis who came at that time, it was in vogue to play a lot of classical gestures. Garib Dass initially felt insecure about his playing. The director Bhag Singh, however, reassured him, saying that he should just play in his folk style. Further, the fashion-following players were allegedly reprimanded by the likes of bhangra dance master Harbhajan Singh to play "real folk *tāls* and *toṛās*."[27] Garib Dass's aesthetics were thus validated by two of the most authoritative figures in Punjabi dance. Another anecdote involved a performance in Bombay that included some of the dancers from the PEPSU team. They asked the dholi present, Harbans Lal Jogi, to play for their dance, to which he responded with some "jazzed-up stuff."[28] The dancers became irked and told the dholi to play the rhythm in straightforward desī style.[29] It is notable that in both these stories the dancers' preferences underlined Garib Dass's position. The value of unadorned dhol lay in its functional application as dance accompaniment. In essence, Garib Dass shunned flashiness in favor of appropriateness. He said that, on request, he would play ornate fills and classical-style *tāls*, and I saw him do so many times in mahifal settings. But when accompanying a dance performance, he abstained from any ornamentation, feeling that it would detract from the integrity of the dance and his professional role. In my lessons with him, he occasionally indulged my interest in learning fills, but if he caught me practicing them he would request that I abandon them in favor of practicing the accuracy and aesthetic nuances of the basic rhythms.

Minimal ornamentation was the approach of dholis from all the qaums whose work centered on the rural, functional applications, whether they were a Valmiki at a Gugga shrine or a Rai Sikh playing for jhummar. An elder of the Bharai village drummer community, Majid Ali, forcefully expressed appreciation of desī style and its approach of playing pure rhythm to match action.[30] He was saying this, however, in contradiction to the fact that his young nephews, brought up in the Mirasi-dominated city of Malerkotla, were keen on classical gestures. This was a pattern: the younger generation, regardless of community, tended to value ornamentation more than the older generation. Elder Bazigar dholi Dev Raj of village Bad Majra, like his cousins, preferred the approach of more rhythms and less ornamentation. He acknowledged that his sons played with a lot of "fast stuff," but he did not disparage them for it, reasoning instead that "classical came from folk."

The clash of stylistic perspectives was revealed once when I introduced a student of another tradition to Garib Dass. On a long train ride to Chandigarh, a Canadian friend, Jag Poonia, and I had an excited debate about the value of classical figures in dhol playing. Jag was a student of Vancouver's Rayman Bhullar, who was the disciple of a Mirasi. Like many young players in the diaspora, Jag interpreted the playing of classical figures as a mark of excellence to be aspired to, while I, under the tutelage of Garib Dass, did not understand them to be important. Jag felt confident, however, that, once he met Garib Dass, the renowned master would dazzle him with such play. When we reached Garib Dass and put the debate to him, both Jag and I were surprised by the decisiveness of the master's response. He granted that classical music is good, and tabla playing is good. But, he opined, classical figures (as one finds in tabla playing) were not relevant to dhol, which should be approached on its own terms. "Dhol is dhol, and tabla is tabla."[31]

The most dramatic difference in ornamentation style appeared between Pakistani and Indian dholis broadly. Even granting that some dholi communities and some individuals in India leaned toward the classical end of the spectrum, Indian dholis as a whole represented desī approaches to style and intent. I suspect a correlation between such folk style and historical style; that is, folk styles are the older styles of playing. This statement is not invalidated by the fact that much content in the Indian dholis' repertoire is "new" (i.e., created since Partition). Intellectual honesty, however, demands some reservation. I have not surveyed dhol in Pakistan with the breadth that I have in India. The unanswered question concerns the extent, historically, to which a classical style may have been in vogue in pre-Partition Punjab. Still, I believe it is reasonable to say that, by the start of the twenty-first century, dhol in Pakistan had become more classical-oriented.

The difference related to the contemporary role and image of the dholi in each country's society. The folk arts have been valued in Indian Punjab, and for their role in them, dholis gained prestige. As I shall elaborate in the next chapter, Punjabi identity in the Indian state context has transvalued folk life;

products of the common people have shifted from low status to a place of pride. By contrast, while Pakistan does have its intelligentsia that subscribes to a folk heritage ideology, a state ethos has rejected folk forms as a sort of backwardness. In that environment, the earthy quality of Punjabi (regional) identity has been comparatively suppressed by the project of looking forward through the lens of "Pakistan," a country in which a unified nation of Muslims might flourish on the joint basis of state and religion. So, despite the contentious relationship between secular music (*mūsīqa*) and Islam, art music's connotations of sophistication and education are arguably more compatible with the perception of Islam as an enlightened faith.

In Pakistan's atmosphere of devaluation of folk heritage, dholis did not receive the same kind of endearment and celebration as India's players. Pakistani dholis effected their own transvaluation of tradition. Appealing to the value of art music, they "elevated" dhol through adopting classical characteristics and aesthetics. On the Pakistani spectrum, the Bharai, those drummers most connected to village-based traditions, were most oriented toward folk aesthetics. Wolf relates how other drummers, including those I have referred to as Shaikh, disparaged Bharai dholis for their perceived lack of sophistication. Even while Shaikh dholis accompanied traditional dances, they interspersed improvisation around classical *tāl* frameworks (Wolf 2014, 31). I argued in Chapter 3 that Shaikh dholis negotiated their predisposition to art musical structures in the context of Sufi worship. Perhaps to mediate the conflict between Islam and musicking "for its own sake," the newer generations of Shaikh dholis presented their artistic playing, in the more liberal Islam of Sufism, as a tribute to the Divinity. Moreover, the Shaikh, composed of individuals from historically low-status qaums, could raise their status by hitching their wagon to the value of art, rather than lowering it by engaging (solely) in the low-prestige work of folk musicians. A key figure in this movement, Pappu Sain, made no pretense about the conscious act of change. He acknowledged that the original purpose of dhol was to accompany things like bhangra dance. But "We have put tabla inside the dhol" (Wolf 2014, 163). Even the Bharais of Pakistan had inclinations toward classical values. Muhammad Boota, who thought about the purpose of dhol playing as functional message sending (see Chapter 2), was, by virtue of his nearly three decades of living in the United States, absent during much of the trend of classicization that took place in Pakistan. Nevertheless, he, too, put a certain emphasis on sophistication. He caricatured what he perceived to be the playing style of "our Indian brothers." He demonstrated versions of rhythms and a *toṛā* as he believed Indian dholis played (though I suspect his information was based on what he had heard from Indian dholis in the diaspora). In actuality, few dholis in India play such simple forms as he claimed. He then proceeded to play "our" (Pakistani) versions of rhythms, which were more complex. Although this broad preference for classical style marked a difference between Pakistani and Indian dholis, I believe a similar logic of giving preference to art musical characteristics is currently driving a trend among Indian dholis of younger generations as they negotiate the value of being seen as purveyors of an artistically valuable product against the value of representing a desī social subject.

PREFERENCES AND ATTITUDES

"Taste . . . classifies the classifier" (Bourdieu 1984, 6). So it was that differences in dholi identity were also evident in players' individual or subculture-based tastes, the expression of which finely distinguished them as individuals or members of subcultural formations. They expressed taste in their attitudes to treatment of the instrument-object, its construction, and decorum during the act of playing.

Some dholis regarded dhol playing as a spiritual act and others preferred to see it as a secular activity. Valmikis, whose playing centered on the worship of Gugga Pir, and traditional Bharais of India, who remembered their role as servants of Sakhi Sarvar, were examples of those who treated the dhol as an object of religious practice. Yet even professionals like Garib Dass, who mostly played the instrument to accompany dance, invested the dhol with spiritual significance. We saw this in the earlier-described treatment of the dhol as a sacred object to which Garib Dass, a Hindu, prayed before playing. Muhammad Boota, a Muslim, took exception when I told him that Garib Dass regarded the dhol as a sort of deity. It conflicted with his belief in Allah as the singular divinity. Boota did, however, believe that it behooved a dholi to practice a sort of clean living, including abstaining from drinking and smoking and maintaining personal hygiene while in his role. He compared it to the ritual ablutions one undertakes before entering a mosque. Yet this, too, put him at odds with the Sain dholis of Pakistan who facilitate Sufi devotion. Boota said that dhol is mostly for entertainment, that he played to make others dance. He disapproved both of Sain dholis making a show of themselves and their apparent *faqīr* lifestyle, popularly associated with a propensity to intoxication and a lack of productive contribution to society. Speaking again to a subtle spiritual dimension of dhol playing, Mali Ram stated that one should first play dhamāl, a rhythm with spiritual connotations, when beginning a playing session. Boota, by contrast, dismissed the notion of any such opening supplications as superstition.

Similarly, Muslim dholis appeared to handle their instruments with less coddling than their Hindu counterparts. Concerning aesthetics, while most Hindu dholis respected the dhol object by maintaining its appearance in the fashion of a dignified being, the Mahasha notably transgressed such a sensibility. Professionals from that qaum painted their names and even their phone numbers on their instruments. The dhol of Dev Raj of Amritsar included the phrase "jai mātā dī" ("praise to the Mother Goddess") and the religious swastika symbol. The practice dated at least to the early post-Partition period, presumably as a means of advertisement. Charan Das can be seen in the film *Jija Ji* (1961) with his name painted on his dhol in Arabic script. Writing on a dhol was a sure way to identify its player as a Mahasha.

The physical features of the setup of a dhol were a fairly reliable indicator of the qaum affiliations of its player, though at times they simply reflected his economic status. These features reflected aesthetic values that cohered within qaums. Therefore, they frequently correlated to values along the classical-folk continuum.

The two methods of attaching drumheads, by rope-lacing or by bolts, allowed for variations in setup. Each had its merits and adherents and related to whether the dholi used natural skin heads or plastic ones.

One variation, the preference of most Indian dhol masters of late, entailed bolts on the treble side and rope on the bass side. Most dholis, further, selected a plastic head for the treble while retaining a skin head for the bass. The rationale for this setup was that bolts should be used on the treble head because they make it possible to fix its tuning at a more or less satisfactory level. This conveniently eliminated the need to tune the head before each playing session, provided one was satisfied with an approximate pitch. In contrast, the bolt system, which required using a wrench, made it less convenient to quickly adjust pitch immediately before or during a performance, and so it was useful only to those dholis (e.g., Bazigar) who did not concern themselves with very fine tuning. As for the bass side, bolts were not significantly advantageous because tuning that head is not necessary; rather, one needed only to roughly tighten the head to obtain adequate bass resonance. Players with this setup pulled on the tightening rings attached to the rope lacing to ready the bass head.

The second variation also had its merits: a bolted bass side and roped treble side. The philosophy behind that setup was that the treble side of a dhol *did* need to be fine-tuned and, in some cases, even matched to a given performing circumstance, which was most conveniently done through quick adjustment by hand. One can see why some players, such as those with inclinations toward classical music (compare the tuning method of the tabla), including Jogis and Mirasis, could not accept the relatively crude bolt-tuned treble head.

A third variation was the original method of roping both sides; reasons similar to those above can be argued.

And the fourth variation, the least common, was the use of bolts on both sides. Although it was in some ways the most convenient setup, dholis opposed to it thought it showed too little regard for aesthetic considerations. It suggested neither concern for fine tuning of the treble nor a tasteful resonance of the bass. Moreover, most dholis associated the tightening rope and its manipulation with the beautiful material form of the dhol and with good etiquette of practice. Because the double-bolted setup negated those aesthetic concerns, it signified a debased appreciation of traditional values. The double-bolted setup was found among two extremes. Some dholis did not appear to care at all for the art of dhol, and just used the instrument for solicitation. Then there were individuals like Samim Muhammad, a classically trained Mirasi whose mindset was so oriented toward practicality and rejection of formal aesthetics that he even took to playing a transparent fiberglass dhol.

Skin and ropes on both sides of the dhol, the historical form, represented the loftiest aesthetics of those dholis who valued the constructs of both art and tradition.

The sticks dholis used were also indicators. A homemade ḍaggā, in the Bazigar community, was carved from the naturally bent branches of the *kikkar* tree (prickly acacia, *Acacia nilotica*). It was small with a rustic appearance; one could identify a Bazigar dholi by this stick. Jogis liked thinner, more refined-looking ḍaggās made of straight pieces of *kaū* (*Olea ferruginea*). Their makers created the bend by soaking the wood in water, bending it, and temporarily holding the bend in place with twine until it dried. Mirasis of Ludhiana district thought cane, rather than wood, was the best material. There were other variations. Most ḍaggās of Indian dholis formed the shape of straight lines intersecting at a bend of around 45 degrees, a shorter portion constituting the striking surface. Ḍaggās having more rounded, crook-shaped ends were common among Pakistani dholis.[32] The differences in material related to community habits and environment, and the differences in shape related to different ways of striking the beater on the instrument, according to the aesthetics of play.

Differences in aesthetics were more evident in the case of the treble switch, *chaṭī*. Most Indian dholis preferred cane (*baint*) for its flexibility and strength. The cane was split to create a thin, flat strip. Recent generations in Pakistan, however, used stiff, rodlike *chaṭī*s made of *kaū*. Saghir Ali, of the new school, insisted that such a *chaṭī* was necessary to achieve his aggressive, precise classical style.[33] Muhammad Boota, a time capsule of Pakistani dhol history, used a cane *chaṭī*, thicker than the Indian style yet similar in other respects. A few Indian dholis had begun to use a plastic store-bought *chaṭī*, heavy and rod-shaped like the new Pakistani one, yet still flexible. They were in fact sticks manufactured for the *tāshā* kettledrum. Like his brothers in Pakistan, Samim Muhammad of Jarg claimed they helped him achieve a hard attack.[34] A young Bharai from nearby Malerkotla cited its imperviousness to breakage.[35]

I observed various *chaṭī* size preferences ranging in length from around 12 inches to 22 inches. Bal Kishan of Jammu's Jogi community used a very short *chaṭī*, which had to be grasped at the end,[36] as indeed did Boota, whose family origins lay nearby. The Jogis in far off Ludhiana also preferred smaller *chaṭī*s. Mahasha dholis used some of the longest and widest, which translated to a heavier style of playing. Mirasis also seemed to prefer the longer *chaṭī*s, while the Bazigars' were generally shorter. As one would expect, the shorter ones afforded a lighter sound. Garib Dass used them to attain the sweeter sound of dhol that was once associated with the jungles of western Punjab. I heard dholis from other traditions, however, complain that Garib Dass's style was not assertive enough.

The differences extend to many more than those enumerated here, ranging from the ingredients dholis use to create the *masālā* spread inside their dhols to which rhythm a young dholi learned first. The important takeaway is that dholis' identities, great and small, imbricated in concentric circles or spilling out across boundaries, found representation in endless, though sometimes only minutely expressed, ways. And yet, all were more specific than, and in local contexts took priority over, the identity of being Punjabi.

6 DHOL PLAYERS IN A NEW WORLD

In the early twentieth century, the practice of Hindustani classical music was liberalized. Music making became, as Neuman describes its transformation, "one of the social graces of the bourgeoisie" (1990, 20). Reframed as heritage that transcended social boundaries (19), Hindustani music changed with respect to who acquired the ability to play it and, in tandem, the avenues through which it was learned. High-caste Hindus apprenticed with Muslim hereditary masters (20) and, with the expansion of this phenomenon, educational institutions supported learning by lay individuals (Katz 2017, 125–127).

In the early twenty-first century, dhol playing is similarly becoming the common purview of all, yet with a different valence. In Chapter 1, I differentiated identification in relation to a sovereign territorial entity, a state, and identification in relation to a superethnic population group, a nation. In accord with this formulation, I suggest that Hindustani music became in its association a *state* music more so than a *national* one. When the hereditary musicians of particular qaums lost their entitlement as the exclusive purveyors of Hindustani music, that music transcended ethnic boundaries. Indians, understood as citizens of the republic (India), acquired the right to perform it as cohabitants of the state, not as people necessarily composing a superethnic group ("Indians"). An obvious problem with this interpretation lies with the fact that India may be viewed as a nation-state; to various degrees, "Indians" identifies a nation of people perceived to be the basis of the state. Yet, by the same token, Hindustani music as music of India (rather than of Indians) has opened it to people without any ties to even the broadest interpretation of Indian nationality. The salient distinction I wish to make with respect to dhol's comparable liberalization is that it is occurring in the absence of the notion of a legitimizing state. Conferment of the right to perform it is delineated with respect to the national (superethnic) group, Punjabis.

In tandem with dhol playing's stronger connection to nation, and that which also distinguishes its liberalization from Hindustani music, is its situation as folk rather than classical music. This is not to imply that folk music may not be state music. Both classical and folk musics might be coopted by the state, and, as Fiol states, "Folklorization and classicization have been the twin processes of modernist reform in modern India" (2017, 72). The process for coopting either differs, however, according to the ways art music (classical) and folk music are conceptualized in a modern discourse that blends an indigenous distinction between a transregional canon (*mārga*) and a localized vernacular (desī) and the European colonial distinction of classical versus folk or popular (see Allen 1998, 23–25). For the art music construct, one is encouraged to disregard ethnicity, supposed to be a vulgar barrier to the transcendence of artistic appreciation. The liberalization of Hindustani music reformed what might be construed as its backward characteristic of limitation by ethnicity. In the folk-music construct, the formula is reversed. Folk embraces the vulgar, which is transvalued as something positive. It represents the perceived essential traits of a people, the ethnic nation. The architects of folk-music study, including the Briton Cecil Sharp and his cohort, who established the Folk-Song Society, rejected art music, not on aesthetic grounds but rather for its perceived distance from the supposed unadulterated or original essence embodied by unlettered common people of specific "racial" groups (Sharp 1907, 1–4).[1] They thought that art music, which valued transcending society in favor of supposed universal beauty, muted particular national expressions and so was antithetical to the preservation of nations in the face of modernity's changes. The academic folklorists' ideology thus gave value to formerly low-status music for an authenticity conceived foremost as a reflection or expression of ethnic identity. An implication is that conceptualizing folk, rather than disregarding ethnicity, must always emphasize it. Doing so is not necessarily at odds, however, with the reformist goals of a state such as India, where regions, especially through their mapping to languages, are correlated to ethnicity. Both the classical—the broadly canonical or *mārga*—and the folk—conceived as regional or desī—collude to form the vision of a pluralistic yet unified entity. I distinguish, therefore, the state-centered notion of Punjabi music as a regional music (inclusive of dhol) and a nation-centered notion of dhol as cultural property of a people not limited to the state.

Fiol's study on drumming in the Indian Himalayas, including a regional version of dhol, offers a comparative case by which to parse similarities and differences in the development of Punjabi dholis' framing as folk musicians. Addressing folklorization as parallel to the changes that occurred in classical music in India, Fiol asks how the folk performer has his or her musical tradition "converted into understandings of a generic folk heritage accessible to anyone in the society" (2017, 4). Fiol explains the transvaluation of "folk," noting that, in the early twentieth century, labeling ethnic performers as "folk" was pejorative (4). At midcentury, however, the "folk music" concept was revalued in the frame of leftist politics as "music for the masses" (57). India followed the pattern of many postcolonial states, in which music producers sought to include the common people of the state through sounds representative of them both essentially and broadly.[2] Fiol found, however, that studio producers took advantage of selected sounds of Himalayan regional music for this purpose without, however, including the low-status traditional musicians (the Shilpkars) in their productions (2017, 106). Visual representations of folk ethos, as in music videos, did include the images of traditional drummers, but the musicians only pantomimed the sounds that had been prerecorded by others on genteel instruments (127). I observe similar phenomena with respect to Punjab's dholis, yet I also observe a greater flourishing of Punjabi dhol itself, as opposed to its musical forms, in the hands of both traditional and lay performers. I attribute the flourishing to a higher profile of Punjabis as a nation. Fiol is writing about regional musicians in relation to a state (India). Transposing his question from state to nation, I find it insightful for thinking about how the construction of Punjabi dhol as generic folk heritage could situate its new players as purveyors of a valued product while, to a degree, protecting them from the devalued aspects of the identities of its historical players. Although also coopted as folklorized music within India, Punjabi dhol as folk music is poised to effectively represent Punjabis, a superethnic nation, in the absence of a Punjabi state.

The liberalization of dhol has expanded access to individuals beyond an exclusive set and has simultaneously maintained folk authenticity by limiting it to a nation—albeit a reformed one. The qaums of traditional dholis were the nations, in a sense, to which the dhol traditions previously belonged. The close genetic descent of their members did much to bind them. What happens, however, when the sharing of broad cultural formation, of similar lifestyles and habits among people of a place, constitutes the idea of nation? Punjabi nationalism emphasizes regional origin and certain broad cultural features over narrow descent in the construction of ethnic boundaries, deemphasizing the boundaries of qaum. This, to reiterate, does not negate ethnicity but rather redraws its boundaries according to a broader set. Retaining ethnicity is important here to retain the valued formula of folk authenticity.

According to the logic of Punjabi nationalism, a Jatt may feel entitled to (all) things of Punjab and to occupy the space of authenticity by virtue of his nationality. The connection between dhol and the Punjab region, that enfranchising concept, offers admission to dhol playing in a special way denied, for example, non-Punjabi Indians. Still, whereas through this view a Jatt (using the example) may feel entitled to dhol as a Punjabi, a smaller group nevertheless excludes him, also based on their concept of national identity, that of a qaum. Thus, we find competing ontologies of authenticity, both of which are founded in ethnic essentialism but that differ in their bases. One, the minoritarian, finds its basis on inheritance conferred by descent. The other, majoritarian, is based on (historical) cohabitation of region.[3]

The following account of dhol in diaspora contributes to the argument that the latter ontology, that of the Punjabi (folk) nation, cleared the ground for the liberalization of dhol through its extension to a broader, albeit nonetheless ethnically based, group. It brings together the phenomena that facilitated the development of the dhol outside Punjab. The phenomena were the divergent cultural landscape and social composition of diaspora communities, an earlier begun process of opening professional musical performance to lay Punjabis, the greater importance of dhol in the popular music that functioned to connect diaspora Punjabis and residencies abroad by traditional dholis. These phenomena gave birth to an unprecedentedly large population of lay dhol players who have legitimized seeing dhol as the common heritage of members of a global Punjabi nation.

LIFE IN THE DIASPORA

In what sense is being in the diaspora—in Punjabi communities outside the land of Punjab—like being in Punjab? The answer depends on the specific place as well as the time. Walking among the crowds of some half a million mostly Punjabi people at the Visakhi celebration in Surrey (British Columbia) in the late 2010s, it was easy for me to forget I was *not* in Punjab. Recent immigrants from Punjab could slip into life in Surrey without missing a beat. When Garib Dass's grandson, Jass, moved to Surrey in 2019, he remarked that it was "just like Chandigarh"—just like his hometown.[4] Canada did not present the shock of something different.

Because of the increasing alignment of Punjabi lifestyles both inside and outside Punjab, the Punjabi individual may perceive a common stratum of Punjabi culture operating both at home and in the diaspora, which buffers feelings of estrangement and, indeed, challenges the continued usefulness of such a spatial dichotomy. This has not always been the case. Narrators of the bhangra music scene of the 1980s–1990s in Britain emphasize, for example, the feelings of difference and alienation expressed in song lyrics (Kalra 2000). The sense now, however, that Punjabi diaspora sites are more developed in their Punjabi character and that lifestyles in Punjab are more connected to those in the West contributes to a sense that Punjabis are less divided by their geographic positions and more a part of a global Punjabi community. Still, the uneven patterns and unequal effects of migration force us to consider the continuing social differences that affect how Punjabi culture operates in diaspora spaces.

Consider first the early experiences of migration, such as the case of Punjabi men in early-twentieth-century California. In stark contrast to the homeland-diaspora networks maintained today, these men had essentially left Punjab behind them. Subject to prohibitive immigration laws (which did not allow Indian wives and children to immigrate) and economic necessity, they were compelled to abandon families in Punjab, to marry Mexican women, and to start new families (Leonard 1992, 62–66). After World War II, Punjabi men also migrated alone to labor in factories in the United Kingdom. Expecting to return to Punjab after earning money in the former British Empire, these men often led lives of minimal engagement with the local culture.

With the second wave of migration in the mid-twentieth century, the character of the emigrant community changed. Communities developed more cohesively as emigrants found the opportunity to bring family members—women and children—to live with them. With the idea of staying came the need to reproduce culture and community life within the confines of a different society.

The third act of this migration story featured the children of immigrants born in the diaspora. Children born in diaspora again changed the community's relationship with Punjabi heritage. Parents tried to raise their children as they would in Punjab while the children often found it challenging and unhelpful to divide Punjabi culture from English culture. Still, they were subject to the dominant discourse that, as Baumann found in his study of 1980s London, "equates culture with community and indeed ethnic identity" (1996, 97). Second-generation Punjabi immigrants supposed themselves to be heirs to two discrete cultures, and they were ascribed the burden of negotiating the identities associated with each one. Reading the history of 1980s–1990s diaspora Punjabi popular music as a cultural text, I have argued that the effort to negotiate identity through sound resulted in a juxtaposition of sonic indices. The explicit presentation of hybridization, syncretism, or fusion not only depended on recognizing essentialized indices of cultural identity but also, perhaps, reinforced the associations between the sounds and cultural identities (Schreffler 2012b). One had only to add the sound of *tūmbī* (discussion to follow) to a hip-hop groove to tell listeners that, although the music was informed by Western taste, it was nevertheless Punjabi. In environments outside Punjab, such intensely essentialized signs take on greater importance as representatives of Punjabiness than they do in the local society of Punjab.

Punjabi emigrants of recent decades experience migration differently from their forbears. With rapid communication, transportation, and mass-media distribution, the emigrant can keep close touch with Punjab or frequently travel back there. Yet the weighted importance of certain signs remains, such as the pursuit of dhol for its value as embodied Punjabiness. This pursuit entails bending the social rules of traditional Punjabi society to expand access to dhol.

ANTECEDENTS TO THE DIASPORA DHOL PHENOMENON

Dhol playing in the diaspora developed through the advent of lay, nonminority individuals into the cultural space earlier occupied by traditional dholis. The transgression or dissolution of ethnic boundaries in the musical performance sphere had a precedent in the folk revival that began in the middle of the twentieth century in the Mediated Field. Such boundary crossing worked both in the direction of proscribed performers' identities becoming cleansed for mainstream consumption and in the direction of mainstream subjects gaining the ability to perform without becoming tainted by the act of performance.

An exemplar of the first direction of boundary crossing is Lal Chand Yamla Jatt, who was born in western Punjab to a Hindu Chamar family in the first decade of the twentieth century. His family's practice of music developed in the ghetto that sprang up from the Jawaharnagar refugee camp. By the 1950s, Lal Chand had recorded many compositions in a style that synthesized the rustic timbres of traditional ballad singers' vocals and plucked lute—modified as the one-stringed *tūmbī*—with a concise popular song format. Lal Chand was his name of address, which omits his caste-clan surname. "Yamla Jatt" (meaning "the crafty Jatt") was his adopted stage name, a reference to the musical film *Yamla Jat* (1940). What was the effect of his choice of name? It is unlikely that all listeners hearing Lal Chand's voice on record assumed he was a Jatt, and yet the name obscured his outcaste identity, minimizing its potential harm to his appeal. As Stokes writes, media industries, to sell their product to a broad base of consumers, characteristically promote "disintegration of history and authenticity" (1994, 21). The new, Mediated Field of Punjabi music had created an environment where one's ethnic identity was more flexible than it had been.

A prior cited exemplar of a figure transgressing boundaries in the other direction was Surinder Kaur. Her career engaged the repertoire of folklorized *lok gīt* or "folk songs" that could represent Punjabi heritage in an idealized form. Surinder Kaur was born into a landowning family of religious Jatt Sikhs who did not approve of singing. Her uncle said that singing was the work of Kanjars (a qaum associated with prostitution and dancing-girls) and that girls of *sardar* (landowner) families do not sing. Her parents said, "Good girls sing only kirtan [Sikh hymns]."[5] Yet she persisted, first studying classical vocal music during an era when laywomen had newly acquired access and then moving on to singing in the film industry. In settling on the revived *lok gīt*, Surinder Kaur may have been successful not despite her nontraditional social position but rather because of it. Her repertoire, partly drawn from the Amateur Field, was not associated exclusively with proscribed minority communities. Indeed, being a minority woman might have limited her acceptance by mainstream audiences who understood this repertoire to be part of their common heritage and preferred the consonance of one of their own voicing it. It was Surinder Kaur's performance within the Professional Field that would have created conflict, and so she had to negotiate the stigma of public performance by avoiding material and minimizing performance contexts that evoked the traditional professionals. The carefully maintained image of Surinder Kaur was an example of the new option of being a performer while maintaining one's respectability. And mainstream Punjabis had in Surinder Kaur a performer of their own social class who represented them through their folk heritage.

The activity of such lay singers in a commercial format was the precedent for the Punjabi popular musicians who emerged in the late 1960s in Punjabi diaspora communities in the United Kingdom, who initially modeled their sound on recorded *lok gīt*. Unlike bands in Punjab, however, British bands also needed laypersons to play the instruments. Their performance initially included nonfolk instruments, suggesting an easier transition. Electronic keyboards, guitars, drum sets, and the lay *ḍholkī* made up the British bands whose sound came to be dubbed "bhangra music" in the 1980s. Concurrent development of bhangra music at multiple sites and the idea that Punjabi popular music was something related to folkloric bhangra dance increased, despite the tenuous connection between these musical forms and the traditional dance accompaniment. This association eventually suggested the addition of the dhol to the musical ensembles that produced bhangra music, especially as popular music shifted from a product chiefly for listening (e.g., to the poetry of lyrics) to one suitable for dancing at wedding parties and in nightclubs. The dhol was not, however, used in dance-oriented popular music at first. For example, the "disco-bhangra" pioneered on records by Gurdas Mann in India in the 1980s did not include the instrument. Outside the studio environment of the Bombay film industry, where modified dhol playing was used to colorful effect, dholis were not called on to play their "outdoor" instrument on recordings. The shift to regularly incorporating dhol in popular recordings occurred only after the work of Malkit Singh, a singer who moved back and forth between the musical scenes of Britain and of India. Malkit Singh's albums (from 1986), including the standout hit "Hey Jamalo" (1988), were crossover successes.[6] They used stripped-down instrumentation and forms evocative of the sound of folkloric bhangra dance, including the dhol of ustād Harbans Lal Kaku from Malkit Singh's hometown of Jalandhar.

Still, it was not until the 1990s that the characteristically "folk" instruments associated with hereditary musicians were significantly incorporated into diaspora music, driven by the second generation's efforts to hybridize essentialized indices of East and West. Of note is the Punjabi-British music producer Sukhshinder Shinda (Bhullar) who learned dhol from an ustād in residence in the diaspora, Lal Singh Bhatti. The notes to Shinda's album *Dhol Beat* stated, "Shinda has employed the traditional folk instruments of Punjab, the key instrument being the 'DHOL' and blended them with the sounds of today, to produce a new hard-core rhythm for the dance floor. He has used instruments that have not yet been fully exposed to the western bhangra market."[7] As the example of Shinda's production illustrates, the crossover of lay Punjabis to traditional instrumental performance was neither immediate nor wholesale but rather initiated by exceptional individuals and made possible through instruction from well-placed hereditary performers.

TRADITIONAL DHOLIS IN THE DIASPORA

Less than a dozen dhol masters emerging from Punjab have settled in the Anglophone diaspora. The reasons for the low number are clear. The families from which traditional dholis come are generally too impoverished, poorly connected, and undereducated (i.e., outside their traditional professions) to win opportunities to live in the West. This section sketches the small set of traditional dholis located in the diaspora with attention to selected sites in North America and Britain. Its outlook, by necessity, is historical, as it would not be possible to account for the more contemporary players springing up in various countries.

In the earliest phase, dholis from Punjab were called over for special, one-time events. I have already enumerated some international visits by Garib

Dass, including his half-year residence in Canada in 1986. Harbans Lal Jogi of Amritsar toured multiple countries, including the United Kingdom and the United States, in the late 1970s and early 1980s, accompanying performances by the singer Jagmohan Kaur.[8] His visit in 1982 was the first of its kind to the communities of northern California—brief, but having a lasting impact on the memories of those who developed a scene there.[9] Several more masters marked their careers through engagements abroad, such as Malkit Singh's drummer Harbans Lal Kaku, who visited New York and California. Such visits have become more frequent of late.

Though most dholis returned home after the invited function was complete, some found a way to stay. Among the first to reside in the diaspora was Piare Lal (1949–2011), who first came with a bhangra team visiting Vancouver in 1979. He was a Bazigar from a village in the Hoshiarpur district. After subsequent visits, Piare Lal settled in Canada to fill the void for bhangra accompaniment in British Columbia and Alberta in the early 1980s.[10] As local dhol player Rayman Bhullar remembered, Piare Lal's position as the only traditional dholi allowed him to earn much money. Bhullar also remembered the precarious existence of this singular dhol master. One of the Sikh social organizations in the historical Punjabi section of Vancouver, the Khalsa Diwan Society gurdwara, set up Piare Lal in a nearby apartment. But in the tense atmosphere after the violent events in Punjab of 1984, some pro-Khalistan individuals, apparently disapproving of Piare Lal's musical activities (which were in discordance with their vision for a Khalsa Sikh society), seized the master's dhol.[11]

Elsewhere in Canada, dholi Amar Nath (born in Lahore, 1946) followed a similar path. He was the brother of Harbans Lal Jogi and the disciple of Jalandhar ustād Charan Das (his maternal uncle-in-law). Amar Nath had been the accompanist for the top bhangra team of Gursar Sudhar College. He appeared in this capacity in the film *Long da Lishkara* (1986), after which the team visited Canada to perform in 1987.[12] Amar Nath returned to Canada the following year for another engagement, after which he remained, first residing in Surrey and Calgary.[13] He finally settled in Toronto for the last dozen years of his life, before passing away from deteriorated health related to alcoholism.

The role of traditional dholi in Toronto after Amar Nath was partially filled by Jolly Bawa (d. 2018; son of Harbans Lal Kaku). For 4–5 five years in the 2000s, Jolly provided a model for a maturing crop of diaspora players. Jolly's tenure, however, was rife with controversy, and his attempt to immigrate permanently was unsuccessful.[14] Since that time, Toronto's need for traditional dholis has been filled by frequent short-term visitors like Ravi Dana of the Ludhiana Jogis.

The first master to take up residence and stay in the United States was Lal Singh Bhatti (b. 1944) (Figure 6.1). He started his life in Jalandhar, his ancestors' native region, as Lal Chand. Because Lal Chand's orientation leaned toward the more functional style of the Mahashas, he was at first rejected when he sought discipleship with the classical-oriented master Harbans Lal Jogi. Harbans Lal later observed a performance, however, in which Lal Chand executed classical gestures well and agreed to become his ustād.[15] Nevertheless, Lal Chand established his career in the growing field of folkloric bhangra accompaniment, first becoming attached to Khalsa College in the 1960s and playing at Republic Day events in the 1970s. Significantly, in 1971 state arts promoters chose him over his contemporaries to accompany the group who toured the Middle East and North Africa and developed a new

FIGURE 6.1 Lal Singh Bhatti, Claremont, California, 2020. Photo by the author.

set of bhangra steps and rhythms (see Chapter 2). His success allowed him to visit Hawaii (1975) and Washington, DC (1976), and to get residencies in Germany (1980) and the United Kingdom (1983–1984).[16] He found professional opportunities as hymn-singer (*rāgī*) in gurdwaras, embraced the Sikh faith and its concomitant appearance, and changed his name to a Sikh form, Lal Singh. Finding similar opportunities in northern California, Lal Singh was able to immigrate there in 1988 with the support of the Sikh diaspora community and he has lived there ever since.[17] Lal Singh's singular position as the US dhol master west of the Mississippi led to his becoming a significant shaping force of the diaspora dhol. Lal Singh adapted to the Western paradigm of music lessons, wherein a student subscribes to a limited number of learning sessions. Scores of young people in North America availed of this opportunity to take a lesson with a master. Yet, in seeing Lal Singh as a model, diaspora dhol players remained unaware of the challenging lives of most traditional dholis. The diaspora players, the majority of whom were Sikh if not also Jatt, learned to envision a Sikh as a dhol master—a rarity in Punjab. What is more, Lal Singh's (Mahasha) family name, Bhatti, also happens to be a common name among Jatts, so it does not obviously signify a Scheduled Caste. Being unaware of the ethnic landscape of dholis in Punjab and able to presume their teacher's social identity was adjacent to their own, Lal Singh's North American students did not experience the intercaste friction that is so endemic to dhol culture.

In New York, the pioneering dhol master was Muhammad Boota. Because he was from Pakistan and a Muslim, he was not as integrated into the Indian-Sikh-Jatt landscape that dominates the North American Punjabi diaspora. Boota was born a few years after Partition in the Gujrat district, the son of Navab Khan, in the village of Bhagowal Kalan. His maternal relatives belonged to Akhnoor, a center for Jogi dholis in the Jammu district. Yet Boota was from a Bharai community. Learning to play from his elders, he began training in 1961. He got the opportunity to come to New York in 1992 as a performer in an annual celebration of Pakistani Independence, the Brooklyn Mela (Amna 2017). During his first decade in New York, Boota lived alone, sending remittances to family while working jobs like limousine driver. His entire nuclear family eventually settled in Coney Island. All his children are American success stories, established in professional careers. The youngest son, Sher Boota, followed his father in the dhol tradition while studying to be an architect. As the only dholi on the scene in the Northeast in the 1990s, Boota was poised to support some of the developments in bhangra music that emerged in the city, and he interacted with Pakistani and American dignitaries.[18] By the same token, however, political divisions between Pakistani and

Indian communities meant that Boota's sphere of activity was based more in functions concerning the former, while his significance was underappreciated by the Punjabi community that originated in India.

Jarnail Singh, son of Chandigarh's Mali Ram, was another dholi settled in New York who followed a trajectory like Boota's. He, too, first came to the United States with a visiting group, in 1997. And he, too, returned to India before coming back to stay in 1998. In those years, he remembered, there was not so much of a cultural scene to support a dholi's work. Jarnail became a driver while playing dhol engagements and providing DJ services. Like his father, he lamented the attrition in dhol players' knowledge of repertoire, but his attitude was practical. Citing the inconvenience of playing for youth bhangra teams in a limited market (in contrast to the plethora of groups in Lal Singh Bhatti's California), he was content to provide basic dhol services at celebratory events. By the mid-2000s, he noted, everyone wanted dhol at their weddings. In 2017 he was able to bring his father Mali Ram and the rest of his nuclear family over to settle permanently in Queens.

Returning to British Columbia, the residency by Bazigar dholis has most recently continued with Garib Dass's son, Des Raj. After almost yearly visits to Canada beginning in 1996, Des Raj took up residency in Surrey in 2009. He began with the long-standing exhibition dance team, Surrey India Arts Club, and, after it folded, was taken aboard the staff of BC Cultural Academy.[19] At the time of this writing, Des Raj had not returned to India, but his dholi son Jass had come to join him.

LAY DHOL PLAYERS IN THE DIASPORA

A flourishing dhol scene in the diaspora was not possible until a large number of lay individuals had taken up the instrument. The precedent set in the Mediated Field for ethnic outsiders to play professional folk instruments, along with the more liberal social atmosphere of diaspora communities gave laypersons greater access to the "right" to play dhol. Yet their number could not grow until they obtained the knowledge of *how* to play, not something acquired through recordings. Rather, their knowledge derived from a base of traditional dholis, either those who came to the diaspora or whom returnees visited in Punjab. Only a few ustāds were scattered in the diaspora in the 1970s–1990s, giving few diaspora residents access to masters from which to learn, and knowledge spread slowly. Therefore, before the millennium, most Punjabis abroad had to make do without dholis for their functions.

The dhol instrument itself was in short supply. When members of Nachdi Jawani bhangra team from Patiala came to settle in San Francisco in 1960, they may have been the first to bring a dhol to the continent—though without a dholi to play it (Schreffler 2013, 401). Paul Binning, an immigrant to Vancouver who started a bhangra team there in 1968, remembered not having a dhol in the early years, in place of which his group had someone beat on a garbage can behind a curtain.[20] After finally acquiring an instrument, Binning and some lay tabla players tried their hand at playing it, until the arrival of Piare Lal at last solved the group's issue.[21]

In the early 2000s, however, interest in playing dhol exploded among young diaspora Punjabis. Even though interest in playing dhol tended to have a short life span—a youthful pursuit before one got "serious" in life—the large number of individuals involved allowed the population to grow. Learning was facilitated by internet discussion forums, including (now defunct) Dholis.com, on which members traded information and rhythms. Learning was further facilitated by the growing ubiquity of college bhangra dance competitions and shows. In 2001, when I used my amateur skills to accompany such a performance by University of California at Santa Barbara's team at a show in Fresno, I was the only dhol player in the event. At that time, it was only in the densest Punjabi centers, in northern California and Vancouver, that one or two dhol players appeared in these productions. Moreover, their task was mainly to play along to a prerecorded music track. Yet by the middle of the decade, after the explosion in dhol learning, it was common for many dance teams to perform with an auxiliary dhol player, and this, in tandem with the fashion for "live" bhangra (i.e., without a prerecorded track, in the fashion of folkloric bhangra of India), meant many became infected with the desire to learn dhol.

With the growth of YouTube after 2006, North American dhol players gained access to information that they had hungrily sought: how dholis play *in Punjab*. The access came mainly in the form of videotaped bhangra dance competitions in India but also from individuals who had filmed dholis while in Punjab visiting family. The influx of lay players and the double-edged phenomenon of being color-blind to the social implications of playing dhol most drastically effected the dhol tradition's liberalization. New generations of players did not intend to adopt a professional identity; diaspora Punjabis still harbored some reservations about the appropriateness of middle- and upper-class individuals becoming musicians. Yet, as a path to embracing heritage and culturally iconic arts, dhol playing became a bourgeois (youth) pastime.

Before this explosion, the few students of the immigrant masters, acting like older siblings, had established a small base from which other young people began to pick up dhol informally. Lal Singh Bhatti's early disciples, like Teginder Singh Dhanoa, from 1991, and, not long after, Raju Bangar, were the first generation of US-born, traditionally taught dhol players. They and other students of Lal Singh, in California and elsewhere, formed one group of diaspora Punjabi pioneers. Another was formed in British Columbia, where a leader was Rayman Bhullar. In 1991 Bhullar's father, who was involved in Vancouver's Punjabi arts scene, located an ustād for his son.[22]

That ustād, Ramju Muhammad Khawra, merits his own introduction. Ramju was the leading studio musician supplying dhol playing for the Mumbai film-music recording studios. His family origins are in a Mirasi-related community of the state of Gujarat. In short, he was a non-Punjabi professional musician, a multi-instrumentalist, valued by the recording industry for his ability to reproduce facsimiles of various Indian drumming styles. Garib Dass believed that it was the occasional visits by Punjabi dholis such as himself, to present programs in Mumbai, that informed Ramju's knowledge of Punjabi style.[23] Ramju used a smaller, cylindrical dhol, which he played seated and with the reverse grip on the *chaṭī*. His goal was not to be part of the Punjabi dhol tradition but to efficiently create its sounds for countless Bollywood films as well as the bhangra-pop music of widely popular artists like Daler Mehndi.

In 1993 Rayman Bhullar began his training under Ramju, making visits to Mumbai during summer vacations.[24] This way, he acquired the sophisticated classical methods that would elevate his technique beyond the basic *tāls* informally acquired by lay dhol enthusiasts. In 2003 Bhullar took part in a solo dhol competition that was part of a bhangra competition in Toronto, Bhangra Nation 7. It was a milestone event of the diaspora dhol explosion because of its timing, its setting amid the flourishing North American Bhangra Circuit, and the consequent effect it had on people wanting to learn dhol. The hereditary dholi in residence, Jolly Bawa, took first place and Rayman Bhullar took second. Bhullar's name was thence uttered alongside traditional players when the diaspora dhol fans shared their opinions, in online forums, of "the best dholis in the world." Bhullar acquired the skill set of dance accompaniment after joining Surrey India Arts Club in 2003.[25] Bhullar's one-time teaching institution, Dhol Nation Academy, nurtured the next generation of students while providing group exhibition dhol showcases that coincided with major bhangra competitions.

The dhol scene in Toronto was considered younger, sparser, and necessarily less developed than its Canadian West Coast counterpart. Millennial generation dhol player Gaurav Sharma was first inspired as a child by seeing Amar Nath play for devotional events at the oldest Hindu temple in Toronto, the Prarthana Samaj Mandir.[26] When, as a teenager, Sharma took an interest in playing dhol for bhangra, Jolly Bawa was his idol. Whereas most of his peers take an interest in elaborating figures on the two main *tāls*, which serve to impress audiences in solo performances and music concerts, Sharma likes to play in the complex system of bhangra dance accompaniment. This skill set has allowed him opportunities to play with several live teams on the continent, including the honor of filling the shoes of Jolly Bawa for the Punjabi Lok Nach Academy team.[27]

Washington, DC, was another base of activity. Satinderjit Singh, a dance enthusiast, became interested in dhol and, returning to India for some months, apprenticed himself to Mali Ram in 1991.[28] Although on his return to the US capital he played dhol only for amateur functions, he was nonetheless among the few with the ability to play dhol there in the 1990s. This gave Satinderjit's sons a head start in playing dhol during the early years of the dhol boom. Soon, the names of these up-and-coming brothers, Nana and Gopi, were being spoken alongside Jolly, Rayman, Raju, and others of the North American–born generation. Amrinder Singh Pannu (Nana) first got the opportunity in 1992 to travel to India to experience the dhol of Ludhiana's Sewa Ram, and that of other ustāds thereafter.[29] Amrinder finally settled on making Lal Singh Bhatti his master in 2003, through whom he not only cultivated aesthetic playing but also gained the practical knowledge of accompanying bhangra teams.[30] Following close behind, younger brother Gurpreet Singh Pannu (Gopi) leaned toward classical gestures and, appropriately, studied with the Jogi Ravi Dana in India.

The development of lay dhol players began earlier in the United Kingdom. A pioneer was an immigrant from Ludhiana, Gurcharan Mall, who moved to Birmingham for studies in 1963. Mall remembered that it was difficult to acquire a *ḍholkī* in those days, let alone a dhol, yet he was able to pick up the former in order to accompany a bhangra team he formed with his schoolmates (Sahota 2014, 88). Eventually becoming self-taught on the dhol, Mall had an enormous influence on the development of UK dhol players (Leante 2009, 199–200). Following a similar path was a young immigrant from Jalandhar, Harbinder Singh Ghattaora, who developed as a dhol player out of the need to accompany a folkloric bhangra collective, the Great Indian Dancers, which he founded in Southall in 1966 (Daboo 2018, 26). Harbinder Singh had the occasion to meet master Harbans Lal Jogi during the latter's tour to the United Kingdom in 1978 (Sahota 2014, 94), and in the 1980s he made several expeditions to India to study as Harbans Lal's disciple.[31]

An important resource for traditional dhol in the United Kingdom has been the British-born player Gurvinder Kambo (b. 1967). Kambo followed the path of his uncle, Satinderjit Singh of Washington, DC, in seeking discipleship. His maternal grandfather was an acquaintance of Garib Dass in Chandigarh and, through the connection, aided in setting up Kambo as a disciple of the ustād. As noted previously, Kambo became the only formal disciple of Garib Dass in 1994. He could visit Garib Dass in India only once more, a dozen years later. In the interim, however—as Garib Dass delighted in recalling—the master and disciple were able to meet during flight layovers at London's Heathrow Airport, where Kambo was employed. Kambo gained experience both with folkloric bhangra accompaniment, first while playing for the Great Indian Dancers, and with music bands. Two things set Kambo apart from other dhol players in the developing UK scene. The first was his commitment to his Bazigar master's desī style. The second was that he acquired the ability to construct dhols, having studied the handiwork of Garib Dass.

The UK scene bore a crop of lay dhol players faster and earlier than across the pond. Until recently, however, the aspirations of most UK dhol players did not include accompanying folkloric dance, nor did their training include much information on how to function in that area. Their playing was music-oriented, and the instrument itself was often their focus. The concentration can be explained by the rapidness with which the first generation of players disseminated dhol instruction to others, not through the master-disciple system but classes. There were programs whereby, usually for a fee, any interested individual could receive group lessons from appointed instructors. Among such schools were the Dhol Blasters (informally, from 1985), based in Birmingham and led by Gurcharan Mall; Ministry of Dhol (1993), based west of London and led by Pritpal Rajput; and the Dhol Academy (1992) of London. The most prolific was the Dhol Foundation (TDF), founded in 1989 by Johnny Kalsi, formerly with the bhangra music band Alaap. In that he came from a nonmusician Punjabi immigrant background via Kenya (the Ramgarhia community), one might observe that Kalsi's connection with the culture of Punjab was oriented differently from those in the more conservative, predominantly Jatt communities from rural Punjab that one finds in North America. Kalsi, who was not trained by a traditional ustād, began drumming on the drum kit. In this way, his style and method of playing dhol formed in an idiosyncratic way (Leante 2009, 200). Indeed, Kalsi's proud embrace of being self-taught appeared unusual when viewed in the framework of the traditional Dhol World, where linking one's identity to a master was of great symbolic import. One arm of TDF was a performing ensemble that presented dhol-ensemble music to diverse audiences. In addition, as a soloist, Kalsi was involved in groups like Transglobal Underground, the Afro-Celt Sound System, and the Imagined Village. One can read Kalsi's unique career in this respect as an outgrowth of the 1990s trend of world fusion music, consumed less by audiences centered on Punjabi heritage and more by those who sought the indexical mixture of Britain's various ethnic traditions to create a sound representing the country's hybridity. While in a cinema watching Martin Scorsese's *Gangs of New York* (2002), I was surprised by the sound of the *bhalvānī* rhythm in the soundtrack. Through this track from TDF's recent album *Big Drum, Small World*, the sound of dhol was recontextualized as if it might belong to an Irish war march.[32]

TDF established a network of dhol-learning schools with an enrollment in the hundreds. Branches in several towns in England and the Canadian commonwealth conducted weekly classes, to which South Asian parents sent their children as a form of after-school enrichment activity. In contrast to the master-disciple system, TDF's methodology was based on the concept of a standard syllabus for learning and structured methods of transmission and progression. Uncharacteristic in comparison with instruction in Punjab, the rhythms were rendered in strict adherence to a consistent system of vocables (*bol*). Students kept the rhythms, rendered in *bol* notation, in personal notebooks. The syllabus began with rhythmic patterns that are of value as exercise and warm-up.[33] Eventually, the first full rhythmic cycle was introduced, corresponding to the popular dance rhythm, luḍḍī, dubbed "chaal." Further lessons taught variations on this groove, followed by solo fills called breaks, that might be played along with it. A student who mastered enough of this standardized material could join the group at occasional public performances and play along with the bhangra music tracks of which chaal makes up the predominant groove. In 2009 I observed a class at the local Community Centre in Southall. Jas Bhambra was the instructor of this once-weekly evening session.[34] Eleven students were in attendance, from quite young (7–9 years old) to late 20s. As the session finished, students scrambled off to join their waiting parents. The location was within walking distance to both JAS Musicals and Bina Musicals, two retail purveyors of dhols. It could not have been more convenient for local families to equip their children with supplies and drop them for this weekly lesson.

The group-class model was subsequently adopted in Canada and came to dominate, even as the competitive bhangra dance scene waned in the 2010s. There, it was organized within commercial learning centers called "academies," tucked into industrial parks, that taught both dhol and dance, and which were often attached to bhangra teams. It included some exported TDF activity. For example, Rajvir Reehal and Rahul Singh of Brampton (in greater Toronto) had learned from UK instructor Jatinder Saund, who brought the TDF method to Toronto.[35] Rahul Singh went on in 2010 to teach for House of Bhangra, a local academy attached to the long-established team

Sonay Gabroo Punjab De (founded 2001). Another longtime bhangra team of greater Toronto, Nachdi Jawani (founded 2000), created the first academy in the area, Punjabi Virsa Arts and Culture Academy (founded 2001).[36]

In the greater Vancouver area, 1990s–2000s institutions like Surrey India Arts Club formed the base of knowledge for the academies flourishing in the 2010s.[37] Gurp Sian, a former dancer on the team VIBE and codirector (with Rayman Bhullar) of South Asian Arts, pointed out that while the many formal places of instruction were a phenomenon of the last decade, less publicized forms of instruction had been happening earlier.[38] The Royal Academy of Bhangra, directed by an immigrant from Patiala, Hardeep Sahota, had a state-of-the-art studio in Surrey. They were committed to bringing instructors only from India, including guest spots by dholi brothers Meshi and Ravi and the all-around musician and grandson of Yamla Jatt, Vijay Yamla.[39] At the end of the 2010s, Sahota had high aspirations for instruction, including diversifying the repertoire of folkloric dances, bringing in video instructional materials from India and asking students to write essays. Not far off was Rupee Kainth's BC Cultural Bhangra Academy, with permanent resident dholi Des Raj. The ustād took a class of a dozen young boys through a routine of mixed dhol rhythms, which they played while coordinating movement displays and showcasing solos. Such routines were exhibited at community events like a celebration of the life of Garib Dass in 2015 and the academy's annual show for parents. There appeared to be little camaraderie between the dholis functioning at various academies, however, in part because of the politics of favoritism.[40] Moreover, dhol professionals, as in Punjab, needed to maintain a competitive advantage, and simply playing the instrument was not enough to encourage bonds.

One might imagine internet-based instruction to be the next logical step, but it had not emerged as a significant medium aside from the haphazard observation by diaspora dhol players of video-recorded performances. Manvir Hothi of Brampton was, therefore, striking new ground with his YouTube project, *Simply Dhol*.[41] Hothi, a student of DC's Amrinder Pannu, has to date produced roughly 100 video lessons focusing on specific rhythms and techniques, which he breaks down for viewers. The fact that Hothi also offers in-person lessons, however, suggests that online learning is not yet seen as a substitute for direct instruction.

A NEW WORLD OF DHOL

The Punjabi diaspora has brought dhol to ever-wider audiences. Few listeners aware of global music trends have failed to notice Punjabi popular music, rendered as "bhangra," and its characteristic dhol-based rhythms. When the

Canadian prime minister wants to show his recognition of citizens of Punjabi heritage, he does it by dancing to dhol.[42] In the United Kingdom, where South Asian representation is fairly coterminous with Punjabi representation, public dhol playing forms an iconic display of the British Asian community. These occasions would not be possible without the massive dissemination of dhol, now through multiple generations, to perhaps thousands of lay practitioners.

This new world of dhol has a different character from the traditional Dhol World. The demographics of the diaspora contributed to the unique character. Consider, first, an incidental factor: religious identity. The composition of the Anglophone diaspora communities was heavily Sikh. Or, more precisely, those individuals who engaged most with Punjabi national identity were Sikhs. This fact had implications for how dhol developed in the diaspora because, in the Dhol World, Hindu and Muslim devotional functions were among its most ubiquitous. Whereas in Punjab these devotional spaces often included or were easily visible to Sikhs, such was far less the case in the diaspora. When I was in Toronto seeking to know something about the local pioneer Amar Nath, it was only a player in the Hindu minority, Sharma, who knew of the old ustād, and that was because of his participation at the temple where Amar Nath played. The Sikh Punjabis in diaspora have been more inclined to hire dhol players for secular applications like folkloric dance, which was the side of the dhol repertoire to which Sikh dhol players, in turn, have been most exposed.

A demographic dimension with further-reaching implications is the cluster of ethnicity and social class. Traditional dholis descend from marginalized outcastes but most diaspora dhol players belong to the opposite side of the social spectrum. The appropriative sense of entitlement, justified by Punjabi cultural nationalism, on one hand, has empowered the latter to occupy the position of dhol players. On the other hand, they have been compelled to beat the drum for themselves in the absence of traditional dholis. Transgressing ethnic borders within the Punjabi community, which operate despite nationalistic ideals, requires gradual erosion in both social act and concept. This chapter has cited social acts that permeated the border. For example, Lal Singh Bhatti met the community halfway. His minimizing of qaum-based difference in social interaction and personal identity has allowed him to better blend into the Jatt Sikh landscape of California, and his open attitude and embrace of American values has made him accepting of lay students. Johnny Kalsi, a mediator of a different sort, came from a cultural perspective (East African "twice migrants") and indeed a class position—the artisan-class Ramgarhia is neither the landed ruling class nor the outcastes—in which being self-taught and teaching others poses no patron-client anxiety. Still, these drips through perforations have multiplied in the diasporic context through the momentum of media, peer networks, and academies. They do not, however, amount to the dissolution of boundaries, such that the waters mingled and the dhol worlds became one ocean. Rather, while mitigated by the Punjabi national culture concept, the perception of social class means that playing dhol persists to be problematic. Lingering anxiety is attached to the idea of being a professional dholi. Internet instructor Manvir Hothi, for example, shares the common experience of being told by his Punjab-born parents not to be a "Mirasi."[43]

This point in the discussion brings us to the fundamental difference in character between the worlds. In the Dhol World, to be a dholi is to be a professional, whereas in the lay diaspora world it is to be an enthusiast. Playing dhol as a hobby is appropriate to young people, as part of their interest in heritage, but the same young people would not be encouraged to develop their playing into their life's work, their career identity. Dhol playing, paradoxically, has reinforced diaspora Punjabis' very Punjabi identity, but it keeps them at arm's length from the native dholi identity.

If demographics explain one part of the unique character of the new world of dhol, the other piece is the concept of what dhol means. The need to maintain Punjabi identity and thus community in the diaspora has engendered a greater demand for heritage products. Diaspora Punjabis exist at some remove from the day-to-day interactions that, in Punjab, can frame everything as Punjabi. They need "Punjabi" stuff to provide reference points to frame a Punjabi existence. The more concise and powerfully signifying these reference points are, the better. Those products that help the reformation of Punjabi identity after Partition include bhangra and its metonym, dhol. And they continue to be the basis in the diaspora, first re-created from memory, later resown from seeds brought by visitors and returnees. But in putting so much burden on dhol to represent Punjab, less attention has been allocated to the breadth and diversity of its content. As dhol has been played more while saying less, it has set the stage for a crisis of aesthetics.

Let us return to the traditional dholis' own notion of folk when they use the term. The notion of folk authenticity is not calibrated for them according to the ethnicity of those who play, for all traditional dholis embody ethnic authenticity. Rather, it is based on the content and style of playing, the stuff of tradition. *Folk* describes, for them, a set of values subscribed to, to one degree or another, by dhol artists. Lal Singh Bhatti often said to his students, accompanying an example of play, *ih fok āh*—"this is folk." For the traditional dholi, folk is in the playing manner and style. It refers to those aesthetic forms and practices—such as the amount of ornamentation used or the way one wears the instrument—that the speaker considers authentic to the native traditions of dhol. One sees, however, that for diaspora players *folk* is, simply, playing. Dhol *is* folk. Bhangra *is* folk. Performers proclaim they are "keeping it folk" even though their aesthetic values may not conform to what the tradition-bearers call folk. It is important to them to understand what they are doing as folk because folk means authenticity. Yet their authenticity is based on the correspondence to ethnic identity—that ethnic identity writ large as Punjabi.

Punjabiness may be thought of as an essence sought by those identifying with Punjabi culture with a strength proportional to their distance from the center position. Strong visual indices of Punjabiness are the turban and beard, prescribed for Sikh men, and bhangra dancing—one religious, the other secular. Both are embodied signs representing a Punjabi subject. The dhol is a visual index, too, as well as a sonic index, making it doubly powerful. And when lay diaspora subjects play dhol, they also engage the sign through embodiment. Yet this act of embodiment crosses a line, occupying the body of dholis. Crossing that frontier, to occupy the embodied identity of dholis, is at the root of the identity-based morale crisis of traditional dholis that I address in the final chapter.

7 RETURN TO PUNJAB, TURNING PUNJAB

I returned to Punjab, after a 12-year absence, in 2019. Punjabi friends in the diaspora had warned me to prepare for how much Punjab had changed. During my previous residences, Wi-Fi had not been available. Smartphones had not been in use. And YouTube had not yet emerged as a platform engaged by my interlocutors. In my absence, however, I noted that a handful of dholis had appeared on YouTube and a number had accounts on the photo-sharing website Instagram. A few dholis were using the platform to sell dhols to players in the diaspora and following the goings-on there. Lay dhol players in the diaspora were connected socially (albeit in mediated fashion) to traditional players. One dholi even knew me before we met, from my own Instagram page. Much larger was the presence of traditional dholis on Facebook; most of the younger generations had accounts. I hypothesized that the introduction of new media had done something to dissolve the boundaries between dhol-playing communities—not only between the worlds of diaspora and homeland but also between the qaums of traditional players. In the past, dhol playing was entirely an aural tradition and one heard and formed one's conception of dhol only from direct experience. Because dholis tended to interact only with other dholis of their community (or indeed, their local area), each community and locality had developed idiosyncratic traditions of the sort I discussed in Chapter 5. Surely, I thought, if dholis were seeing what other dholis were doing, they would have borrowed ideas. For example, Indian players might have seen the many videos now existing of dhol-accompanied dance in Pakistan and might have come to reform their presentations of such forms. One of my goals in returning to Punjab was to document the effects of new media.

At my first meeting while back in Punjab, however, Anil Sharma, an old friend and officer at the arts institution Kala Bhawan, told me that nothing had changed among Punjab's dholis. I was incredulous, suspecting he was holding onto previously formed notions. I found in the next 2 months, however, that, as to the effects of new media, Sharma's assessment was accurate. All the dholis now had smartphones, to be sure, but phone use to access global trends was limited. For example, younger generations were avid users of the messaging application WhatsApp, yet one dholi advised me that, because he was illiterate, he could use the application only to send photos and voice messages. Indeed, the technology had skipped over the phase of computers and e-mail. Individuals went from no forms of written communication straight to smartphones and, being further limited by data plans and language barriers, were not in the habit of engaging much of what was posted online. Those dholis who did have an online presence were exceptions to the generalization that technology had minimal influence on the dholis' art. Boundaries between insular ethnic communities remained. Moreover, the average dholi had no sense of what was going on with dhol outside Punjab. On several occasions, dholis of diverse backgrounds asked me whether there was potential work for dholis (such as themselves) abroad and responded with amazement when I told them plenty of players were already filling those roles. In fact, the dhol profession was changing, but my hypothesis of technology as the direct agent was not proven. As in the anecdote with which I began this book, about Amritsar's dholis facing tough times, the advent of new technologies did not appear to threaten the distinctiveness of dhol traditions. One traditional dholi, considering my question whether YouTube was affecting dhol, supposed that maybe it had, but he was unconcerned. One will not find "real" dhol on that platform, he opined, and so those who attempted to learn dhol through that medium, learning only "fake stuff," were not a threat.[1]

WORK GOES ON

"The work goes on." Time and again I received this statement when asking dholis the state of their profession. They did not say it optimistically but rather with some resignation and even politeness, as the way someone might reply "I'm fine" to the question "How are you?"—even after a personal loss. The work goes on because it *must* go on. There are always ups and downs, and it was not appropriate to overdramatize one's situation. Anil Takhi of Jalandhar, who had lost his father Kala Takhi only a few months prior, said the dhol scene was "level" and that the number of dholis had remained the same, yet there was weariness in his expression.[2] A Jogi from Ludhiana was ambivalent, suggesting that his community's opportunities for work had decreased a bit, and yet "work goes on."[3]

Dholis had made minor shifts to gain employment, following fashions in the market. One fashion was a call for a service known as *jāgo*. In village contexts, an upcoming wedding was made known to the inhabitants the night before in the form of a procession, a *jāgo*, which means "wake up!" The custom was for females attached to the groom's family to parade through the neighborhood, disturbing the rest of residents through noise, pranks, and minor acts of vandalism, ultimately feeding sweets to those awakened by way of receiving their blessings. At the center of the procession was the trademark feature of *jāgo*, a waterpot with lighted oil lamps attached, which young women took turns carrying on their heads. The historical practice was semifolklorized in communities like the Bazigars' (audiovisual example 29), who were among the first artists employed to lead folklorized versions. A fully folklorized version, requiring the service of dholis, was a feature of some urban weddings, to which it was added as one more event, hosted in a banquet hall, in the roster of wedding-related celebrations. By 2019, the call for such events had increased and more dholis of various communities found work at them.

Another new fashion was particular to Mahasha dholis, probably because of their involvement with wedding-band services. They adopted the playing of the shallow kettledrum called *tāshā*, which has been part of such bands elsewhere in India but had not been used formerly in Punjab. In 2019 every band shop in Jalandhar prominently advertised *tāshā* as a feature of their services, and the business cards of dholis in both Jalandhar and Amritsar indicated that they belonged to a "dhol-tasha group." Having adapted to these newly popular services, the ever-challenging means of earning a living by the average dholi had stayed "level."

For younger dholis who inherited opportunities and a path to employment, there was no reason to sound pessimistic. They were growing into their careers, gaining status with each year. In the 2000s, Vijay Kumar was one of the entrepreneurial young dholis who advertised their services on the guardrail in Mohali (see Figure 4.5). The practice of roadside advertising continued in 2019, with Bazigars hanging their dhols on trees, on lampposts, or propped on rocks. One of them, a middle-aged man named Mahinder from Garib Dass's neighborhood, said "The work goes on." Young Vijay, however, had moved on to bigger work. He had taken part in three or four Punjabi and Hindi films and was getting wedding party engagements of a more prestigious sort. Life was a hustle but not filled with despair.

Yet another means of income for some was to supply the dhol instrument. The volume of the dhol trade had grown to be enormous, in contrast with the way it was years ago. As I described in Chapter 2, Indian professional dholis of the 2000s and earlier acquired their instruments in the raw form of shells manufactured outside the state of Punjab and completed their construction themselves, according to their own methods. The ready-made dhols sold in a few shops in Delhi or Amritsar were of no interest to them. Moreover, dholis had no need of more than a single instrument that could be made serviceable and that they obtained either through inheritance or the personal journey of self-construction. As interest in dhol began to boom in the diaspora, however, a network of music shops with their ready-made instruments, expanding from Delhi to London, supplied a mail-order trade. Some diaspora players sought the telephone numbers of Indian ustāds and sent their "uncles" in India requests to meet ustāds and persuade them to part with dhols. Even though they would not become professionals, they sought the "best" dhols. Types of wood were fetishized, and cost was no object. Meanwhile, professional dholis were limited by cost and the availability of dhols made of superior wood. A top dholi like Garib Dass was patching up the main dhol that he acquired only after a life of growing into his position. In 2019 Garib Dass's grandsons proudly showed me the two instruments they inherited, part of their wealth. They had become even more patched and repaired but were cherished like a part of the family. At the same time and in contrast to this traditional mindset, it had become possible to acquire professional-style dhols with much greater convenience through dholis who were meeting the demand.

Notable among the dhol suppliers for his prolificness and attention to scrupulous practices is the Jogi Naresh Kukki. As a performer, Kukki specializes in studio recordings in the manner of Mumbai maestro Ramju Bhai. He is the proprietor of Kukki Music House in Ludhiana; his business in some sense carries on that of his late father Sewa Ram, who had supplied dhols to his local community. Now, however, Kukki sells dhols far and wide to players oriented toward accompanying sangīt and to the international market. His Instagram account, with thousands of posts about dhols offered, helps to advertise to the latter. He must farm out the work of manufacturing the shells, the sources of which he keeps close to his chest. Knowing his customers will spare no expense, he seeks out the best materials.[4] To make the dhols more attractive to customers abroad, who are sometimes interested in acquiring—even collecting—dhols as material objects, Kukki and similar suppliers have fancy designs carved into the shells by furniture makers.

Garib Dass's grandsons were puzzled by the role of such dhol suppliers. Even though Kukki made some claim to being among the few with the knowledge of dhol construction, thus justifying the need for his service, Bazigars had always done their own work. They did not understand why one would purchase a ready-made dhol when they could create their own for far less cost. We can conclude, therefore, that the substantial market for these dhol suppliers is made up of players outside the traditional world. For this reason, more dholis have acted as middlemen reselling dhols to enthusiasts. Older ustāds disapproved of treating dhols as commercial objects, but can we fault the dholis who engage in trading in them? They, as always, are adapting to the market.

DHOL HAS GONE DOWN

Although some dholis said the work goes on, others lamented that the dhol profession had "gone down," yet without resorting to drama. They were not thinking of the market but dhol traditions and aesthetics. Manak Raj of the Bazigars near Sanaur (Patiala), among those who voiced a lament, was still gaining employment at several local educational institutions, but the tradition had diminished from what it had been for his father, the influential Biru Ram (d. 2011). One reason, he believed, was that young dholis were playing a lot with "songs." In other words, they were accompanying popular music, which was not one of the traditional applications of dhol. Accompanying popular songs meant employing just one or two of the most common rhythms, which leaves little room for modes of engagement native to dhol. Sewa Singh of Chandigarh, who also lost his father, Prem Chand, in 2011, also said things had gone down. Dholis nowadays, he said, play a lot with wedding processions, another application that limits the range of dhol. What today's dholis did less of was playing with staged bhangra, an art form that requires knowledge of how to apply dozens of rhythms and breaks. The comments bore on the rise of popular song and the iconic representation of dhol in parties and the decrease in fashion for bhangra team performances. Vijay Yamla of Ludhiana opined that bhangra was, properly, the main application of dhol, adding that few of the dholis in his locality were cultivating bhangra accompaniment skills.[5]

A change in playing content and style was thus interpreted as part of the decline. In the case of those dholis who valued desī repertoire, they noted the decrease in variety of rhythms and, indeed, the lack of knowledge of many rhythms among the younger players. This trend was increasingly tied to the focus on newer contexts (i.e., popular music and wedding parties), a trend already growing in the 2000s. The newer aggravating factor was the popularity of playing "classical" style. Interlocuters hastened to add that the objection was not to classical music in itself. The implication was that focus on elaboration was to the detriment of cultivating a diversity of rhythms that made up the traditional dhol styles of engagement. The increase in "classical" was not, indeed, an expression of dhol playing in the mode of classical (art) music, as, for example, what the new breed of dholis in Pakistan had promulgated. Rather, it was an accompanying effect of playing to popular song, with its particular presentational mode (for listening) and limitation to a few rhythms played continuously. So, even dholis from communities associated with desī playing had taken to classical stylings. In mixed contexts of older and younger generations, the older were more comfortable stating that "classical" playing was not harmonious with dhol, while the younger acquiesced to the comments of their elders uncomfortably. It was the younger who had adopted the fashion of "classical" play, excited by the brilliance of the style and the attention it brought them.

It is no coincidence that the sentiments about decline were well represented among Bazigars, the community that combines the greatest investment in folk aesthetics with professionalism. The Bazigar community around Chandigarh, whose families had found their way from western Punjab, had been a resource for the rejuvenation-through-folklorization projects based, since the mid-twentieth century, in the capital and nearby Patiala. They gained a reputation for working with institutions, for being fair and reasonable, and for having an attractive, authentic knowledge of diverse cultural forms. By 2019, most of the senior artists who had been carrying the folk ethos—the memories of community events, of rambling, of living in huts—were out of the picture. The Vartia clan's dholi cousin-brothers, Garib Dass, Prem Chand, and Mangat Ram had all died, and the youngest, Mali Ram, was in America. Their own sons were much engaged abroad. It was Dev Raj (Figure 7.1), son of Mangat Ram, who was the oldest remaining. But he had suffered an illness that caused a palsy affecting his treble hand, and he was no longer capable of controlling the *chaṭī* well.[6] He said without bitterness—more as a matter-of-fact observation—that dholis these days simply did not know the particular rhythms for such past applications as *kabaḍḍī* and *kushtī*.[7]

Other dholis spoke directly about the decline in morale and even what they perceived as a moral decline. As might be expected, these individuals were older, the few still-living senior masters, who had experienced the meteoric rise of dhol in the twentieth century. Sitting with Charan Das, age 86, took me back to the previous era. He warmed to me when he remembered I was a student of Garib Dass. Despite being from different qaums, both masters had participated in the camaraderie of the national events that elevated bhangra and they shared older values. He showed me the trophies he earned at milestone events. Most striking, as we perused his photo albums, was his constant attention to noting who the "chief guests" were at the events

FIGURE 7.1 Dev Raj Vartia (left) and son, Charni, Jujhar Nagar, 2019. Photo by the author.

pictured—the politicians and dignitaries in attendance. Through emphasis, these seemed the most important features of the events in which he took part. It was something that the old masters always did in the 2000s, rather than boasting of themselves directly, as if their honor were heightened through association with these officials. I wondered why the recent generations of dholis made few such gestures. Perhaps they had lost faith in their leaders, whereas for the older generation, whatever the politics of the leaders, they felt connected with them and the project of state building. Charan Das had harsh opinions about the younger generations of dholis' conduct. He spoke with aesthetic revulsion against dholis playing along to songs, complaining that they do not know bhangra anymore. And he rejected the practices of selling dhols and selling dhol lessons.[8]

Yet Charan Das's heart seemed more troubled by the moral climate, evincing something more than an old timer's perennial lament about cultural change or a wish to turn back the clock. His face showed sadness when he said, "Punjab is gone. There is nothing left." Here he shifted away from the parochial concerns of dholis to a concern with the national body. And yet his lament was voiced from the particular position of the dholi community. When I first met him in 2004, the ustād mentioned that he had once gone abroad to England (1972), but he had returned quickly because he was disturbed by drug abuse and other social ills he saw there. He decided at that point that he wanted to stay in India so that he could care for and guide his family.[9] He had once drunk his fair share of alcohol, especially when work had waned, but he had given up drink. Two of his noted disciples, Des Raj (Jalandhar) and Amar Nath (Toronto), had died from alcohol-related causes. In 2019 Charan Das was even more adamant. As I mentioned to him dholis who had passed on, he discretely made gestures of drinking and smoking "smack." "Nobody is left."

The old masters still around were survivors, and they appeared isolated and alone. In Ludhiana, near the adjacent offices where Jogis make their market, master Pappu sat in a separate shop the size of a guardhouse. When I entered, he was sitting in silence, as if meditating. Pappu was happy to chat about the old days, referring to photos on the walls as he reminisced. Yet, even in this neighborhood of dholis, he was isolated, merely marking time. His generation was not well connected to the younger. The latter were not seeking value from their elders. The gap between the oldest and youngest dholis was not being bridged by the intermediary generation, lost to excess.

When I first visited Amritsar's dholi neighborhood in 2004, I interacted with the lower-tier players who plied their services along the main road outside Sultanwind Gate. It was a difficult meeting, for the cohort of dholis and their neighborhood friends had pressured me to purchase liquor for them and to go to a bar to consume it. When I returned to the area in 2019, dholis were still set up on the roadside. Gosha Shiva, a disciple of Ghuggi, was a familiar face. "The work goes on," he said. But the conversation turned gloomy when I produced the photo of his gang that we had taken those years earlier at that very spot. Most men in the photo had died in the intervening years.

Amritsar's alley of dholi offices was less vibrant than it had earlier been, and I noted only three or four offices. One master around was Dev Raj, son of Munshi Ram (d. 2001) of the Mangluria clan, a disciple of Charan Das. Noticeably absent, however, was Tilak Raj, who, barely middle-aged, previously had the habit of staying in his open-air office all day. Now his office looked like it had been gutted. When I asked a relative nearby where Tilak

Raj was, he replied, evasively, "He's at home." Master Dev Raj was similarly ambiguous: "He comes less often."[10] I put the inquiry to the dholis outside the gate, pressing on: "Has Tilak Raj retired?" They laughed heartily at the notion of "retired," in part because retirement as such is not really a phenomenon among dholis, whose careers are not clearly marked by working versus nonworking life. They suggested that, yes, *retirement* could be a euphemism for it, and I inferred that Tilak Raj was, in fact, fading into the oblivion of substance abuse.

Harbans Lal Jogi (Figure 7.2) was another ghost from Amritsar's past. I had been surprised to find him alive in 2006, and even more surprised when I stumbled on him in 2019 on a second pass by Tilak Raj's derelict office.

FIGURE 7.2 Harbans Lal Jogi in Tilak Raj's vacated office, Amritsar, 2019. Photo by the author.

Harbans Lal, like Charan Das, was embittered. Whereas Charan Das was discouraged by the decline in bhangra activity, Harbans Lal, who had always identified with classical aesthetics, clung with pride to the sophistication in his lineage. Still, he felt the same morale drop. Alone in his late 80s, Harbans Lal's three sons had all died already. He screwed up his face, making silent gestures of pouring a bottle and drinking.

EXIT OF USTĀDS

The Indian dhol-playing population was particularly vulnerable to the public-health crisis of substance abuse. The middle generation was most hurt by it directly. The oldest generation was most troubled by it as they looked back. And the youngest generation, though less concerned and less directly affected, was nonetheless affected by the break in the continuity of tradition and deterioration of social support. That crisis, however, is a problem in much of South Asia and is not unique to dholis. The changes that are particular to dholis are those related to the institution of *ustādī*. First and in simplest terms, ustāds are a dying breed. Those model figures have exited the landscape.

The start of the second decade of this century marks the time by which most of the model ustāds had passed away or ceased activity. Everywhere I went, I found garlanded portraits of lost masters hanging on the walls. And just before I left Punjab, Bahadur Singh—the son of modern bhangra originator Bhana Ram—crossed over.[11] In the case of Ludhiana's Jogis, for example, a vestige of such models was Janak Raj. He was a master about whom the consensus is, among the entire dhol-playing population, that he was a true ustād. Since 2017, he was incapacitated and battling cancer. Because this meant that Janak Raj was now effectively out of sight, his power of influence as a model was diminished. Neither had anyone in the area become a successor to his position. As Vijay Yamla opined, no one of Janak Raj's stature remained.[12] Dholis of Ludhiana's younger generation, perhaps as a result of this vacuum, were among the most prominent to adopt newer strategies of sustenance: supplying dhols, offering lessons, and accompanying music recordings. In the absence of the older generation and much of the middle generation, Punjab's youngest dholis were fending for themselves without a strong connection to prior practice.

Garib Dass's own family household felt similarly incomplete. The ustād, now gone, had been the head of this multigenerational household who directly disciplined his dholi grandsons. By this time, Garib Dass's one dholi son, Des Raj, had been settled in Canada for a decade. The fruit of the master's long career, their house, which the family owned free and clear, now had three floors. The grandsons had an entrepreneurial spirit and supported each other's career goals. Jass, now in his mid-20s, was the most likely inheritor of Garib Dass's dhol-playing line. Notably, the investment in his education that his family made paid off, for he became the first in the family to graduate from the university. He hoped to diversify by becoming a music store owner, a DJ, or a producer using digital media, although the cost of the necessary start-up equipment was far beyond his means.[13] His younger brother, Jasbir, who was encouraged to play dhol as a child, had decided not to pursue music as a career, becoming instead a taxi driver. Their cousin, Sandeep, continued to play dhol for seasonal jobs like *jāgo* events and he had performed in Malaysia. The grandsons had been bequeathed a great inheritance of opportunity. Still, without older figures (Garib Dass and Des Raj), the household felt empty. The young men were without ustāds, and the future of the lineage appeared uncertain.

Ironically, the application of the label "ustād" had become more liberal by 2019. Earlier, it sufficed to call a professional player a dholi. One tended to reserve the use of *ustād* as an address to one's own master, or else to refer to an established senior master. It is now common to call many more ordinary dholis ustāds. The usage is driven by outsider players who are overeager to address any professional with the title, according to the notion that anything otherwise would be disrespectful. I first observed this in the early 2000s among the growing legion of diaspora dhol players, who took great care, when discussing dholis, to include *ustād* and the additional honorific *jī* in the dholis' names. Yet, having met many of the professional dholis referred to thus, the practice was amusing to me, for I knew they themselves were not always comfortable with the appellation. Indeed, such dholis, who subscribed to the ideals of *ustādī*, would feel awkward in that they might not think they filled the criteria to be called ustād—and the responsibility that comes with it. Dholis, among whom humility is a value, are not eager to adopt a title that they have not earned. In the comparable context of classical tabla players, Kippen notes that it was gauche for a younger player to call himself ustād (2008, 127). Further, it has been seen that dholis from various qaums like Bazigar and Bharai considered there to be a category of *ustād-lok*, which they ascribed to Mirasi and Jogi individuals exclusively.

In the Punjab of 2019, it was commonplace for outsiders to call any professional an ustād, including younger players. Begrudgingly adopting this development in language, I, too, began to use *ustād* more liberally. I was corrected in one instance by the dholi Kukki. He being internationally known, his reputation preceding him and, because I had heard diaspora dhol players refer to him as ustād, I decided to play it safe and follow suit. When I first encountered Kukki, however, and asked (to confirm his identity), "Are you Ustad Kukki?" the musician laughed and said he was indeed Kukki, but not so sure if he was an ustād![14] Kukki, to be sure, is a master of his craft and does have disciples. But he is a younger man living in the shadow of eminent senior masters. Kukki elaborated that he observes many young people calling dholis ustād nowadays when it is not appropriate. Whether or not Kukki "really" is an ustād, by questioning the label for himself, he was enforcing the code of *ustādī* and that, paradoxically, brings him closer to being an ustād.

If youngsters and outsiders were applying the label of ustād liberally, the use did not correspond to the sharply hierarchical power relationship customarily assumed to adhere between the addressor and addressee. This is not to say that true ustāds were no longer masters in the relationship but rather, simply, that the relationship, in many cases, was rather more equal. Outsider collaborators with masters acted more informally, even chummy, with the dholis they called ustād. Previously, and despite the dholi's lower rank in the social order, in the space of collaborative performance (e.g., bhangra presentations) he had clear authority over youths from landowner communities (e.g., college students). But in the case of Kartar Singh, for example, he had an easygoing relationship with the students of a Chandigarh college. After a bhangra rehearsal, we all sat together as equals, and the dholi was keen about my meeting and appreciating the talents of the students. Kartar Singh exercised the humility associated with *ustādī*, downplaying his own importance. But he did not exercise a display of authority over the students, even though doing so would have once been considered appropriate and not at odds with humility toward the guest (myself).[15]

DETERIORATION OF THE MASTER-DISCIPLE SYSTEM

In Chapter 5, I argued, speaking largely in reference to Punjab of 15 or 20 years ago, that the master-disciple system enforced the borders of dholi identity by maintaining ideal aesthetic, economic, and moral parameters that make up the Dhol World. According to that system, the identity of ustād carried with it more than just a description of a dholi who plays well or who teaches others to play dhol. Serving as role models, ustāds were upholders of values and saddled with the responsibility of appearing as dignified objects of community esteem. Their gravitas commanded respect. The presence of such figures, modeling the ideal, was something that maintained a sort of discipline in local dhol-playing communities. These ustāds were like father-figures in a traditional household.[16] They also represented their particular communities among the wider dhol-playing body. Even while dholis from a given qaum generally disregarded the players of other qaums (or locales)—cultivating a feeling of superiority of their own people—they respected other qaums' ustāds. *Ustādī*, a sort of brotherhood, was the institution that transcended ethnic difference. Most important, nurturing and sustaining the crop of professional dholis was the ustād's prerogative. I suggest further that the existence of ustāds, or rather "true" and "good" ustāds, contributes to the morale of the dhol-playing community. One might reason from that proposition that a dearth of such ustāds contributes to poor morale. The fact that ustāds are recently wanting may be looked to as the deeper cause of the decline of the Dhol World. Despite the popularity of dhol, the disappearance of ustād-based transmission contributes to a spiritual decline. It is not only the death of the last generation of masters but also changes in the application of the master-disciple system that suggests that the era of the ustād is coming to an end.

The master-disciple system regulated the economically meager, yet relatively stable, ecology of the dhol-player community. It limited the number of professionals, preventing the market from becoming oversaturated. It did something to help ensure that professionals were committed and of high quality. All this was good for the preservation of the guild as a whole. The era of the ustād being over, the dhol profession is less stable. A result is that dholis have more freedom to act outside the traditional bounds of ustāds. By this, I do not mean practicing newer forms of work. I am referring, rather, to work that would have been discouraged by ustāds and which is supported by the newly expanded market of dhol players as consumers. This work, most notably, includes teaching dhol lessons.

The ideal model of *ustādī* included adherence to a code wherein lessons were not sold, where one's teaching was reserved for select recipients of the master's legacy. Lessons as such were foreign to the Dhol World, wherein hereditary players would learn through that combination of enculturation and discipleship. Because offering instruction in direct exchange for compensation was frowned on, and because training outsiders to the professional community made no sense in the economic structure, a lesson system had no proper place. The notion of offering lessons, therefore, implies teaching people outside the dhol-playing qaums. We may recall the unusual scenario where Sansis received instruction from the Bazigar master Prem Chand. There was some logic to the scenario in that, although Sansis were technically outsiders to the historical qaums that played dhol, their qaum was of similar social status and they had the intention of adopting dhol as a service profession. Nonetheless, the arrangement had some element of selling out dhol, and, if it was acceptable to Prem Chand, it was not considered to be a best practice by the likes of Garib Dass. The teaching of more distant outsiders, who were unlikely to form a paramparā, was an even greater transgression of the code, for which the consensus was clearer. It was not appropriate under usual circumstances.

Despite being considered inappropriate, informal instruction in the style of lessons for nonprofessionals did have an irregular place at the tail end of the ustād era. The emergence of dhol as Punjabi national culture was followed by that new and peculiar phenomenon of dhol as hobby among a modest number of outsiders. The smattering of ethnic others was met with amusement, charity, or friendship. Teaching these individuals occurred in cases when an ustād, usually of some prestige, was in the position of an ambassador for Punjabi culture. It was sharing of Punjabi culture as opposed to indoctrination into the guild of dholis. The case might come up that a lay, foreign participant in a cultural exchange took an interest in playing dhol. The ustād of a relatively secure economic position would recognize the sincerity of the individual desirous of learning and would give instruction as a sort of philanthropy, giving the gift of Punjabi culture. For example, the senior master Biru Ram, who was widely employed by educational institutions around Patiala, taught some outsiders. In his case, it was clear that the learners were doing so "for fun."[17] In the case of foreigners like myself studying with Garib Dass or of Fiol learning the Garhwali dhol from Sohan Lal (Fiol 2017, 108), we learned for the purpose of research; the ustāds preferred sharing their knowledge with us cultural outsiders to sharing it with high-caste neighbors.

The dynamic took a turn when the interest of outside learners reached a critical mass and some professional dholis saw the outsiders as a market. In this scenario, the dhol teachers were seeking direct financial gain through offering lessons. Having established a vision of outsiders playing, the practice became more acceptable in Punjab as well. My estimate that the global critical mass was sufficient to realize the phenomenon back in Punjab by the 2010s was corroborated by the Ludhiana dholi Kala, whose sense it was that teaching local laypeople had begun around the beginning of that decade.[18] A middle-aged individual still trying to survive by the old model, Kala was amused by the notion. The advent of outsider players to the dhol scene in Punjab was not, however, facilitated only by the precedent of a handful of diaspora players receiving instruction. I believe that it depended, as well, on the earlier-rooted delinking of dhol from proscribed qaums that was influenced by media in the Punjabi culture industry. To see this, we must take a step back.

THE NONETHNIC DHOLI

Two interrelated barriers guarded the exclusivity of dholi identity: ethnicity and professionalism. Access to becoming a dholi in the traditional sense had historically meant being born into a particular qaum whose members generationally practiced dhol or, in some cases, a qaum that was socially adjacent to those qaums. Actually becoming a dholi meant following the occupation of playing to support oneself in accordance with the norms modeled by ustāds. I have already begun to discuss how an erosion of rules for training (becoming a professional) effected changes to the master-disciple system. The changes weakened the barrier to the professional criterion of the dholi identity, yet, before that, one had to cross the barrier of ethnic identity.

The barrier of ethnic community membership began to erode as dhol was reduced to a generically Punjabi tradition. Performances of Punjabi national identity, as in presentations of folkloric music and especially through media, make the argument that musical traditions are the shared property of all Punjabis. In this process, dhol sheds some of its minoritarian ethnic baggage. The liberation from ethnicity is not as democratic as it might first appear, because, despite its ostensible inclusiveness, the Punjabi national identity is not ethnically neutral. The majority peoples of Punjab, especially agriculturalists like the Jatts, are more privileged to become representatives of Punjabi identity. Moreover, although their majority status at once makes them seem neutral in the sense of a default—nonethnic, in the colloquial sense—being Jatt (etc.) brings its own ethnic signification. The image of the dholi is first neutralized in public culture through the mediated portrayals of commercial Punjabi music and culture promotion. Then this neutralization allows dhol to be mapped onto new identities, and such is their centrality in media that dhol players may be portrayed as Jatt or Sikh (or both). The reductive view of dhol as a generically Punjabi tradition, therefore, entails both stripping away the ethnic identities of historical players and adding Jatt-like qualities to dhol. The latter include values like being the center of attention, machismo, brashness, and an attitude that considers dhol as the locus of carefree fun, lacking reverence for devotional temperament, and overlooking minority cultural aesthetics.

Figure 7.3 is a photograph of bhangra performers at the 1970 Republic Day celebration in New Delhi. On the left is the dhol accompanist, Garib Dass. One may observe, especially after examining numerous photos of this sort, that the Bazigar drummer looks different from the others in the photo, the dancers. Note, for example, his smaller physique, darker skin tone, and lack of beard. The performance was not meant to highlight difference, of course; on the contrary, bhangra aims to present a unified Punjabi front. Figure 7.4 is an illustration, clearly adapted from the 1970 photograph, that appears on the cover of a music cassette.[19] The original dholi has been cropped from the image and an inaccurately rendered dhol has been put into the hands of one of the dancers. Whatever the intentions of the artist, the picture makes

FIGURE 7.3 A bhangra dance team at the 1970 Republic Day celebration.

a tacit argument that mainstream-ethnicity, bhangra-dancer types commonly play dhol. The irony is that Jatt people were the clients of dholis and held a diametrically opposite social position. Unlike dhol playing, amateur dancing was not a proscribed activity. The former is a profession; the latter is a pastime. In bringing them together in visual representation, their difference is eroded. The casual viewer or, alternatively, the viewer looking for Punjabi unity, has no trouble imagining a dancer changing roles to become a drummer. In social practice, however, the notion of a Jatt playing dhol was ridiculous to most ustāds and only slightly less ridiculous to most Jatts. Most ustāds were against taking on a Jatt as a student. And so, such images were fantasy. The fantasy, however, approaches reality in the perception of people on the receiving end of media who are increasingly unable to spot its incongruities.

In observing that ustāds were against teaching local ethnic outsiders, we must again remember that the rules of engagement had much to do with economics, the preservation of earning potential for the guild. Ethnic group membership might not be prioritized if it had no bearing on earning potential. The bar of ethnicity might therefore be lowered provisionally, which helps to explain inconsistent and evolving reactions among dholis to the acceptability of the practice. Once, while I was visiting with Kala Takhi in 2004, two soldiers and a police captain came to his shop. They wanted to learn bhangra and dhol. Takhi cautioned them that it would take several

FIGURE 7.4 Cassette cover with artist's revisions.

years to learn these arts. Takhi was doing his due diligence in maintaining skepticism of outsiders and gently dissuading them. Indeed, the surprised police captain replied they had only intended to study for a month or two. A pure traditionalist might have rejected the clients outright. Takhi, however, was willing to haggle over a fee for a couple of months of lessons. After the officers left, Takhi, embarrassed in my presence, rationalized his actions to me by citing the need to make money and "fill one's stomach."[20] Assuming the students would pose minimal threat to the guild's sustainability, the economic foundation of the rule of not teaching outsiders could be considered irrelevant, thereby justifying breaking the rule. Takhi's embarrassment, however, revealed his sense that there was more to the rule than could be nullified by a local economic exchange.

Because, it can be presumed, older dholis possessed an intuitive sense of the value of their communities' discouragement of giving access to outsiders, breaking custom necessitated such rationales. It was mentioned earlier that Mali Ram had taught many, including outsiders, and for this his status as an ustād suffered in the eyes of traditionalists like Garib Dass. In 2018 I asked Mali Ram whether he had any problem with teaching lay Punjabis, and he replied that he did not. In this case, I believe Mali Ram's economic status and reputation among dholis was considerably greater than Kala Takhi's, and so he could not offer the rationale that he would need to lower the barrier to survive. Perhaps for this reason, he added that "art has no caste."[21] It should be noted that such a statement has popular appeal within the framework of modern Punjabi culture. Here, the notion of art is being used to neutralize the phenomenon of caste, although, critics might argue, in potential service of economic gain. It was rare for a dholi to truly believe that an ethnic outsider, especially one from among their historical clients, could occupy the identity of dholi. So, such rhetoric as "art has no boundaries" and "I am financially compelled to share" mitigated the tension that accompanied the exchange of capital for status across the social boundary.

Another sort of rationalizing rhetoric minimized the threat of outsiders. The Jogi Kala scoffed at the idea of lay dhol players, whom he referred to as *paṛhe-likhe* ("reading-writing") people. He downplayed the issue by saying that these "children of big people" take an interest yet they do not really know much.[22] Dhol players outside the traditional qaums were, in a certain sense, "nobody." They were pretenders. Few in number, they posed no threat. Other dholis, like Bharai master Akhtar Dhillon, reacted to the topic with a mixture of dismissal (they do not know much) and ambivalence (it does not matter).[23]

Perhaps dholis did not make more explicit their feelings about outsider players because it is not politically sound to bite the hand that feeds one. In the company of Kartar Singh and the lay Punjabi students whose bhangra he was accompanying, I raised the issue of the sons of landowners playing dhol. One of the students remarked that, indeed, a lot of changes had taken place in the musical landscape. Kartar Singh, however, had nothing to add. Maybe it was best that he did not opine. What is most notable is that none of the dholis interviewed said that it was a *great* thing that outsiders were adopting dhol. They were not excited about the popularity of the instrument in the hands of many; they did not praise its spread across the globe, as if a victory for Punjabi culture's preeminence.

In diaspora communities, being situated as minorities within other countries, Punjabis had compelling reasons to subscribe to the notion of a globalized Punjabi community and to affirm their membership in it through associating with the constructed signs of Punjabi identity—including dhol. Images such as Figure 7.4 suggested a potentiality. Playing dhol, at least as a hobby, was transmuted from the degrading work of service provider to the laudable pursuit of staying in touch with one's roots. Early on, such activities did not threaten the economics and social observances of professionals in Punjab. Even as, throughout the 2000s, outsider players multiplied in the diaspora, they carried on far away from the traditional dholis' environment—in another land—and could be disregarded. The worlds of ustāds and the diaspora dhol enthusiasts would, however, come into increasing contact. We have seen that into the 2000s, travel abroad was limited to the cream of the crop of dholis called to present brief programs. By the 2010s, a greater number of professionals were being called, with more regularity, and for longer periods. Ongoing links were forged between ustāds and diaspora learners of outside ethnic communities, wherein the diaspora player might expect to acquire training. And yet such an exchange could be mutually beneficial. It solved the problem of diaspora dhol players, all but a few of whom previously had no access to instruction from a professional. It contributed to the income of dholis from Punjab who compete in a flooded home market. The market created by diaspora Punjabis creates some incentive to waive the requirement of traditional qaum membership.

The tradition-minded ustād could, nevertheless, reason that to give outsiders instruction was acceptable—barring rationalizations—only if he firmly maintained that an outsider may not become a disciple in the traditional sense. For the outsider to become a disciple would mean entering into the sacred contract without any intention to fulfill his obligations to the qaum. Or rather, the false disciple would put the ustād in a situation where he cannot fulfill his own. Hence, offering dhol lessons, especially in exchange for payment, is paradoxical. A virtual taboo discouraged ustāds from engaging in direct monetary compensation, for it went against the ideals of the master-disciple system. At the same time, teaching in the form of lessons was a virtually nonexistent system, because the master-disciple system was the model that made sense to support the dholi guilds. And although teaching outsiders also went against the system, if one *is* to make that exception—if one is to teach an outsider—it virtually necessitates a music-lesson system. Further, if one were to teach outsiders in greater numbers, one would have to receive compensation for one's labor and time because, again, the outsider learners could not be expected to contribute to the guild, because they could never really become professional dholis. The paradox is that, if offering lessons for pay violates the behavioral prescriptions of how to be a good ustād, at the same time it succeeds to an extent in maintaining the exclusivity of the guild by denying true discipleship—by denying a pathway to professionalism even after the barrier of ethnicity has been removed.

Returning to where we started, barriers of ethnicity and professional status (being a disciple) guard the exclusivity of dholi identity, an identity that can be considered under threat. The dissolution of both barriers is occurring, but the weakening of ethnic exclusivity was the starting point. The outsider-ethnicity dhol players, who achieved critical mass in the diaspora, amassed the force (or created the incentive) to lessen ethnic exclusivity, and the non-ethnic dholi of media representations aided their growth. This set a precedent for instruction outside the master-disciple model. Once the master-disciple model began to erode, enabled by individual short-sighted and economically motivated rationalizations, the whole structure of dholi identity began its collapse. The staunchly traditional ustāds of older generations frown on the practice of giving lessons for pay, but younger entrepreneurs are engaging in such a neoliberal business model, increasingly free from the regulations of their absent "fathers."

FUTURE LANDSCAPES OF DHOL PLAYER IDENTITY

Amritsar's Harimandir Sahib, at its center the iconic Golden Temple, is the holiest of holies, the political center of the Sikh community and a lynchpin for the imaginary of place engaged through Punjabi cultural nationalism. One is not considered to have visited Punjab unless one—on every visit, really—has visited the Golden Temple. In 2016 the city of Amritsar "cleaned up" the chaotic bazaar and community network that had developed around this gurdwara to create something called Heritage Street. Now one can stroll the environs without dirtying one's shoes, without the risk of colliding with a rickshaw, without experiencing the confusion of a hundred shop owners hawking their wares. The heritage of Punjab has been cleaned up, streamlined, into a pedestrian shopping mall, some say approximating a touristic Disneyland that includes other familiar icons like a McDonald's restaurant. In the middle of Heritage Street are three statues. One depicts men dancing bhangra; a second depicts women doing one of "their" dances, *kikklī*. Between these is the third statue, a dhol player. As in the depiction of a dhol player in Figure 7.4, the details are off. The player resembles the archetypal bhangra dancers of the nearby statue in his stature, dress, and grooming, and his dhol, the way he holds it, and the way he strikes it are equally unrealistic. The modern icons of bhangra and dhol are brought together here under the rubric of Punjabi heritage, appropriately placed in the shadow of, yet nevertheless near and complementary to, the Sikh-dominated locus of Punjab. The dhol has been moved from the peripheral alley of dholis, a hard-to-locate neighborhood of Amritsar's downtrodden residents, to the city's center and its visual focus. Does the dhol benefit from such deep enfranchisement, from this elevated position scoured of the filth of its lowly and problematic past? And if the dhol has been moved to this honored place, what about the dholi?

As any place that contains a copy of the Sikh scripture is transformed into a *gurdvārā*—a gateway to the divine Guru—any place with the sound of dhol is transformed into a space of Punjabiness. Dhol works to instruct us about where we are, though interpretations of the borders and contours of that place vary. This book has shone a light on the local places where dhol resounds and creates spaces for particular cultural formations while arguing that the space has been broadened to encompass an expansive imaginary of Punjabi national culture. If the sound of dhol is the center from which the surrounding space is created, who inhabits that center, the position of the dhol player? Do people want the traditional dholi to inhabit that space? What happens when the subject of the margins, a Hindu or Muslim of a degraded social class, representing a culture that does not align with archetypes of Punjabi national culture, is placed in the center? It might seem better to keep the dhol but to remove the player.

In Chapter 6 I compared the earlier reformation of Hindustani music to the recent embourgeoisement of dhol playing. Both share the feature of weakening the link between musical practice and ethnic identity. They differ in that the former involved classicization and strengthening the link to state (Indian) identity, while the latter involves folklorization and strengthening national (Punjabi) identity. In the latter case, the aspect of occluding the traditional dholis' identities from dhol's national face bears additional comparison to the predicament of professional female dancers in north India as explained by Morcom (2013). Because their traditional work was stigmatized as inappropriately erotic, these performers, with hereditary ties to marked qaums, were socially marginalized. Yet a similar process of modern reformation of their genre for middle-class dancers did not result only in disentitlement to exclusive practice for their communities. Their concomitant disenfranchisement and the foreclosure of other opportunities pushed them into actual sex work (58). In that traditional dholis now occupy social positions similar to those the dancers had before reformation, more may be at stake for them in dhol's embourgeoisement than disentitlement to practice and social disenfranchisement. Foreclosure of opportunity may be on the horizon. Where will dholis go next?

Sherinian narrates how the Paraiyar, outcaste players of a frame drum, became icons of a Dalit liberation movement (2014, 13–14). By turning to their folk music, Tamil Christian Dalits consolidated and organized their identity in the struggle (34). The frame drum may remain unclean, but Dalits have been able to use it as part of their own political movement. In the case of outcaste drummers of the Himalayas, as analyzed by Fiol (2017), the drums were washed clean by separating them from the players and incorporating their image and repertoire into the heritage of all. Punjabi dholis have not sought their liberation through the dhol as in the Tamil case, although, as in the Himalayan case, their instrument has become part of a national heritage. What is distinct in the Punjab case is the phenomenon of others wanting to reinhabit the vacated space of drummers. The estrangement takes not only the form of removal of the folk sound from the folk body (Fiol 2017, 106) but also the replacement of the folk body.

Punjabi nationalism's valorization of *folk* as an authenticity that confers Punjabiness puts dhol in the middle of a struggle for identity that the traditional players cannot win. For, rather than reclaiming dhol for themselves, Punjabi dholis' struggle for better lives involved a strategy of acceptance of the power of their instrument to represent Punjab. As dholi Charan Das framed his achievement through the national events and figures at and for whom he played, twentieth-century dholis hitched their cart to the provisionally lucrative project of Punjabi nation building. In their struggle for survival and the betterment of their families, dholis participated in the expanding bubble of economic opportunities for people in their inherited profession. As seen in the biography of Garib Dass, the most prestigious opportunities for a dholi were those that engaged with the Punjabi culture industry and its international projection. The ever-increasing prospects of such work allowed the population of dhol professionals to grow. For a time, the enormous popularity of dhol gave dhol-playing qaums a level of prosperity and security that they had never experienced before. Yet all bubbles must burst eventually. As Punjabi farmers thrived during the Green Revolution, they also experienced its aftereffects: the exhaustion of resources and the flatlining of productivity as ecological limits were reached. So goes the ecology of the dhol profession. The dhol boom of the twentieth century was a tragedy of the commons. Its greatest resource, dholis, was taxed by the reduced viability of traditional players to sustain an environment in which all could earn. Yet the demand for dhol as a cultural commodity did not decrease. Other players have come to fill the role unburdened by the need to make a living. Traditional dholis, whose very existence depends on the use of dhol to make a living, are sidelined.

For the traditional dholi, work goes on. It goes on in a damaged ecological environment, which compels changes to the tradition and, ultimately, the loss of identity that individuals once gained from that tradition. The causes and effects are perpetual. The burst bubble, the decline in productivity, can be seen as a contributing factor to substance abuse. Substance abuse, in turn, hastened the departure of a generation of ustāds. To be sure, the older masters would pass eventually, but the social crisis also gutted the generation that would transmit their values to the younger generation. Without these values, invested in sustaining the community, the younger generation employs its own (new) strategies of immediate rather than long-term survival. They face the pressure of betraying the community by sustaining themselves in ways that change the tradition. First and most notable, the disappearance of model ustāds in Punjab facilitates the creeping acceptability (less stigma, less shame) of offering lessons for pay. This practice is on its way to becoming normal. Second, the playing of dhol by outsiders, with the precedent set by diaspora players, becomes more commonplace. Dhol goes on, in a form, but the dhol traditions as they were do not.

How should we respond to this situation, if at all? From a quasi-neutral, anthropological perspective, we witness an unsurprising change to the practice of traditions. From the perspective of someone in support of ending all caste-type distinctions, one may celebrate the chance to obliterate the phenomenon of ethnic or professional exclusivity in its application to "music." My perspective, as an advocate for the dhol-playing communities with whom I have worked, compels an argument that something must be *acknowledged* here. Change may be both productive and destructive, in unequal proportions. Any response to the situation should acknowledge dholis' ethnic and professional identities. Ignoring their identities, whether motivated by so-called color-blindness, visions of unity, or increasing accessibility, erases them. Such an erasure has real-world effects on individuals—individuals in disadvantaged positions. To speak of effects in this fashion engages philosophical debates on "cultural appropriation." A liberal approach to those debates suggests setting a high bar for the application of the label "appropriation" when it concerns the intangible of culture. In this case, the real economic effect precipitated by the stripping of cultural identity meets that bar. As the idea that "anyone may be a dholi" grows, the cultural basis of acquiring capital by dholis, already marginalized in a literal sense, has been reduced. Injury is added to insult.

At a minimum, it is ethically appropriate to cultivate recognition of who the real dhol players are. Dholis *along with* their respective ethnic groups should be acknowledged for their role in shaping the traditions that put the soul in Punjabi culture. The dholis of Punjab are not just anybody who happens to play the instrument. They are people with distinct identities, who have created, maintained, and lived the experiences that are at the heart of modern Punjab. This book has been an effort to write these people into the story of dhol.

NOTES

Introduction

1. As the reader shall discover, Punjabi usage of *ḍhol* encompasses several phenomena and may be taken to include multiple meanings simultaneously. The word may refer not only to an instrument-object (a drum) but also to the genre and repertoire of performance on the instrument, the manifested playing or sound of the instrument, and, more abstractly, a composite of cultural traditions of which the instrument is at the center. Moreover, as revealed in Chapter 2, personification of *ḍhol* further enriches its semantic resonance. The absence of the definite article (i.e., "the") in the Punjabi language colludes to ambiguate the meaning of the word in some contexts, or rather enables such polysemy to thrive. In respect for the Punjabi discourse, in approximation of which this book strives to facilitate a faithful and rich discussion, *ḍhol* is also, by default, used without the definite article. When a narrow denotation is required, the work employs an article ("the dhol," "a dhol"), plural ending ("dhols"), or such phrases as "the dhol drum" and "dhol playing."

2. Fiol defines *folklorization* as "the recontextualized composition or performance of local artistic practices as a means to express cultural identity" (2017, 3).

3. For Sitla Devi, see Bhatti (2000, 133).

4. The Census of India for 2011 (http://www.censusindia.gov.in) and the Census of Pakistan for 2017 (http://www.pbs.gov.pk).

5. In that year, the eastern portion was further divided such that Punjab lost territory to Rajasthan and the new states of Himachal Pradesh and Haryana.

6. Turino, whose work on identity I engage elsewhere, rejects the use of *global* in reference to things that are not universal (2008, 119). I, however, retain it to refer to things widely dispersed across the world.

7. Compare al Faruqi's (1985) analysis of the status of *mūsīqā* in the Islamic world.

8. For an example, see "ghoriyan," *Pannu Punjabi cooking and kahaniyan* YouTube channel, May 4, 2019, https://youtu.be/rF40cO4QnRY.

9. For an example, see "Idu Sharif—Songs of Five rivers," *Rajeesh Kaushik* YouTube channel, November 17, 2010, https://youtu.be/VGsBJjAPtZ4.

10. For case studies of this phenomenon in other regions of South Asia, see also Sakata (1983), Slobin (1976), and Sherinian (2014).

11. They include the Talwandi, Sham Chaurasi, Kapurthala, Saharanpur, and Qasur and the latter's offshoot, the Patiala *gharānās* (Sharma 2006, 57–78). Among the renowned performers belonging to the Patiala *gharānā* was Bade Ghulam Ali Khan (1902–1968). For an example, see "Raag Malkauns," *Syed Wajid* YouTube channel, June 21, 2012, https://youtu.be/sisG8crGoEQ.

12. Kalra (2015, 44) considers the ascription of "classical music" to this repertoire to be the product of "colonial modernity." Bakhle (2005) narrates a process of musical performance becoming marked as "respectable" as, at the end of a process from the eighteenth to the twentieth century, this repertoire came to occupy pride of place in the Indian imagination.

13. It must be acknowledged that, although the focus of this book is divisions along lines of class and ethnicity, one could equally interrogate Punjabi identity's gender divisions. Dhol players, inclusive of the lay and the professional, exist in societies where gender boundaries are significant determinants of one's scope of action. Consider Denise Gill's observation that musical actors, by their practices, partake in learning and shaping their own and others' sense of the world through subjective gender-based lenses (2017, 141). Factoring in the ways that gender intersects with identity professionally, ethnically, and nationally, however, requires a scope too vast for the present work to address.

Chapter 1. The Short End of the Stick

1. Prejudice among some Sikhs has prompted "low-caste" Sikhs to search for alternative religious spaces, such as their own gurdwaras, syncretistic sects like Radhasoami and Dera Vadbhag Singh, or the shrines of Muslim saints (Puri 2004b, 218).

2. For discussions of *tribe*, see Hasnain (1983, 12–18) and Tapper (1997, 5–6).

3. Tribal people of Punjab are not to be confused with the Adivasi (indigenous), to whom state discourse refers as "tribals" and who make up an insignificant portion of the population.

4. Commander (1983, 284–288), Eglar (1960, 28–41), and Wiser (1936).

5. See Grewal (2004a, 4–8) for a sketch of this history of peoples moving into Punjab.

6. See, for example, Latif (1891).

7. A fuller analysis appears as Schreffler (2012b).

8. Note, e.g., Banerji (1988) and Banerji and Baumann (1990), which set the stage for many reflections on bhangra music and British Asian identity in the 1990s.

9. Herzfeld extends Anderson's idea by adding that the imagined-community effect is not limited to the imagination of nation-states (2005, 5).

10. Herzfeld uses the concept of cultural intimacy to refer to "the recognition of those aspects of a cultural identity that are considered a source of external embar-

rassment but that nevertheless provide insiders with their assurance of common sociality" (2005, 3).

11. Mooney observes that although Jatts are the majority group among Punjabis, their position in India and host societies in other countries compels them, simultaneously, to "cultivate a sense of marginality" (2013, 283).

12. As Lipsitz writes, "Members of dominant social groups might not feel the same anguish of invisibility that oppresses ethnic minorities, but cultural identity has become an exercise in alienation for them as well" (1986, 159).

Chapter 2. Dhol Manifested

1. Interview, February 25, 2005.

2. Hands folded and against the forehead, the player bows to dhol (*matthā ṭekṇā*). He makes a supplication, a sample content of which Garib Dass describes: *One must pray to one's God, "May my work be good; May the rhythm that I play be true."*

3. For a comparative discussion of these forms, see Schreffler (2010, 341–356).

4. Verse 390, sourced from a Perso-Arabic script edition (Khan 1986, 134) and a Gurmukhi excerpt (Kang 1994, 93).

5. A typical line states, "Dhol and kettledrums were beaten and the forces clashed" (*vajje ḍhol nagāre dalāṅ mukāblā*; Sri Dasam Granth, p. 248).

6. See, e.g., verse 230 (Nijjhar 2000, 90) and verse 184 (78), respectively.

7. For the remainder of this chapter, I employ the present tense when describing general affairs that may be considered more or less extant to date. Most of the data were gathered in the 2000s and it is to this period that such general statements strictly pertain, although most can be presumed to have continued since. Directly reported events and personal statements, by contrast, are voiced here in the past tense.

8. Other, less-used woods include *sarīṅh* (*siris*, *Acacia speciosa*), *akhroṭ* (Indian walnut, *Aleurites moluccana*), and *tūn* (Indian red cedar, *Cedrela toona*).

9. For a comparable view of an Indian drumming community's negotiation of modern drumhead options, see Manuel (2015, 153–158).

10. As historical evidence of this role, an 1880s observer remarked, "The women only are allowed to use cymbals *(tambal)* and a small drum *(dholkí)* on special occasions, the practice in their case being sanctioned by the example of certain holy women of old" (Tucker 1884, 75).

11. Mirasis of the village Jarg all played with the reverse grip. Among them, Samim Muhammad (Gaga) could play with either grip but felt the reverse grip offered a technical advantage (Samim Muhammad, interview by the author, Jarg, March 29, 2005).

12. A Bharai dholi, Sultan Dhillon, once played with the reverse grip and an affected, sloppy technique to lampoon the way he thought Bazigars played (interview by the author, Malerkotla, January 21, 2005). However, the Bazigar Garib Dass said proudly that none from his immediate community used the reverse grip and that, if they had, their elders would chastise them (interview by the author, Chandigarh, March 30, 2005).

13. Kippen's metalabel for this phenomenon, "groove," is useful (2006, 86). In restricting my discussion here to dhol, however, it is sufficient to use the dholis' own Punjabi and English terms, i.e., *tāl* and *rhythm*.

14. Potential confusion arises from the fact that one may perform on the dhol while employing the classical *tāl* concept. Doing so was not the norm, however, and therefore it is recognizable as a "classical" style adapted to a "folk" instrument.

15. The reader may compare the treble strokes in my simple meter representation of dhamāl (Figure 2.1) and in audiovisual example 25 to the rendition of dhamāl in "Un groupe de Dhamal," *Local Traditional Artist—Topic* YouTube channel, June 19, 2018, https://youtu.be/kfmsAlr-gxY. In this example, the treble strokes suggest compound meter.

16. A conversation between Wolf and his interlocuter Baksh, a *naqqārah* player (2014, 86), suggests Baksh had an explicit awareness of the phenomenon of not subdividing *tāls* that I present here.

17. The term *tirakaṭ* is derived from the classical *bol* sequence for a ubiquitous four-stroke pattern, but the dholis' concept does not correspond to that specific pattern, being rather a general impression of that sort of ornamental gesture.

18. *Laggī* corresponds to a technique used in art music (Stewart 1974, 130–48).

19. *Ḍabal* patterns corresponding to various *tāls*, unknown to many Indian dholis, can be heard played by Indian dholi Garib Dass and Pakistani dholi Muhammad Boota in audiovisual examples 4, 9, and 15.

20. *ḍhol mār ke te dhāṇāṅ jhang utte, nahīoṅ haṭdā hāṭh dā mohrā ve*. Verse 167 in Nijjhar (2000, 70).

21. Rajpal Singh, interview by the author, Chandigarh, December 23, 2004.

22. Garib Dass, interview by the author, Chandigarh, June 5, 2005.

23. "Babur's boats," reproduced in Wade (1998, Plate 9).

24. For Punjabi wrestling, see Jogi (1990, 4).

25. Wolf, during the *'urs* at Shah Hussain's shrine (*melā cirāgāṇ dā*) in 1997 and 2003, found that dholis played three or four rhythms, such as dhamāl, bhangṛā, *tīntārā*, and *lahirā* (2006, 254). The dhamāl rhythm is thought to have originated at the Sevan Sharif shrine in Sindh, where it was played to stimulate dancers honoring the thirteenth-century saint Lal Shahbaz Qalandar (Baloch 1975, 35).

26. Garib Dass, interview by the author, Chandigarh, March 19, 2005.

27. Garib Dass, interview by the author, Chandigarh, March 20, 2005.

28. Bal Kishan, interview by the author, Jammu Cantonment, May 21, 2005.

29. Bahadur Singh, interview by the author, Sunam, April 25, 2005.

30. Balbir Singh Sekhon, February 23, 2006 (in privately shared video interview by Teginder and Surinder Dhanoa).

31. Like the swing earlier discussed in bhangṛā rhythm, the swing in luḍḍī is noticeable between pairs of successive treble strokes. In this case, however, the variation in each second stroke's placement ranges between the second part of a duplet and the third part of a triplet—as with the eighth notes in jazz. Figure 2.12 represents the rhythm in duple subdivision to correspond to Hindustani music's *kahirvā tāl* and analogously to the practice for jazz scores.

32. Lal Singh Bhatti, interview by the author, Claremont, California, February 25, 2020.

33. Women's giddhā is described in works including Dhillon (1998), Nahar Singh (1988), and Satyarthi (1998 [1936]). For men's giddhā, see Nahar Singh (1998).

34. Some conscientious dholis in this role elect to play a *ḍholkī*, but most prefer the volume and convenience of the dhol they have brought along to accompany other items.

Chapter 3. Asking Rude Questions

1. "Other Backward Classes" constitutes a dynamic list of groups "socially and educationally backward," whose welfare, per Article 340 of the Constitution of India, the government is obligated to promote. See Ghurye (2016 [1932], 216).

2. Their explanation for their lack of knowledge was that they had no need of identifying *specific* castes. Individuals with Scheduled Caste status came to them with a previously verified card stating that they qualify, without having to reveal their specific background.

3. Garib Dass, interview by the author, Santa Barbara, California, May 22, 2003.

4. The disclaimer applies that these descriptions include a necessary amount of generalization and that they are meant to highlight the notable and distinctive while acknowledging fluidity. Further, the majority of data being collected in the past, albeit relatively recently (the 2000s), the descriptions should not be taken to imply that the communities continue unchanged. On the contrary, the exposition based in that time period provides a point of reference to a state of affairs to which more recent changes subsequently will be observed.

5. K. Singh (1998, 4: 861).

6. See, e.g., Baines (1912, 85), Blunt (1969 [1931], 151), Elliot (1976 [1859], 84), and Risley (1969 [1908], 134). This line of conventional thought depends on the hypothesis that the Indo-Aryan language family, which, evidence suggests, originated outside South Asia, was introduced with the advent of a certain group of peoples to the region. Evidence may, however, be insufficient to make such a conjecture. On this, see Bryant (2001).

7. This was the case, for example, in the mountains northeast of Punjab (Chandola 1977, 5; Fiol 2017, 40).

8. For examples of jogi music makers in other parts of India, see Henry (1991) and Natavar (2000, 643).

9. Bal Kishan interview.

10. Ramesh Chand, interview by the author, Dharival, February 23, 2005.

11. Pappu, interview by the author, Ludhiana, February 2, 2019.

12. Punjab's caste schedule indicates "Doom," "Dumna," and "Mahasha" together in a single entry. In the 2011 census, this group numbered some 202,000 (Government of India, "State and District-wise Scheduled Castes Population for Each Caste Separately [*sic*], 2011—PUNJAB," https://data.gov.in/resources/state-and-district-wise-scheduled-castes-population-each-caste-seperately-2011-punjab).

13. Kala Takhi, interview by the author, Jalandhar, November 19, 2004.

14. Madan Lal, interview by the author, Purkhu, May 21, 2005. I did hear one Jogi consider Mahashas to be of his same *birādarī* (Des Raj, interview by the author, Ludhiana, February 17, 2005). However, this view was an exception to the rule that Jogi and Mahasha were separate qaums.

15. Garib Dass, interview by the author, Chandigarh, May 18, 2005. "Dove" is the meaning of the name "Ghuggi."

16. Anonymous dholi outside Baba Kishan Singh music shop, interview by the author, Amritsar, February 19, 2005.

17. Garib Dass interview, May 18, 2005.

18. Chabli Nath "Babbi," February 27, 2006 (in privately shared video interview by Teginder and Surinder Dhanoa).

19. Harbans Lal Jogi, interview by the author, Amritsar, February 15, 2019.

20. Harbans Lal Jogi, interviews by the author, Amritsar, June 18, 2006, and February 15, 2019.

21. Charan Das, interview by the author, Jalandhar, November 20, 2004.

22. Harbans Lal Kaku, interview, in *Lok Sāz: Folk Instruments of Punjab*. Punjabi University DVD, 2015.

23. Harbans Lal Kaku, interview by the author, Jalandhar, November 21, 2004.

24. Vishnu, interview by the author, Bathinda, April 27, 2005.

25. Sher Khan, interview by the author, Jarg, May 14, 2005.

26. Salamat Ali, interview by the author, Malerkotla, February 7, 2019.

27. Muhammad Boota, interview by the author, New York, October 9, 2018.

28. Recall the reference by Nahar Singh to "Dum, Jogi, Shekh, or Bharai." It might be more accurately parsed as "Dum/Jogi or Shekh/Bharai." In the census of 1881, Bharais in the Lahore division were subsumed under "Shekh" [*sic*] (Ibbetson 1995 [1983], 229). And in the 1901 census, the Bharai were counted only under the rubric of Shaikh (Baines 1912, 91). A later, Pakistan-based study calls Sheikh a "Family or lineage name of bharain" (Faruqi et al. 1989, 35). In June 2006 my informants at the village of Dhaunkal (an important Sakhi Sarvar pilgrimage site) hardly recognized the word *Bharai*, referring instead to the dholis as Shaikh. In February 2019, at the shrine of Haider Shaikh in Malerkotla, Mirasis referred to the local Bharais both as Bharai and Shaikh.

29. Boota interview. See also Wolf (2014, 29).

30. Boota interview.

31. Akhtar Dhillon, interview by the author, Malerkotla, May 13, 2005.

32. Both Sakhi Sarvar and Haider Shaikh may appear in green clothing and on horseback. Artwork depicting both saints surrounded by common Sufi symbols and captioned with ambiguous titles freely circulates among Haider Shaikh's devotees.

33. Muhammad Sabi, interview by the author, Malerkotla, April 14, 2005.

34. Akhtar Dhillon interview, May 13, 2005.

35. Akhtar Dhillon, interview by the author, Malerkotla, February 5, 2019.

36. Akhtar Dhillon, interview by the author, Malerkotla, April 15, 2005.

37. Ibid.

38. Akhtar Dhillon interview, May 13, 2005.

39. Sultan Dhillon, interview by the author, Malerkotla, April 15, 2005.

40. Though they are sometimes called *Bhangī* in other areas, Ibbetson noted in the late nineteenth century that *Bhangī* was considered derogatory and that group members themselves preferred "Chuhra" in Punjab (1995 [1883], 293). In recent years, "Chuhra" has been designated as offensive speech, such that using the term *with abusive intent* can be a criminal offense (Judge 2003, 2990).

41. Taken together, the Sweepers and Chamar make up around 80 percent of the Scheduled Caste population in East Punjab (Jodhka 2004, 65).

42. One might suspect the word should be *mahṛī* ("shrine erected at a cremation site"), but the precise word in use for Gugga's temples is indeed *māṛī* ("mansion").

43. For an example of a song text, see S. Bedi (1991, 1254).

44. This idea arose out of a conversation with Dr. Harvinder S. Bhatti (November 9, 2004) and partial credit goes to him.

45. This information largely derives from a pilgrimage to Goga Meri (Rajasthan) in September 2004, which I undertook along with *bhagat*s from Dadu Majra Colony.

46. The shrine was demolished in 2007, being deemed by the local government to have encroached on public land.

47. Gulab Singh, interview by the author, Chandigarh, April 17, 2005.

48. Balbir Singh interview by the author, Malerkotla, April 14, 2005.

49. In the original Arab context, *shaykh* refers to a chief or elder. Imported into the Indian context, it retained that meaning but also gained use as a respectful title for people of Arab descent. By the nineteenth century, the term had "degraded to a much more vulgar use" (Rose 1914, 399).

50. A list of such castes calling themselves Shaikh in the Gujrat district in the late nineteenth century included the musician groups Dohli (dholi), Mirasi, Rababi, and Nakarchi (Rose 1914, 400–401). In 1931, the Mirasis in Uttar Pradesh gave Shaikh as their new name (Ansari 1960, 38). Neuman later recorded that Mirasis in Delhi rarely called themselves Mirasi, saying instead their caste was Shaikh (1990, 124). Still more recent data show that Mirasis in Chandigarh were called Shaikh (K. Singh 1998, 5: 2300).

51. For *malang*, see Ewing (1984, 359).

52. Saghir Ali, interview by the author, Jhelum, June 21, 2006.

53. According to Thind, the Sansis comprised more than fifty subgroups (1996, 22). The Sansi's oral history begins, like many itinerant tribes', with a Rajput ancestor. Their namesake was said to have been Raja Sans Mall of Rajasthan (Ibbetson 1995 [1883], 158; Sher 1965, 4). There are about 60,000 speakers of the Sansi language. Few Sansis under the age of 40, however, are competent speakers (Gusain 2002). The so-called Sansi language documented by Rose (1914, 369–370) was not this language (which would be fairly comprehensible to local outsiders) but rather a secret language of the community he studied. It mostly consists of Punjabi words tempered by semi-systematic sound shifts to obscure recognition.

54. I did speak to a Dakaunt in Chandigarh (2005) who said that his relatives in a nearby village played dhol.

55. Joginder Chota, interview by the author, Chak Khiva, May 1, 2005.

56. Founded in the 1920s by a Chamar scholar, Mangoo Ram, the movement sought to uplift Dalits and to carve a niche for them distinct from the Vedic Hindu population, in the process characterizing the Dalits as heirs to the original faith of India (Ram 2004, 329–331).

57. Jagdish Yamla, interview by the author, Ludhiana, February 17, 2005.

58. Vijay Yamla, interview by the author, Surrey, British Columbia, April 19, 2019.

Chapter 4. A Portrait of a Dholi and His Community

1. Biographical information on Garib Dass and statements made by him are drawn from innumerable conversations with the author in Chandigarh, India, and in Santa Barbara, California, and South Windsor, Connecticut, between 2000 and 2007.

2. Son of Makkhan Ram, interview by the author, Ludhiana, February 27, 2005.

3. Garib Dass, interview by the author, Chandigarh, May 19, 2005.

4. In this and other aspects of social position and structure, the Bazigars may be compared with the Sansis of Punjab (Chapter 3) and the Bedia of Madhya Pradesh, Uttar Pradesh, and Rajasthan (Agrawal, 2004, 225–226).

5. Garib Dass interview, March 30, 2005.

6. Garib Dass, interview by the author, Chandigarh, December 27, 2004.

7. Government of India, "State and District-wise Scheduled Castes Population for Each Caste Separately [*sic*], 2011—PUNJAB," https://data.gov.in/resources/state-and-district-wise-scheduled-castes-population-each-caste-seperately-2011-punjab.

8. Garib Dass interview, March 30, 2005.

9. Several other Scheduled Castes are reported to have "secret" languages (Grierson 1968 [1922], 8–11; Rose 1919, 369).

10. Garib Dass interview, May 19, 2005.

11. See Rose's observations on dancing in colonial Punjab: "It is, as a popular pastime, confined almost entirely to the hills and the Indus valley. Elsewhere it is a profession, and confined to certain castes. Further where it is allowable for people to do their own dancing, without calling in the professionals, it is more or less confined to religious or ceremonial occasions" (Rose 1919, 920).

12. For a representative clip, see "Bhangra scene from Naya Daur," *wujatt36* YouTube channel, April 21, 2009, https://youtu.be/5yoiLOfjdaQ

13. Garib Dass, interview by the author, Chandigarh, December 12, 2004.

14. Bahadur Singh interview, April 25, 2005.

15. Theater director Neelam Man Singh Chowdhry related how, in 1984, she happened on the group performing in a village. She subsequently invited them to perform both new and revamped classic stage pieces in conjunction with modern artists (interview by the author, Chandigarh, July 29, 2004).

16. Prem Chand and Party, "Nakkālāṅ de Sāng." Live performance audio cassette, Kala Bhavan, Chandigarh, March 27, 1992.

17. Among the films are *Jagte Raho* (1956), *Naya Daur* (1957), and *Mirza Sahiban* (1957).

18. Biru Ram, interview by the author, Sanaur, November 25, 2004.
19. Saroop Singh, interview by the author, Chandigarh, November 28, 2004.

Chapter 5. Becoming and Being a Dholi

1. In recognition of significant changes in progress—addressed particularly in Chapter 7—this chapter will speak predominantly in the past tense, to indicate that the phenomena pertain to an earlier period of observation (the 2000s) and history of the previous century.
2. Compare Baily's (1988, 101–103) discussion of amateur musicians in Afghanistan.
3. See also Neuman (1990, 204) on hereditary classical musicians as guilds.
4. Pappu interview.
5. Neuman's study (1990, 44) distinguishes the use, in Hindustani music, of *gurū* and *ustād* for Hindu and Muslim masters, respectively. By contrast, in Punjabi vernacular music-culture, *ustād* was commonly used for Hindu masters as well.
6. Mali Ram, interview by the author, New York, October 8, 2018. See also Neuman on love of the disciple in classical music (1990, 45).
7. Neuman notes, similarly, "a guru will not transmit his knowledge promiscuously" (1990, 48). The master would rather have no students than one who misrepresents him.
8. Mali Ram stated on record that he made Garib Dass his master in 1968 (Jaimalvala 2008).
9. I was one of those distant Others, as I suggest in Chapter 7, whose playing dhol as a veritable hobby was of little consequence. Yet I strove to offer a degree of service while Garib Dass, convinced of my admirable intentions, agreed to provide nurturing. The relationship was a facsimile of *ustād-shagird*, but could never really be more. We never formalized the relationship, sharing an understanding that the case was exceptional.
10. Garib Dass interview, May 22, 2003.
11. Mali Ram interview.
12. Ibid.
13. I obtained this side of the story from Amit Aulakh, October 6, 2018.
14. Regarding becoming a musician in the classical tradition, from the perspective of Delhi in the 1970s, see Neuman (1990, 43–58).
15. See also Neuman (1990, 50): "The guru enculturates the shishya [disciple] into musical life."
16. Ramesh Chand interview.
17. Chabli Nath "Babbi," February 27, 2006 (in privately shared video interview by Teginder and Surinder Dhanoa).
18. Wolf's consultant, a Pakistani Bharai named Niamat Ali, said that one cannot receive formal teaching from a family member (2014, 55).
19. See also Kippen's description of a discipleship ceremony in a classical tradition (2008, 130–131).
20. Meaning "paternal grandfather," the metaphoric usage of *dādā* is like the prefix "grand-." See also Neuman (1990, 45).

21. This is complicated by the fact that the Muharram festival, as problematized by Wolf, may at once be construed as a period of grieving or a time of grateful remembrance. One of Wolf's interlocutors conceded the right of the dhol to be played during that time because its dark timbre and deep pitch were believed to suit the mood of sadness (2000, 105).

22. Boota called the rhythm *ḍhaḍḍ*. See also Baloch (1975, 32) for mention of this rhythm in the Sindhi dhol tradition. Wolf documented a death-related rhythm of Pakistan dholis called *mārū*, in 7 beats (2014, 285).

23. Gulab Singh, interview by the author, Chandigarh, January 13, 2005.

24. Ravi Malhotra, interview by the author, Ludhiana, May 22, 2005.

25. Variations of luḍḍī swing as a function of stylistic difference (as well as tempo difference) may be heard in audiovisual example 28. The rhythm is familiar globally, after the fashion of Indian players, in the style of loping, long-short pairs of treble strokes that approach a 2:1 ratio of duration. Whereas the first player in the example, the Indian Dev Raj, plays closer to that ratio, the second, Pakistani Muhammad Boota, plays the pairs that more approximate a straight feel (1:1 ratio).

26. Harbans Lal Kaku interview, November 21, 2004.

27. Garib Dass, interview by the author, Chandigarh, March 1, 2005.

28. Garib Dass interview, May 18, 2005.

29. Ibid.

30. Majid Ali, interview by the author, Malerkotla, February 5, 2019.

31. Garib Dass, interview by the author, Chandigarh, December 9, 2004.

32. Bharais of the nineteenth century used "a curiously shaped stick, like a short crook shape," considered particular to their identity (Rose 1911, 86). One Bharai dholi whom I met, who followed the traditional routine of his community, did use such a distinctive ḍaggā.

33. Saghir Ali, interview. Pappu Sain, in conversation with Wolf (2014, 164), ascribed the origin of the stiff stick to Baba Lal Magpur, a dholi from Gujrat. Pappu said it was he who then introduced this style to the dholis of Lahore.

34. Samim Muhammad interview.

35. Ehsan Dhillon interview by the author, Malerkotla, February 5, 2019.

36. Bal Kishan interview.

Chapter 6. Dhol Players in a New World

1. Sharp characterized folk music as "a communal and racial product, the expression, in musical idiom, of aims and ideals that are primarily national in character" (1907, x).

2. This is Turino's idea of modernist reformism (2000, 16).

3. The rhetorical binary I present here is complicated by the fact that, as Chapter 3 showed, minority communities have adopted dhol in recent generations and, in that sense, may have weaker claim to the position of authenticity by descent. Local conflicts between these actors and dholis from communities with longer dhol traditions are mitigated by shared class position.

4. Des Raj, telephone interview by the author, August 2019.

5. Surinder Kaur, interview by the author, Chandigarh, July 30, 2004.
6. See Malkit Singh and Golden Star, "Hey Jamalo," on the album Up Front. Oriental Star Agencies cassette, 1988. A music video for the song, including folkloric dress and dance actions, can be seen at https://youtu.be/7c4P__CoGgw.
7. Surinder Singh Shinda, *Dhol Beat.* Fantronic cassette, 1993.
8. Harbans Lal Jogi interview, February 15, 2019.
9. Teginder Dhanoa correspondence, January 3, 2010.
10. Sodhi Lal (son of Piare Lal), telephone interview by the author, April 14, 2019.
11. Rayman Bhullar, interview by the author, Surrey, British Columbia, April 17, 2019.
12. Gaurav Sharma, interview by the author, Brampton, Ontario, October 16, 2018.
13. Tejinder Singh, interview by the author, Surrey, British Columbia, April 18, 2019.
14. Rayman Bhullar interview.
15. Gurvinder Kambo, telephone interview by the author, October 23, 2018.
16. Lal Singh Bhatti interview.
17. Ibid.
18. Boota has photos in which he posed with Pakistani prime minister Benazir Bhutto and Pakistani president Pervez Musharraf, as well as with US secretary of state Hillary Clinton. He was included in Maira's 1990s study of the nightclub bhangra scene (2002, 33).
19. Des Raj, interview by the author, Surrey, British Columbia, April 14, 2019.
20. Shiraz Higgins, dir., *Bhangra City.* Victoria, British Columbia: Made You Look Media video, 2017.
21. Rayman Bhullar interview.
22. "Gopi Sian and Rayman Bhuller," *The Harpreet Singh Show*, October 5, 2015, https://youtu.be/a6RVK3vyOa8.
23. Garib Dass interview by the author, Chandigarh, May 30, 2005.
24. "Gopi Sian and Rayman Bhuller."
25. Before Bhullar, the group was accompanied by Kam Johal, a student of Lal Singh Bhatti and another in the history of lay players of British Columbia (Tejinder Singh interview, April 18, 2019).
26. Gaurav Sharma, interview by the author, Brampton, Ontario, October 14, 2018.
27. Ibid.
28. Amrinder Singh Pannu correspondence, April 22, 2014.
29. "Meet Our Staff," DCMPAA.com, accessed October 15, 2020, http://www.dcmpaa.com/staff.
30. Ibid.
31. Gurvinder Kambo interview.
32. The Dhol Foundation, *Big Drum: Small World.* Shakti CD, 2001. Listen to the track "Drummers' Reel" here: https://youtu.be/99zLwC6krjc.
33. The course begins with a pattern affectionately called "Mummy Daddy," which, rendered in *bol* as "na ge ge na," simply alternates between the treble and bass sides of the instrument.
34. Jas Bhambra, interview by the author, Southall, UK, April 20, 2009.
35. Raj Reehal, interview by the author, Brampton, Ontario, October 14, 2018.

36. "Culture + Passion + Fitness," Nachdijawani.com, accessed May 7, 2021, http://www.nachdijawani.com/about-us.php.

37. Tejinder Singh interview.

38. Gurp Sian, interview by the author, Surrey, British Columbia, April 17, 2019.

39. Hardeep Sahota, interview by the author, Surrey, British Columbia, April 18, 2019.

40. Hardeep Sahota, Tejinder Singh interviews.

41. Manvir Hothi, *Simply Dhol*, accessed May 7, 2021, https://www.youtube.com/manvirhothi

42. "Bollywood Bhangra Blunder?" (2018).

43. Manvir Hothi, interview by the author, Brampton, Ontario, October 13, 2018.

Chapter 7. Return to Punjab, Turning Punjab

1. Manak Raj, interview by the author, Sanaur, January 27, 2019.

2. Anil Takhi, interview by the author, Jalandhar, February 3, 2019.

3. Kala, interview by the author, Ludhiana, February 2, 2019.

4. Naresh Kukki, interview by the author, Ludhiana, February 2, 2019.

5. Interview.

6. Dr. Narinder Nindi, a Chandigarh theater director, was working to accommodate Dev Raj at the time, feeling that he was the only person left in the area with knowledge of folk forms (interview by the author, Chandigarh, February 13, 2019).

7. Dev Raj, interview by the author, Chandigarh, February 12, 2019.

8. Charan Das, interview by the author, Jalandhar, February 3, 2019.

9. Charan Das interview, November 20, 2004.

10. Dev Raj, interview by the author, Amritsar, February 15, 2019.

11. Bahadur Singh died on February 20, 2019.

12. Vijay Yamla interview. Vijay Yamla is the grandson of Yamla Jatt of the Chamar community. He has carried on the dhol practice initiated by his uncle Jagdish, having learned dhol from Kukki.

13. Jass Vartia, interview by the author, Chandigarh, February 10, 2019.

14. Naresh Kukki interview.

15. Kartar Singh, interview by the author, Chandigarh, February 13, 2019.

16. See also Neuman's remarks on masters maintaining discipline (1990, 48). My consultant Gurvinder Kambo (interview) likened dholis without teachers to wayward children.

17. Manak Raj interview.

18. Kala interview, February 2, 2019.

19. *Dhol: The Power Rhythm of India*. Tips cassette, 2001.

20. Kala Takhi interview, November 19, 2004.

21. Mali Ram interview.

22. Kala interview, February 2, 2019.

23. Akhtar Dhillon interview, February 5, 2019.

BIBLIOGRAPHY

Abul-Fazl-i-'Allámí. (1872 [c. 1590]). *The Á'in-i-Akbarí: In the Original Persian* (Vol. 1). H. Blochmann (Ed.). Calcutta: Baptist Mission Press.

———. (1873 [c. 1590]). *The Ain I Akbari* (Vol. 1). (H. Blochmann, Trans.). Calcutta: Baptist Mission Press.

———. (1894 [c. 1590]). *The Á'in-i-Akbarí* (Vol. 3). (H. S. Jarrett, Trans.). Calcutta: Baptist Mission Press.

Agawu, Kofi. (2003). *Representing African Music: Postcolonial Notes, Queries, Positions*. New York: Routledge.

Agrawal, Anuja. (2004). "The Bedias Are Rajputs": Caste Consciousness of a Marginal Community. *Contributions to Indian Sociology* 38(1–2), 221–246.

Ahmad, Saghir. (1977). *Class and Power in a Punjabi Village*. New York: Monthly Review Press.

Ali, Imran. (1988). *The Punjab Under Imperialism*. Princeton, NJ: Princeton University Press.

———. (1997). Canal Colonization and Socio-economic Change. In I. Banga (Ed.), *Five Punjabi Centuries* (pp. 341–357). New Delhi: Manohar.

Allen, Matthew Harp. (1998). Tales Tunes Tell: Deepening the Dialogue between "Classical" and "Non-classical" in the Music of India. *Yearbook for Traditional Music* 30, 22–52.

Ambedkar, Atul, Ravindra Rao, Alok Agrawal, Ashwani Mishra, Rajesh Kumar, and Manish Kumar. (2016). *Punjab Opioid Dependence Survey*. New Delhi: AIIMS.

Amna, Dur e Aziz. (2017, June 22). The Ramadan Drummer of Coney Island. *Roads and Kingdoms*. https://roadsandkingdoms.com/2017/the-ramadan-drummer-of-coney-island/.

Anderson, Benedict. (1991). *Imagined Communities: Reflections on the Origin and Spread of Nationalism*. Rev. ed. London: Verso.

Ansari, Ghaus. (1960). Muslim Caste in Uttar Pradesh: A Study of Culture Contact. *Eastern Anthropologist* 13(2), 5–80.

Axel, Brian K. (2001). *The Nation's Tortured Body: Violence, Representation, and the Formation of a Sikh "Diaspora."* Durham, NC: Duke University Press.

Bagga, Neeraj. (2005). DJ Culture in Full Blast, Dholis in Doldrums. *Tribune*, October 13. Amritsar ed. Retrieved from https://www.tribuneindia.com/2005/20051013/aplus.htm#2.

Baily, John. (1988). *Music of Afghanistan: Professional Musicians in the City of Herat.* Cambridge: Cambridge University Press.

Baines, Athelstane. (1912). *Ethnography (Castes and Tribes).* Strasbourg: Karl J. Trübner.

Bakhle, Janaki. (2005). *Two Men and Music: Nationalism in the Making of an Indian Classical Tradition.* Oxford: Oxford University Press.

Baloch, Nabi B. K. (1975). *Musical Instruments of the Lower Indus Valley of Sind.* 2nd ed. Hyderabad, India: Zeb Adabi Markaz.

Banerji, Sabita. (1988). Ghazals to Bhangra in Great Britain. *Popular Music* 7(2), 207–213.

Banerji, Sabita, and Gerd Baumann. (1990). Bhangra 1984–88: Fusion and Professionalization in a Genre of South Asian Dance Music. In P. Oliver (ed.), *Black Music in Britain: Essays on the Afro-Asian Contribution to Popular Music* (pp. 137–152). Milton Keynes, UK: Open University Press.

Banga, Indu. (1996). *Cultural Reorientation in Modern India.* Shimla, India: Indian Institute of Advanced Studies.

Barth, Fredrik. (1998). Introduction. In Fredrik Barth (ed.), *Ethnic Groups and Boundaries: The Social Organization of Cultural Difference* (pp. 9–38). Prospect Heights, IL: Waveland.

Baumann, Gerd. (1996). *Contesting Culture: Discourses of Identity in Multi-ethnic London.* Cambridge: Cambridge University Press.

———. (1999). *The Multicultural Riddle: Rethinking National, Ethnic and Religious Identities.* New York: Routledge.

Bedi, Rahul. (2018, July 9). Drugs Crisis in Indian State "More Deadly Than 15 Years of Conflict." *Telegraph.* Retrieved from https://www.telegraph.co.uk/news/2018/07/09/drugs-crisis-indian-state-deadly-15-years-terrorism-government/.

Bedi, Sohindar Singh. (1971). *Folklore of the Punjab.* New Delhi: National Book Trust.

———. (1991). *Panjābī Lokdhārā Vishvākosh* (Vol. 5). New Delhi: National Book Trust.

Berland, Joseph C. (1982). *No Five Fingers Are Alike: Cognitive Amplifiers in Social Context.* Cambridge, MA: Harvard University Press.

Bhag Singh. (1992). Pradhānagī Shabad. In G. Singh (ed.), *Panjāb de Lok Nāc* (pp. 65–67). Patiala, India: Punjabi University.

Bhai Gurdas. (2009 [1610s-1620s]). *Vārāṅ Bhai Gurdas Ji* (Vol. 1). (Shamsher Singh Puri, Trans.). Lilburn, GA: Academy of Sikh Studies.

Bhatti, Harvinder Singh. (2000). *Folk Religion: Change and Continuity.* Jaipur, India: Rawat.

al-Biruni. (2000 [1910]). *Alberuni's India* (Vol. 1). (Edward C. Sachau, ed., trans.). London: Routledge.

Biswas, Prophilla Chander. (1960). *The Ex-criminal Tribes of Delhi State*. Delhi: University of Delhi.

Blacking, John. (1971). Deep and Surface Structures in Venda Music. *Yearbook of the International Folk Music Council* 3, 91–108.

———. (1973). *How Musical Is Man?* Seattle: University of Washington Press.

Blunt, Edward Arthur Henry. (1969 [1931]). *The Caste System of Northern India*. Delhi: S. Chand.

Bollywood Bhangra Blunder?: India Not Impressed with Trudeau's Dancing. (2018, February 23). *CTV News*. https://www.ctvnews.ca/politics/bollywood-bhangra-blunder-india-not-impressed-with-trudeau-s-dancing-1.3816130.

Booth, Gregory D. (1991). Disco Laggi: Modern Repertoire and Traditional Performance Practice in North Indian Popular Music. *Asian Music* 23(1), 61–83.

Bourdieu, Pierre. (1984). *Distinction: A Social Critique of the Judgment of Taste*. (R. Nice, Trans.). Cambridge, MA: Harvard University Press.

———. (1985). The Social Space and the Genesis of Groups. *Theory and Society* 14(6), 723–744.

Brown [Schofield], Katherine Butler. (2007a). Introduction: Liminality and the Social Location of Musicians. *Twentieth-Century Music* 3(1), 5–12.

———. (2007b). The Social Liminality of Musicians: Case Studies from Mughal India and Beyond. *Twentieth-Century Music* 3(1), 13–49.

Bryant, Edwin. (2001). *The Quest for the Origins of Vedic Culture: The Indo-Aryan Migration Debate*. Oxford: Oxford University Press.

Census of India. (2013, April 30). *Primary Census Abstract*. Registrar General and Census Commissioner, India.

Chand, Gurnam. (2016). Drug Menace in Punjab: Politics and Position. *DAV Shodhdhara* 4(1), 116–124.

Chandola, Anoop. (1977). *Folk Drumming in the Himalayas: A Linguistic Approach to Music*. New York: AMS Press.

Chatrik, Dhani Ram. (2006). Panjāb [1931]. Reproduced in *Journal of Punjab Studies* 13(1–2), 6–11.

Chaturvedi, Jagdish, and Chandramani Singh. (2000). Professional Performers of Rajasthan: A Sociological Study. In C. Singh (ed.), *Performing Arts of Rajasthan: Lok-Rang* (pp. 47–57). Jaipur, India: Jawahar Kala Kendra.

Chauhan, Monica K. (2018). Per Capita Alcohol Consumption More Than Doubled in India From 2005 to 2016. *Tribune*, September 22. Retrieved from https://www.tribuneindia.com/news/health/per-capita-alcohol-consumption-more-than-doubled-in-india-from-2005-to-2016/657173.html.

Chowdhry, Neelam M. S. (2011). The Naqqals of Chandigarh: Transforming Gender on the Musical Stage. *Journal of Punjab Studies* 18(1–2), 203–216.

Commander, Simon. (1983). The Jajmani System in North India: An Examination of Its Logic and Status Across Two Centuries. *Modern Asian Studies* 17(2), 283–311.

Cross, Ian. (2003). Music and Biocultural Evolution. In M. Clayton, T. Herbert, and R. Middleton (Eds.), *The Cultural Study of Music* (pp. 17–27). New York: Routledge.

Daboo, Jerri. (2018). *Staging British South Asian Culture: Bollywood and Bhangra in British Theatre*. London: Routledge.

Daler, Avtar Singh. (1954). *Panjābī Lok-Gīt (Baṇatār te Vikās)*. Jalandhar, India: New Book Company.

Darling, Sir Malcolm. (1947). *The Punjab Peasant in Prosperity and Debt*. 4th ed. Bombay: Oxford University Press.

Darshan, Abdul Ghafoor. (1996). *Sakhī Sarvar kī Loriāṅ*. Islamabad, Pakistan: Lok Virsa.

Deb, P. C. (1987). *Bazigars of Punjab: A Socio-economic Study*. Delhi: Mittal.

Dhami, Sadhu Singh. (1996). *Piplanwala: Stories and Reminiscences*. Patiala, India: Punjabi University.

Dhillon, Iqbal Singh. (1998). *Folk Dances of Punjab*. Delhi: National Book Shop.

Dick, Alastair. (1984). The Earlier History of the Shawm in India. *Galpin Society Journal* 37, 80–98.

Dick, Alastair, and Geneviève Dournon. (1984). Ḍhol. In S. Sadie (ed.), *The New Grove Dictionary of Musical Instruments*, Vol. 1 (pp. 560–562). London: Macmillan.

Dusenbery, Verne A. (1989). Introduction: A Century of Sikhs Beyond Punjab. In N. G. Barrier and V. A. Dusenbery (Eds.), *The Sikh Diaspora: Migration and the Experience Beyond Punjab* (pp. 1–9). Columbia, MO: South Asia.

Eglar, Zekiye. (1960). *A Punjabi Village in Pakistan*. New York: Columbia University Press.

Elliot, Henry M. (1976 [1859]). *Memoirs on the History, Folk-lore, and Distribution of the Races of the North Western Provinces of India*. Osnabrück, Ger.: Biblio.

Ewing, Katherine. (1984). Malangs of the Punjab: Intoxication or Adab as the Path to God? In B. D. Metcalf (ed.), *Moral Conduct and Authority: The Place of Adab in South Asian Islam* (pp. 357–371). Berkeley: University of California Press.

Farmer, Henry George. (2000). Ṭabl-khāna. In P. J. Bearman, Th. Bianquis, C. E. Bosworth, E. van Donzel, and W. P. Heinrichs (Eds.), *The Encyclopaedia of Islam* (Vol. 10, pp. 34–38). New ed. Leiden, Neth.: Brill.

Faruqi, Farhana, Ashok Kumar, Anwar Mohyuddin and Hiromi Lorraine Sakata. (1989). *Musical Survey of Pakistan: Three Pilot Studies*. Islamabad, Pak.: Lok Virsa.

al Faruqi, Lois Ibsen. (1985). Music, Musicians, and Muslim Law. *Asian Music* 17(1), 3–36.

Fiol, Stefan. (2010). Sacred, Polluted, and Anachronous: Deconstructing Liminality Among the *Baddī* of the Central Himalayas. *Ethnomusicology Forum* 19(2), 137–163.

———. (2017). *Recasting Folk in the Himalayas: Indian Music, Media, and Social Mobility*. Urbana: University of Illinois Press.

Gera Roy, Anjali. (2010). *Bhangra Moves: From Ludhiana to London and Beyond*. Farnham, UK: Ashgate.

———. (2014). Imagining Punjab and the Punjabi Diaspora: After More Than a Century of Punjabi Migration. *South Asian Diaspora* 6(2), 137–140.

Ghurye, G. S. (2016 [1932]). *Caste and Race in India*. Bombay: Popular Prakashan.

Gill, Denise. (2017). *Melancholic Modalities: Affect, Islam, and Turkish Classical Musicians*. New York: Oxford University Press.

Gill, Sucha Singh. (2005). Economic Distress and Farmer Suicides in Rural Punjab. *Journal of Punjab Studies 12*(2), 219–237.

Government of India. (2007). *Constitution of India (As Modified up to the 1st December, 2007)*.

Grewal, J. S. (1998). *The Sikhs of the Punjab*. Rev. ed. Cambridge: Cambridge University Press.

———. (1999). Punjabi Identity: A Historical Perspective. In P. Singh and S. S. Thandi (Eds.), *Punjabi Identity in a Global Context* (pp. 41–54). New Delhi: Oxford University Press.

———. (2004a). Historical Geography of the Punjab. *Journal of Punjab Studies 11*(1), 1–18.

———. (2004b). *Social and Cultural History of the Punjab*. New Delhi: Manohar.

Grierson, George Abraham. (1968 [1922]). *Linguistic Survey of India*. Vol. 11, *Gipsy Languages*. Delhi: Motilal Banarsidass.

Gurdit Singh. (1960). Mele te Tiuhār. In M. S. Randhava (ed.), *Panjāb* (pp. 193–213). Patiala, India: Bhasha Vibhag.

Gurvinder Kaur. (2002). A Village That Lives on Shani's Bounty. *Tribune*, July 30. Retrieved from https://www.tribuneindia.com/2002/20020730/punjab1.htm.

Gusain, Lakhan. (2002). Endangered Language: A Case Study of Sansiboli. *Language in India* 2(9). Retrieved from http://www.languageinindia.com/dec2002/sansi.html.

Habib, Irfan. (2005). Jatts in Medieval Punjab. In R. Grewal and S. Pall (Eds.), *Precolonial and Colonial Punjab* (pp. 63–74). New Delhi: Manohar.

Harjinder Singh. (1977). Caste Ranking in Two Sikh Villages. In Harjinder Singh (ed.), *Caste among Non-Hindus in India* (pp. 84–90). New Delhi: National Publishing House.

Harjit Singh. (1949). *Naiṅ Jhanāṅ*. 2nd ed. Ropar, India: Harjit Singh.

Harkirat Singh. (1995). *Yādāṅ Ganjī Bār dīāṅ*. Patiala, India: Punjabi University.

Hasnain, Nadeem. (1983). *Tribal India Today*. New Delhi: Harnam.

Henry, Edward O. (1991). Jogis and Nīrgun Bhajans in Bhojpurī-speaking India: Intra-genre Heterogeneity, Adaptation and Functional Shift. *Ethnomusicology* 35(2), 221–242.

Herzfeld, Michael. (2005). *Cultural Intimacy: Social Poetics in the Nation-State*. New York: Routledge.

Husain, Mahdi. (1976). *The Reḥla of ibn Baṭṭūṭā (India, Maldive Islands and Ceylon)*. Vadodara, India: Oriental Institute.

Hutchinson, John. (1987). *The Dynamics of Cultural Nationalism: The Gaelic Revival and the Creation of the Irish Nation State*. London: Allen and Unwin.

Ibbetson, Denzil C. J. (1995 [1883]). *Panjab Castes: Being a Reprint of the Chapter on "The Races, Castes and Tribes of the People" in the Report on the Census of the Panjab*. Patiala, India: Language Department Punjab.

India Today State of the States 2018: Complete Rankings. (2018, November 22). *India Today*. Retrieved from https://www.indiatoday.in/state-of-states-conclave/story/india-today-state-of-the-states-2018-complete-rankings-1394303-2018-11-22.

Jaimalvala, Ikbal Singh. (2008). Ḍholī Mālī Rām. *Panjabi Tribune*, November 16, 1.

Jalal, Ayesha. (1995). *Democracy and Authoritarianism in South Asia*. Cambridge: Cambridge University Press.

Jensen, Joan. (1988). *Passage from India: Asian Indian Immigrants in North America*. New Haven, CT: Yale University Press.

Jodhka, Surinder S. (2004). Dissociation, Distancing and Autonomy: Caste and Untouchability in Rural Punjab. In H. K. Puri (ed.), *Dalits in Regional Context* (pp. 62–99). Jaipur, India: Rawat.

Jogi, Jugindar. (1990). *Panjāb de Prasiddh Khiḍārī*. (Vol. 1). Patiala, India: Bhasha Vibhag Panjab.

Jones, Kenneth W. (1976). *Arya Dharm: Hindu Consciousness in 19th-Century Punjab*. Berkeley: University of California Press.

———. (1989). *Socio-religious Reform Movements in British India*. Cambridge: Cambridge University Press.

Judge, Paramjit S. (2003). Hierarchical Differentiation among Dalits. *Economic and Political Weekly* 38(28), 2990–2991.

Juergensmeyer, Mark. (2004). Cultures of Deprivation: Three Case Studies in Punjab. In H. K. Puri (ed.), *Dalits in Regional Context* (pp. 43–61). Jaipur, India: Rawat.

Kalra, Virinder Singh. (2000). Vilayeti Rhythms: Beyond Bhangra's Emblematic Status to a Translation of Lyrical Texts. *Theory, Culture and Society* 17(3), 80–103.

———. (2015). *Sacred and Secular Musics: A Postcolonial Approach*. London: Bloomsbury.

Kamble, N. D. (1982). *The Scheduled Castes*. New Delhi: Ashish.

Kang, Kulbir Singh. (1994). *Hīr Damodar: Itihāsak te Sāhitik Mullānkaṇ*. Amritsar, India: Ruhi Prakashan.

Katz, Max. (2017). *Lineage of Loss: Counternarratives of North Indian Music*. Middletown, CT: Wesleyan University Press.

Khan, Muhammad Asif (ed.). (1986). *Hīr Damodar*. Lahore, Pak.: Pakistan Panjabi Adbi Board.

Kippen, James. (2006). *Gurdev's Drumming Legacy: Music, Theory and Nationalism in the Mṛdaṅg aur Tablā Vādanpaddhati of Gurdev Patwardhan*. Aldershot, UK: Ashgate.

———. (2008). Working with the Masters. In G. F. Barz and T. J. Cooley (Eds.), *Shadows in the Field: New Perspectives for Fieldwork in Ethnomusicology* (pp. 125–140). New York: Oxford University Press.

Kirpal Singh. (1972). *The Partition of the Punjab*. Patiala, India: Punjabi University.

Kumar, Pushpesh. (2002). Only 6 Bazigar Families in Punjab. *Tribune*, July 4 (online ed.). https://www.tribuneindia.com/2002/20020704/punjab1.htm#24.

Latif, Syad Muhammad. 1891. *History of the Panjáb from the Remotest Antiquity to the Present Time*. Calcutta: Calcutta Central.

Leach, Edmund Ronald. (1962). Introduction: What Should We Mean by Caste? In Edmund Ronald Leach (ed.), *Aspects of Caste in South India, Ceylon and Northwest Pakistan* (pp. 1–10). Cambridge: Cambridge University Press.

Leante, Laura. (2009). "Urban Myth": Bhangra and the Dhol Craze in the U.K. In B. Clausen, U. Hemetek, and E. Sæther (Eds.), *Music in Motion: Diversity and Dialogue in Europe* (pp. 191–208). Bielefeld, Ger.: Transcript.

Leonard, Karen Isaksen. (1992). *Making Ethnic Choices: California's Punjabi Mexican Americans*. Philadelphia: Temple University Press.

Lipsitz, George. (1986). Cruising Around the Historical Bloc: Postmodernism and Popular Music in East Los Angeles. *Cultural Critique* 5, 157–177.

Lybarger, Lowell H. (2011). Hereditary Musician Groups of Pakistani Punjab. *Journal of Punjab Studies 18*(1–2), 97–129.

Maira, Sunaina Marr. (2002). *Desis in the House: Indian American Youth Culture in New York City*. Philadelphia: Temple University Press.

Manuel, Peter. (2015). *Tales, Tunes, and Tassa Drums: Retention and Invention in Indo-Caribbean Music*. Urbana: University of Illinois Press.

McCord, Susan. (1996?). *Natha Singh's Story*. Unpublished manuscript, in private collection of Gibb Schreffler.

Merriam, Alan. (1964). *The Anthropology of Music*. Evanston, IL: Northwestern University Press.

Ministry of Social Justice and Empowerment, Government of India. (2018). *Magnitude of Substance Use in India*. New Delhi: National Drug Dependence Treatment Centre and AIIMS.

Minorsky, Vladimir. (1964). Gardīzī on India. In V. Minorsky (ed.), *Iranica: Twenty Articles* (pp. 200–215). Tehran: University of Tehran.

Moffatt, Michael. (1975). Untouchables and the Caste System: A Tamil Case Study. *Contributions to Indian Sociology* 9(1), 111–122.

Mooney, Nicola. (2013). Dancing in Diaspora Space: Bhangra, Caste, and Gender among Jat Sikhs. In M. Hawley (ed.), *Sikh Diaspora: Theory, Agency, and Experience* (pp. 279–318). Leiden, Neth.: Brill.

Morcom, Anna. (2013). *Illicit Worlds of Indian Dance: Cultures of Exclusion*. Oxford: Oxford University Press.

N. Kaur. (1999). *Bol Panjābaṇ de*. (Vol. 1). Patiala, India: Panjabi University.

Nahar Singh. (1988). *Panjābī Lok-Nāc: Sabhiācārak Bhūmikā te Sārthaktā*. Sarhind, India: Lokgit Prakashan.

———. (1998). *Bāgīṅ Cambā Khiṛ Rihā: Suhāg, Ghoṛīāṅ, Vadhāve ate Chand Parāge*. Patiala, India: Panjabi University.

Natavar, Mekhala Devi. (2000). Rajasthan. In A. Arnold (ed.), *The Garland Encyclopedia of World Music*. Vol. 5, *South Asia: The Indian Subcontinent* (pp. 639–649). New York: Garland.

Nayyar, Adam. (2000). Punjab. In A. Arnold (ed.), *The Garland Encyclopedia of World Music*. Vol. 5, *South Asia: The Indian Subcontinent* (pp. 762–772). New York: Garland.

Neuman, Daniel M. (1990). *The Life of Music in North India*. Chicago: University of Chicago Press.

Newton, John. (1854). *A Dictionary of the Panjábi Language*. Ludhiana, India: Mission Press.

Nijhawan, Michael. (2006). *Dhadi Darbar*. New Delhi: Oxford University Press.

Nijjhar, Bakhshish Singh (ed.). (2000). *Hīr Vāris Shāh*. Jalandhar, India: New Book Company.

Oberoi, Harjot. (1994). *The Construction of Religious Boundaries: Culture, Identity, and Diversity in the Sikh Tradition*. Chicago: University of Chicago Press.

Peirce, Charles Sanders. (1932). *Collected Papers of Charles Sanders Peirce*. Vol. 2, *Elements of Logic*. Edited by C. Hartshorne and P. Weiss. Cambridge, MA: Harvard University Press.

Pritam, Amrita. (2006). Ākhāṅ Vāris Shāh nūṅ [1947]. Reproduced in *Journal of Punjab Studies 13*(1–2), 78–79.

Punjab Government. (1990 [1921]). *Gazetteer of the Sialkot District, 1920*. Lahore, Pak.: Sang-e-Meel.

———. (2002 [1907]). *Ludhiana District and Malerkotla State Gazetteer, 1904*. Reprint ed. by Jagmohan Singh Hans. Chandigarh, India: Revenue and Rehabilitation Department, Punjab.

Puri, Harish K. (2004a). Introduction. In Harish K. Puri (ed.), *Dalits in Regional Context* (pp. 1–20). Jaipur, India: Rawat.

———. (2004b). The Scheduled Castes in the Sikh Community: A Historical Perspective. In Harish K. Puri (ed.), *Dalits in Regional Context* (pp. 190–224). Jaipur, India: Rawat.

Qureshi, Regula Burckhardt. (1986). *Sufi Music of India and Pakistan: Sound, Context and Meaning in Qawwali*. Cambridge: Cambridge University Press.

———. (1997). The Indian Sarangi: Sound of Affect, Site of Contest. *Yearbook for Traditional Music 29*, 1–38.

Ram, Ronki. (2004). Untouchability, Dalit Consciousness, and the Ad Dharam Movement in Punjab. *Contributions to Indian Sociology 38*(3), 323–349.

———. (2017). Castes within Caste: Dilemmas of a Cohesive Dalit Movement in Contemporary East Punjab. *Panjab University Research Journal (Arts) 44*(2), 45–62.

Ravinder Kaur. (2008). Narrative Absence: An "Untouchable" Account of Partition Migration. *Contributions to Indian Sociology 42*(2), 281–306.

Rice, Timothy. (1994). *May It Fill Your Soul: Experiencing Bulgarian Music*. Chicago: University of Chicago Press.

Risley, Herbert. (1969 [1908]). *The People of India*. 2nd ed. Delhi: Oriental.

Rode, Ajmer. (2006). Ducittīāṅ [1993]. Reproduced in *Journal of Punjab Studies 13*(1–2), 160–165.

Rose, Horace Arthur (ed.). (1911). *A Glossary of the Tribes and Castes of the Punjab and North-west Frontier Province* (Vol. 2). Lahore. Pak.: Civil and Military Gazette Press.

———. (1914). *A Glossary of the Tribes and Castes of the Punjab and North-west Frontier Province* (Vol. 3). Lahore, Pak.: Civil and Military Gazette Press.

———. (1919). *A Glossary of the Tribes and Castes of the Punjab and North-west Frontier Province* (Vol. 1). Lahore, Pak.: Superintendent, Government Printing, Punjab.

Sahota, Hardeep Singh. (2014). *Bhangra: Mystics, Music and Migration*. Huddersfield, UK: University of Huddersfield Press.

Saini, Manvir, and Bharat Khanna. (2019, June 2). Punjabi Dhol Not Economic Supporter Anymore. *Times of India*. https://timesofindia.indiatimes.com/city/chandigarh/nothing-upbeat-about-it/articleshow/69615241.cms.

Sakata, Lorraine. (1983). *Music in the Mind: The Concept of Music and Musician in Afghanistan*. Kent, OH: Kent State University Press.

Salim, Ahmad. (2004). Migration, Class Conflict and Change: Profile of a Pakistani Punjabi Village. In I. Talbot and S. Thandi (Eds.), *People on the Move: Punjabi Colonial, and Post-colonial Migration* (pp. 159–176). Oxford: Oxford University Press.

Saran, Rohit. (2004, August 16). India's Best and Worst States; North and South Lead. *India Today*, 21–31.

Sarmadee, Shahab. (1975). Ameer Khusrau's Own Writings on Music. In Z. Ansari (ed.), *Life, Times and Works of Amir Khusrau Dehlavi* (pp. 241–269). Delhi: Amir Khusrau Society.

Satyarthi, Devindra. (1998 [1936]). *Giddhā*. New Delhi: Navayug.

Schreffler, Gibb. (2010). Signs of Separation: Dhol in Punjabi Culture (PhD diss., University of California-Santa Barbara). Available from ProQuest database. (AAT 3428015).

———. (2011). The Bazigar (Goaar) People and Their Performing Arts. *Journal of Punjab Studies 18*(1–2), 217–250.

———. (2012a). Desperately Seeking Sammi: Re-inventing Women's Dance in Punjab. *Sikh Formations* 8(2), 127–146.

———. (2012b). Migration Shaping Media: Punjabi Popular Music in a Global Historical Perspective. *Popular Music and Society* 35(3), 333–358.

———. (2013). Situating Bhangra Dance: A Critical Introduction. *South Asian History and Culture 4*(3), 384–412.

———. (2014). "It's Our *Culture*": Dynamics of the Revival and Reemergence of Punjabi Jhummar. *Asian Music* 45(1), 34–76.

Schwarz, Henry. (2010). *Constructing the Criminal Tribe in Colonial India: Acting Like a Thief*. Chichester, UK: Wiley-Blackwell.

Seeger, Anthony. (1983). *Why Suyá Sing*. London: Oxford University Press.

Sewa Singh. (2015). *Masterji: A Sansi Saga*. Bloomington, IN: Partridge.

Sharma, Manorma. (2006). *Tradition of Hindustani Music*. New Delhi: APH.

Sharp, Cecil J. (1907). *English Folk-song: Some Conclusions*. London: Simpkin.

Sher, Sher Singh. (1965). *The Sansis of Punjab*. Delhi: Munshiram Manoharlal.

Sherinian, Zoe C. (2014). *Tamil Folk Music as Dalit Liberation Theology*. Bloomington: Indiana University Press.

Singer, Milton. (1984). *Man's Glassy Essence: Explorations in Semiotic Anthropology*. Bloomington: Indiana University Press.

Singh, Indera Paul. (1977). Caste in a Sikh Village. In H. Singh (ed.), *Caste Among Non-Hindus in India* (pp. 66—83). New Delhi: National Publishing House.
Singh, Kumar Suresh. (1998). *India's Communities* (Vols. 4–6). New Delhi: Oxford University Press.
———. (1999). *The Scheduled Castes*. Rev. ed. New Delhi: Oxford University Press.
Slobin, Mark. (1976). *Music in the Culture of Northern Afghanistan*. Tucson: University of Arizona Press.
Small, Christopher. (1998). *Musicking: The Meanings of Performing and Listening*. Middletown, CT: Wesleyan University Press.
Spivak, Gayatri Chakravorty. (1999). *A Critique of Postcolonial Reason: Toward a History of the Vanishing Present*. Cambridge, MA: Harvard University Press.
Sri Dasam Granth. c. 1690s. https://www.searchgurbani.com/dasam-granth/page-by-page.
Sri Guru Granth Sahib. 1604. http://www.srigranth.org/servlet/gurbani.gurbani.
Stewart, Rebecca Marie. (1974). *The Tablā in Perspective* (PhD diss., University of California-Los Angeles). Available from ProQuest database. (AAT 7412474).
Stokes, Martin. (1994). Introduction. In Martin Stokes (ed.), *Ethnicity, Identity, and Music: The Musical Construction of Place* (pp. 1–27). Oxford, UK: Berg.
Stronge, Susan (ed.) (1999). *The Arts of the Sikh Kingdoms*. Trumbull, CT: Weatherhill.
Sumbly, Vimal. (2007). The Vanishing Art of Bazigars. *Ludhiana Tribune*, July 24. https://www.tribuneindia.com/2007/20070724/ldh2.htm#6.
Tapper, Richard. (1997). *Frontier Nomads of Iran*. Cambridge: Cambridge University Press.
Tatla, Darshan Singh. (2004). Rural Roots of the Sikh Diaspora. In I. Talbot and S. Thandi (Eds.), *People on the Move: Punjabi Colonial, and Post-colonial Migration* (pp. 45–59). New York: Oxford University Press.
Temple, Richard. (1977 [1884, 1885]). *Legends of the Panjáb* (Vols. 1–2). Bombay: Education Society's Press.
Thandi, Shinder S. (2015). Punjabi Diasporas: Conceptualizing and Evaluating Impacts of Diaspora-Homeland Linkages. In S. Rajan, V. Varghese, and A. K. Nanda (Eds.), *Migration, Mobility and Multiple Affiliations: Punjabis in a Transnational World* (pp. 234–259). Cambridge: Cambridge University Press.
Thind, Karnail Singh. (1996). *Panjāb dā Lok Virsā*. Patiala, India: Punjabi University.
Thuhi, Hardial. (2002). *Tūmbe nāl Joṛī Vajdī: Ravāitī Panjābī Lok Gāikī*. Chandigarh, India: Panjab Sangit Natak Akademi.
———. (2017). *Panjāb dī Lok Kalā: Nakalāṅ te Nakalīe*. Chandigarh, India: Punjab Sangeet Natak Academy.
Tucker, G. (1884). *Report of the Settlement of the Kohat District in the Panjáb*. Calcutta: Calcutta Central Press.
Turino, Thomas. (2000). *Nationalists, Cosmopolitans, and Popular Music in Zimbabwe*. Chicago: University of Chicago Press.
———. (2008). *Music as Social Life: The Politics of Participation*. Chicago: University of Chicago Press.

Turner, Victor. (1966). *The Ritual Process: Structure and Anti-structure*. London: Routledge and Kegan Paul.

———. (1973). Symbols in African Ritual. *Science 179*(4078), 1100–1105.

Wade, Bonnie C. (1986). Playing for Power: Drum and Naubat, the Symbols of Might. In M. Honegger and C. Meyer (Eds.), *La Musique et le Rite Sacré et Profane* (pp. 28–32). Strasbourg: Presses Universitaires de Strasbourg.

———. (1998). *Imaging Sound: An Ethnomusicological Study of Music, Art, and Culture in Mughal India*. New Delhi: Oxford University Press.

Wiser, William H. (1936). *The Hindu Jajmani System*. Lucknow, India: Lucknow Publishing House.

Wolf, Richard K. (2000). Embodiment and Ambivalence: Emotion in South Asian Muharram Drumming. *Yearbook for Traditional Music* 32, 81–116.

———. (2006). The Poetics of "Sufi" Practice: Drumming, Dancing, and Complex Agency at Madho Lāl Husain (and Beyond). *American Ethnologist* 33(2), 246–268.

———. (2014). *The Voice in the Drum: Music, Language, and Emotion in Islamicate South Asia*. Urbana: University of Illinois Press.

INDEX

Ādi Dharm, 125
advocacy: for dholis, xvi, 4, 215; for small groups, 57
agriculture, 2, 17–18, 23, 35, 40, 42, 45, 47, 53, 76, 80–81, 123–24, 134, 147, 207
Ā'īn-i-Akbarī, 63, 106
algozā, 9, 136
Amar Nath, 180, 185, 190, 200
Amateur Field, 22–27, 178
Ambala, 100
Ambedkar, Bhimrao Ramji, 43
Amir Khusro, 63
Ampadu, Nana, 20
Amritsar, 1–4, 6, 13, 52, 102–4, 132, 141, 143, 157, 169, 180, 194–96, 200–201, 212–13
Amroha, 64
Anderson, Benedict, 50, 218n9 (chap. 1)
antiessentialism, 52–53
appropriateness: of dhol playing, 74, 89–90, 161–62, 165; of musical performance, 8, 24, 184, 191; of teaching techniques, 204, 206
appropriation. *See* cultural appropriation
Art Field, 26–27, 164
Arya Samaj, 100
audience, 21–23, 135, 178; catering to, 6, 186; diverse, 187–89; of mass media, 26, 49
authenticity, 2, 22, 87, 173–75, 177, 191–92, 198, 214, 226n3
Axel, Brian, 47, 52–53
Bachan Ram, 9
Bagga, Neeraj, 1, 4–5
Bahadur Singh, 138, 202
Baines, Athelstane, 96, 221n6, 222n28
Bakhle, Janaki, 218n12
Balgotra, Madan Lal, 97
Bal Kishan, 79–80, 98–100, 152, 171
ballad, 23, 48–49, 84, 97, 136, 177
Balochistan, xvi, 109, 141
Banerji, Sabita, 49, 218n8
Bangar, Raju, 185–86
Barkat Ali, 107
Barth, Fredrik, 37
Bathinda, 104, 132
Baumann, Gerd, 19, 38, 49, 56, 176, 218n8
Bawa, Jolly, 104, 180, 185–86
Bawa, Manish, 104
bāzī, 77, 130, 134, 134–35, 141–42, 147
Bazigar, 9–10, 33, 77, 81, 94, 114, 118, 120, 123–25, 128–47, 149, 158, 163–66, 169–71, 180, 183, 187, 195–98, 203, 205, 207, 219n12 (chap. 2), 224n4; history, 130–33
Bedi, Rahul, 17
Bedi, Sohindar Singh, 117, 123, 223n43
bhagat, 116–18, 223n45
Bhag Singh, 126, 143, 165
Bhai Gurdas, 105–6
bhalvānī, 67, 77, 85, 188
Bhambra, Jas, 188
Bhana Ram, 137–38, 140, 161, 202

Bhand, 106
bhangra: choreography, 12, 182; competitions, 9, 82–83, 85–86, 101–2, 143, 184–85; dholi accompaniment, 81–88, 99, 101–2, 104, 113, 129, 135–44, 147, 167, 186, 188, 197; in diaspora, 85–86, 176, 189; folkloric, 18, 29, 46, 60, 80–87, 129, 135, 139, 143, 165, 179–81, 183–84, 186–87, 197, 208; history of, 1–2, 49, 80–87, 138, 147, 178–79, 202; and identity, 51–52, 60–61, 192, 207, 212, 218n8; live, 184; music, 2, 49, 51–52, 86, 144, 176, 178–79, 185, 187–89, 218n8; repertoire, 90; representation of, 207–10, 212; university, 85–86, 139, 141–43
bhangṛā rhythm, 12, 69, 74, 80–82, 87, 89, 91, 220n25
Bhanjra, 101
Bharai, 41, 94, 109–14, 116–17, 119, 121, 158, 165, 167–68, 171, 182, 203, 210, 219n12 (chap. 2), 222n28, 225n18 (chap. 5), 226n32
Bhatkhande, V. N., 30
Bhatti, Harvinder Singh, 109–10, 116, 223n44
Bhatti, Lal Singh ("Lal Chand"), 83, 179, 181–84, 186, 190–91, 227n25
Bhula Nath, 101
Bhullar, Rayman, 166, 179–80, 185, 189, 227n25
Bhupinder Singh (Maharaja), 107
Billa. *See* Muhammad Shukardin
bīn, 97–98, 111
Binning, Paul, 184
Birmingham, 186–87
Biruni, al-, 43, 96
Biru Ram, 124, 138–39, 197, 206
Blacking, John, 21, 70
bol, 98, 156, 188
bolī, 49, 133
Bombay, 143–44, 165
Boota, Muhammad, 72–74, 113, 161, 167–68, 171, 182–83, 220n19, 226n22, 226n25, 227n18
Boota, Sher, 182
Bourdieu, Pierre, 21, 24, 168
brass band, 65, 75, 103, 108
British Columbia, xvi, 53, 175, 180, 183, 185
British Empire, 14, 16, 46–47, 176
Brooklyn, 73, 182

cāl, 83–84
Calgary, 145, 180
California, xvi, 176, 180, 182–85, 190
Canada, 47, 54, 85, 145–46, 175, 180, 183, 188, 202
canal colonies, 46, 81, 129, 131
caste system: dissolution of, 30–31; evading, 114; friction, 182; history, 43–44, 114; and identity, 37–38, 40–42; of musicians, 39, 210. *See also* Dalit; Jatt; Scheduled Caste
chaal, 188
Chabli Nath Babbi, 101
Chamar, 44, 114, 125–26, 177, 223n41, 224n56, 228n12
Chandigarh, 9–10, 118, 124, 136, 140–43, 145–46, 162–63, 166, 175, 183, 187, 197, 223n50, 223n54, 224n1, 228n6
Charan Das, 103–4, 169, 180, 198–200, 202, 214
chaṛī, 66, 116. *See also chaṭī*
chaṭī, 66–67, 143, 170–71, 185, 198
Chatrik, Dhani Ram, 14
Chindu, Surindar Kumar, 99
choreography, 10, 86–87, 90, 142
Chuch Mahi, 102
cimṭā, 9
circumcision, 111
citizenship, 19, 29, 35–36, 38, 50, 59, 172, 190
class issues, 29–30, 32, 39–40, 42, 57, 92–93, 95, 114–15, 149, 190
college, 12, 21, 30, 81–83, 99, 101–2, 104, 113, 121, 139–40, 142–43, 146, 180–81, 184, 204
colonial era, 26, 46, 55, 73, 76, 114, 147, 218n12, 224n11
Criminal Tribes, 43, 122, 133
cultural appropriation, xv, 32, 55, 190, 215
cultural capital, 8, 21, 24, 215
cultural intimacy, 51, 218n10 (chap. 1)
cultural nationalism, xv, 8, 18–19, 32, 38–39, 55–58, 190, 212
culture, 37, 39

ḍabal, 71–72, 74, 220n19
Dadu Majra Colony (DMC), 118–19, 123, 145, 223n45
daff, 115, 123
ḍaggā, 66–67, 74, 85, 101, 170, 226n32
Dakaunt, 124, 223n54
Dalit, 42, 44, 94, 114, 145, 214, 224n56
Damodar Gulati, 64
ḍamrū, 99, 117
Dana. *See* Ravi Kumar Dana
dance: Bazigar, 135–36; conceptions of, 49; and dhol, 32; and dhol style, 165; events, 9–12, 66; forms, 80–88; and mass media, 49; schools, 183, 188–89; social, 178. *See also* Bhangra; *jhummar*; *luḍḍī*
ḍanḍās, 9–10

ḍaurū, 117
death, 63, 79, 123, 152, 161–62, 202, 205, 226n22
Delhi, xvi, 13, 16, 49, 76, 81, 103, 132, 139, 145, 165, 196, 207, 223n50, 225n14
Delhi Sultanate, 63
desī, 165–66, 168, 173, 187, 197–98
Des Raj (dholi of Chandigarh), *88*, 146, 183, 189, 202–3
Des Raj (dholi of Jalandhar), 200
Des Raj (dholi of Ludhiana), 99
devotional practice, 12, 25–27, 78–80, 85, 89, 97, 115, 120–21, 150, 168, 185, 190, 207
Dev Raj (dholi of Amritsar), 169, 200–201, 226n25
Dev Raj (dholi of Chandigarh), 142, 166, 198–99, 228n6
ḍhaḍḍ, 23, 85, 117, 226n22
ḍhāḍī, 23, 25, 27, 84
dhamāl, 11–12, 70, 72, 75, 79–80, 85, 89, 91, 120, 164, 168, 220n15, 220n25
Dhanoa, Teginder Singh, 185
dharma, 31
Dhillon, Akhtar, 112–13, 210
Dhillon, Sultan, *112*, 219n12 (chap. 2)
dhol (*ḍhol*): accent, 70–71; as accompaniment instrument, 1, 9–10, 29, 34, 60, 72, 76, 80, 84, 89–90, 101, 104, 122, 165, 167, 186, 197; anthropomorphizing, 62–63; as art, 160–62, 164, 167–68; and change, 2–3, 5–6, 28–29, 89–90, 119, 129, 167, 193, 197, 210, 213, 215; competitions, 101–2, 185; construction, 32, 64–66, 99, 168–71, 187, 196; contexts for, 72–91; as cultural phenomenon, 1–2, 59, 66, 91, 122, 173; and dance, 80–88; defining, 32; decline, 2–3, 6–7, 34, 197–98, 205; democratization of, 30, 207; in diaspora, 29–30, 55, 145; drumhead, 62, 65–68, 85, 102, 117, 155, 169, 219n9; drumsticks, 62, 66, 111, 170, form, 62, 64–66; function, 60, 66, 73, 159–61, 159–62, 164–65; group classes, 187–89 ; history, 63–64, 145; as index, 60, 91, 188, 192; learning, 150, 156, 158, 184–87; lessons, 123, 154, 157, 165, 182, 187–89, 199, 202, 204–6, 209, 211–12, 215; meanings of, xv, 2, 7, 29, 32–33, 59–61, 62, 111, 191–92, 212, 217n1; and message, 68–70, 73–74, 89–90, 161; as object, 4, 28, 32, 60–64, 71, 159, 168–71, 196–97, 217n1; ornamentation, 11, 70, 109, 162, 164–66, 191, 220n17; as pastime, 184, 191; performance practice, 29, 33, 62, 65–74, 108, 121–22, 161, 163–64, 168, 170–71, 186; and Punjab, 1–2, 13, 18, 175, 177, 207; repertoire, 29, 32, 90, 150, 157, 183; and ritual, 9, 120; sales, 98, 112, 188, 195–97, 199, 202; schools, 185–89; secular, 12, 25, 168, 190; shoulder strap, 65–67; as sign, 8, 59–61, 89; and space, 10, 90; stigma, 31, 109, 113, 120, 122, 215; tuning, 65, 169; use of, 64, 73–88, 113, 116–17, 120, 123, 125, 134, 137, 144, 179, 197
ḍholak. See *ḍholkī*
Dhol Foundation (TDF), 187–88
dholi(s) (*ḍholī*): aesthetics, 6–7, 29, 88, 102, 160–71, 191, 197–98; as authorities, 10, 139, 204; Bazigar, 9–10, 33, 77, 81, 94, 114, 118, 123–25, 128–30, 136–42, 149, 158, 164–65, 169, 198; Bharai, 111–14, 119, 121, 158, 165, 167, 226n32; and class, 29–31, 36, 39–40, 42–43, 93–94, 149, 190–91; in diaspora, 29–30, 34, 73, 175–92, 203, 211, 215; diversity amongst, 150; economic conditions of, 5–6, 30, 34, 89–91, 101–2, 151–52, 156, 169, 179, 194–95, 208, 211, 214; ethnicity, 6, 8, 27, 33–34, 92–127, 162–71, 192, 206–16; existential issues, 6, 8, 28–29, 31–32, 39, 72, 91, 102, 113, 122, 160, 191, 205, 211, 213–14; as hereditary musicians, 5, 7, 29, 31, 105, 114, 151, 160, 174, 202; identity, xv-xvi, 7–8, 19–20, 27–29, 31, 33–34, 52, 62–63, 71, 92–129, 148–52, 162–71, 191, 212–16; individualism, 163–64, 168; Jogi, 79, 94, 97, 99–102, 111, 157–58, 162–71, 191; Mahasha, 100–105, 149, 157–58, 164, 169, 195; Mirasi, 107, 111–13, 121–22, 149, 157–58, 164–65, 170; movement of, 36; narratives about, 2–3, 150; as occupational group, 33, 150–51; Pakistani, 65, 71, 73, 88, 113, 120, 122, 166–68, 170–71, 182–83, 226n22; professionalism, 150–53, 198, 206, 212; religiosity, 119, 152, 168; representations of, 1, 8, 32, 92, 95, 212; roles of, 9–12, 27, 29, 33–34, 65, 68, 72–80, 82–88, 103–7, 110–11, 118, 121, 123, 138, 166; Shaikh, 94, 113, 119, 167; on social media, 193–94; and social relationships, 27, 160, 177; spiritual decline in, 7, 205; style, 162–71, 191; and technology, 4–5; tensions, 87, 210, 226n3; training, 152–59; values, xvi, 8, 12, 18, 27, 33–34, 54, 63, 88, 98, 102, 113, 149–50, 157, 160, 162–63, 167, 169–70, 190–92, 198–200, 202–54, 211, 215
ḍholī galī (alley), 98–99, 101–2, 200, 213
ḍholkī, 66, 87–89, 123, 127, 178, 186, 219n10, 221n34

Dhol World, 27–28, 30, 34, 71, 162, 187, 190–91, 204–5
disciple, 30, 34, 101, 104–5, 120–21, 136–37, 143, 146, 153–59, 166, 180–81, 184, 187–88, 200, 202, 204–5, 207, 211–12, 225n6, 225n15, 225n19 (chap. 5)
disco, 49, 179
displacement, 45, 90, 147
DJ, 5–6, 183, 203
Dom, 96, 105, 109, 113–14
drum kit, 70, 178, 187
duhul, 63, 106
Dum, 41, 94, 96–97, 99–102, 105, 222n28
Dumna, 96–97, 100–102, 221n12

ektālā, 88, 101
embellishment, 71, 85, 101
emblem, 1, 31, 33, 37, 61–62, 111, 116–17, 129, 147
enculturation, 33, 156, 205, 225n15
essentialization, 32, 48, 50, 52–55, 130, 175–77, 179
ethical issues, xv-xvi, 2, 4, 32, 95, 151, 155, 161–62, 192, 216
ethnicity, 18–19, 25–28, 32–33, 37–41, 92–114, 149, 173–74, 177, 182, 188, 190, 206. *See also under* dholi

faqīr, 11, 23–24, 97, 113, 120, 168
Faqir Ali, 107, *108*
film, 2, 49, 81, 86, 103, 135, 138, 141, 143–45, 165, 169, 177–80, 184–85, 195, 224n17
Fiol, Stefan, 33, 173–74, 206, 214, 217n2
folk: instruments, 9, 112, 179, 183, 220n14; meaning of, 173–74, 191–92, 198, 214; music, 94, 164, 214, 226n1, 228n6; musicians, 109; revival, 48, 177; songs, 178; style, 166–67
folklorization, 10, 18, 129, 135–36, 173–74, 178, 198, 207, 213, 217n2
folklorized dance performances, 9–10, 29, 33, 46, 60, 82–87, 89–90, 93–94, 122, 135, 147, 189–90, 195
frame drum, 115, 214

Gaga. *See* Samim Muhammad
Gandhi, Indira, 52
Gardizi, 96
Garib Dass, xvi, 5, 31, 33, 62–63, 69–70, 72–76, 78–84, 87–88, 94, 101, 128–33, 135, 140–47, 154–58, 161, 165–66, 168, 171, 175, 179–80, 183, 185, 187, 189, 195–96, 198, 202–3, 205–7, 210, 214, 219n2, 219n12 (chap. 2), 220n19, 224n1, 225nn8–9; career, 141–45; and Punjabi music, 20; as teacher, 146; upbringing, 140–41
gatkā, 77
gender issues, 23, 27, 36, 45, 66, 74, 87–88, 106, 117, 123, 129, 142, 152, 176, 213, 218n13
Gera Roy, Anjali, 12, 19, 52
ghaṛā, 9
gharānā, 26, 107, 218n11
Ghattaora, Harbinder Singh, 186
ghoṛī, 22, 27, 116
Ghuggi, 101–3, 143, 157–58, 164, 200, 222n15
giddhā, 87, 89, 146, 221n33
Gill, Denise, 218n13
Gill, Gaurav, *118*, 158–59
Gill, Sucha Singh, 17
gīt, 73, 178
Goaar, 130–31, 133, 136. *See also* Bazigar
Goga Meri (Gogā Meṛī), 115, 117, 119, 223n45
Golden Temple. *See* Harimandir Sahib
Gorakh Nath, 97, 99, 115, 117
Gosha Shiva, 200
Great Indian Dancers, 186–87
Green Revolution, 17, 91, 214
Grewal, J. S., 14, 18, 43, 52, 218n5
Gugga Pir, 80, 115–18, 168, 223n42
guild, 64, 121, 151, 153–54, 205–6, 208–9, 211–12, 225n3
Gujrat (Pakistan), 99–100, 128, 136, 182, 223n50, 226n33
Gulab Singh, 118
Gunga Sain, 121
Gurdaspur, 99, 132
gurdwara, 53, 112, 180, 182, 212–13, 218n1
gurū, 31, 97, 143, 153, 155, 157, 159, 225n5
Guru Granth Sahib. See *Sri Guru Granth Sahib*
Gypsy Tribes, 43, 131

Harbans Lal Jogi, 102, 164–65, 180–81, 186, 201–2
Harbans Lal Kaku, 104, 164, 179–80
Harbhajan Singh, 99, 139, 165
Harimandir Sahib, 13, 52, 212
Harjit Singh, 45, 73, 76, 161
Haryana, 13, 100, 217n5
havan, 116, 159
Herzfeld, Michael, 51, 218n9 (chap. 1)
Himalayas, 14, 173–74, 214
Hindu(s): communities, 107; conversion, 100; in East Punjab, 16; as Hindustani

musicians, 30; ideology, 40; perspectives, 79; practices, 158–59, 190; temple, 12, 97, 185
Hindustani classical music, 26–27, 30, 68–69, 71, 85, 88–89, 98, 101–2, 107, 109, 112, 120–22, 153, 156–57, 164–74, 178, 181, 185–86, 197–98, 202–3, 213, 218n12, 220n14, 220n17, 220n31, 225n3, 225nn5–6, 225n14
Hīr-Rānjhā, 56, 64, 137
Hoshiarpur, 61, 115, 180
Hothi, Manvir, 191
Hutchinson, John, 38
hybridity, 86, 176, 179, 188

Ibbetson, Denzil, 23, 131, 222n28, 223n40, 223n53
identity: definition of, 37–39; and emblems, 61; and place, 59; state, 172. *See also under* dholi; Punjabi
India: Bazigar migration to, 132; castes within, 43–44; Independence of, 1; musical identity of, 172–74, 213; regional culture in, 57; relationship with Punjab state, 16, 52
Indo-Aryans, 43, 45, 96, 221n6
itinerant communities, 11, 23, 43–44, 114, 117, 122, 124, 128, 132, 133–34, 223n53

Jagat Ram, 135
Jagmohan Kaur, 180
jāgo, 195, 203
jajmānī, 42
Jalandhar, 100, 103–5, 134, 164, 179–81, 186, 194–95, 200
Jammu, xvi, 64, 79, 97–98, 100–101, 111, 152, 171, 182
Janak Raj, 99–100, 146, 202
Jangli (*jānglī*), 45–46, 141
Jangvir, 125
Jarg, 10–11, 25, 108, 171, 219n11 (chap. 2)
Jarnail Singh, 183
Jatt, 25, 35, 47, 81, 106, 108, 110, 112, 123–25, 175, 177–78, 182, 187, 190, 207–8, 219n11 (chap. 1); culture, 52, 54–55; and land ownership, 42; politics, 57; and Punjabi identity, 18–19
Jatt Sikhs, 18, 25, 190
jhuggī, 45, 134
jhummar, 9, 67, 73–74, 87, 90, 125, 135–36, 142, 165
jogī, 24, 97, 115, 119, 221n8
Jogi (qaum), 23, 41, 79, 94, 97, 99–102, 105, 111, 142, 146, 152, 157–58, 162, 164–65, 170–71, 180, 182, 194, 200, 202–3, 222n14, 222n28

kabaḍḍī, 77–78, 134, 141, 198
kahirvā, 82–84, 220n31
Kainth, Rupee, 189
Kalra, Virinder Singh, 25–26, 176, 218n12
Kalsi, Johnny, 187, 190
Kambo, Gurvinder, 154, 186–87, 228n16
Kamboj, 81, 124
kammī, 42
Kanjars, 178
Kartar Singh (dholi of Chandigarh), 204, 210
kasbī, 102
kathak, 106, 137
Katz, Max, 30, 172
kettledrum, 75–76, 78, 112, 171, 195, 219n5
Khalistan, 52–54, 57, 180
Khalsa, 53–54, 99, 101–2, 104, 142, 180–81
Khalsa College, 99, 101–2, 104, 181
kikklī, 212
kinship, 41
Kippen, James, 153, 203, 220n13, 225n19
kīrtan, 25–26, 53, 75, 106, 178
Kukki, Naresh, 196, 203–4, 228n12

Lacchman Singh, 73, 125, *126*
laggī, 71, 85, 220n18
lāgī, 106, 110
lahirā, 88
lahirīā, 88, 220n25
Lahore, 14, 16, 74, 100, 102, 112, 120–21, 180, 222n28, 226n33
Lal Chand Yamla Jatt, 127, 177
Lalka, Jagat Ram, 136
language issues, 14, 16, 51, 59, 133, 225n5
lay dhol players, 175, 183–89, 193, 210
liberalization, 172–75, 184
Lipsitz, George, 219n12 (chap. 1)
Lohri, 75–76, 123, 143
lok gīt, 178, 203
London, xvi, 176, 187, 196
loss, 4, 27–28, 31, 91, 194, 215
Luddan Sain, 120
luḍḍī, 11–12, 74, 82–84, 86–87, 91, 188, 220n31, 226n25
Ludhiana, 11–12, 99, 101, 107, 126, 137, 146, 162, 164, 170–71, 180, 186, 184, 196–97, 200, 202, 206
Lybarger, Lowell, 105–6

Madan Lal, 99, 164
Maharaja of Patiala, 107, 136
Mahasha, 41, 97, 100–105, 149, 157–58, 164, 169, 171, 181–82, 195, 221n12, 222n14
māhīā, 136
mahifal, 88–89, 164–65
Majid Ali, 165–66
malang, 79, 120, 223n51
Malerkotla, 106–8, 111–13, 166, 171, 219n12 (chap. 2), 222n28
Malhotra, Ravi, 162–63
Mali Ram, 10, 73, 78, 142, 153–56, 164–65, 168, 183, 186, 198, 210, 225n8
Malkit Singh, 179–80
Mall, Gurcharan, 186–87
Malvaī giddhā, 9
Manak Raj, *139*, 197
Mangal Singh Sunami, 136
Mangat Ram, 142, 198
Mann, Gurdas, 104, 144, 179
Mann, Surjit, 142
Mardana, 105–7
marginalization, xv-xvi, 4, 8, 18–19, 25, 28–32, 42–44, 46, 54, 57–58, 119, 129, 145, 151, 190, 213, 215, 219n11 (chap. 1)
māṛī, 116–18, 141, 159, 162, 165, 223n42
masālā, 62, 65, 171
masculinity, 66, 90
master-disciple practice, 30, 34, 101, 105, 143, 146, 153–59, 166, 180, 181, 184, 186–88, 200, 204–7, 211–12, 225n5–8, 225n15, 225n19 (chap. 5), 228n16
mast/mastī, 11, 79, 120
Mazhbi, 106, 114, 119, 124, 133
Mediated Field, 26–27, 177, 183
melā, 10–12, 25, 86, 220n25
Merriam, Alan, 24
meter, 68–69, 71, 73, 85, 220n15
migration, 7, 13, 32, 35–36, 44–48, 50, 52, 73, 81, 90, 96, 98–99, 102, 104, 119, 125, 131–33, 138, 141, 176–77, 180, 182
military, 11, 47, 63–64, 76–77, 81
Milkhi Ram, 99, 102
minorities: Dalit, 42, 44, 94; diaspora, 210; identities of, 19, 52, 92, 178, 207, 226n3; Jatts as, 54; Muslims as, 16; ontologies of, 28–29, 175, 219n12 (chap. 1); and Punjabi cultural nationalism, 51, 55–58, 130
Mirasi, 23, 25; community 11–12; qaum, 94, 97, 105–7, 110–13, 121–22, 136–37, 148, 157–58, 164–66, 170–71, 185, 191, 203, 219n11 (chap. 2), 222n28, 223n50
mirzā, 84–85
Mirzā-Sāhibāṅ, 84–85, 224n17
modernity, 1, 3, 28, 30, 49, 147, 173, 218n12, 226n2
Mohali, 140, 195
Mooney, Nicola, 18, 219n11 (chap. 1)
Morcom, Anna, 23, 213
Mother Goddess, 79, 165, 169
Mughals, 14, 24, 45, 76, 78, 131
Muhammad Shukardin (Billa), 107–8
Mukhtiar Singh, 5
Multānī luḍḍī, 84
Mumbai (Bombay) film industry, 49, 165, 179
Mundri Lal, 137
Munshi Ram, 99, 102, 200
Musalli, 114, 119
music: as activity, 21–22; as art, 26; as entertainment, 25; valuing of, 24, 150
musicians: status of, 24–26, 42, 151
musicking, 21, 24–25, 150, 167
music production, 48, 50, 174, 179, 203
Muslim: communities, 107; devotional practice, 78–80, 190; dhol practices, 169; identity, 105
Muslims: in East Punjab, 16; as Hindustani professional musicians, 30; theology of, 41; in West Punjab, 46

nacār, 106, 126, 142
nagāṛā, 75, 104
nagar kīrtan, 53, 75
Nahar Singh, 61, 94, 221n33, 222n28
naqal, 106, 136
Naqqalia, 106–7
naqqārah khānah, 63, 78
Naseeb Singh, 142
Natha Singh, 122–23
nation, 38–39
nationalism. *See* cultural nationalism
nationalists, 18, 38–39, 51, 55–57
Nawab Ghumar, 136
Naya Daur, 135, 224n12, 224n17
Nehru, Jawaharlal, 101
Neuman, Daniel, 30, 107, 157, 172, 223n50, 225n3, 225n5–7, 225nn14–15, 225n20, 228n16
New Delhi. *See* Delhi
new media, 193–94
New York, xvi, 35, 73, 164, 180, 182–83
Niamat Ali, 120, 225n18 (chap. 5)
Nigaha, 109–10

Nijhawan, Michael, 25
Nikka Ram, 103
1986 World Exposition, 145, 180
Noora, 105
norms, 11, 22, 24–27, 207

Oberoi, Harjot, 52, 150
offerings, 74, 79, 98, 111, 116, 118–20, 124, 143, 158–59
Other Backward Classes, 94, 124, 221n1
ownership: of cultural practices, xv, 8, 22, 30–31, 40; by dholis, 10; of geographic areas, 14; of land, 35

pakhāvaj, 98
Pakistan: after Partition, 46, 73, 132; politics in, 121–22; Punjab region in, 13–14, 16. *See also under* dholi
Pakistani identity, 57, 167
Pammi Bai, 99
Pannu, Amrinder Singh (Nana), 186
Pannu, Gurpreet Singh (Gopi), 186
Pappu Sain. *See* Zulfikar Ali
Paraiyar, 214
paramparā, 96, 120, 122, 125, 127, 206
parshād, 116, 159
Partition, 18, 46, 48, 55–56, 73, 80–81, 87, 89–91, 99, 102, 107, 109, 113–14, 116, 120, 125, 131–33, 135–37, 140, 142, 151, 166, 169, 182, 191; and Punjabi cultural nationalism, 55–56
Pathani Ram, 142
Patiala, 6, 76, 81, 83, 104–5, 107, 124, 130, 132, 136, 139, 183, 189, 197–98, 206, 218n11
Patiala and East Punjab States Union. *See* PEPSU
Pawandeep Kaur, 25
Peirce, Charles Sanders, 60–61
PEPSU (Patiala and East Punjab States Union), 81, 83, 135–37, 139, 165
phuhmmaṇ, 62, 65–66
Piare Lal, 180, 184
piṇḍ, 13, 129
Pokhar Singh, 125
postcolonial period, 47, 174
Prem Chand, 123, 135–36, 142, 197–98, 205, 224n16
prerecorded music, 5–6, 26, 86, 104, 174, 184
Pritam, Amrita, 55–56
professional female dancers, 213
Professional Field, 23–27, 119, 178
prosperity, 16–17, 91, 214
Punjab: addiction in, 17; caste in, 39–40; current conditions in, xvi, 2, 7, 16–17, 30; description of, 12–20, 35; difference in, 29; discourse on, 35–36, 39, 45, 129; diversity in, 35, 39, 42, 48, 51–52; ethnic groups in, 18–19, 23–24, 32, 39, 92; feudal structure in, 42; gender in, 23–24; history, 45–47, 89, 218n5; as homeland, 48; identity in, xv, 1–2, 4, 8, 13, 18–20, 32, 35–36, 39; and land, 35, 38, 42, 129, 117n5; as nation, 38–39; Pakistani, 13, 16, 46; as a political entity, 14, *15*, 16, 18–19; population movement in, 45–46; and *qaum*, 40; representations of, 49, 208; Scheduled Caste members in, 44; topography of, 13–14
Punjabi community, 50, 190, 176–77, 210
Punjabi cultural nationalism, 32, 38–39, 55–57, 174–75, 190, 212, 214
Punjabi culture, 54, 57–59, 77, 90, 175–77, 206, 210, 213–14, 216
Punjabi dance, 80–88, 224n11
Punjabi heritage, 1–2, 4, 18–21, 38–39, 80–81, 85, 147, 167, 174–76, 178, 188, 190–91, 212–14
Punjabi identity, 1, 14, 18–20, 28–29, 32–33, 35–36, 38–40, 48–54, 56, 58–59, 61–62, 81–82, 90–91, 127–29, 145, 148–49, 166–67, 173–75, 191–92, 207, 211, 213
Punjabi language, 16, 18, 133
Punjabi music: defining, 20–23, 27, 48–50, 173; excitement for, 5; as marked activity, 22; norms, 26; patronage of, 23; popular, 48–51, 86, 176, 178, 189
Punjabi national identity, 8, 36–39, 50–51, 54, 174, 190–91, 207
Punjabiness, 18, 32, 48, 50, 60–61, 91, 95, 177, 192, 213–14
Punjabi politics, 55–58
Punjabis: British, 49–50; under British rule, 47; in diaspora, 7, 46–47, 49–50, 52, 55, 176–79, 189–93, 210–12, 215; Indian, 57; military service of, 47; ontologies of, 28; Pakistani, 57; subaltern, 4, 28–29
Puran, *118*, 119, 158–59

qaum, 40–42, 45, 48, 54–55, 71, 95–97, 100, 105–6, 108, 110, 112–15, 122, 127, 130, 149–53, 156, 158, 163, 167, 169, 172, 174–75, 190, 193, 198, 203, 205–7, 213–14
qavvālī, 106–7, 122
Qureshi, Regula, 61, 79

Rababi, 106, 223n50
Rafi, 11–12, 108
rāg, 26
Rahul Singh, 188
Rai Sikh, 124–25, 165
Rajasthan, 6, 115–17, 119, 124–25, 131–33, 217n5, 223n45, 223n53, 224n4
Rajpal Singh, 76
Rajput, 115, 131, 223n53
Rajput, Pritpal, 187
Ram, Ronki, 115
Ramadan, 73–74
Rāmdāsīā, 125–26, 133
Ramesh Chand, *84*, 99, 158
Ramesh Kumar (Meshi), 99, 142, 189
Ramgarhia, 187, 190
Ramju Muhammad Khawra, 185, 196
Ranjit Singh (Maharaja), 14
Ravīdāsīā, 125–26
Ravi Kumar Dana, 99, 164, 180, 186
Rawalpindi, 14, 119
Reehal, Rajvir, 188
refugee, 48, 81, 132, 135
refugee camp, 107, 137–38, 141, 177
religious issues, 12, 56, 59, 79–80, 112–14, 132, 150, 158, 168–69, 190
representation, xvi, 20, 28, 32, 36, 49, 52, 55, 58, 81, 89, 92, 95, 174, 207
Republic Day, 81, 103, 139, 143, 165, 181, 207, *208*
rhythmic patterns, 10–11, 60, 68–73, 89, 101–2, 111, 121, 161, 164–65, 188, 198, 220n17, 227n33
Rice, Timothy, 70
river, 12–14, 16, 35, 63, 125, 128, 218n9 (Intro.)
Rode, Ajmer, 35
Rose, Horace, 96, 105, 109–10, 115–16, 123, 223nn49–50, 224n11, 226n32

Sabi, Muhammad, 111, 113
Sacred Field, 26–27
sadd, 73–74
Sadhu Khan, 107
Saghir Ali, 88, 121–22, 170
Sahota, Hardeep, 186, 189
Sain dholis, 119–22, 168
Sakhi Sarvar, 80, 109–11, 113, 116, 168, 222n28, 222n32
samā', 79
Samim Muhammad (Gaga), 12, 108–9, 170–71, 219n11 (chap. 2)
sammī, 9, 84, 136
Sandal Bar, 46, 136
sangīt, 23, 27, 66, 88, 109, 186
Sangrur, 107, 119, 132
Sansi, 122–24, 145, 205, 223n53, 224n4
sārangī, 9, 23, 106, 117
Sardari Lal, 135, 142
sarnāī, 64
Saroop Singh, 142
Satinderjit Singh, 186
Satpal Bovi, 99
Satta and Rai Balvand, 105
Saund, Jatinder, 188
Scheduled Caste, 42–44, 94, 97, 119, 124–25, 133, 182, 221n2, 223n41, 224n7, 224n9
Schofield Brown, Katherine Butler, 24–25
seasonal festivals, 75
secular music, 11–12, 25, 167–68, 190, 192
Seetal, Sohan Singh, 25
Sekhon, Balbir Singh, 83, 220n30
Sewa Ram, 99, 186, 196
Sewa Singh, 142, 197
Shaikh, 11, 94, 110, 113, 119, 167, 222n28, 223nn49–50
Shani Dev, 124
Sharif Idu, 23, 218n9 (Intro.)
Sharma, Anil, 194
Sharma, Gaurav, 185–86, 190
Sharp, Cecil, 173, 226n1
Shekhupura, 131, 137
Sherinian, Zoe, 39, 214, 218n10 (Intro.)
Sher Khan, 108
Sialkot, 84, 99–101, 103, 131
siālkoṭī, 84
Sian, Gurp, 189
Sikh: community, 13, 53; devotional practice, 25; identity, 52–54; musicians, 11; politics, 16, 52–54; theology, 14, 41
Sikhs: beliefs of, 119; dholi, 182; in diaspora, 51, 190; in East Punjab, 16; Jatt, 18–19, 47, 190; prejudice, 218n1; prominence of, 51, 213
Sindh, 14, 16, 125, 220n25, 226n22
Singer, Milton, 61
singing, 66, 74–75, 84, 87–88, 97, 109–10, 127, 136, 178; as ritual, 21–22, 25–26
Sitla Devi, 10
Small, Christopher, 21
social justice, 30–31
Sohan Lal, 104, 206
Sonu, *77*, *78*, 104, *118*, 119
sound recording, 4–5, 21, 48, 70, 108, 144, 179, 183, 185, 196, 202

Southall, 186, 188
Spivak, Gayatri, 4
sports, 76–78, 89, 130, 134
Sri Dasam Granth, 64, 219n5
Sri Guru Granth Sahib, 53, 75, 105
Stokes, Martin, 59, 177
substance use, 17–18, 101–2, 104, 152, 180, 200–202, 215
Sudagar Ram, 136
Sufi: practices, 85, 116, 119, 167–68; shrine, 12, 79, 104, 107–13, 115–17, 119–22, 159, 165, 218n1, 220n25, 222n28, 223n42, 223n46; symbolism, 222n32
Sukhshinder Shinda, 179
Sunam, 137, 139
Surinder Kaur, 49, 178
Surrey (Canada), 53, 145, 175, 180, 183, 185, 189
Sweepers, 44, 114–17, 119, 223n41
swing, 69–70, *75*, 82, *83*, 164, 220n31, 226n25

tabla, 27, 65, 69, 89, 98, 102, 121, 127, 142, 153, 166–67, 169, 184, 203
ṭabl khānah. See naqqārah khānah
Takhi, Anil, 194
Takhi, Kala, 104, 164, 194, 208–10
tāl, 26, 68–72, 74, 79, 88–89, 101, 112, 143, 159, 164–65, 167, 185–86, 220nn13–14, 220n16, 220n19, 220n31
Tara Chand, 118–19, 158
tempo, 69–70, 72, 82, 87, 226n25
Thandi, Shinder, 44, 46
Thuhi, Hardial, 107, 136
tihāī, 101, 121
tīhlī. See *chaṭī*
Tilak Raj, 102, *103*, 104, 200–201
tinn tāl, 88, 164
tirakaṭ, 71, 164, 220n17
toṛā, 11, 72, 74, 82, 165, 167
Toronto, 145, 180, 185, 188–90, 200
tradition: narratives about, 2–3
trance, 11, 70, 79, 117, 120
tribal communities, 9, 18, 33, 41–46, 110, 114, 122–24, 128, 131, 133–34, 136–38, 147, 218nn2–3, 223n53
tūmbī, 127, 176–77
tuṇkā, 83
Turino, Thomas, 21, 37, 217n6, 226n2
Turner, Victor, 25, 59

United Kingdom, 13, 47, 154, 176, 178, 180, 182, 186, 190
United States, 47, 61–62, 85, 113, 145, 167, 180–81, 183
untouchables, 42–44, 96, 113–14, 133
ustād, 6, 10, 34, 63, 74, 76, 94, 99, 112, 128, 153–58, 179–81, 183, 185–87, 189–90, 196–97, 200, 210–12, 215, 225n5; current state of, 202–8
ustādī, 157, 202–5
ustād-lok, 99, 112, 158, 203
Uttar Pradesh, xvi, 64, 223n5, 224n4

Vaishno Devi, 79, 97
Valmiki, 106, 115, 117–19, 122, 145, 158–59, 162, 165, 168
Vancouver, 145, 166, 180, 184–85, 189
variant (rhythmic), 71, *72*, 82, *83*, 164
Varis Shah, 56, 64, 76
varṇa system, 43
Vartia, Jass, 146, 175, 183, 203
Vedas, 43, 96, 100
Vijay Kumar, 195
Visakhi, 53, 80, 90, 143, 175

Wade, Bonnie, 78, 220n23
warfare, 76–77, 131, 188
wedding, 21, 49, 73, 97–99, 102–3, 105–6, 110, 120, 123, 135, 142, 146, 178, 183, 195; procession, 1, 45, 64, 74–75, 197
Westernization, 49, 55
Wolf, Richard, 74, 112, 120–21, 161, 167, 220n16, 225n18 (chap. 5)
women's dance, 86, 136, 212, 221n33
women's musicking, 21–25, 27, 63, 66, 74, 87, 178, 195, 219n10
wrestling, 74, 76–78, 85, 98, 111, 118, 134, 141, 220n24

Yamla, Jagdish, 126–27, 228n12
Yamla, Vijay, 189, 197, 202, 228n12
youth festival, 9, 21, 82
YouTube, 86, 184, 189, 193–94

zikr, 79
zimīndār, 42
Zulfikar Ali (Pappu Sain), 101, 120–21, 167, 200, 221, 226n33

GIBB SCHREFFLER is an associate professor of music at Pomona College. He is the author of *Boxing the Compass: A Century and a Half of Discourse about Sailors' Chanties*.

The University of Illinois Press
is a founding member of the
Association of University Presses.

University of Illinois Press
1325 South Oak Street
Champaign, IL 61820-6903
www.press.uillinois.edu

Printed by Printforce, United Kingdom